OAKWOOD LIBRARY OF RAILWAY HISTORY

RAILS TO TUR
AND
HEADS OF AYR

The Maidens & Dunure Light Railway and the Butlin's Branch

by
David McConnell & Stuart Rankin

THE OAKWOOD PRESS

British Library Cataloguing in Publication Data
A Record for this book is available from the British Library
ISBN 978 0 85361 699 3

Typeset by Oakwood Graphics.
Repro by PKmediaworks, Cranborne, Dorset.
Printed by Cambrian Printers, Aberystwyth, Ceredigion.

Front cover: A Glasgow & South-Western Railway Girvan-Ayr train at Turnberry station, *c.* 1920. *GNSR Association: Barclay-Harvey Collection*

Title page: The Doon viaduct, looking west from the 'new' road bridge, reproduced from G&SWR's *Carrick Coast Tourist Guide*, showing the large northern arch, the castellated parapet and the two adjoining and stepped retaining walls of the tunnel that were also castellated and symmetrical. *S. Rankin*

Rear cover, top: A colour-tinted postcard view looking east to Maidens station and containing an Ayr postmark of 1907 on the back. The sheeted wagons of what looks like a potato train are seen at the nearer or western side of the island platform but partly hidden behind Jameston farm, while possibly the brake van is indistinctly seen at the end of the train on the right. In the left foreground is the Maybole road, while the road ahead leads to the station. *M. Chadwick*

Rear cover, bottom: A colour-tinted postcard view of Dunure station in the rock cutting below the goods yard, looking north-east. On the back of the postcard, containing postmarks of Dunure and Ayr of 1908, was the message 'Nice big station isn't it?' The goods shed on the higher ground of the yard looms over the station in the rock cutting, while the perspective provides the illusion that the yard is on a rising gradient; but, like any yard, it is effectively level, whereas the main line is descending at 1 in 80 north-east of, and at 1 in 100 through, the island platform. Entry to the yard from the Ayr direction was by facing points 400 yards beyond the platform. *M. Chadwick*

Rear cover: A G&SWR stamp-sized label, attractively depicting an aerial view of the hotel, bay and lighthouse at Turnberry and the Carrick coast to the north. The artwork was in existence by 1911 because the same view appeared as a poster that was illustrated in a *Railway Magazine* special G&SWR issue for April of that year. *M. Chadwick*

Rear cover: A G&SWR first class ticket from Glasgow St Enoch to Turnberry for the 1921 Ladies, Open Golf Championship. *NAS, Edinburgh*

Published by The Oakwood Press (Usk), P.O. Box 13, Usk, Mon., NP15 1YS.
E-mail: sales@oakwoodpress.co.uk
Website: www.oakwoodpress.co.uk

Contents

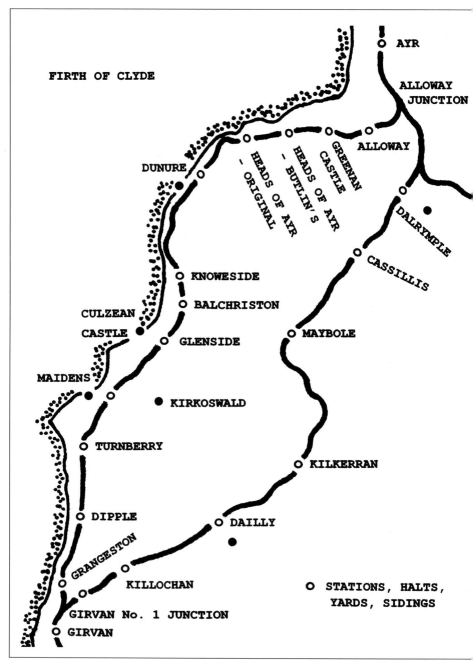

The route of the Maidens & Dunure Light Railway and the main Ayr-Girvan line through Maybole, showing the stations.
Drawn by D. McConnell

Introduction *by David McConnell*

It was in late 2001 that I had the idea of writing a little book about the Maidens & Dunure Light Railway, along the highly-scenic Carrick coast of Ayrshire through Turnberry; and my aim was to commemorate 100 years of the line in 2006, though the publication was initially intended to be available before the centenary date. I had bought a little book called *The Cairn Valley Light Railway*, written by Ian Kirkpatrick and published by Oakwood Press in 2000; and, about the same time, I had bought a booklet called *G&SWR Ayr and Cumnock Branches*, written by Stuart Rankin and published by the Glasgow & South-Western Railway Association also in 2000. The latter production was the fourth issue in a Sou'West Profile series that concentrated on a specific theme. With both the Oakwood and the G&SWR Association publications before me, I thought that, if the story of the G&SWR's Cairn Valley Light Railway, running north-west of Dumfries, was able to be publicized in book form, so could - and so *should* - a book be published about the G&SWR's Maidens & Dunure Light Railway, running south-west of Ayr. Then, with the idea of a larger-than-usual 'Sou'West Profile' in mind, I contacted the G&SWR Association to ask whether the project could be accomplished with the help of any members, but, of course, I did not know whether there would be anyone in the association who was sufficiently interested and knowledgeable to be able to collaborate in such a publication.

My plan for the book was based, firstly, on information that I had acquired from having written articles about the line for the popular *Scots Magazine* and the specialized *British Railway Journal* in 1985, and, secondly, in the hope that someone from the G&SWR Association would respond in having the prerequisites of enthusiasm and knowledge to complement mine. Stuart Rankin, as the archivist of the G&SWR Association and the editor of the Association's annual *Sou'West Journal*, contacted me and offered to assist, as he was enthusiastic and knowledgeable about aspects of the Maidens & Dunure line and had written numerous articles on railways, particularly about the G&SWR but also about the Caledonian Railway. Inevitably over the next few years, the booklet size was rapidly and greatly exceeded, becoming a volume, to the extent that we look back and wonder how we thought that a small book could have done justice to what the line was to present in its fascinating, extensive and varied history.

At the beginning of the project, I could not have realised the amount of material that would be available and the analysis that would be required and, therefore, to what extent the publication could develop. Nevertheless, I should have known better, because my previous book, *Rails to Kyle of Lochalsh*, for Oakwood Press, was originally intended to have been a small publication that I estimated would take two years to complete. Instead, it became a large book that took six years from the start in research to the completion in print, containing detailed text and many photographs and other illustrations, in telling the story of that highly-scenic line. Thus, during the seven years from 2002, I co-ordinated what has now been published about the Carrick coast railway, which was produced through extensive and intensive research, collation, analysis and writing, and through editing and blending with Stuart's written contributions, resulting from his analysis in addition to his knowledge of the line and of railways in general.

However, unlike my book about the Kyle of Lochalsh railway, which was published in time for its centenary in 1997, the book on the Maidens & Dunure line could not be published in time for its and Turnberry Hotel's simultaneous centenary in 2006. Although it was our intention to have achieved this, we were not able to succeed because much additional and vital information about the line was discovered only shortly before the centenary, leaving insufficient time to finish the book. The extra information was partly in the form of interesting memories of the line from several helpful ex-railway and non-railway people and partly from the discovery of other important historical material about both the original Turnberry period and the more recent Butlin's era. We had no doubt about deciding on a late and larger publication being preferable to an incomplete version being rushed in time for the Turnberry centenary celebrations; while another positive consequence of the delay was that several more photographs, other illustrations, and yet more significant historical material, were subsequently found and analysed much more recently, such that all these valuable components of the line's history would not have appeared in the book if it had been published in 2006.

Indeed, during the earlier period of our work, the subject of a limited number of available photographs for the book could have provided a serious obstacle to publication because the Carrick line was much less photographed than other railways, especially in the early years. Fortunately, we obtained an acceptable number, though it should be realised that the absence of specific photographs of the line most likely means that such photographs do not exist, and, if at one time they did exist, they have long been lost or destroyed. Perhaps one day, lost photographs may re-appear from the dusts of history.

So here is the outcome: a book on what was a vastly under-publicized railway and its associations with Turnberry Hotel and golf courses, amid the historic, historical and present-day environment of both Carrick and Ayrshire. Stuart and I therefore feel that justice has been done, at long last, in capturing the invigorating and romantic spirit of this scenic line and its fascinating and varied trains, services and embracing history – all astounding in relation to a small rural branch with no intermediate towns. The story of the Carrick coast railway, through the country of Robert the Bruce, the Clan Kennedy and Robert Burns, has now been told.

Turnberry Hotel and Turnberry golf clubhouse, with their striking red-tiled roofs, in the early era of the railway, from a colour-tinted postcard view.   *G. Clark*

Chapter One

Historic Ayrshire and Carrick, and their Railways

The part-lowland and part-upland maritime county of Ayr in south-western Scotland is bounded by the five counties of Renfrew to the north and north-east, Lanark to the north-east and east, Dumfries to the south-east, Kirkcudbright to the south-east, and Wigtown to the south; and by the sea expanse of the Firth of Clyde to the west. Ayrshire is crescent-shaped, of greatest length 58 miles in a straight line by the sea from the northernmost to the southernmost coastal points, but with the concave coastal distance adding another 30 miles; and of greatest width 30 miles west to east. The most northerly stretch of the boundary is formed near and along the course of the Kelly Burn that, in reaching the Firth of Clyde, separates the adjacent small towns of Skelmorlie in Ayrshire and Wemyss Bay in Renfrewshire. The southern extremity of the boundary is along the short Galloway Burn that reaches the sea a mile south of Finnarts Bay, at the head of Loch Ryan, where Wigtownshire begins. The greatest west-east distance of 30 miles extends from two locations on the coast, south-west of Ayr: from Fisherton and from Turnberry Point, due-east to their respective boundaries with Dumfriesshire. In general, Ayrshire is hilly in the north, flat in the centre and hilly in the south, but with the highest ground in the extreme south-east, attaining a peak of 2,565 ft at Kirriereoch Hill, precisely on the Ayrshire-Kirkcudbrightshire border, and a summit of 2,520 ft entirely within Ayrshire at the summit of nearby Shalloch on Minnoch. Of Scotland's 33 original counties, Ayrshire is the seventh largest in area, the fourth largest in population, and the largest outside the Highlands; and while there are counties in the Highlands and in the Lowlands that are greater than Ayrshire in area or population individually, there is no county in Scotland that is greater in both combined.

In centuries past, the area that eventually acquired the overall name of 'Ayrshire' had comprised four districts that were known as 'bailliaries' or 'provinces', with each having its own jurisdictions and baillies or magistrates. These bailliaries were, from north to south, Cunninghame, Kyle Stewart, Kyle Regis or King's Kyle, and Carrick, under the successive reigns of the Norman rulers David I, Malcolm IV and William I during the 12th century. The kings had recruited warriors from Norman England and France to acquire feudal control of more regions, and the warriors had been rewarded with extensive lands and had become royal agents within the expanding administration over south-western Scotland. Thus, Cunninghame had been awarded to Hugh de Morville, in having become High Constable of Scotland, with his family castle and administration located at Irvine; while Kyle Stewart had been presented to Walter Fitzalan, in having become the High Steward of Scotland, with his castle at Dundonald and administration at Prestwick, and with his family having become known as the Stewards or Stewarts. However, Kyle Regis had not been given to any family, in having remained directly under royal control at Ayr. Cunninghame, Kyle Stewart and Kyle Regis originally formed part of the region of Strathclyde within the Kingdom of Scotland; but Carrick had not been initially part of Strathclyde and Scotland and, instead, was a constituent of the independent region of Galloway, under Fergus MacDowall, Lord of Galloway, and his successors. Carrick had remained so until 1186, when it was separated from Galloway and became affiliated to Scotland while still under the inheritance of the MacDowall clan; and that year also, William I, who was known as William the Lion and who was the

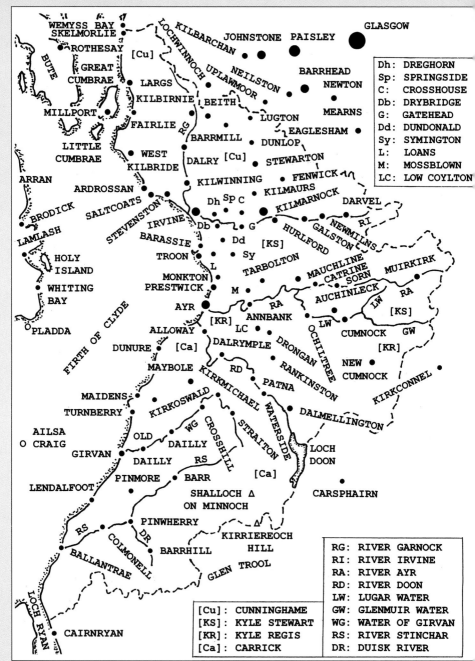

Ayrshire, showing towns, villages and the four original bailliaries and their river boundaries, with some small villages omitted owing to lack of space. The county was densely populated by railways, with most places served directly or indirectly, and some by both the G&SWR and the CR. Geographically, Ailsa Craig is part of Ayrshire; but Bute, Great Cumbrae, Little Cumbrae, Arran, Holy Island and Pladda are not, and they formed the pre-1975 county of Bute.

Drawn by D. McConnell

brother of David I, awarded a new title of Earl of Carrick to Duncan MacDowall, grandson of Fergus. The seat of the MacDowall clan was Turnberry Castle.

The three boundaries of the four bailliaries had been decided by principal water courses, flowing from east to west or from south-east to north-west: the River Irvine, separating Cunninghame and Kyle Stewart; the contiguous Glenmuir Water, Lugar Water and River Ayr, separating Kyle Stewart and Kyle Regis; and the River Doon, separating Kyle Regis and Carrick. At the mouth of the River Ayr, William the Lion built a castle in 1197, establishing a king's or royal burgh, and the importance of the settlement of Ayr increased in 1207 with the incorporation of the four bailliaries into the larger judicial region as the sheriffdom of Ayr, under the authority of a sheriff or judge in the town of Ayr. However, the names Cunninghame, Kyle and Carrick - with the two Kyles uniting - remained in permanent use for reasons of tradition, geography and local administration.

Turnberry Castle was the birthplace in 1274 of Robert the Bruce, who was to become Scotland's king. His father, of Norman origin, was Robert Bruce, Lord of Annandale in the south-western border country of Scotland; and his mother, of Celtic origin, was Marjorie MacDowall, Countess of Carrick and the granddaughter of Duncan, the first Earl of Carrick; while his grandfather of the same name had been one of the claimants to the Scottish throne after the death of King Alexander III of Scotland in 1286 had left no heir. In that year, a meeting took place at Turnberry Castle of the nation's noblemen who were supportive of the claim of the Bruce family in having the nearest male heir to the throne. Unfortunately, the peaceful and prosperous period in Scotland under Alexander's rule was soon to change dramatically, when a provisional ruling council for Scotland ill-fatedly asked King Edward I of England for guidance in choosing the next Scottish monarch, and Edward saw this as an opportune and devious plan for his subjugation of Scotland. An invasion in 1296 by Edward's army and the capture of strategic Scottish castles resulted in the Wars of Independence, whereby powerful resistances were led by William Wallace of Elderslie near Paisley and Andrew Moray of the Moray province in north-eastern Scotland, in the determination that Scotland would never submit to Edward and English domination. The cause was maintained by Robert the Bruce, who had inherited the title of Earl of Carrick from his mother as the Countess of Carrick, and, with the approval of some of the Scottish noblemen and church representatives, he was crowned King of Scots, as King Robert I, in 1306, in spite of the English invasion.

With the support of James Douglas of Douglasdale, south of Lanark, he sought to recapture the Scottish castles, including his home at Turnberry that was under the command of Henry Percy, Lord of Northumberland, on behalf of Edward. However, after battles lost at Methven, west of Perth, and at Tyndrum, north of Loch Lomond, he had no option but to flee; but he found further support from Angus MacDonald, Lord of the Isles and Kintyre, and in 1307, he made another attempt for Scottish liberty. Edward I had vowed to destroy the Scots but he did not, for he died in 1307, succeeded by his son as Edward II. In darkness, the freedom fighters of Robert the Bruce and James Douglas crossed from the isle of Arran to land at the bay of Port Carrick, north of Turnberry, and they terrorized the English soldiers, with the stunned Henry Percy thereafter abandoning Turnberry and fleeing to the safety of Ayr. The freedom army proceeded through Galloway, making Robert's headquarters at the Forest of Buchan in Glen Trool, and defeating much larger English armies in that location and at Loudon Hill in Cunninghame. Through 1307 and 1308, Robert and James regained most of the Scottish castles, encompassing as far north as Aberdeen and Inverness, such that Robert was able to hold the first free parliament in Scotland for 18 years, in 1309 at St Andrews, and among the successes was Ayr Castle in 1312, where he convened a parliament that year. His greatest battle for liberty occurred in 1314 when his 6,000 fighters, assisted by James Douglas, defeated the 20,000 trained soldiers of Edward II at Bannockburn, south of Stirling.

Robert the Bruce - Earl of Carrick and King of Scots, from Turnberry Castle - was a hero not only because he had won back freedom and independence for Scotland but also for his other achievements: rebuilding, uniting and stabilising the nation; restoring integrity and law and order; and re-establishing the economy through trade with other countries. Furthermore, he had treated his English captives with humanity, to their own and England's general astonishment, in spite of the brutal behaviour and the legacy of the tyrannical Edward I, who had left the Scots long in hatred and distrust of the English nation.

King Robert died in 1329, aged 54, and his son David, from his second wife Elizabeth, succeeded him as David II. However, David died in 1371 and he was succeeded by King Robert's grandson, Robert Stewart, from his first wife Isobel and their daughter Marjorie, whose husband was Walter Stewart, the High Steward of Scotland, of Dundonald Castle. At the late age of 55, Robert Stewart became King of Scots as Robert II, and the significance of his appointment lay in the fact that he became the first monarch of the Stewart dynasty, which eventually succeeded to the English throne as Stuart in addition to the Scottish sovereignty and which originated at Dundonald in Kyle Stewart as part of the sheriffdom of Ayr.

Before the Wars of Independence, the principal clan of Carrick was the MacDowalls, as the Celtic Lords of Galloway, but after the era of the Bruce dynasty of Robert I and David II, the dominant clan became the Kennedys, who were resident in Carrick at the time of Robert the Bruce, and who supported him in his fight for Scottish liberty. In 1357, John Kennedy of Dunure Castle had been granted a charter by David II, confirming the lands and dwellings already in his possession and allowing the acquisition of the estate of Cassillis (pronounced formally as 'Cassillis' and less so as 'Cassills'), north-east of Maybole a few years later; and then in 1372, Robert II, on a visit to Ayr, bestowed upon him the title of Chief of the Clan Kennedy. In 1405, John Kennedy's grandson, James, married Princess Mary Stewart, granddaughter of Robert II; and thus, in addition to attaining the Royal Stewart lineage, the right to the claim of descent from Robert the Bruce and the Earls of Carrick was established. The Kennedys remained loyal to the House of Stewart, and a reward as an honour for the family name was granted by King James IV of Scotland in 1509, with the creation of the title of Earl of Cassillis for David Kennedy, the third Lord Kennedy and clan chief.

The fourth Earl of Cassillis was Gilbert Kennedy, who was a greedy tyrant and became infamous for his cruel treatment, in 1570, of the trustee or Commendator of Crossraguel Abbey, south-west of Maybole. Gilbert wanted the Crossraguel land that was in the interim possession of the Commendator, Allan Stewart, who would not release the land, and Gilbert resorted to brutal actions. He imprisoned Allan in the vaults of Dunure Castle and, stripping him of his clothes, he tied him to a spit and roasted him over a fire, as the servants poured oil on him so that he would not burn in flames. After much suffering, Allan had no option but to surrender the land, and he was intended to be kept a prisoner until his burns had healed, but he was soon rescued by another branch of the Kennedy family who were in a feud with Gilbert. They were the Kennedys of Bargany (pronounced 'Barginny' - hard 'g'), nearby in the valley of the Water of Girvan, who also wanted the Crossraguel land but who, on hearing of Allan's plight, had the decency to free him by storming the castle, and Gilbert was sent to prison at Dumbarton Castle. Ironically, he purchased the Crossraguel land legally the following year, and he paid Allan, who was crippled from the roasting, an annual payment as a pension in compensation, but the episode cast a large and enduring stain on the Kennedys of Cassillis.

While the seat of the Kennedys was Cassillis House, the family owned another structure on the coast, called Coif or Cove - from the Norse, meaning 'cave', because of six large caves directly below its site on the top of cliffs. This building, having become a ruined tower or castle, had been in existence by or before the 15th century, and the notorious Gilbert had granted a charter there in 1569 to his brother Thomas, who renovated and enlarged the ruin into an L-shaped tower in the 1590s. Thomas named his new castle Cullean (pronounced 'Cull*ain*') - from the Gaelic, meaning 'nook of the birds', because of the many seabirds nesting in the caves.

The rise of the Kennedys continued through the reign of the Stewarts in Scotland as far as Mary Queen of Scots and her son James VI, who, as the successor to Queen Elizabeth of England, became James I of England by the Union of the Crowns in 1603 that united the monarchies of the two countries. The influence of the Kennedys in Carrick, and ultimately over all the land southwards to encompass western Galloway, occurred because a central government in Scotland was ineffective for the whole country in implementing administration and law, with the monarchy having appointed local or regional landowners for such purposes.

Like much of Ayrshire and southern Scotland during the mid-to-late 17th century, Carrick was staunch Covenanter country, and John Kennedy, as the sixth Earl of Cassillis and as Lord Justice-General of Scotland from 1649 to 1651, and his son, John, as the seventh Earl, were ardent Covenanters. They were Presbyterians or Protestants who courageously resisted the tyrannical attempts of the Stuart kings Charles I and Charles II, of both Scotland and England, to enforce the English Episcopalian religion in Scotland. The signing of the National Covenant of 1638 and of the Solemn Covenant of 1644 - hence the Covenanter name - portrayed the determination of the Scottish people to fight for the retention of their religion. From the signing of the 1638 Covenant, there occurred a 50-year period that was marked by increasing unrest, fighting, persecution, brutality and killings during the reigns of Charles I and Charles II against the Covenanters. Presbyterianism was made illegal but ministers continued to preach in secret in houses, barns and other outbuildings and on the slopes and tops of hill slopes that were remote from the government authorities. Ministers who preached at these open-air 'conventicles' (originating from 'place to convene'), which attracted large crowds, risked execution. In 1678, the largest conventicle in Scotland was held on the 830 ft-high Craigdow Hill (pronounced 'Craig*doo*), three miles south-west of Maybole, when 7,000 people gathered from various parts of Carrick and beyond for two days, while 600 armed men were positioned around the hill to guard them from possible attack by government soldiers.

Particularly from 1680 to 1685, the extent of the atrocities and executions was such that the period became known as 'The Killing Time', when the widespread murder of the Covenanters was despicably sanctioned under the religious 'blessing' of the Stuart monarchy. In 1685, Charles II was succeeded by his younger Catholic brother as James VII of Scotland and James II of England, but from his attempts to catholicize the United Kingdom, he was replaced after the 'bloodless revolution' of 1688, which was the called the 'Glorious Revolution' by Protestants, because it resulted in the Protestant monarchy of Mary Stewart and her Dutch husband Willem Hendrik,

A dark and stormy view of the ruins of Turnberry Castle (*above*), the birthplace of Robert the Bruce; and a serene twilight view of Culzean Castle (*below*) and the nearer Culzean Home Farm, perched over the cliffs and coves, with Ailsa Craig in the distance to the south.

Carnegie Library, Ayr

Prince of Orange, while also ensuring that the persecution of the Covenanters was at an end. The era of Scotland's Covenanters, having extended for 50 years during the 17th century, encompassed a significant but distressing and terrifying episode in the history of Carrick, and many people died as martyrs, with graves and other memorials throughout Carrick and southern Scotland honouring their bravery.

A new landmark in the history of the Kennedys was heralded in 1762 because, in place of Cassillis House, Cullean Castle was adopted as the principal seat of residence for the family, who were now the Kennedys of Cullean. David Kennedy, the 10th Earl of Cassillis, commissioned the renowned Scottish architect Robert Adam to enlarge and transform Cullean, which involved the caves below the cliffs having to be filled or strengthened with supports to accommodate the extra weight of the new structure. The work was carried out in four stages between 1777 and 1792, and the new Culzean Castle (by now, generally spelled with the 'z' and still pronounced 'Cull*ain*') was a magnificent part-Gothic and part-Classical mansion, dramatically perched on 100-feet-high vertical cliffs, commanding the spectacular setting of the beautiful expanse of the outer Firth of Clyde that was dominated by the isle of Arran.

Archibald Kennedy, the 12th Earl, was created Baron Ailsa in 1806, having taken his title from the island rock of Ailsa Craig, which was his property and which was prominently seen south-westwards from Culzean in the outer Firth of Clyde. A quarter of a century later in 1830, King William IV of the United Kingdom presented to him the title of Marquis of Ailsa, and the new Marquis spent large sums of money improving the castle and estate, including experimenting with new methods of agriculture and horticulture and in introducing new flowers, plants and trees.

The first Marquis was succeeded in 1846 by his grandson, also Archibald, who lived at Reigate in Surrey, in sometimes staying at Culzean, but the second Marquis and the Marchioness moved there permanently in 1852. The Marquis began to make further improvements at Culzean, at his other properties in Carrick, including Cassillis house, Maybole Castle and Newark Castle, south-west of Alloway, and at the hamlet of Douglaston (now the village of Maidens) by Maidenhead Bay, though debts restricted his collective success. The family were the first of the Culzean inheritors who were able to make convenient use of the revolutionary transport through the Kennedy country of the steam-locomotive railway, which, having reached Ayr from Glasgow in 1840 and from London to Glasgow via Dumfries and Kilmarnock in 1850, had been extended into Carrick from Ayr to Maybole in 1856. Little could the second Marquis have realised that, as the railways continued to expand through Ayrshire, his eldest son - Archibald, the 14th Earl of Cassillis, who was born at Culzean in 1847 - would become involved in promoting a railway that would run through the Kennedy country along the Carrick coast from Ayr to Girvan, in passing close to Culzean Castle and Turnberry Castle - thereby effectively symbolizing the connection between the Kennedys and Robert the Bruce.

Before the appearance of the railways in Ayrshire, horse-drawn vehicles on the roads had been the only public land transport for passengers. Affluent members of society, like the Marquis of Ailsa, could travel by their own horse-drawn coaches, but the vast majority of the people were served by public coaches that also carried the mails, while carrier firms used horse-drawn vehicles to transport agricultural produce and manufactured goods to the markets in Ayrshire's largest towns and to Glasgow and Edinburgh. Steamboats - the other regular form of transport for passengers and goods before the railways - plied the length of the Firth of Clyde to connect Glasgow and Stranraer by way of the Ayrshire coast, with services - daily or weekly, or twice- or three-times-weekly - calling at Largs, Ardrossan, Troon, Ayr, Girvan and occasionally Ballantrae; while there were also services between Ardrossan and Brodick and Lamlash on the isle of Arran.

For the conveyance of minerals, several horse-drawn wagonways had been established in the county, which was rich in coal and ironstone, and such valuable minerals for local industries and for export at local harbours were carried much easier on rails than could be done on the roads, while they also allowed the mineral owners to evade turnpike, or toll-gate, charges that only applied to carts on the roads. Coal was especially important for export to other areas of Scotland and to Ireland, and an efficient means for coal and iron-ore to reach harbours was vital. During the decades between the second half of the 18th and the early 19th centuries, wagonways for minerals had been constructed in the following locations of the county: in the vicinity of Ayr, at Newton, Wallacetown, Holmston, Auchincruive and Annbank, for coal; at Muirkirk, for coal and iron-ore; between Kilmarnock and Troon, for coal; at Saltcoats, Stevenston and Kilwinning, for coal and iron; at Shewalton, by Irvine, for coal; and at Mansefield, by New Cumnock, for coal and limestone. Of these horse-drawn wagonways, the most sophisticated and, by far, the longest, at 10 miles, was the Kilmarnock & Troon Railway (K&TR), which, in opening partly in 1811 and completely in 1812, was a precursor of the locomotive railways that were to emerge throughout Britain two and three decades later. The K&TR also carried passengers, as did another wagonway, or railway, between Ardrossan and Kilwinning, which, after opening from Ardrossan to Stevenston in 1830 and to Kilwinning in 1831 for coal traffic, started conveying passengers in 1834. This 5½ miles-long line was part of the Ardrossan & Johnstone Railway that was not completed beyond Kilwinning, but the locomotive railway was soon to follow and form the connection with Johnstone, Paisley and Glasgow.

In 1836, businessmen from Glasgow and Ayrshire formed the Glasgow, Paisley, Kilmarnock & Ayr Railway Company (GPK&AR), with a proposed capital of £550,000, on a scale that would make it the most extensive railway system in Scotland, and the most advanced, in being worked by locomotives. The project would unite the potentials of the large city of Glasgow, with a population of 280,000, and its neighbouring large town of Paisley, containing 60,000 people, to the economic advantages of Ayrshire. In addition to its resources in minerals, the county possessed expanses of land that were used for dairy, arable and sheep farming - the Ayrshire breed of cattle being remarkable for the large quantity and high quality of milk output - and many farms were involved in two or all three types of agriculture; while fishing was another principal industry of Ayrshire that would benefit from the new railway, as would the increasing population generally. In essence, the railway would provide a fast connection with the principal ports and the manufacturing, commercial, industrial and rural towns and villages of northern and central Ayrshire. Back in 1755, the total number of people of the county was 59,000, when Irvine was the largest town, with 3,000, followed by Kilmarnock, with 2,500, and Ayr, including Newton and Wallacetown, with 2,000. However, as the county population continued to grow to 73,500 in 1790, to 84,000 in 1801, to 104,000 in 1811, and to 150,000 when the GPK&AR was proposed in 1836, the populations of Kilmarnock and Ayr had risen greater in proportion to the county's population. Having accounted for less than a tenth of the total in 1755, both towns together now contained about a quarter. Each had greatly superseded Irvine, and the county's largest towns in 1836 were: Kilmarnock, 19,000; Ayr, 16,000; Irvine, 7,000; Girvan, 5,000; Saltcoats, 4,000; and Maybole, 3,000.

An Act of Parliament in 1837 authorized the GP&KR by Johnstone and the Garnock Valley to Dalry, where the one line would continue southwards to Ayr via Irvine and the other would branch south-eastwards to Kilmarnock; while at Kilwinning on the Ayr line, a new Ardrossan Railway would connect the important harbour of Ardrossan with the GPK&AR. The first section of the line over the 11 miles between Ayr and Irvine was opened on 5th August, 1839, with the rest of the route opening in sections during 1840, resulting in the whole 40 miles between Ayr and Glasgow being opened on 12th August, 1840. The station in Ayr was located at Newton on the northern side of the River Ayr, and the station in Glasgow was Bridge Street, in the city centre on the southern side of the River Clyde. The 5½ miles of the Ardrossan line opened on 17th August, 1840, in connection with the GPK&AR, but the construction of the 11¾ miles of the Kilmarnock line from Dalry did not begin until the summer of 1841, and the opening was on 4th April, 1843.

The line to Kilmarnock - ironically called 'the Kilmarnock branch' and making the town a circuitous 34 miles from Glasgow - was intended to be continued through Nithsdale to Dumfries and Carlisle to form part of the proposed trunk line from Glasgow, by Lancaster and Birmingham, to London, and the success of the GPK&AR was believed to have increased the chances of the extension materializing. However, the optimism was accompanied by anxiety because of a competing line between Glasgow and Carlisle that was proposed to run by a more direct, if steeper, route through Clydesdale and Annandale. Ultimately, two new railway committees were established in 1844: of the Glasgow, Dumfries & Carlisle Railway (GD&CR), reinforcing the strength and success of the GPK&AR and its continuation by Nithsdale; and of the Caledonian Railway (CR), having government support for Annandale and allowing the opportunity of establishing a line for Edinburgh from it in Clydesdale.

The Caledonian Railway Act of 1845 authorized the incorporation of the large ambitious company and the construction of a valuable railway system from Carlisle by Annandale and Clydesdale to Glasgow and Edinburgh. In the same year, the GPK&AR, undaunted in competition with the CR, presented a Bill for the extension of its railway system from Kilmarnock to Cumnock and the GD&CR presented a Bill, in conjunction with the GPK&AR proposal, for the extension from Cumnock through Nithsdale, Dumfries and Gretna to Carlisle. While the GPK&AR Bill was successful, the GD&CR Bill failed, and the strong case for the CR route was proved in Parliament as the shortest and most direct line for Scotland generally. The GD&CR promoters were advised by Parliament that if their Bill was modified to 'terminate' by a junction with the CR line at Gretna, the outcome would likely be different. Thus, in 1846, at the second attempt, the GD&CR presented its revised Bill that sought running powers over the CR line from Gretna to Carlisle, and the Bill was sanctioned on the stipulation that the Nithsdale line would, in effect, be a local line that was not intended to compete with the CR route for traffic between Carlisle and Glasgow.

The CR was opened throughout from Carlisle to Glasgow and Edinburgh on 15th February, 1848, when the first 'west-coast' railway services commenced between Scotland's two largest cities and London. The combined and extensive GPK&AR and GD&CR scheme from Kilmarnock to Gretna, in completing the whole distance from Glasgow to Carlisle via Nithsdale, opened in sections from 1848 and the whole stretch was completed on 28th October, 1850, granting Kilmarnock and Ayrshire an unprecedented fast communication with Carlisle over the 91 miles of railway distance from Kilmarnock, and, thereby, with London by way of the London & North Western Railway (LNWR).

The date of 28th October, 1850 was significant in another respect. Back in 1847, an Act of Parliament had been passed, in conjunction with the GD&CR Act of 1846, for the eventual incorporation of a new railway company from the amalgamation of the GPK&AR and the GD&CR, and this Act sanctioned the vesting of GD&CR in the GPK&AR on the date of opening throughout of the GD&CR, when the GD&CR Company would be dissolved and the GPK&A Company would be called the Glasgow & South Western Railway Company (G&SWR). The amalgamation occurred as intended, when the G&SWR, with its headquarters at Bridge Street station in Glasgow, officially came into existence on 28th October, 1850. The train livery of the G&SWR both for the locomotives and the coaches was dark green, which had been maintained from the most recent livery of the GPK&AR.

Progress was next made in the establishment of railways beyond Ayr - south-eastwards to Dalmellington and southwards to Maybole and Girvan. The Ayr & Dalmellington Railway, from a junction with the GPK&AR at Newton-on-Ayr, was opened to Dalmellington on 15th May, 1856 for goods and minerals, in serving the Dalmellington Iron Company's works at Waterside, and on 7th August, 1856 for passengers, with a new but incomplete station opened at Townhead on the south-eastern side of Ayr. The Ayr & Maybole Railway was opened to Maybole, the administration centre and 'capital of Carrick', on 15th September, 1856 for goods and on 13th October, 1856 for passengers. The distance from Ayr to Maybole was eight miles, but with the first three miles shared with the Dalmellington line, and a new permanent station at Ayr Townhead, opened on 1st July, 1857, served the two routes. The natural continuation of the railway from Ayr to Maybole was down the valley of the Water of Girvan to reach the town of Girvan, which was Carrick's largest fishing port and the Maybole & Girvan Railway, 13 miles long, was opened on 24th May, 1860 for passengers and goods.

It was never intended that the railway system would cease at Girvan, and a line southwards to reach Stranraer and connect with Ireland by steamboat communication was further encouraged by the opening of other lines in south-western Scotland. These were principally the Castle Douglas & Dumfries Railway in 1859, and the Portpatrick Railway from Castle Douglas to Stranraer and from Stranraer to Portpatrick in 1861 and 1862 respectively. In 1865, an Act was obtained for the Girvan & Portpatrick Junction Railway (G&PJR) to build a line that would run southwards and inland from Girvan, up the valley of the Duisk River and by the village of Barrhill, over the expanse of hill country and bleak and empty moorland, to reach the gentler land by the village of New Luce, down the fertile valley of the Water of Luce, and join the Portpatrick Railway at the head of Luce Bay, two miles east of Glenluce village. Unfortunately, the scheme lay in abeyance for five years, and another Act was required in 1870. Finally, the single-track line of 30¾ miles was opened throughout on 5th October, 1877 from Girvan to Challoch Junction to join the Portpatrick Railway's route to Stranraer. The G&PJR, which united Carrick and Galloway, contributed a sizeable fraction of the 100 miles of railway that now connected Glasgow, Ayr, Girvan and Stranraer harbour.

The opening of the Gothic-styled St Enoch station in Glasgow in 1876 was one of three significant and co-incident developments in association with the G&SWR that year - the other two being the establishment of an alliance with the large Midland Railway Company (MR), based in Derby, and the opening of the MR's 72 miles-long Settle & Carlisle Railway to convey Anglo-Scottish services over the new 'Midland route' between the company's St Pancras station in London and St Enoch. The new Glasgow station, as part of the City of Glasgow Union Railway, was jointly owned by the G&SWR and the Edinburgh-based North British Railway (NBR) as allies, and the date of 1st May, 1876 for the St Enoch and Settle & Carlisle Railway openings heralded the introduction of joint G&SWR-MR express through services between London and Glasgow over the 'Midland route' via Luton, Leicester, Nottingham, Derby, Sheffield, Leeds and Carlisle, and then via Dumfries and Kilmarnock. The G&SWR's agreement for the London service consisted of operating the trains between Glasgow and Carlisle, and they ran by the Glasgow, Barrhead & Kilmarnock Joint Railway (GB&KJR) that had been authorized by an Act of 1869 and had been co-financed by the G&SWR and the large Caledonian Railway, from the logic in avoiding two competing lines by this route.

The GB&KJR opened on 26th June, 1873 and provided a shorter route between Glasgow and Kilmarnock, via Lugton and Stewarton in Ayrshire, to reduce the Glasgow-Carlisle distance to 115 miles, instead of 125 miles by Paisley and Dalry. The GB&KJR was greatly significant to both companies, because, from it, the G&SWR had acquired a more direct and natural line as part of its trunk route to Carlisle and London and the CR had obtained its first access to Ayrshire by reaching the important manufacturing town of Kilmarnock. The G&SWR's Glasgow-London services used 'Midland Scotch Joint Stock' coaches that were equally-owned and operated by the G&SWR, the MR and the NBR, as an alliance in opposition to the Glasgow-London partnership of the CR and LNWR.

Nevertheless, apart from the necessity of the GB&KJR, the situation had become imperative for the G&SWR during the mid-1860s to prevent the threat of an invasion into Ayrshire by the CR, and this resulted in the company having acted with speed and determination in the building of two cross-country branch railways eastwards from Ayr. These lines, via Annbank and Tarbolton to Mauchline and via Annbank and Ochiltree to Cumnock, had opened in 1870 and 1872 respectively, allowing connections with Muirkirk and Lanarkshire, and encompassing the districts between Ayr and Lanarkshire that were rich in coal and iron ore.

On 12th January, 1886, a new and much larger passenger station, built of red freestone, was opened at Ayr on the site of its Townhead predecessor, and, like Glasgow St Enoch station, it was built in conjunction with a grand hotel of 60 bedrooms, with the station comprising four platforms and four sets of rails. Two of each were through platforms and tracks, on the eastern side of the station, and two were dock or bay platforms and tracks, facing north, on the western side.

In northern parts of Ayrshire from the late 1870s to the late 1880s, two more sets of railway extensions had taken place, separately - one by the G&SWR and the other by the CR. In sections between 1878 and 1885, the G&SWR had completed the extension from Ardrossan through West Kilbride and Fairlie to Largs; but by the early mid-to-late 1880s, the CR had been intent on capitalizing on mineral and passenger traffic by way of Ardrossan. The result was the CR-backed Lanarkshire & Ayrshire Railway (L&AR) of 1884 that would allow the CR to reach, from Glasgow and Lanarkshire, the northern Ayrshire coast by way of the GB&KJR and by the construction of a new line from there to Kilwinning and Ardrossan, with branches to Kilbirnie and Irvine. The L&AR main line opened from near Barrmill, on the GB&KJR's Lugton-Beith branch, to Kilwinning and Ardrossan town in 1888, reaching Kilbirnie in 1889 and Ardrossan harbour and Irvine in 1890.

The arrival of the CR directly into the lucrative Kilbirnie-Ardrossan-Irvine triangle, in the domain of the G&SWR, not only had a profound effect on the G&SWR but necessitated certain action by the G&SWR much further south, on hearing that the CR were considering the purchase of the line between Girvan and

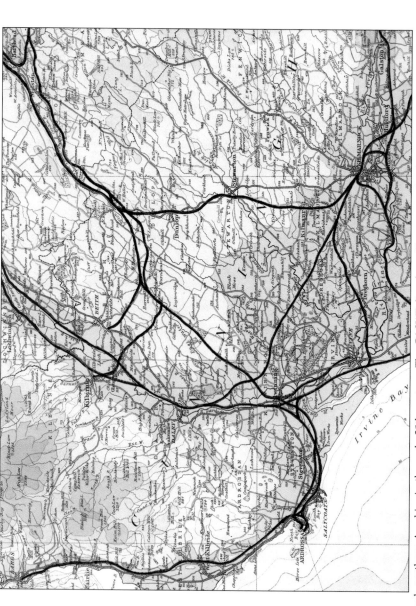

Railways through northern Ayrshire in the early 20th century. The G&SWR line from Glasgow via Paisley runs (*from top centre*) south to Kilwinning, branching west to Ardrossan and turning north to Largs, with the line to Ayr continuing south via Irvine. The G&SWR and CR joint line from Glasgow via Barrhead runs via Neilston, Uplawmoor and Lugton south to Kilmarnock (*from top right to bottom right*); but in 1903, the CR opened a parallel direct line from Glasgow, running east of the joint line, and then west to Barmill, where it joined the existing CR route of 1888 from Barmill south-west via Kilwinning

Challoch Junction, as part of an ambitious expansion plan of expansion through Ayrshire from Glasgow to Stranraer. The G&PJR had already been sold cheaply in 1887 to a new company of London businessmen under the name of the Ayrshire & Wigtownshire Railway (A&WR), which from that year had become the new name for the G&PJR, and they had sold it in 1890 to a lawyer from Edinburgh, John Blair, who was a Director of the A&WR and who, like his London predecessors, had no interest in the line other than for the financial reason. After trying to sell it in 1891 and 1892, he was fortunate that the G&SWR had shown a sudden interest, by the latter year, because of the CR threat. Fortunately for the G&SWR, the CR was in no hurry to proceed south of Irvine, and the G&SWR purchased the A&WR in early 1892, permitting the company full control of the stretch from Girvan to Challoch Junction, and this outright ownership greatly decreased the CR's incentive for reaching Stranraer.

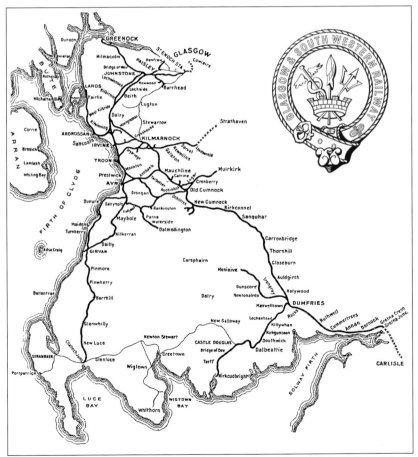

The system of the G&SWR. Routes entirely owned are indicated heavy; those jointly owned are light; and those having running powers are dotted. For towns and villages served, part of this map can be compared with the Ayrshire map on page 8.

G&SWR Association

Robert Burns (*above*); and Burns' Cottage at Alloway (*below*), on the right of this south-looking view.   *(Both) Carnegie Library, Ayr*

Chapter Two

Rails for Alloway, 1896-1897

In the six decades since the arrival of the locomotive railways to Ayrshire, the population of the county had increased from 150,000 to nearly a quarter of a million. By the early 1890s, Kilmarnock was still the largest town, containing 29,000 people, followed by Ayr, with 25,000, and then Irvine and Saltcoats, with 9,000 and 6,000. South of Ayr, in Carrick, Maybole's general increase to 5,000 had overtaken Girvan's more significant decrease to 4,000, because Girvan's population had temporarily risen from 5,000 in 1836 to 7,000 in 1850 and had then fallen during the second half of the 19th century. This change originated from a significant immigration by Irish refugee families because of the island's disastrous potato famine in 1845 and from the growth in Girvan of the cottage industry of cotton-weaving, but then with a gradual decline in the traditional industry during the second half of the century, as it was superseded by mechanized factory weaving, particularly in Glasgow and Paisley.

The spread of the railways had greatly helped - and had been greatly helped by - the growth of the population and commerce of Ayrshire, and also by the early 1890s, the county had been densely criss-crossed by railways that served most of the towns and villages. There were lines for minerals - coal and iron ore - and for other industries, especially agriculture and fishing; there were lines for the vital 'commodity' of passengers; and there were lines by two rival companies: of the Glasgow & South Western Railway, displaying a train livery of dark green for locomotives and, from 1884, crimson for passenger coaches; and of the Caledonian Railway, consisting of dark blue for passenger locomotives, with black for goods locomotives, and brown and white, or brown, for passenger coaches.

Again by the 1890s, most of the trunk railways, subsidiary main-line railways and additional cross-country branches - those originally considered of greatest priority - had already been constructed in Scotland and in the British Isles generally, with a large proportion of the lines having materialized during the 'railway mania' period of the mid-to-late 1840s, while a similar ratio had applied to Ayrshire as had occurred nationally. However, railway-building, while certainly well past its peak, had still not ceased by this time, neither nationally nor in Ayrshire, and the G&SWR was still intent on laying new lines.

In November 1896, the G&SWR provided the required notices for the 1897 session of Parliament to announce a number of other lines were intended to be made in Ayrshire. Included in the 1896 G&SWR notices for the 1897 session - if to the astonishment of much of the town and neighbourhood of Ayr - was the planned construction of a short branch to the village of Alloway, to commence from the Ayr-Maybole-Girvan line and to terminate at the Burns Arms Hotel. The idea of this branch was induced by the centenary commemorations, on 21st July, 1896, of the death of Robert Burns, Scotland's national poet, for Alloway, two miles south of Ayr on the Kyle side of the River Doon, was the birthplace of the poet; and a railway into the very heart of the Burns Country highlighted the immense tourist potential; but, not surprisingly, such a line was also seen by many as an intrusion through the very heart of the sacred district. However, there was also support for the line, and an example appeared in the twice-weekly *Ayr Observer* newspaper of 17th November, 1896:

The 'haunted' Auld Alloway Kirk and graveyard (*above*); and the Auld Brig o' Doon, looking northwards from Carrick to Kyle, and to Burns' Monument (*below*). *(Both) Carnegie Library, Ayr*

A Bill is to be promoted, containing among other clauses a branch line to Burns' Monument. This new line will form a junction with the main line south of Ayr at a point beyond Belmont, and will run round behind Rozelle, with a terminus at Alloway. Though no active agitation has been raised for the promotion of this line, the wonder is that it has not been carried out long ago. The thousands of visitors to the Land of Burns and the desire of numerous residents to visit the Cottage and Monument might have suggested this long ago.

The village of Alloway, the town and the county of Ayr, and the town and county of Dumfries constituted 'the Burns Country' or 'the Land of Burns' that encompassed the poet's places of residence, livelihood, escapades and admiration in south-western Scotland during his 37½-years' lifespan. Robert Burns was born on 25th January, 1759 in the dwelling-house which became famously known as Burns' Cottage and which was built by his father, William Burnes, as the surname was originally spelt (pronounced '*Burn*-niss'), who originated from near Stonehaven, Kincardineshire, in north-eastern Scotland.

However, in late 1896, the G&SWR's planned branch to Alloway was not the only form of transport that was being considered in that direction because of the widespread fame of Robert Burns. For the previous one and a half decades, there had been much discussion about the formation of a tramway for Ayr that would embrace Prestwick and the Burns Country at Alloway; and the tramway topic, originating this time not from local enterprise but from London, had re-emerged concurrently with, but independently of, the idea of the railway to Alloway that had been mentioned in the *Ayr Observer* of 17th November, 1896. The paper recorded in its issue of 20th November:

There is something singular in the almost simultaneous announcement that a London company propose to make a tramway from Ayr to Burns' Monument and that the Glasgow and South Western Railway Company intend to construct a branch railway to the same place. It is about 15 years since it was first proposed to form this tramway, and for several years past the Town Council have been talking of doing it - only getting the length of talk, however. Already it is announced that the proposed line [the branch railway] is to be opposed, but it is not said on what grounds. It will be a novelty in railway history to hear of successful opposition to a scheme giving railway accommodation to any district.

In reality, the promotion of the two schemes was not 'singular', if seemingly so, because the reason for their simultaneous emergence was the Robert Burns connection, and a steam railway and an electric tramway to Alloway were seen as essential in providing the means to convey numerous sightseers quickly and conveniently to the various Burns shrines at and in the vicinity of the village - in particular, Burns' Cottage, the Burns Monument, the Auld Brig o' Doon, and the 'haunted' Auld Alloway Kirk and graveyard.

Of the planned railway to Alloway and an alleged ulterior motive for it by the G&SWR, the weekly *Ayrshire Post* newspaper, published in Ayr, was in opposition to the new scheme, as stated in its issue of 20th November:

The proposal of the Glasgow & South Western Railway Company to run a branch line from Belmont Junction or thereabouts to Burns' Monument, we regard with unconditional hostility; it is bad for Ayr, it has no compensating advantages, and it will have to be opposed. To begin with, it is part and parcel of the policy of the South Western to draw its cordon a little closer and a little tighter about the town, and to shut out, if it only can, competition from any and every quarter. It may not mean an absolute perpetuity of the existing railway monopoly, but it tends in that direction, for it makes it worse for any competing line to break through the sacred circle with which the South Western are gradually shutting us in.

Adjacent on the page to the paper's assertions were further words of disapproval from a regular correspondent under the pseudonym of 'Oculeus':

No! no! anything but that! Here [is] this - There is a proposal by the G&SW Railway Coy to run a branch railway to Burns' Monument. Not if I can prevent it. The very idea of such a thing knocks all the romance and poesy out of the hallow'd spot. We cannot afford to have our classic Burns country despoiled, or the romance of Auld Alloway's Kirk brought to naught by 19th century trains steaming past the place. Oh! let us have one small spot left to the calm and repose of rural quietness free from the thunder, noise, and bustle of railway enterprise. Leave, O! leave us our 'To the monument' drive. Carriage hirers, too, must live as well as railway shareholders. If this scheme is persisted in I'll - I'll - Yes, I will.

In contrast to the preceding newspaper sentiments, the weekly *Ayr Advertiser* had not involved itself in an opinion about whether or not the line should be made, and, instead, in early January 1897, helpfully indicated the route:

The proposed new railway to Burns' Monument branches off the main line to Girvan a short distance beyond Annfield farm - about a mile and a half from Ayr - and curving to the south-west crosses over the public road to Maybole a little below Laigh Glengall farm. The line will afterwards cross Rozelle Glen near to the home farm, but it will not interfere to any great extent with Rozelle policies. Another bridge will be required at Doonholm Road, which it crosses near Doonholm gates, and then curving round behind Alloway new school terminates on the side of the public road near Alloway new church and about 100 yards from Burns' Monument. The line, which is to be about a mile and a quarter in length, will pass over part of the estates of Belmont, Rozelle, Doonholm and Cambusdoon.

Nevertheless, opposition to the Alloway branch was officially lodged in early 1897. In mid-January, the G&SWR Directors were made aware of the discontent when a meeting was arranged at St Enoch station with a deputation from the vicinity of the proposed line at Alloway, and they were met by Sir William Renny Watson, the Chairman of the G&SWR since 1890 and a Director since 1883. Sir Renny Watson, as he was referred to, was a partner in the sugar-machinery engineering firm of Mirrlees, Watson & Yaryan Company Limited of Glasgow. At the meeting,

Mr Shaw, solicitor, Ayr, agent for Miss Hamilton of Rozelle and other members of the deputation, addressed the meeting and pointed out that the railway was not being promoted by local request, and that the district, being principally a residential one, it would, in their opinion, prejudicially affect the amenity of the district to have a terminal station.

Then, in February, petitions against the railway were deposited in the House of Commons by Miss Christian Ann Dundas Hamilton of Rozelle, sole daughter of the late Alexander Hamilton, and by William Baird and Mrs Isabella Baird of Cambusdoon. However, Mr Baird and Mrs Baird were not husband and wife. Mrs Baird, as the resident, or tenant for life, of the estate, was the second wife of the late James Baird, an illustrious Lanarkshire ironmaster and philanthropist who died in 1876 without having children, while William Baird of Elie, Fife, as the non-residing heir, was his nephew. Mr Baird and Mrs Baird lodged separate petitions in regard to Cambusdoon being affected by the proposed railway.

Chapter Three

Rails for the Carrick Coast, 1897

Plans for the Alloway branch dissipated during early 1897 - not because of local opposition but because such a short stretch of railway being of little consequence in its own right, and later, because a much longer line, still by way of the village, was already in mind by the early spring of that year. Indeed, the matter had been mentioned back in late 1896 in the *Ayr Observer* of 20th November, from a suggestion by third Marquis of Ailsa, who was a Director of the G&SWR:

> Will Alloway remain a terminus for the new branch railway? Lord Ailsa, one of the most enterprising peers in the country, is a railway Director. He is known also to be in favour of railway communication along the Carrick shore, of which he is the largest proprietor. The Maidens [as it was known locally] and Turnberry present a locality which is unequalled anywhere for summer residents, golfers, etc, etc, and the whole district is productive and could be made remunerative for a railway. An extension of the new line from Alloway to the shore would take up much ground left out by the present Maybole and Girvan railway; and Ayr at least would have no reason to regret the improvement it would make in its position as a railway centre.

How right the statement was; for, by the spring of 1897, communications were in progress between the G&SWR and the Marquis of Ailsa about a proposed new railway along the coast from Ayr to Girvan. By mid-March, a plan of the possible route was made available to the Marquis by the G&SWR; and, at the end of May, in London, the Marquis met David Cooper, the G&SWR's General Manager, when the coastal extension to Girvan was seriously discussed. It was agreed at the meeting that David Cooper and William Melville, the G&SWR's Engineer-in-Chief since 1891, would go over the proposed line; and at the beginning of June, the Marquis, having thought over the route through Culzean, sent a letter from London to his factor, Thomas Smith, informing him of the intended route but suggesting an alternative that Mr Smith should put to the G&SWR.

David Cooper, having diligently worked his way through the railway ranks, was familiar with the district of the proposed Carrick coast railway. He was an Ayrshireman, born in 1855 at Waterside near Dalmellington, and he had been in the employment of the G&SWR since 1867, having begun work at the age of 12 as a booking clerk at Waterside station, to move two years later to Maybole station, where he remained for three years. In 1872, after just five years' service and while only 17 years old, he received a post in the Superintendent's Office at St Enoch station, and this was followed by transfer and promotion to the General Manager's Office as chief assistant in 1884. He was next promoted to the position called superintendent of the line in 1889, remaining there for five years, until he became General Manager in 1894.

William Melville was born in 1850 at Dunoon, on the Cowal peninsula by the Firth of Clyde in Argyllshire. Originally apprenticed as a joiner and then given the opportunity at the age of 16 to work for a civil engineering firm in Glasgow, he next entered as an apprentice in the engineering office of the North British Railway in Glasgow, where he was later entrusted to important works, such as the 1878-79 rebuilding and extension of Queen Street station and the construction of its iron-

Archibald Kennedy, the third Marquis of Ailsa.
Carnegie Library, Ayr

David Cooper, the General Manager of the G&SWR. *G&SWR Association*

William Melville, the Engineer-in-Chief of the G&SWR. *G&SWR Association*

Patrick Caird, Chairman of the G&SWR. *G&SWR Association*

and-glass arched roof. In 1882, he joined the Caledonian Railway as assistant to the Engineer-in-Chief - the long-serving George Graham - and Mr Melville took on the task of extending the railway from Greenock westwards to Gourock through Scotland's longest tunnel under the streets between central Greenock and Fort Matilda for a distance of 6,300 feet, or nearly a mile and a quarter, with the line having opened in 1889. Two years later, he was selected from a large number of applicants for the position of Engineer-in-Chief of the G&SWR, and one of his best known early works for his new company was also in Greenock - the construction of the grand Princes Pier station, completed in 1894 as the new terminus of the G&SWR's Greenock line via Bridge of Weir and Kilmacolm that opened in 1869.

The proposed Carrick coast line of 1897, which David Cooper and William Melville were now intently considering, was originally planned to run through the Culzean estate on the western side of the Maybole-Maidens road and then cross this road immediately after passing the Culzean Kennels, beside Thomaston Castle, to head by Morriston farm to Maidens. However, the Marquis had reconsidered this plan, and now wanted the line to proceed on the western side further beyond the kennels until after Morriston farm because it would be in cover through 'comparatively valueless land', as he described it, and he thought that it could cross over the road again somewhere between Morriston farm and Morriston Cottages. This, the Marquis stated, would avoid cutting up valuable fields and would save a crossing over the Morriston approach, and he added that the hills on the main road were already very uneven and a railway crossing at the only level spot, at the kennels, would not improve matters. The understanding was that the railway, in running close to the Pennyglen or main approach road into Culzean, was to be in a deep cutting with a bridge to carry the approach road over it. The Marquis requested his factor to ask David Cooper and William Melville to 'consider a convenient spot for a siding for goods and possibly a private station for Culzean', and he supposed that 'somewhere about the kennels would be as good a place as any', if the road to it from the castle was improved. Accordingly, Mr Melville and Mr Smith met on 14th July, 1897 to drive over and discuss the proposed line through Culzean, with the modifications of the Marquis now in consideration; and in late September, Mr Melville sent a plan to Mr Smith of the amended route of the line through the estate.

The third Marquis of Ailsa and 14th Earl of Cassillis was Archibald Kennedy, who was born at Culzean in 1847 as the eldest son of the second Marquis of the same name, whose death in 1870 resulted from being thrown by his horse while hunting near Kilmarnock. The third Marquis, who was aged 22 when he succeeded his father that year, was educated at Eton in Berkshire from 1860 to 1865, emerging as a brilliant scholar and enlisting in the army in 1866 as an ensign in the Coldstream Guards, to become a lieutenant and a captain before resigning his commission on the death of his father. In 1871, he married Evelyn Stuart, daughter of Lord Blantyre of Erskine House in Renfrewshire and of Lady Evelyn Leveson-Gore (pronounced 'Looson-Gore'), who was the daughter of the second Duke of Sutherland, of Dunrobin Castle in the far north-eastern Highlands. Like his father, the Marquis was enthusiastic about yachting and boatbuilding, and he secured a master's certificate in navigation in 1874, thereafter winning numerous prizes for yachting. In 1878, he established a small yard at the little Culzean Harbour, by the castle cliffs, for the construction of small racing yachts and steam launches to his designs and supervision. Larger orders meant that a new dockyard on a more ambitious scale was completed at Port Murray, on the western side of the fishing village of Maidens in 1883, under the name of the Culzean Shipbuilding & Engineering Company, and a suitable dwelling-house was erected for the boatyard's workers. Unfortunately, the lack of railway communication rendered the yard unprofitable because of the expense of the carriage of construction materials, such that the business was enlarged and transferred again in 1886 - this time to Troon and called the Ailsa Shipbuilding Company, having the Marquis as Chairman.

The Marquis was deeply involved in the agriculture and fisheries of Carrick and Ayrshire generally, being a member of the Ayrshire Agricultural Association, and, as a considerate landlord, he held a personal interest in the welfare of his tenant farmers and fishermen. He played an active role in the inauguration of the early-season potato industry along the Carrick coast that soon developed into a large enterprise for his tenant farmers. When the Marquis inherited the Culzean estate in 1870, the village of Maidens consisted mainly of old and small thatched cottages, but he set himself the task of rebuilding them, such that Maidens became one of the neatest villages in Carrick. In conjunction with his love of the sea, he provided further help for the fishing community of the village by spending a large amount of money from 1878 to 1880 in building a safe harbour in the form of a pier and breakwater from the west, because, previously, the harbour had only been protected by a line of rocks from that direction.

During the late 1870s and early 1880s, under the Marquis's plans for the development of the district, Evelyn, the Marchioness of Ailsa, had played a significant part in the improvement of the living conditions of the Culzean tenant farmers, fishermen and the other local working people, by the building of cottages and blocks of houses for them. As an evangelist who conveyed her convictions regularly at Maidens, Kirkoswald and Maybole, and as a supporter of the temperance movement, the well-liked Marchioness was devoted to persuading people to abstain, and she paid for the building of a mission church at Maidens, which also served as a school during the day and as a reading room during the evening. She established a reading room and a coffee room in Maybole that provided free coffee for those who signed the pledge to refrain from alcohol, and she arranged for the construction of a block of workmen's houses in the town. Unfortunately, the mid-1880s were sad for Evelyn and the Kennedy family, beginning with her own ill health and then the death from diphtheria, in 1886, of their elder daughter, Evelyn, aged nine. It was in the little girl's memory that the Marchioness founded a convalescent home in the same year at Ardlochan, north of Maidens, for working men who were recovering from illness - again representing her concern for the proletariat - and engraved on the building was the biblical quotation: 'Come unto me all ye that labour and are heavy laden and I will give you rest.' The second tragedy in two years for the Marquis and his family was that Evelyn died from tuberculosis in 1888, aged 40, and she was buried beside her daughter in the family cemetery at Culzean.

In reaction to Evelyn's death, the grieving Marquis virtually closed Culzean, leaving the decision-making of the estate entirely to his loyal and efficient factor, Thomas Smith, and he spent most of the next three years in solace in Africa and India. Eventually, and happily, a new era began in the life of the Marquis, in consequence of his visit to India from 1890 to 1891. He returned to Culzean in 1891 with Isabella, daughter of a Scottish missionary and market gardener, Hugh MacMaster, from near Blairgowrie, Angus, who was stationed in India. The Marquis married Isabella later that year, and she became the Marchioness of Ailsa.

In August 1892, the Marquis officially became involved with the G&SWR, in having been 'unanimously elected a Director of the company' to fill the vacancy that resulted from the resignation of the Earl of Glasgow, of Kelburn Castle near Largs. This meant that Carrick now had a representative on the railway board, and, as such, there were hopes for improvement to the agriculture and fisheries of the district; while it was of great advantage - and even of necessity - for the Marquis to increase the prosperity of his tenants and, therefore, his own income, because of this being less than the expenditure in the management of the Culzean estate. Eventually, his direct connection with the G&SWR led to the discussion during 1897 of the proposed coastal railway through his lands, with the aim of invigorating the whole district in respect of its under-developed industries, markets and tourism, but especially, from the standpoint of the Marquis in regard to the feuing, or leasing, possibilities, both seasonal and permanent. From the route and environs of the projected line, the likelihood of new feuing potential offered the most promising source of revenue, because increased income that would be received from the existing agriculture and fishing, resulting from the new project, was expected to take many years to be significant. For the establishment of a railway, the beautiful and rugged, but also fertile, Carrick coastal land between Ayr and Girvan, with its magnificent sea views, was seen to offer considerable potential in the form of produce to be taken away and tourists to be brought in.

One important source of summer revenue for a railway and for the tenant farmers along the Carrick coast from Ayr to Girvan was the Carrick component of the crop of the Ayrshire 'early potatoes'. Before the 1880s, farmers throughout Scotland had been experimenting in various ways to increase the yield from potatoes, for one of the hopes of greater production lay in the possibility of being able to start the growing season earlier, and it was eventually realised that the Ayrshire coast provided an ideal location for this to be attempted. In 1875, two Carrick farmers, Quintin Dunlop of Morriston farm, a mile north-east of Maidens, and John Hannah of Girvan Mains farm, ¾ mile north of Girvan, decided to investigate the matter, and they visited Jersey in the Channel Islands to see evidence of the early potato-growing successes for many years. They came to the conclusion that the mild and moist Gulf Stream climate and the heavy sandy soil of their own farms, and of the Carrick coast generally, would be equally suitable for growing early potatoes, and it was Mr Dunlop who first made arrangements for growing early potatoes. To do so, he had to obtain large quantities of manure, and his inquiries led him to making arrangements with the cattle boats plying between Belfast and Ayr and Glasgow for the manure to be offloaded onto barges that he had hired from Maidens to meet the boats in the Firth of Clyde, with the manure conveyed in carts from Maidens to his farm. Then he and several other farmers of the Carrick coast eagerly became involved in the prosperous but foul-smelling venture on a larger scale, with the railway from Ayr to Maybole and Girvan transporting large quantities of what was referred to as 'Glasgow dung' from the material of the city's dry closets, to Maybole and Girvan stations. This waste had previously posed a problem for Glasgow, and an ideal solution came in the form of its transfer to the Carrick coast, to be piled high at the farms to decompose before being spread over the fields. From the success in Carrick, early potatoes were developed in the northern part of the county, especially in the coastal vicinity of West Kilbride.

The growing of the Carrick early potatoes meant that the farmers were able to have them carted by horses from their coastal farms to Maybole and Girvan stations, from where the railway was able to expedite them to Ayr, Glasgow, Edinburgh, and throughout Scotland and England. The planting of the early potatoes was in March instead of May, as with potatoes in other parts of Scotland generally, and the result was that the Ayrshire crops were dug in June and July, instead of August and September. Furthermore, a second crop of Carrick potatoes was able to be planted in April and May, though not as extensive as the first and main crop, which presented the situation of the second crop being able to be dug at about the same time as the main crop in other parts of Scotland. The Carrick early potatoes were usually slightly ahead in readiness than those further north in Ayrshire, and they were enthusiastically awaited, with great interest shown in the specific date on which they would first be dug, which was dependent on the recent and present weather conditions; and then their conveyance by the railway allowed them to be eaten in various parts of the Lowlands on the same day that they were dug from the Carrick fields. The sooner that the Ayrshire early potatoes were able to be transported to the markets in Scotland and England, the higher would be the prices obtained by the local farmers; and thereby, from the significance of the potatoes, a proposed railway to convey the Carrick crop along the coast was now considered essential.

The majority of the potato diggers, or 'tattie howkers' (pronounced as in 'how'), were from the west of Ireland, including women, who invaded Ayrshire in their hundreds; and, being indispensable for the work, they were very much appreciated by the farmers and the potato merchants who ensured that they were provided with comfortable shelter in the form of barns and other suitable outbuildings, and with bedding in the form of straw-filled pillows and covers. The Irish workers were industrious and frugal because most of their payment was reserved to help their families and smallholdings back home; but they were allowed to eat the fresh potatoes during their sojourn at the 'howking', which they could supplement by the purchase of provisions from the travelling carts of the local shopkeepers, who transacted a lucrative extra business from their temporary customers. When they were paid for their work, the Irish workers headed to the nearest post office to send money orders home, so that they would not lose it or have it stolen. When their work in Ayrshire was complete, they drifted inland to the later potato fields of the other counties, such as in the Lothians, Stirlingshire and Perthshire, returning to Ireland after staying as much as five months in Scotland. Some of the Irish workers had been coming to the Ayrshire coast for nearly 20 years, since the introduction and development of the early potatoes by Mr Dunlop in the mid-to-late 1870s.

In addition to the other types of agriculture in coastal Carrick - in particular, dairy farming - the sea was also expected to bring revenue to a railway and to the local fishermen of the coast between Ayr and Girvan. The two quaint little fishing villages of Dunure and Maidens, in spite of harbour improvements, were much in need of nearer railway facilities to revolutionize their under-developed fishing industry, by transporting the produce conveniently and quickly to the markets at Ayr and beyond.

Seven miles south-west of Ayr was Dunure, with its neat little harbour, constructed in 1811 at a cost of £50,000, which provided shelter for the small fishing boats - with the name of the village originating from the small headland called Dunure Point, half a mile to the south. For the making of the harbour, an opening of 150 feet was cut through the solid rock of the coast, to form a quadrangle basin, with from 700 to 1,000 feet of quay along the sides, to provide easy and safe access and shelter in most conditions. The water outside the harbour at Dunure had a good depth that varied from 24 to 120 feet, with a level, clean and sandy bottom, and good anchorage, and the depth of water in the harbour itself was 12 feet at ordinary spring tides that could be artificially increased to nearly 30 feet. The harbour was financed by the estate owner, Thomas Kennedy of Dunure House, 200 yards to the north, and of Dalquharran Castle (pronounced 'Dal*whirran*'), in the valley of the Water of Girvan. He was a relative of the Kennedys of Culzean, and his wife was the niece of Robert Adam, the famous architect, who had been commissioned in 1781 to design Dalquharran and who had finished it in 1790, which was ahead of his work on Culzean Castle, lasting from 1776 to 1792, for David Kennedy, the 10th Earl of Cassillis. Immediately south of the harbour lay the neatly-arranged fishermen's cottages that constituted the village of Dunure; and beyond the cottages was the ancient ruined castle, perched on the cliffs, which was the historic birthplace of the Kennedys of Cassillis and Culzean.

Two miles south of the Kennedy family's majestic Culzean Castle and seven miles north of Girvan was Maidens, having taken its name from the rocks in the bay which were originally called 'The Maidens of Turnberry' or 'The Maidens', and which, by the late 1800s, were known as the Maidenhead Rocks. However, the name of Maidens for the village - or locally 'The Maidens' - began to appear only after the third Marquis of Ailsa had transformed the fishermen's cottages and the harbour during the 1870s, and it was also referred to as 'The Marquis' village'. Previously, the little settlement had the general name of Douglaston, from a small farm there, with this and the nearby larger farm of Jameston commemorating James Douglas of Robert the Bruce alliance and their historic and heroic landing in this area to herald the fight to regain Scotland's freedom. In 1850, only a few old cottages had been in existence at Douglaston, and beside the Ardlochan road, where it joined the Maybole-Girvan road, there had been a chemical works, belonging to the second Marquis, for the production of an acid that was used in the process for dyeing cloth. It was at Douglaston farm that Douglas Graham, the inspiration for Robert Burns' famous poem 'Tam o' Shanter', was born in 1738, becoming the tenant of nearby Shanter farm, under the ownership of the Kennedys of Cassillis and Culzean. Another Robert Burns connection, if indirect, in Maidens was a building called 'The Cellars', 350 yards along the Ardlochan road, which was not only the oldest building of the village, and by far, but was formerly an alehouse that was believed to have been used by Robert during the summer of 1775. This was when he was 16 years old, in attending a school for a few weeks in Kirkoswald to learn mathematics and surveying.

In 1873, a new landmark had become part of the Carrick coastline, a mile south-west of Maidens, at Turnberry Point, to be seen at a distance of several miles during the day from the land, and discernible even further at night from the sea. This was the Turnberry Lighthouse, which was considered necessary because of the increased number of shipwrecks during the 19th century, having resulted from the growing maritime traffic along the Carrick coast. These shipwrecks were most frequent at Turnberry Point and at the Brest Rocks a mile further south, as was recorded by the gentleman who was the Receiver of Wrecks at Ayr, and in 1869, he had recommended to the Board of Trade that a lighthouse be built on the Brest Rocks. The Board of Trade referred the recommendation to the Northern Lighthouse Board, whose engineers David and Thomas Stevenson - brothers from a famous Scottish lighthouse-engineering family - examined the vicinity of Turnberry and advised that the lighthouse should be placed at Turnberry Point, beside the ruins of Turnberry Castle. The Board of Trade approved the decision later in 1869, though it was not until 1871 that the construction was begun, with the lighthouse, to the design of the Stevenson brothers, brought into use on 30th August, 1873. The tower of the structure was 80 feet high, with the light, 96 feet above the high-water mark, beaming flashes of 235,000 candlepower every 12 seconds across the Firth of Clyde.

Dunure village and castle, *c.* 1900, looking south-west, with the harbour and its quadrangle basin immediately to the right of the view.   *G. Clark*

Culzean Castle, *c.* 1900, looking south-west, showing some of the coves on the left.   *G. Clark*

The family name of Stevenson was also made famous by Thomas' son, who was Robert Louis Stevenson and whose popular novels, during the 1880s, included *Treasure Island*, published in 1883; *Kidnapped*, 1886; *The Strange Case of Dr Jekyll and Mr Hyde*, 1886; *The Black Arrow*, 1888; and *The Master of Ballantrae*, 1889. Thomas Stevenson had also gained scientific fame in having designed a special wooden box-shaped structure - the Stevenson Screen - for housing thermometers at weather stations to allow accurate readings of air temperatures; and it was ironical that the father was very disappointed that the son had shown no interest in engineering and science but that Robert Louis became the most renowned Stevenson of all - worldwide - through his writing.

From a clear light having been established in the literal sense at Turnberry Point during the mid-1870s, there had next emerged, during the 1890s, a figurative clear light for the promotion of a railway that, in serving the 20 miles of the scenic Carrick coast between Ayr and Girvan, would run near Turnberry Point - the district of Turnberry consisting mainly of a scattering of farms and hardly constituting a hamlet. The initiator of the new enterprise was Archibald Kennedy, the third Marquis of Ailsa, in convincing his fellow G&SWR Directors of the need for such a railway; and it was certainly from the original G&SWR intention of 1896 for a short branch to Alloway that the idea had then come from the Marquis to develop the farming and fishing industries of Carrick. Fortunately, to increase the possibility of the line materializing, other circumstances within and even beyond the British Isles resulted in new legislation from the government that would offer rural areas, which were not suitably served by existing railway communication, the opportunity to be connected to the railway system, if considered to be sufficiently merited by local circumstances. This legislation - in effect, having the intention of creating another but smaller railway revolution, or 'railway mania' - was the Light Railways Act of 1896, which was passed on 14th August of that year: 'An Act to facilitate the Construction of Light Railways in Great Britain'. It was this Act that inspired the G&SWR, after the initial encouragement by the Marquis, to reconsider its plans for the Carrick coast in the form of a light railway, even if the G&SWR Directors, by their own admission, had little idea of what was meant by the term 'light railway'.

The Light Railways Act emerged from, and was intended to alleviate, a prolonged and serious general economic, but largely agricultural, depression in the British Isles that had occurred during the early- to mid-1870s and was still in evidence by the mid-1890s. Following the already-damaging economic consequences of the Franco-Prussian War of 1870-71, this depression - having affected much of the world and having been strongly felt in western Europe and in the United States - commenced immediately after the financial collapse of the Vienna stock exchange in 1873, producing a panic by the withdrawal of European capital from America. In the British Isles, the agricultural industry suffered worst because of a series of very poor harvests, owing to inclement weather, and also because of the plentiful supply of cheaply-imported cereals - especially wheat from America and Canada, and other food and animal products, such as mutton and wool, from Australia and New Zealand - that produced falling prices at home. The dismal harvests were not readily noticed by people in the towns because the cheap and plentiful imported food greatly reduced the visible effects of the depression there; but the farmers were certainly aware of the dire situation, augmented by a series of cold and wet summers in the late 1870s, which the urban population had certainly noticed - particularly an intensely-cold winter of 1878-79 and a dreadfully wet and cold summer of 1879. Some of the worst conditions occurred in Ireland, leading to deaths from starvation, and, with rural poverty present throughout the British Isles, two royal commissions were appointed to inquire into the long-ongoing agricultural depression - the first of these, in 1879, under the Conservative government of Prime Minister Benjamin Disraeli, and the second, in 1893, under the Liberal government of Prime Minister William Gladstone. Furthermore, by the mid-1890s, a transport impetus was seen to be one of the means of remedial action by the Conservative government of Prime Minister Robert Gascoyne-Cecil, who was the Marquis of Salisbury, and this assessment produced the Light Railways Act. Encouragement to the Board of Trade for the development of light railways, as opposed to the standard type, was provided by their success in France and Belgium.

The building of light railways was intended to be a cheaper way of providing rural areas with appropriate transport and improving the depressed state of the agricultural industry. There were important agricultural districts that had unfortunately been excluded from the earlier periods of railway connection, because the main or parent railway companies were not financially able or were not interested in building new lines to these locations, such that the landowners and farmers had been placed at much disadvantage from the want of easy conveyance for their produce. Rural areas were expensive to serve, which was why many of them had never become part of the railway network, and the Light Railways Act had the aim of changing this situation by providing the incentive for country lines to be built in an era when railway-making had decreased significantly. The establishment of light railways was to be effected by the relaxation of the Board of Trade railway regulations, in respect of application, construction and operation, and by the possibility of financial help from the government by loans or grants to the promoters. With the easing of the regulations came the basic stipulation that only lighter trains could be used on any proposed light railways and only at reduced speeds, while sharper curves and steeper gradients than normal would be permitted.

The Light Railways Act created a Light Railway Commission of three members, who were appointed by the Board of Trade with the consent of the Treasury, to assess the applications for new lines under the legislation and, thereby, approve or reject them on the gathered evidence that would originate locally. Applications could be made by any railway companies or local authorities or even individuals, either separately or jointly, and the Treasury would also consider the advance of a loan not exceeding a quarter of the projected cost of the light railway. Furthermore, this financial support could be increased to an amount not exceeding one half of the cost of the light railway, on two conditions: if the making of the line was considered essential to benefit agriculture and fishing in a district where such a project would not otherwise be constructed without special assistance from the Treasury; and if reasonable financial contributions and co-operation from the local area were guaranteed before Treasury assistance was requested. The Light Railways Act was a general Act that would apply to all proposed lines under the legislation, and it was not an Act that would authorize any specific line. If a line was approved by the Light Railway Commission, it would be provisional only, and would require to be confirmed by a separate Light Railway Order by the Board of Trade under the terms of the Light Railways Act.

Chapter Four

The Carrick Coast Railway Meetings, 1898

At a meeting of the G&SWR Directors on 25th January, 1898, the subject of the 'Dunure Light Railway' was discussed, and William Melville was instructed to prepare plans and estimates for the line so that the matter could be considered further. It was in the spring of 1898 that the locality of Ayr became aware of the intention of the G&SWR to construct the line along the Carrick coast, when notification from the G&SWR, dated 19th April, was placed in the three Ayr newspapers and headed 'Maidens & Dunure Light Railway - Application for Order under the Light Railways Act 1896'. This stated that an application was to be made to the Light Railway Commissioners in May 1898 by the G&SWR for an Order

> ... to authorize the company to make and maintain the light railway hereinafter described, to form a railway connection for passenger, goods, mineral, and other traffic from the company's line near Girvan station along the coast, for the accommodation of Dipple, Maidens, Kirkoswald, Dunure, Greenan, Doonfoot, Alloway, and the surrounding districts to the company's line near Ayr station, with stations, sidings, and other works and conveniences in connection therewith.

The railway at its southern end was to commence 'at a point about 280 yards or thereabouts south-eastwards from Girvan Mains farm steading' and it was to terminate at its northern end 'at a point about 380 yards southwards from Kincaidston farm steading'.

On 17th May, 1898, a Special Meeting of the 'proprietors of the Glasgow & South Western Railway' - meaning the company's Directors and shareholders - was held at St Enoch station to consider the application to be made to the Light Railway Commissioners for the Maidens & Dunure Light Railway (M&DLR). The G&SWR Chairman, Sir Renny Watson, explained that a draft order was being submitted for the light railway, about 20 miles long, and that there was a general desire throughout the district of the Carrick coast for additional railway facilities, such that, after careful consideration, the Directors thought that these facilities would be met by the proposed line. It would provide an alternative route, by the coast, between Girvan and Ayr; it would serve the villages and districts of Dipple, Maidens, Kirkoswald, Dunure, Greenan, Doonfoot and Alloway; and it would afford great assistance in the development of the agricultural, fishing and other industries in this important part of Ayrshire. The industries were probably not of such magnitude to justify the construction of an ordinary railway, added Sir Renny, but the Directors believed that the industries were sufficient to provide a fair return upon the more moderate cost of a light railway. Sir Renny also informed the meeting about the anticipated expense of the line, in that the capital to be raised for the works was £120,000, 'with the usual borrowing powers that amounted to an additional £40,000'. The proposal was unanimously confirmed at the meeting - even if Sir Renny 'confessed to a little ignorance on the matter [of light railways]', adding on behalf of the Directors that 'they hoped to learn more during the time occupied in the making and equipping of this line'.

Five weeks later, on 24th June, a public meeting took place in Alloway to consider the position of the village and locality in relation to the proposed railway. The meeting was called and chaired by John B. Fergusson of Balgarth House, Doonfoot, as a member of the Ayr Parish Council, though he was also a member of Ayr Town Council. He stated that he would use his best endeavours to put the views of the majority, either in favour or against the railway, before the Light Railway Commissioners on behalf of the Board of Trade; and after outlining the route of the line, he drew attention to some of its legislation and specifications:

> Where the stations are to be, we are not informed. That is another thing the promoters are not bound to tell us, and they have not told us where they intend to make the stations. You will notice this is called the 'Maidens & Dunure Light Railway'. Well, what exactly a light railway is I do not think it necessary for me to enter into, because there might be a considerable amount of legal argument on that point. But so far as the scheme is described by the promoters, it seems not to differ in very many respects from an ordinary railway; and it is a light railway in so far as it is made under the Light Railways Act. They have not to go to Parliament, but there is a special procedure provided, under which the Light Railway Commissioners hear the application in the first instance, after which it is referred to the Board of Trade. So far as I can understand, the railway is of the ordinary construction. In its gauge, it is 4ft 8½in, which, I think I am right in saying is the ordinary gauge. It is provided that heavy running stock can be used on it, not exceeding the weight of 16 tons upon any one pair of wheels, which I understand is a considerable weight.

Mr Fergusson also noted several other aspects about the proposed light railway: that trains would not be permitted to run at more than 25 miles per hour; that the G&SWR were not bound to use any special electrical apparatus for working the trains upon the block system; that no signals other than those at the two junctions with the main line need be interlocked with the points; that platforms would be provided, unless all the carriages on the line were constructed with proper and convenient means of access between the carriages and the ground, in which case, added Mr Fergusson, there need not be platforms; and that there was no obligation on the G&SWR to provide shelter or conveniences at any station or stopping place. Having remarked that such aspects were not what was found on an ordinary railway, he concluded by saying that he did not wish to express an opinion and only wanted to hear the views of the meeting.

Mr Shaw, son of the solicitor who represented Miss Hamilton of Rozelle, stated that his father was in France on holiday or he would have been at the meeting to represent his client and he added that the railway could do an incalculable amount of harm to the Rozelle estate. From Mr Shaw's remarks, it seemed that the G&SWR had not intended to build a station for Alloway on the northern side of the River Doon, and, instead, there was talk of a station on the southern side at Longhill Avenue, the road that connected Alloway and Doonfoot. However, Mr Shaw thought it ridiculous to place a station at Longhill Avenue to accommodate tourists, when they could have better accommodation directly from Ayr itself, and here he meant by the existing horse-drawn carriages. He was of the opinion that it was a one-man railway, but it was not clear that the Marquis of Ailsa would benefit as much as he thought to warrant his capital for the railway or to risk spoiling the noble mansions of the neighbourhood and driving away the wealth and prosperity of that part of the county.

In contrast, Mr Lees, of Lagg farm near Heads of Ayr, spoke for all the tenant farmers along the shore who anxiously wanted the line and who viewed the question in a broader light than the people of Alloway, simply because the whole district would benefit:

About Dunure, and further on, they have no access to any place unless by driving six or seven miles, while poor people have to walk. It is easy for people about Alloway, who can pop into Ayr without difficulty, to talk; and the great bulk of you have your machines and your carriages and pairs. You know nothing about a wet day at all or about toiling along a dirty road. If we had a railway, we would consider it a great improvement. I have no hesitation in saying that if a meeting were held at Dunure, there would not be a single dissentient voice.

Mr Turnbull, schoolmaster at Alloway, was against the railway, but, with a hint of contradiction or even hypocrisy, he added that if there was no station on the northern side of the river, he would rather walk to Ayr than go to Kate's Avenue - the popular alternative name for Longhill Avenue and supposedly referring to the last occupant of a leper colony in the vicinity. Therefore, Mr Turnbull implied that he would indeed use the railway if it had a suitably-placed station; and after saying that he understood the position of the shore farmers, he asked whether it would be better for them to have their railway connection from Maybole. Certainly, as a schoolteacher but with a selfish lack of knowledge and understanding, it was better for Mr Turnbull that the Carrick coast farmers should have the connection by Maybole, and, furthermore, he seemed more concerned about how many ice cream shops would spoil Alloway when the railway was introduced than with the needs of the farmers further south.

Mr Fergusson remarked that the railway would be detrimental to Alloway but that it was not necessary for it to come to Alloway to give the farmers their conveniences; and he was astonishingly and unjustifiably derisory towards the many sightseers who would generate trade and prosperity for the village in arriving at Alloway by the proposed railway:

First of all, it will bring a very large number of cheap trippers down here. They will be shot out in large numbers at the station, wherever it may be. Do you think that any district is benefited by cheap trippers? You know what they are! You see them in many other places. They arrive, many of them - well, they have a good deal to drink; and most of them are provided with a bottle, and certainly very few of them go away sober. They will come in their thousands, and they will roam over your fields; your gates will be left open, and your stock will be run in heaven knows where! I cannot think it will be an unmixed blessing even to the farmers.

Resolutions were then submitted for and against the making of the railway through Alloway, and, on a show of hands, there were 17 votes to 14 respectively, such that the meeting was officially recorded to be in favour of the line.

The *Ayr Advertiser* responded admirably by blending a balanced summary of the sentiments of the meeting with its own sound opinion:

It is impossible not to feel a considerable amount of sympathy with the strong objection which the dwellers in and around Alloway, and the admirers of the Burns Land generally, have to the invasion of the district by the new light railway. It is natural that they should have a great dislike to anything that will mar the beauty or lessen the attractiveness of the locality, and that they should view with apprehension the bringing of shoals of trippers upon the classic scene. We think the fears on the latter are a little exaggerated.

But while it is natural that the Alloway people should desire to guard their district against a threatened danger, it is equally natural that the farmers and other dwellers along the shore should wish to be no longer excluded from the benefits of a railway. It will be a great help to them in getting the produce of their farms and fisheries to market; while they may reasonably expect that in course of time the many fine sites along the shore may be utilised for feuing.

   The people of Alloway did not turn out in large numbers to oppose the railway, and they were outvoted by those from the shore district.

The disturbance to Alloway was indeed the principal objection to the railway for the people of that district; but, to counter the opposition, the G&SWR was intending to construct the line under the public road beside the Auld Alloway Kirk and almost directly below the kirkyard. Thus, the line would be out of sight from that point for a distance that was longer than necessary, in relation to the engineering requirements, until it would emerge immediately before crossing the River Doon. The bridge was to span the river at the western end of the little wooded island that would be used for one of the piers, and it was hoped that the bridge would be constructed in an ornamental character that was in keeping with the nature of the surroundings; but the intended concealed and camouflaged stretch from the kirkyard to the bridge was no consolation to some of the local people. 'From the Burnsianic point of view, this is vandalism of the very worst sort', warned the *Ayrshire Post*. 'Alloway Kirk will have lost much of its charm if its ghosts are to be scared away by the railway engine.' Nevertheless, in referring to what was effectively the same railway to Alloway as had been planned in 1896, the paper had now softened its vehement opposition - perhaps, in reality, conceding to a previous excessive reaction against the initial short branch:

> We held then, and we are still of the same opinion, that there was no justification for a mere extension to Alloway, and we hold as strongly as ever still that no extension should be sanctioned that is certain to destroy the amenity of the Burns Country. But when to the original proposal is added the opening up of a new reach of country, and when there is a chance of materially benefiting the people of the district, we cannot do otherwise than take in one sense a modified view of the undertaking.

Although progress had been made at the Alloway meeting - if not to the liking of almost half of those present - an extra and unexpected involvement in the proposed Carrick coast railway had also begun to materialize in the summer of 1898. On 1st July, a meeting of the merchants of Maybole was arranged with the Burgh Commissioners of the Town Council for the purpose of obtaining support for petitioning the G&SWR to provide the town with a connection to the new line, to the effect that 'there should be action taken at an early date for the purpose of obviating the inconvenience it was going to do Maybole if a branch were not put into the town'. The merchants were unanimous that the line, as planned solely along the coast, would cause serious injury to their town by excluding it from the benefits of a railway connection with Maidens - meaning that, whatever advantage the new line would offer the district, they were entitled to that advantage too. There were rumours that the Marquis was prepared to feu the route of the line and also the land at Turnberry to the G&SWR, such that there was likely to be a considerable amount of trade. The merchants explained that it was essential to have a branch from the new line to Maybole, which was the administration and market centre of the wide surrounding rural district and was significant because of its manufacturing industries, primarily of footwear - employing 1,500 people, producing a million pairs of shoes and boots per year, and representing £250,000 per year - followed by agricultural implements for the surrounding rural fertile country of Carrick and beyond. In using a railway term to describe their feelings about the situation, the Maybole people felt that 'they were shunted', and Provost Ramsay, replying on behalf of the Burgh Commissioners, acknowledged the great advantage of the proposed branch to the town, adding that a public meeting would firstly be desirable in promoting their aim. John Latta, a local stationer, who had convened the meeting, stated that the branch need not be any more than 2½ to 3 miles long and that there were no serious difficulties in the way. Sadly, and especially at such an early stage, Mr Latta asserted - seemingly with spite - that the merchants would object to the coastal railway if the G&SWR were not agreeable to their proposal.

A public meeting took place in Maybole on 8th July, before a large attendance and with Provost Ramsay presiding. The aim was to highlight to the public the advantages of the suggested branch to Maybole and to have the town's sanction in petitioning the G&SWR to construct the line. Maybole consumed a large amount of agricultural produce, and, therefore why should the town not have the benefit of the railway in that respect? Mr Latta repeated his words from the earlier meeting of the merchants and the Burgh Commissioners that the branch would only be 2½ to 3 miles long - 'a comparative trifle', he thought, with no great engineering difficulties and only one cutting. He provided a rough indication of the route in that it would leave the main line near the station and proceed south-westwards by Cultezeoun (pronounced 'Culti-yowan' - hard 'u', and 'ow' as in 'now') and Mochrum Loch; along the lower ground on the southern side of the 886 ft-high Mochrum Hill; and then south-westwards from there to join the proposed coastal line somewhere north-east of Maidens. The meeting resolved to appoint a committee to bring the matter before the G&SWR Directors, in the hope that they would listen and provide the railway facility that Maybole desired.

No further details of the route were supplied at the meeting, but the branch, even in taking the easiest and most direct course possible between Maybole and Maidens, would have to be a mile or more longer than the 2½ to 3 miles by Mr Latta's reckoning.

At a Board meeting of the G&SWR on 12th July, a letter, dated 9th July, from the Town Clerk of Maybole was submitted for the Directors' consideration, and they resolved to receive a deputation from Maybole at the next Board meeting. The letter was accompanied by a copy of the resolutions that had been passed at the public meeting of 8th July, and, therefore, the Directors were clearly aware of the intended opposition from Maybole if their desired branch railway was rejected.

In late July, a joint committee of magistrates and merchants of Maybole, which had been appointed to promote the branch, agreed to lodge objection to the Light Railway Commissioners, in so far as the coastal line did not provide a connection for Maybole; and it was further resolved to request a meeting with the Marquis of Ailsa, to encourage him to use his influence for establishing the Maybole branch. This meeting took place on 1st August at the council chambers in Maybole, when Provost Ramsay, on behalf of the other members of the joint committee, explained the advantages of the Maybole connection to the Marquis, who showed support for the scheme and expressed the hope that it would receive the serious consideration of the other G&SWR Directors. Then, on 9th August, the joint committee from Maybole met with the G&SWR Directors at St Enoch station, when the necessity and advantages of the branch were reinforced to the Directors, who were pressed by the Maybole committee to take a favourable view of the proposal. The Directors informed the committee that, in the event of the coastal railway receiving authorization, they would carefully consider the Maybole proposal but they refused to make any promises in the meantime, until their present scheme for the coastal line was passed and completed.

Other opposition had threatened the establishment of the M&DLR - this time from the Ayr Burns Club, in terms of a circular that was issued to the members on 15th August:

> As you are no doubt aware, the council of the club sometime ago resolved to object to the proposed light railway in the vicinity of Alloway as injuring the amenity and destroying the scenery in the immediate neighbourhood of the birthplace of the national bard, and instructed the secretaries to intimate these objections to the Light Railway Commissioners and ask to be heard in support of them at the forthcoming local inquiry. Intimation has now been received from the secretary to the Light Railway Commissioners that our objections are in order, and that the club will be heard for their interests in regard to the proposed route of the railway in the neighbourhood of Alloway Kirk, Mungo's Well, the little island in the River Doon before the Monument bridge, the Banks and Braes o' Bonnie Doon, and Longhill Avenue.

A Special Meeting of the Ayr Burns Club was convened for 22nd August in the King's Arms Hotel, High Street, Ayr, to consider the matter and take action in the interests of the club. However, as the meeting progressed, the prevailing opinion became more a case of acknowledging that no material harm was intended to be done by the railway in passing through the district. Nevertheless, a resolution was moved that the club should take the necessary steps to be represented at the forthcoming local inquiry of the Light Railway Commissioners.

It was felt that a great deal could often be obtained by quiet negotiation. If the Ayr Burns Club told the G&SWR that they wished the Burns Country to be interfered with as little as possible, they would be surprised if Mr Cooper, the General Manager, would not meet them in a kind and courteous manner. Would not the G&SWR be very foolish to kill the goose that laid the golden egg? The Burns Country was a perfect mine of wealth to the company. Could they imagine Mr Cooper and his officials willingly setting themselves to destroy a bit of scenery that brought hundreds of thousands of passengers to the railway, with all the revenue to be derived from it? Opposition would also mean financial expenditure for the club, and the opinion was expressed that the Light Railway Commissioners would not for one moment entertain any objections that the Ayr Burns Club could put forward. Two resolutions were proposed: to ascertain more details from the G&SWR, and to do nothing further; and, on a show of hands, there were 21 votes for the resolution and 5 for no further action, with a committee thereby appointed to approach the railway company.

The meeting heard the view that Robert Burns himself would have been against the iron horse in the district because he was a lover of nature and sought places of repose; but - inappropriately - this 'sureness' ignored the fact that Robert was a progressive thinker and traveller who would have been delighted to see the iron horse and its benefits to the public.

'Oculeus' of the *Ayrshire Post*, in disagreeing with one aspect of the resolution of the Ayr Burns Club meeting, offered a possible and logical compromise between the club and the G&SWR in the paper's issue of 26th August:

> The resolution was right enough, but not the deputation - as the most of its members are either indifferent to or in favour of the proposed route of the railway - an unusual mode of advocation. I do not think it would interfere much - if any - with the levels, or cause

engineering difficulties, for the railway company to have their station midway between the Cottage and the Monument - a low-level station on the east side of the road, and the railway continued underneath the road and crossing the river further down [more westwards] - quite out of sight of the Monument and away from Alloway Kirk. This would be the most convenient site for the station. Visitors coming from where the station is presently proposed, to the Cottage, would almost be as near to walk into Ayr, as to go back from their train to this station at Longhill Avenue. The railway company must appreciate this point. It means money.

Unfortunately, the one problem that would be created by this otherwise-admirable suggestion was that the line would be placed slightly nearer to Cambusdoon House and the already-existing objections of Mr Baird and Mrs Baird. On 31st August, a deputation from the Ayr Burns Club met David Cooper and William Melville. The deputation brought four points to Mr Cooper's attention:

(1) the desirability of (a) altering the line of deviation of the proposed railway so that it may pass at a greater distance from the Auld Alloway Kirk, and (b) of crossing the River Doon further to the west than shown on plans; (2) the bridge over the River Doon should be of a character in consonance with the surrounding scenery; (3) if possible, the gradients should be altered in passing under Longhill Avenue so that the level of the road should remain undisturbed; and (4) cuttings, where visible to the eye, should be ornamented with trees and shrubs.

Mr Cooper, in receiving the deputation in a friendly and courteous manner, explained that he could not meet their requests in regard to the first point, because the suggested alteration would mean an encroachment on the Cambusdoon estate. However, in referring to the second and fourth points, Mr Cooper said that he would see that the wishes of the deputation were carried into effect; and, for the third point, he informed them that Mr Melville 'would endeavour to alter his gradients so that the raising of the road would be lessened, if not removed altogether, and that the trees in the avenue should be disturbed as little as possible'.

Shortly afterwards, from what Mr Cooper had said at the meeting, the deputation unanimously agreed that no further action in the matter should be taken by the club, and a circular to that effect was sent to each of the members in early September. Therefore, the opposition to the M&DLR from the Ayr Burns Club was withdrawn.

However, other objections still remained - from Alloway and from Maybole - and such opposition, if justified by the Light Railway Commissioners, would be given the opportunity of expression at a forthcoming public meeting at an appropriate venue in the district, in the presence of the Light Railway Commissioners in accordance with the terms of the Light Railways Act. No meeting would take place if no opposition was received, but, in mid-August, the announcement had been made that the Light Railway Commissioners would hold a public meeting at Ayr on 21st September because significant objections had been lodged.

Accordingly, at a meeting in Maybole on 30th August, with Provost Ramsay as Chairman, the merchants of the town, having received the required approval from the Light Railway Commissioners, had voted to proceed in raising their objections to the M&DLR at the forthcoming meeting in Ayr, and it had also been agreed at the Maybole meeting to engage legal representation for that purpose. However, an amendment was raised by two members of the Maybole Co-operative store that the objections be withdrawn and no counsel engaged, but this received no other support and the motion, to proceed with the objections, was carried.

An insight into the disapproval towards the railway from residential Alloway was illustrated by 'Objections on Behalf of William Baird of Elie and Cambusdoon and Mrs Isabella Agnew Hay or Baird', in their presentation to the Light Railway Commissioners. Naturally, only the negative aspects of the proposed railway in relation to Alloway were highlighted, with the content being both objective, which could not be disputed as facts by those in favour of the line, and subjective, which left differences in interpretation of the relevant points that were considered, but which decidedly took no account of the possible benefits in the development of the locality from the establishment of such a line.

Mr Baird and Mrs Baird described Alloway as having 'a very sparse population' and mostly of 'country gentlemen in their own or rented mansion houses and a few tenant farmers and their cottages'. Regarding the development of the district, they stated that no less than 14 of the 19½ miles of the railway passed through the estate of the Marquis of Ailsa, and they were of the opinion that the line 'is not bona fide projected to accommodate the district of Alloway, or the insignificant fishing hamlets at Maidens and Dunure, or to give railway connection between Ayr and Girvan [as] no powers are sought by draft order to improve or develop the fishing coves or shelters at these places.' They believed that the railway was intended 'to be constructed for the private purpose of accommodating and opening up Lord Ailsa's estate in his personal interest'; and they submitted that 'it is contrary to precedent and the established practice of Parliament to grant to promoters compulsory powers over a landowner's estate where no public necessity or local want exists and where such powers are sought merely for the private object of accommodating and developing the estate of another landowner'. Furthermore, 'a station with all its appurtenances of station-houses, goods and locomotive sheds, turntables, water tanks, coal and manure depots and the like', in addition to creating an injurious effect upon all the residences in the vicinity, 'will wholly destroy the privacy of Cambusdoon as a residential property and will also greatly injure it as a feuing subject and cause great loss to the objector'.

The Maidens.   Maybole.

Maidens village and bay, c. 1900, looking east.   M. Chadwick

Chapter Five

The Meeting with the
Light Railway Commissioners, 1898

The official meeting - in reality, a public inquiry - before the Light Railway Commissioners was arranged for Wednesday 21st September, 1898 in the Station Hotel, Ayr. This was the meeting that would decide whether or not the M&DLR would be authorized, even if, on the previous day, the *Ayr Observer* had confidently predicted that the outcome would be that the scheme would be approved: 'Much of the opposition to the proposed line has been withdrawn, and the inquiry is not likely to extend over a day.'

In the formal terms of the Commissioners' duties, the meeting was 'for the purpose of possessing themselves of such information as they might consider material or useful for determining the expediency of granting the application which had been made to them by the Glasgow & South Western Railway Company for an Order to authorize the Maidens & Dunure Light Railway'. The Chairman of the Commissioners, of three members inclusive, comprised Sir Victor Albert George Child Villiers, who was the seventh Earl of Jersey, whose family residence was near Bicester in Oxfordshire, and his two colleagues Colonel Boughey and Mr Fitzgerald, augmented by Mr Steward as secretary. The case for the G&SWR as 'the promoters' was to be directed by Mr Balfour Browne, QC, and by Mr Moon. The cases for the various objectors were to be led by three separate members of counsel. Mr Ure, QC, collectively represented Miss Christian Ann Dundas Hamilton of Rozelle, William Hamilton Dunlop of Doonside, and James Kennedy of Doonholm. Mr Lamond, solicitor, Glasgow, represented William Baird and Mrs Isabella Baird of Cambusdoon. Mr Blackburn collectively represented the inhabitants of the Alloway district and the Maybole Town Council, Burgh Commissioners and traders. In addition to a large attendance of local gentlemen, including the Marquis of Ailsa, there were representatives of the G&SWR by the presence of Chairman Sir Renny Watson, General Manager David Cooper, Chief Engineer William Melville, and the renowned civil engineer Sir Benjamin Baker who, in the summer of 1897, had been 'appointed Consulting Engineer to the company'. Sir Benjamin had gained international fame in co-designing, with Sir John Fowler, the massive and spectacular Forth Bridge that had opened in 1890 as the longest in the world.

The meeting of the Light Railway Commissioners was held in a room that was crowded in eagerness about whether the M&DLR would be sanctioned. Hopes were high from the majority that this would be the case and that the substantial support for the line would indeed be too formidable for the opposition to counteract. At 9.30 am, Mr Balfour Browne opened the proceedings on behalf of the promoters by characterizing the district through which the proposed line would pass, which, he said, was 'eminently suited for a light railway', as there would be considerable traffic but not of an amount to justify a heavy expenditure. He referred to the coast being especially suitable for the growth of early potatoes, followed by a second crop, and the farmers now only needed these to reach a market easily by a railway, as, at present, they had to be carted by road to Maybole, Girvan and Ayr. Similarly, there were fishing stations at Maidens and Dunure, but only in a small way, and it was impossible to carry on this industry with the success that might be achieved by a railway. While the population of the coastal district was not large, at 3,000, the two villages lent themselves well as seaside resorts. There was also a place near Maidens that had the potential to be one of the best natural golfing links in Scotland, and, while Maidens was suitable for residential purposes, the district was important agriculturally, with the beautiful scenery being an attractive place for feuing. However, building was precluded by the difficulty of access to the district.

Mr Balfour Browne referred to land along the route and the majority of support for and the minority of opposition to the project. Starting at the southern end from Girvan Mains, the line passed through the property of John Campbell Kennedy, who also owned land at Dunure, constituting a total length of about four miles. After Mr Kennedy's Girvan property, it ran through the short distance of 78 chains on the land of George Kerr of Chapeldonan, and then on to the estate of the Marquis of Ailsa for 12 miles 28 chains. Next, there was a piece of land of only 44 chains that belonged to Andrew Mitchell of Fisherton, and, in the middle of the Marquis's extent of land, there was also a little strip - merely a field - that belonged to Mr Dunlop of Doonside, Alloway. Every landowner was assenting until Alloway was reached, and Mr Dunlop was also one of the opponents of the scheme through his land at Alloway. However, rather than being against the railway company, he was more in disagreement with Mr Baird of adjacent Cambusdoon about the position of the station for Alloway, in the sense that, as Mr Balfour Browne put it, each very politely wanted the other to have the station! He did not think that Mr Baird was afraid of the railway doing damage to Cambusdoon, as it would run through for a length of only 23 chains mostly in cut and cover, and Mr Baird's fear was simply on the possibility that the station would be placed near the entrance of his estate. Then the line passed through the property of Mr Kennedy of Doonholm but the piece of ground here - again, only a field - was separated from the main part of the estate. This brought the line to the land of Miss Hamilton of Rozelle, the final objecting proprietor. The G&SWR proposed to run the line through Miss Hamilton's property much further from Rozelle House than they had planned for the 1896 line to the Burns Monument, and the present line would be hidden by the trees in purely agricultural land, with no damage done to the property. The areas of ground that were intended to be taken from the landowners were, south to north: Mr Kennedy, 33½ acres; Mr Kerr, 10 acres; the Marquis of Ailsa, 110 acres; Mr Mitchell, 5 acres; Mr Dunlop, less than an acre; Mr Baird, 2¼ acres; Mr Kennedy, 3 acres; and Miss Hamilton, 9 acres.

Mr Balfour Browne listed the petitions in favour of the line. These had come from Girvan Town Council and Burgh Commissioners; from Girvan Parish Council; from the tenant farmers in the parishes of Girvan, Kirkoswald and Maybole; from the people of Kirkoswald parish, signed by 154 people of various occupations, including the fishermen and inhabitants of Maidens; from Kirkoswald Parish Council; from the Landward Committee of Maybole Parish Council; from the fishermen and inhabitants of Dunure; and from Carrick District Committee of Ayr County Council. Indeed, he stressed that everyone was in favour along the route except at Alloway, with its residential properties. Dealing with the other contention that visitors to Burns' Cottage and Monument were already well served by horse-drawn buses and by the new but rare motor cars, Mr Balfour Browne said, 'Fancy going to visit the shrine of Burns in a motor car!', adding that he had never heard such a row as made by one that he had met! Then there was the opposition from the Town Council, Police Commissioners and traders of Maybole, on the basis of the line being of no benefit to them unless there was a connecting branch to the town, but which, he said, was really a petition in favour, because, with no objections to the line itself, only a connection to it from Maybole was desired.

The hearing of the evidence followed, with the questioning of the various witnesses by the counsel, and several tenant farmers were eager to give their support to the line.

Quintin Dunlop, farmer at Morriston, near Maidens, outlined the costs that were involved in his potatoes having to be carted either six miles to Maybole station or seven miles to Girvan station, and he had to bring in large quantities of manure and feedstuffs, such that he felt the proposed railway to be 'a dire necessity'. Other disadvantages were that his workers had to cease work as early as 2 o'clock so that the potatoes could reach Maybole in time for the next day's market, while, for the Ayr market, his cattle had to be walked to Maybole for trucking by rail to Ayr, and his sheep had to be walked all the way to Ayr. A similar story emerged from David Hastings, of both Jameston, near Maidens, and Ladybank, near Dipple, as he had to cart his potatoes from the farms to Bridge Mill siding at Girvan. The distance was 6½ miles from Jameston to Bridge Mill and six miles to Maybole, but he carted to Girvan because of the better road, using as many as 35 carts per day. He explained that Bridge Mill siding was overcrowded; to which Mr Lamond asked, 'Does that not show that it is very convenient?' 'No', Mr Hastings smartly affirmed, 'it shows that there is no other place!' Thomas Crawford of Dowhill (pronounced 'Doohill'), 3½ miles from Girvan, and William Lyburn of Balchriston, four miles from Maybole, gave similar evidence that a railway was needed for their produce. George Richmond at Drumshang, five miles from Maybole and 8¼ miles from Ayr, asserted, with reference to his potatoes and sheep and in response to questions from Mr Ure, that what he wanted was not a better communication by road with Maybole but the proposed railway to Ayr and a station that was convenient for his farm. William Dunlop of Dunure Mains informed the meeting that he raised mainly stock, especially horses, but found it disadvantageous without a railway. In the past, he had a dairy and made cheese, which he had to cart to Ayr, and if he had a railway nearby, he would reconsider dairying and also grow crops. Glasgow was the great market for milk, which had to be reached quickly; and, with early milk trains passing through Maybole, he knew that he would only be able to catch one of them if he had the proposed light railway to Ayr.

The Earl of Jersey was enjoying the discourse on the agriculture of the district, but he thought it necessary to proceed to another aspect, and Mungo Munro, fisherman, Dunure, obliged on behalf of his form of employment. He had lived all his life at Dunure, and, with 50 fishermen and somewhere between 200 and 300 inhabitants now living there, he had seen the fishing industry increase threefold. The fish had to be carted to Ayr, but if they had a railway, the cost of carriage would be a great deal less and they would reach the market quickly and receive a good price. He added that, apart from being involved in fishing, the Dunure people often had to go to Ayr on business and had to do so over the seven miles on foot. After Mr Munro had described improvements to the harbour and more about the fishing itself, Mr Ure asked if he expected the station for Dunure to be right at the harbour. The apt reply was, 'We would not expect to run our boats into the station, and a station about Fisherton school would suit us quite well'. John McCrindle, fisherman, Maidens, echoed Mr Munro's views about the necessity of a railway for the 32 fishermen and 130 inhabitants of Maidens, such that more people would be able to engage in the industry.

Three Glasgow merchants provided evidence in favour of the railway. Mr Fulton, potato dealer, explained the limitations of having to take the Carrick coast potatoes to market at present and how the railway would undoubtedly benefit the potatoes to be brought to the city. Mr Paton, another potato dealer, readily concurred, before Mr Brand, dairyman and milk contractor, spoke about having a large interest in the city, and also in sending milk to Liverpool and other places in England. If the light railway was sanctioned, he would be able to obtain a considerably bigger supply of milk from the district.

Provost Templeton of Ayr said that the railway would allow Ayr to spread out into the surrounding country as villa residences were desired, and the shore near the River Doon would lend itself to these. He had talked about the railway to many people who were in favour of it, and he referred to the Ayr Burns Club having been originally against it, with their members having withdrawn the opposition when all the facts were known. David Brown, solicitor, Maybole, and also factor to Mr Kennedy of Dunure and the legal representative of Mr Mitchell of Fisherton, praised the G&SWR for its enlightenment in asking for authority to construct the line, adding that it would develop the estates. However, after commenting on the need for a railway to improve the services to the Burns shrines, Mr Brown was not so eager to be forthright when challenged by Mr Ure about the circumstances of the estate owners in Alloway. 'Do you think it is a fair proposition that a railway company to serve trippers should set down a railway station in the midst of very picturesque residential properties against the wish of the proprietors?' 'I have no opinion on that subject.' 'Try to form one now.' I am not going to form any opinion.' 'I put it to you: here we have four or five hostile proprietors. Do you think it is a fair thing?' 'I refuse to answer such a question.' 'Well, I am in the hands of the Commissioners; I cannot force it.'

The Marquis of Ailsa, having stated that he was the proprietor of the estates of Cassillis and Culzean and that he was a Director of the G&SWR, emphasised that the railway was not promoted in his private interest, as his Culzean estate would suffer from the route of the line more than that of any other proprietor. The line would pass for about two miles through the Culzean policies, crossing several of the avenues there, but he had consented to this because it was to the public advantage of the district and his neighbours along the coast. In response to a question from Mr Ure, the Marquis expressed with regret that he could not see how the line could avoid passing the residential estates of Alloway; to which Mr Ure next asked, 'Then I gather that you sympathise with the objections which the proprietors of those residential estates have to the railway passing through their estates, with a station designed to serve large crowds of people at their doors?' 'Yes, but I think they are making the most of it.' But you agree with them in their views?' 'To a limited extent.' In response to Mr Lamond, the Marquis answered that he was aware of Doonbank farm on his estate being leased by Mrs Baird of Cambusdoon but that he was not aware of Mrs Baird leasing the farm to preserve the amenity of her Cambusdoon estate. 'You will take it from me if I tell you', said Mr Lamond. 'No, I will not!' said the Marquis. Then, as if still trying to win something from that direction of argument, Mr Lamond asked about the necessity of the line going through the residential properties against the people's will. 'I think there is a strong necessity', replied the Marquis. 'But if there was not a strong necessity?' continued Mr Lamond. 'Then there would be no use for the railway', countered the Marquis, who thought it quite proper to make a railway against the wishes of proprietors, if it was for the benefit of the public.

Mr Balfour Browne stated that the line was to be tunnelled through Cambusdoon, but this decision was to Mr Lamond's surprise, as the latter pointed out that this change had not been made known previously, since the plans showed it as an open cutting. It was the G&SWR's intention to have a tunnel, confirmed Mr Balfour Browne; as John Inglis Davidson, land valuator in support of the G&SWR, next summarized the formation of the line immediately westwards of the tunnel. Coming out of the tunnel, Mr Davidson explained, the line would cross the River Doon by an ornamental bridge, which would be invisible from the Auld Brig o' Doon and would not interfere to any extent with the views obtained from the nearer new road bridge across the river; and then the line would run through a cutting, which, in Mr Davidson's opinion, would not spoil the amenity. The matter of the uncertain position of the station for Alloway was also discussed, with Mr Davidson clarifying that the station site had now been considered for the Alloway or northern side of the river, in a field immediately north of the parish church, such that it would be 16 feet below the level of the ground and entirely screened from Cambusdoon. However, Mr Lamond returned Mr Davidson to the riverside. 'You spoke of a bridge across the Doon which is just brought into view of the windows of Cambusdoon? Do you not think this bridge and the deep cutting in front of Cambusdoon House will be an eyesore for Mrs Baird?' 'The bridge will not be visible from the house. It will be hidden by trees.' 'But you know that the trees will shed their foliage in winter and Mrs Baird will then be able to see the bridge?' 'Yes, if she has nothing else to do!'

Soon afterwards, there was an unexpected change of stance from three members of the Alloway residential opposition, when Mr Ure informed the meeting that his clients - Miss Hamilton of Rozelle, Mr Dunlop of Doonside, and Mr Kennedy of Doonholm - would reconsider their position, on assurance from the G&SWR that the station for Alloway would be placed near the parish church. Mr Balfour-Browne confirmed to Mr Ure that the G&SWR was indeed willing to place the station there; to which Mr Ure replied: 'Then my clients withdraw their opposition.'

While this was indeed good news for the promoters, the proceedings necessarily continued because there was other opposition to be heard from the Alloway vicinity and from Maybole, though there was still evidence to be heard from the promoters.

William Melville, Engineer-in-Chief of the G&SWR, described the route and construction of the line, and stated the total cost, including acquiring the land, to be £157,255, or £8,000 per mile. The steepest gradient was 1 in 60 but there were no engineering difficulties, and he did not think that any part of the works could be seen from the windows of Cambusdoon. To Mr Lamond asking about the weight of the locomotives to be used on the line, Mr Melville replied that they weighed more than eight tons per axle - which referred not to the total weight of the locomotives but to the weight that was supported only by each axle of the locomotives' wheels. Mr Fitzgerald of the Commissioners then informed Mr Lamond that this weight had already been allowed and asked him what his objection was here. Mr Lamond replied that he wanted to show that it was not a bona fide light railway and that the G&SWR was only taking advantage of the Light Railways Act to promote a new branch of its ordinary railway, adding that the methods of signalling, etc, were the same as those of an ordinary railway. Mr Melville denied this, saying, 'The methods of signalling were the same only at the two junctions.' 'The fittings are the same as an ordinary railway', continued Mr Lamond. 'I beg your pardon, they are not! An ordinary railway branch would cost £53,000 more than the light railway.' 'Yes, £500 here and £3,000 there', said Mr Lamond. 'Or £10,000 here and £40,000 there!' countered Mr Melville.

The question by Mr Lamond about the weight of the locomotives had stemmed from the first reference to the term 'light railway' in the Regulation of Railways Act, 1868, when axle loads were restricted to eight tons, but the Light Railways Act, 1896 contained no such stipulation. The Earl of Jersey commented that the Commissioners had already had a case of this kind before them in the Basingstoke & Alton Light Railway in Hampshire, which had been passed by the Commissioners and by the Board of Trade. Mr Moon, for the promoters, then called the attention of the Commissioners to the facts that the weight of the locomotives and the weight of the rails were only to be exercised in cases where the Commissioners thought it necessary to do so. Next, Sir Benjamin Baker gave evidence to show that regulations about the weight of locomotives and rails were not intended to be enforced in every case. For example, the common-sense view that was enforced by the Board of Trade, of which he was a member, was that partly-worn rails on an ordinary railway could be used on a light railway.

David Cooper, General Manager of the G&SWR, was the last witness in favour of the promotion of the line. From his knowledge of the district, he was satisfied that there would be a considerable development of traffic for the railway after a few years, such that it could be made into an ordinary railway. Having been asked a series of questions by Mr Lamond about the potential fish traffic, Mr Cooper felt the need to reciprocate effectively with a question: 'I hope you do not think that we are making a railway purely for carrying fish?' 'Would potato traffic plus the fish traffic justify you making a railway?' asked Mr Lamond. 'Yes, I have seen Maybole and Girvan alone totalling 17,000 tons.' 'But some of the farmers you brought up have spoken only of 500 tons.' 'But', intervened Mr Balfour Browne, 'we only called a few of the farmers'; which was true, because there were indeed other farmers along and close to the route of the coast who would benefit from the railway. However, Mr Lamond returned emphatically to Mr Cooper about the point of the ordinary railway: 'But you have no right to come here before the Commission in the guise of a light railway and at any time put down an ordinary railway!'

On being asked by Mr Blackburn about the requested railway connection with Maybole, Mr Cooper had no objection to a branch, adding that it would be favourably considered but he felt that the G&SWR firstly had to have the coastal line completed. Mr Blackburn then led the evidence in support of the Maybole opposition, with Provost Ramsay describing the importance of the town to the surrounding districts and expressing the view that if a connecting branch was not made, the trade of Maybole would suffer. Other witnesses from Maybole naturally concurred: Mr Goudie, draper; Mr Couperwaithe, draper; Mr Latta, stationer; Mr Fairlie, baker; and Mr McConnell, grocer. However, irrespective of the sincerity of the Maybole beliefs, the audience must have realised that the opposition contained no substance when weighed against the evidence in favour of the line. For the Alloway opposition, Mr Blackburn stated that he had been placed in a hole because of Mr Ure withdrawing but that he would nevertheless follow-on from him. 'Yes, follow him!', cried Mr Moon.

John B. Fergusson of Balgarth, Doonfoot, harked back to the meeting that he had chaired at Alloway and alleged that the vote taken there was not representative of the feelings of Alloway against the railway, as the majority at that meeting comprised the shore farmers. Although this so-called misrepresentation was not further addressed at the present meeting, he was no doubt correct about that majority; but Alloway, nevertheless, had obtained an opportunity to oppose the railway in greater force and had not done so. However, Mr Fergusson informed the present meeting that, after the Alloway meeting, he had assented to a petition against the line, signed by 80 or 90 of the inhabitants of the village and district, and he soon directed himself to his sore topic of the dreaded cheap trippers. He referred to the 'necessity' of having to distinguish between the 'legitimate tourists' and the 'cheap trippers', and it was the latter, he said, who ruined the district; did an immense amount of harm; were terrible people; gave disgraceful exhibitions of themselves; and were not sober when they left. The local people wanted to ward them off, but the railway company wanted to foist them upon the village. He added, with absurdness, that he had suffered from cheap trippers all his life, and, with derision, that it was in Ayr where they could be seen to perfection and where he wanted them to stay! Mr Pollok, Convener of the County of Ayr and the councillor for Alloway, added support against the railway but said that Mr Fergusson had not been strong enough in his remarks! Mr Pollok and Mr Turnbull, schoolmaster, Alloway, both felt that the railway would be of no benefit to Alloway and that there was no demand for it, except in bringing the cheap trippers. 'Have you ever gone a cheap trip yourself, Mr Turnbull?' asked Mr Balfour Browne. 'Yes, I have', was Mr Turnbull's simple confession.

Mr Blackburn then addressed the meeting for his summary of the opposition to the railway, firstly explaining the significance of Maybole, the capital of Carrick and the principal trading centre of the district, having been omitted from the light railway scheme. The Earl of Jersey interrupted him: 'Is your argument that no district is to be opened if the usual run of trade is to be disturbed?' 'No, it does not go that length.' 'It seems to me to go very near it.' However, Mr Blackburn contended that, far from benefiting the district as a whole, the proposed railway would seriously injure the whole trade of Maybole. As for the Alloway case, Mr Blackburn conceded that his case had been weakened by the withdrawal of the Rozelle, Doonholm and Doonside opposition, but that there was still a real objection to the railway because of the cheap trippers who would destroy the amenity of the district.

Mr Balfour Browne began his summary by explaining that Mr Baird's objections, while not absolutely settled, were in the course of being completed. This left only the other Alloway and the Maybole objections, which, he thought, were very trivial. Of the leader who was so against the cheap trippers, he declared ironically, 'Well really, Mr Fergusson was the only stalwart left, and even he came here representing a public meeting that had decided in favour of the railway!' Mr Balfour Browne protested about the statements of the various witnesses against cheap trippers, 'and they had heard that even the exemplary schoolmaster of Alloway sometimes went a cheap trip!' As for Maybole, Mr Blackburn's argument was absolutely ridiculous, and Mr Balfour Browne cleverly paraphrased what Maybole was saying: that 'because we are enjoying the custom of people who have to walk a great distance to our shops, the railway should not be made along the coast to take them to better shops in Ayr or Girvan, unless the company is asked to spend £20,000 more in making a railway to us.' He then sealed his case with a general statement: 'No development whatever could take place if such an argument were listened to for one moment'; and he asked the Commissioners to authorize the Order.

At 5pm, with the Commissioners having heard all the evidence and having readily formed their decision from it, the Earl of Jersey informed the audience that they would certainly be recommending the Board of Trade to issue an Order for the M&DLR.

The next day, the *Ayr Advertiser* was the first of the town's three newspapers to be able to provide reactions of approval to the meeting and the expected verdict, clarifying the position of overcoming part of the Alloway opposition:

A good part of the local objections hinged on the question of where the station at Alloway was to be. Two sites had been indicated - one on the south side of the Doon, in the beautiful Longhill Avenue, and the other on the north side on the Doonholm Road, near the new school house. As it turned out the railway company discarded both, and fixed on a site in the field adjoining the new Alloway Church, at a point where the line will be sixteen feet under the level of the existing ground. So soon as this was made known, three of the principal objectors - viz, the proprietors of Doonside, Doonholm, and Rozelle - withdrew their objections.

The argument from the opposition about the line not being a light railway was briefly explained by the paper, followed by words of optimism for the people of the Carrick coast:

An attempt was made to set up the objection that the proposed railway is not a light railway at all, but it was summarily brushed aside by the Commissioners. No doubt the first idea of a light railway was that of a railway of narrow gauge, and with light engines and carriages. But Parliament deliberately refused to fix a gauge, leaving that to the discretion of the Commissioners. We congratulate the dwellers on the Carrick shore on the prospect of soon being brought into closer touch with the world by means of a serviceable railway.

The *Ayrshire Post*, while sympathizing with the Maybole population and the handful of Alloway proprietors, recognised that private interest had to give way to public interest and that the real benefits of the railway had to be granted to the local people along the coast and to the area's visitors:

The farmers and the fishers alike demand access to the market and the town, and it is just and fair that they should have it. There are not many of them, but that is no reason why they should be kept perpetually shut out from the world. But we take it that the real justification for the extension is to be found in the development of the Carrick coast. It lies there waiting to be exploited. It is made ready to hand for tourists, for watering places, for summer resorts, for cheap trippers. It has a wealth of unexhausted and of unexhaustible ozone. It has historical scenes and spots to repay a visit. It has cliffs to climb and bays to explore, and links to transmogrify into golfing grounds, and beaches whence to bathe. It is all new and fresh to the general tourist, and twenty years hence in all probability its present population will be more than doubled.

In the same issue, 'Oculeus' was pleased to report on the matter of the site for Alloway station:

I am satisfied. In our issue of 26th August last I asked the railway company to place the Alloway station on the proposed new railway 'mid-way between the Cottage and the Monument - a low level station on the east side of the road, and the railway continued underneath the road, and crossing the river further down - quite out of sight of the Monument and away from Alloway Kirk'. The Commissioners on Wednesday fixed upon my site for the station, instead of Longhill Avenue, but brought it nearer the Monument than the Cottage. The railway will skirt Alloway Kirkyard, but sufficiently removed not to disturb the sleepers. The railway will be banked in, and quite out of sight, and the bridge across the river is to be in keeping with the sylvan surroundings, and festooned with evergreens. What more?

The *Ayr Observer* contained praise for the splendid efforts of the local farming and fishing population at the meeting who had helped to ensure the railway's authorization:

Examining witnesses is often a source of great amusement. In many cases these witnesses fall easy victims to the gentlemen of the long robe, who turn them inside out to the cruel satisfaction of both friends and opponents. In this case, however, the witnesses decidedly had the best of it. We have heard of soldiers' victories. At this inquiry it was really a witnesses' victory. Farmers who have not hitherto earned reputation for smartness in the witness-box here came through the ordeal scatheless, and frequently the laugh against the examining counsel turned. The Dunure fishermen, who were probably never cross-examined in their lives, stuck to their guns like veterans. All the witnesses did well, and while under 'cross' came off well. Lord Ailsa made a capital witness, justifying both the company, of which he is Director, and his own action in promoting the line with a clearness which left nothing to be desired. The little reflection cast upon him for any self-interest he has in the matter was repaid with a slating which could not have been surpassed by any one who had had years of experience in witness-boxes, and was warmly approved of by a large audience.

There was also mention of the unfortunate and absurd hostility from Maybole towards the project:

The opposition to this line was a blunder, because, with the promise of favourable consideration from the General Manager and the Lord of the Manor's influence among the Directors, there was a possibility of early attention being given to their wishes, but not now; the prospect is at any rate not so bright. It was a big thing to demand the expenditure of at least £20,000 to give a connection with the Maidens.

The opposition from Maybole was indeed difficult to comprehend, though the town certainly could not be faulted for having tried to obtain a short branch-line connection to the proposed Carrick coast railway. However, the pointlessness was in objecting to the making of the coastal line on what were effectively immature and spiteful conditions; for, until it was made, Maybole could not have a railway connection with the coast - thus, ironically, preventing the very line and that the town was so desperately in need of, judging from the extent of the protests! The ideal and natural course of action would have been for Maybole to have supported the coastal line, and, during its construction, to have made the G&SWR Directors regularly aware of the necessity of the connection, without any demands or protests. Then, when the coastal line was well in process of completion, the urgency of the Maybole connection could have been reinforced to the Directors, who would then have been in a much better position to listen to the Maybole people and to determine the practicability of the connection. Instead, there was the attitude from Maybole of 'if we are not to be immediately connected to the Carrick coast by a railway, then we don't want a Carrick coast railway to be built at all, to benefit people anywhere else'. The inevitable reaction from the G&SWR could only have been one of alienation and rejection - not just for the present and near future but, in all probability, for a long indeterminate period in the future. Moreover, initial support from Maybole towards the coastal line would have unhesitatingly resulted in support for the Maybole branch from the Carrick coast, for a line to the Carrick capital would have been a bonus for the coast after the priority connection with Ayr and Girvan. Without doubt, the misguided pride and principles of the town of Maybole resulted in a wasted opportunity for further railway communication directly from the capital of Carrick to the coast of Carrick.

Chapter Six

Rails and Golf for the Carrick Coast, 1899-1901

As expected, with no difficulty and based on the recommendation of the Light Railway Commissioners from the meeting in Ayr in September 1898, the M&DLR received the sanction of the Board of Trade. This was by a Light Railway Order which was officially known as the Glasgow & South Western Railway (Maidens & Dunure Light Railway) Order, dated 30th September, 1899, and it left the G&SWR free to build the line along the Carrick coast without further objections.

The M&DLR was one of several light railway schemes to have been proposed in Scotland during 1898; and through the same period of promotion as, firstly, for the short branch to Alloway and, secondly, for its extension as the Carrick coast line, another G&SWR light railway had been actively planned south-eastwards in neighbouring Dumfriesshire. Indeed, the parliamentary application for this line appeared in the same G&SWR notices as for the Alloway branch in November 1896, and, like the Carrick line, it was not originally intended to be a light railway. As a standard line, it was to connect the village of Moniaive (pronounced 'Monni-*ive*) with Dumfries through the Cairn Valley and other villages along that pleasant country route, by a junction with the Dumfries-Kilmarnock line; but the G&SWR had decided in late 1897 that the Cairn Valley line - 15¾ miles long, but with Moniaive 18 miles from Dumfries - would be projected as a light railway. The Light Railways Act had encouraged a large number of these schemes before the Light Railway Commissioners, and there were 54 applications in Britain during 1898, with nine of them in Scotland; while, of the 54, there were 32 planned to have electric traction, as in tramways, and 22 to have steam motive power, as in orthodox railways but having the new light railway construction and regulations. The Cairn Valley Light Railway was authorized by a Light Railway Order on 29th December, 1899.

From the Light Railways Act, the Maidens & Dunure line had been contemplated to accommodate the farmers and the fishermen of the underdeveloped but scenic Carrick district of Ayrshire. It was for the alleviation of the difficulties that had been experienced in these two industries - simply for the want of suitable transport communications - that the line was considered a necessity; and, while additional advantages in its establishment certainly lay in the aspects of feuing and pleasure activities, these had been secondary in nature. However, while the value of the line to farming and fishing had always been firmly acknowledged, its value in tourist potential had become ever more appreciated in time, such that the idea of the Carrick coast railway generated even greater significance and interest from this potential source of revenue. Who could say when the first-ever suggestions occurred for the proposed railway being used in conjunction with the increasingly-popular sporting activity of golf, but it had certainly been mentioned back in November 1896 in the *Ayr Observer*: 'The Maidens and Turnberry present a locality which is unequalled anywhere for summer residents, golfers, etc, etc, and the whole district is productive and could be made remunerative for a railway.' The subject of a golf course there had been expressed at the meeting of the Light Railway Commissioners in September 1898 by the Marquis of Ailsa's factor, Thomas Smith: 'There has long been talk of forming a golf course at Turnberry, where there is an admirable site.' Mr Smith had good reason for his statement, because, in the spring of that year, the

Marquis had developed a sudden interest in the game and had now visualized the Carrick coast railway and the popularity of golf working in association - in effect, serving each other, with the line acting as a conduit for a new and specialized passenger traffic.

The pastime of golf in a rudimentary form was established in Scotland three to four centuries earlier than the transport revolution of the railways or even the primitive wagonways. Reaching Scotland from The Netherlands because of strong trading links between the two countries, golf was played in the east of Scotland, and particularly at St Andrews in the Kingdom of Fife, well before the founding of Scotland's first university at St Andrews in 1411, but it was from the 18th and 19th centuries that golf in Scotland developed to the earnest extent that golfing societies came into existence throughout Scotland. In 1860, the first Scottish and British golf tournament was held at Prestwick Golf Club, and from 1862, with the next 10 tournaments also held at Prestwick, professionals and amateurs from anywhere in the world could enter; and, thus, the Open Championship was born.

While St Andrews had been justifiably christened 'the home of golf', there was no question about Prestwick in the west of Scotland being 'the home of the Open Championship'. Accordingly, from the success of the increasingly-popular Open tournaments there, the county of Ayrshire was motivated in the establishment of more golf courses, as greater numbers of people became passionate about the sport, such that, by the end of the century, there was no doubt that Ayrshire was the golf coast of Scotland. The G&SWR Directors were also keenly aware of the popularity of golf in coastal Ayrshire in relation to railway revenue, and it was indeed fortunate that the trains on the iron road were ideally placed for the enthusiasts with the iron clubs.

The Marquis of Ailsa, although having been a non-playing member of Prestwick Golf Club since 1871, did not become a golf player until his interest in the game suddenly developed during early 1898. In February of that year, he and the Marchioness, Isabella, went on holiday to the resort of Pau in south-western France, and he finally decided to learn to play the game at Pau Golf Club. Having taken instruction from the golf professional at Pau, Dominique Coussies, and having become a member of the club, the Marquis had found increasing passion for the game at Pau during March 1898, to the extent that he then made arrangements for Monsieur Coussies to come to Culzean during the summer and autumn, so that he could continue his instruction. He quickly applied to Prestwick Golf Club to become a playing member, and this was agreed by the club the same month. Furthermore, the Marquis intended to involve the French professional in the making of a private golf course at Turnberry, and in April 1898, while still resident at Pau, he reconsidered the location for his private course and decided on Culzean, which would save him travelling to Turnberry.

Monsieur Coussies arrived at Culzean in June to help to establish the golf course and to commence golf tuition to the Marquis, which was ultimately to have a significant impact on the building of a railway along the Carrick coast. The *Ayr Advertiser*, in its issue of 11th August, reproduced a short and humorous account from a London newspaper on the Marquis having acquired his new golfing interest and tutor:

Lord Ailsa and Golf. The Marquis of Ailsa has thrown himself (says the *Daily Telegraph*) into golf with enthusiasm, and has laid down a course on his own estate. To the horror of the Scottish devotees of the sport, he has engaged a Frenchman from Pau to be his instructor. This is held to be a heinous offence. Scotland is still proud of the prowess of professionals like Andrew Kirkcaldy and Willie Park, but it may be mentioned that the Frenchman in question, whose name is Dominique, is a very pretty player, and an excellent and patient master. It would be interesting to see Mons Dominique play some of our well known professionals.

The London paper was soon to have its wish for a contest, for the Marquis, before the impending return to France of Monsieur Coussies, organized a golf tournament for eight professionals at his Culzean course on Saturday 24th September, 1898, and, as such, this event became the first-ever professional golf tournament in Carrick.

With his golfing passion having become established during 1898, the Marquis found himself having a closer association with Prestwick Golf Club; for, in February 1899, he was honoured by an invitation which he accepted, and, in April, he was appointed the club's Captain for 1899, succeeding the Earl of Glasgow, as he had so done in becoming a G&SWR Director back in 1892.

While the Marquis was a large landowner, he still had to keep a careful control of his financial circumstances, because the expenditure on his estates of Culzean and Cassillis during the 1890s was greater than the revenue. These estates were 'entailed' or 'inalienable', which meant that they could not be sold or transferred to anyone outside the Kennedy family, to ensure them being kept within the family from the one generation to the next. Therefore, no sale or feuing of land to the G&SWR could occur without the approval of the supreme court in Scotland, being the Court of Session in Edinburgh, which would decide whether such a sale would be in the interests of the future generations of the Kennedy family. However, by late 1899, a hotel and a golf course at Turnberry were a decided probability, and the M&DLR was already planned to proceed by Culzean and bring benefits to the Carrick coast, including to the tenant farmers and fishermen of the Marquis and, therefore, to the Marquis himself, by developing the agriculture and fishing. The whole of the G&SWR project looked promising from the aspect of enriching the lands of Culzean and Turnberry, and the G&SWR was interested in the novel project of a golfing and seaside resort at Turnberry, which would lead to the development of feuing in its neighbourhood, with the hotel and a connecting railway considered essential for the accommodation of golfing and non-golfing tourists.

Meanwhile, regarding the construction of the railway, a letter, dated 20th July, 1899, from William Melville to Thomas Smith indicated where he and his engineering staff had then been located in the marking of the route, as he acknowledged caution in proceeding through the Culzean estate:

> *Maidens & Dunure Light Railway.* As you are no doubt aware I am at present pegging out this line and having sections and working drawings prepared. My staff are at the north end of Culzean policies, and as arranged with you I now write you so that you may make arrangements with regard to the necessary cutting of trees, etc, through the policies, as I do not wish my staff to be cutting anywhere and any way they may choose for the purpose of staking out the line, and I think it would be better for you to have your forester to do this work.

During the first half of 1900, various agreements were ultimately reached between the Marquis and the G&SWR in regard to the hotel site of 15 acres and the golf course land of 175 acres. The terms for the hotel site were that the G&SWR would feu from the Marquis the ground that was required for the hotel building, which the G&SWR proposed to build at its expense and which would be the G&SWR's

property, with the Marquis receiving a feu duty of £6 per acre, or £90 in total, per year for the use of all the land for the hotel building and its immediate surroundings. The terms for the golf course meant that the G&SWR was able to obtain the following:

> The right and privilege in all time to come of using the links and bent hills shown upon the plan as a golf course and for the purpose of playing the game of golf thereon subject to the payment to Lord Ailsa of ten shillings per acre per annum there for.

This amounted to an annual £87 10s., to be paid by the G&SWR to the Marquis for the use of the golf course, with the G&SWR forming the course at its own expense but being entitled to the use of the course for its guests in the hotel free of charge; while members of the public would also be entitled to use the course by means of a payment. These rates were 1s. per day; 2s. 6d. per week; 7s. 6d. per month; and 20s. per year. Additionally, by the agreement, the Marquis, his family and his guests were to be entitled to the free use of the course and the clubhouse.

At a meeting of the G&SWR Directors on 12th June, 1900, the tenders for the construction of the line were considered, but unfortunately, as the lowest offer at £205,000 was much in excess of William Melville's original estimate, it was resolved to postpone the construction for a year. Six weeks later, the *Ayr Advertiser*, in its issue of 23rd August, reproduced an understandably pessimistic account, headed 'The Light Shore Railway', from the Glasgow newspaper the *North British Daily Mail*, and this account explained the delay in the start of the building of the line:

> There is some reason to believe that the Glasgow & South Western Railway are in no hurry to go on with the light railway along the Carrick coast for which they obtained powers from the Board of Trade some two or three years ago. They recently took certain possible contractors for the construction into their confidence. These gentlemen were taken over the route proposed to be followed and asked to send in estimates, with the result that the Directors have discovered that the undertaking, if proceeded with at once, would involve them in an expenditure of nearly a third more than the original estimate. Wages are high, and material, specially iron, is dear; and to sink an extra hundred thousand pounds sterling in a branch that of itself could hardly be expected to pay for many years to come is a contingency too serious to be faced just at present.
> The delay will occasion no little disappointment along the Carrick shore. And yet in the circumstances it can hardly be wondered at. The coast is not fruitful either in people or in minerals. It fringes a district much in need of being opened up, and that, with its frontage to the Atlantic, its cliffs and its sands, would in all likelihood be extensively feued in the course of ten or twenty years. Beyond Alloway, however, the passenger traffic would of necessity be very limited. Nor can the projected light railway be even regarded as a feeder of any immediate considerable value to the main system; for the Carrick traffic is already wholly monopolised by the G&SW. In the whole circumstances delay, from the Directors' point of view, appears to be next door to unavoidable.

Happily, official notification of intended action by the G&SWR on the new Turnberry project appeared in November 1900 in the Ayr newspapers, under the explanatory heading of 'Power to establish hotel and golf course at Turnberry, and agreements with the Marquis of Ailsa'. This notice stated that application would be made in December to the Secretary of State for Scotland for an Order for a number of powers and agreements in connection with various railways, and one of these was for:

Certain lands at Turnberry in the parish of Kirkoswald in the county of Ayr, lying on the east side of and adjoining the highway from Ayr to Girvan via Dunure and between Turnberry Lodge and Turnberry Wood and certain other lands in the same parish, lying on the west side of and adjoining the said highway and between that highway and the foreshore of the Firth of Clyde.

Furthermore, the application was:

To empower the company on the one hand and the Most Noble the Marquis of Ailsa, as heir of entail in possession of the entailed lands and estates of Cassillis and Culzean or otherwise and his successors, on the other hand to enter into agreements with respect to the acquisition of the lands or easements or servitudes over lands at Turnberry, and the maintenance and use of the same respectively for the purposes of an hotel and golf course, and to authorize the company to erect and maintain an hotel and to lay out, form, regulate and maintain a golf course on all or any part of such lands, and to confirm or give effect to any such agreement which may have been or may be made prior to the passing of the Order or Act conferring the powers aforesaid.

The agreement on the formation of the golf course by the G&SWR at its expense, with the use of the course, was the first of two options that were available to the Marquis. The second option, which the Marquis could bring into effect if he so desired, was to arrange to have the golf course constructed himself earlier than by waiting for the G&SWR to do so. The expenditure would then be reimbursed fully by the G&SWR, when the latter would be given full control of the course under the terms of the feu, with the Marquis able to retain full control until he had received the payment. By late 1900, the Marquis had decided to effect the second option of the agreement that would allow him to form the course himself, because it was expected that a few years would pass before the G&SWR would establish it. Not surprisingly, the G&SWR had no particular desire or incentive to have the golf course formed until the hotel and the railway were constructed, and these had not even been in consideration of commencement by the close of 1900.

The success of both the golf course and the hotel depended on the M&DLR being built, but the railway was now being considered for commencement in the immediate future by the G&SWR. A Special Meeting of the G&SWR Directors and shareholders had already been convened on 5th February, 1901 to discuss, among other separate topics, the 'Proposed New Golf Links and Hotel'. Presiding was Patrick Caird, who had become the Chairman of the G&SWR in March 1900 on the resignation of Sir Renny Watson through ill health, with his death in April 1900. Mr Caird was the General Manager and Chairman of the large Greenock shipbuilding concern of Caird & Company Limited, and he had been appointed a G&SWR Director in 1891 and the Deputy Chairman in 1897. In earlier times, Caird & Co. had also, appropriately, constructed four locomotives, including one for the Glasgow, Paisley, Kilmarnock & Ayr Railway. The meeting confirmed that the Directors considered the erection of a hotel of moderate size and the formation of a golf course to be sources of additional revenue to the company. Nevertheless, two shareholders - John Charlton of Dumfries and Hugh Mayberry of Glasgow - dissented from this view, and Mr Charlton had travelled to Glasgow all the way from his home town specially to make his protest against the G&SWR becoming involved in the project, saying, albeit with some concession:

I think that it is entirely outwith the business of the company. Surely the gentlemen who play golf are sufficiently interested to make a course and erect a clubhouse for themselves. The company may as well propose to run a theatre or a football club. These attract larger attendances than a golf club, and I suppose the only excuse that can be put forward for what is now recommended is that the latter [i.e., golf] would make traffic for the railway.

Mr Caird immediately answered:

Mr Charlton says he presumes that the reason why we have done this is for the purpose of increasing our traffic. It is entirely on that account. The golf courses on the Ayrshire coast are the means of bringing considerable traffic to this company. So far as the Turnberry links are concerned, they have been reported to us, after careful examination, as forming quite an ideal course - a better course almost than exists in Scotland. That being the case, your Directors consider that they are acting entirely in the interests of the company in taking the steps they have done.

Mr Charlton proposed an amendment not to approve of the golf course and hotel, and then he added: 'I presume that Turnberry is not a populous place?' 'Not in the meantime', replied Mr Caird. 'May I ask', said another shareholder to Mr Caird, 'whether you are acquiring ground as proprietors, and what is the extent of it?' Mr Caird's reply was:

The extent of the ground is 15 acres for the hotel and 175 acres for the golf course. The ground has been arranged for with the Marquis of Ailsa on particularly favourable terms for the company. We do not purchase the golf course, but only the right to play over it.

Mr Charlton was not able to make any impression on the shareholders with his amendment. On a show of hands being taken, only he and Mr Mayberry voted for the amendment, and the motion in favour of Turnberry was therefore carried.

Meanwhile, in January 1901, a monthly newspaper called the *Girvan Gazette* had been initiated to serve Carrick, and the March issue provided a summarized communication about the positive outcome of the G&SWR's meeting of February 1901, regarding the proposed hotel and golf course at Turnberry:

Girvan and Golf Links. At a Special Meeting of the Glasgow & South Western Railway shareholders, held in the St Enoch Station offices, on Tuesday, 5th February, a motion was brought forward, and agreed to, having for its object the acquisition of playing powers over the golf course which the company understand is being fitted up at Turnberry by the Marquis of Ailsa. The railway company will erect a hotel on the ground of the golf course when they proceed with the construction of the light railway which they propose building along the Carrick coast between Ayr and Girvan. The hotel will use 15 acres of ground, the golf course 175 acres, and the company consider the Marquis of Ailsa's terms to be particularly favourable.

Back in the late 1890s, Girvan Golf Club had become increasingly concerned about the future of their golf in the town because part of the course had recently been feued by John Campbell Kennedy, the landowner, for the construction of new houses. Consequently, the club had formally asked Thomas Smith, the Marquis of Ailsa's factor, to inquire about the possibility of their members being able to play on the new course that was to be made at Turnberry. Happily, in view of the alternative agreement which the Marquis was now intending to carry into effect with the G&SWR - that he would construct the course himself - an arrangement with Girvan Golf Club for the use of Turnberry was found to be satisfactory to the Marquis. However, it was explained that this had to be tentative because the Marquis would retain the management and maintenance only until the G&SWR took over the course, on completion of the M&DLR, when any arrangement would then have to be made with the railway company.

Thus, in late 1900, with the view of establishing a golf course in the meantime for the local enthusiasts from Girvan and Maybole, the Marquis had invited Willie Fernie, the famous professional golfer and Open Champion of 1883, to be the architect of the new Turnberry course. Mr Fernie, who appropriately originated from the golfing town of St Andrews, was by this time the 'Winner of 22 First-Class Tournaments' and the architect of many courses in Scotland and England. The work commenced in mid-March 1901, with Mr Fernie and a staff of labourers engaged in marking out the new 18-hole course, which was intended to be opened in May of that year. The Girvan members were naturally eager to transfer to Turnberry, and at a Special General Meeting of Girvan Golf Club on 11th June, 1901, 'it was unanimously resolved to remove to Turnberry at the earliest opportunity'. The formal opening ceremony of the impressive Turnberry golf course by Girvan Golf Club was at last able to take place on Saturday 6th July, 1901 in gloriously sunny and calm conditions, when a handicap game was played by the members of the club, with the Marquis donating a gold medal for the winner. Willie Fernie accompanied the members in participation and, not surprisingly, as the Troon professional and as the designer of the Turnberry course, he attained the best score, but, as the only professional present, he was exempt from winning. The winner of the medal was David McConnell, brother of the club's secretary, Robert, who also played in the game.

John Morrison (*left*) and Thomas Mason (*right*), the contractors for the railway and Turnberry Hotel.   *Mitchell Library, Glasgow*

Chapter Seven

Developing Turnberry and
Building the Railway, 1902-1906

While golf had been introduced at Turnberry in the summer of 1901 as part of the plan for the transformation of the quiet, coastal and scenic location, no work had begun on the construction of the M&DLR during the whole of that year to foster the sport there, but the line was still on its course of projection, even if everyone wondered when. At a G&SWR Board meeting on 21st January, 1902, William Melville was authorized to advertise for tenders for the construction of the line, and at a Board meeting on 15th April, 1902, a letter from Mr Melville was read on the tenders received, when the Board authorized the acceptance of the tender of Morrison & Mason Ltd of Glasgow at £201,316 1s. 10d. Established in 1876, the highly respected firm of contractors of John Morrison and Thomas Mason, in the Polmadie (pronounced 'Polma*dee*') district on the southern side of the city centre, specialized in both heavy engineering, such as docks, bridges and railways, and in public and commercial buildings; and among their railway works were the Cathcart suburban line in Glasgow and the Paisley Canal line that took a more southerly course from Glasgow to Paisley than by the original route.

There were to be three sections for the building of the line, all under the contract of Morrison & Mason: Section No. 1 from the junction at Alloway to a quarter of a mile beyond where Dunure station would be, at Fisherton; Section No. 2 from Dunure to the southern end of where Maidens station would be, at Jameston; and Section No. 3 from Maidens to the junction at Bridge Mill sidings, north of Girvan. The constructional work would be under the principal supervision of Mr W.H. Anderson, as resident civil engineer on behalf of the G&SWR, and this work, in turn, would be overseen by William Melville at Glasgow. Additionally, there would be other resident engineers, agents and managers on site, including family members, in Alex Melville, Thomas Mason junior, William Morrison and James Morrison; and there would be the hard-working and resilient navvies, without whose exertions and expertise the line could never be built - a line with many earthworks and bridges, and a line unusually extensive and ironically heavy for a light railway. The work on the construction of the railway was expected to proceed during the summer and autumn of 1902.

Through the later years of the railway's promotional period, the electric tramway from Prestwick to Ayr and Alloway had been successfully financed, completed and operated independently by Ayr Town Council, after much commendable research and diligence from the council members. The start of the construction had been made in late January 1901, and the first and principal section of the Ayr Corporation Tramways had opened along the 3¾ miles from Prestwick Cross to St Leonard's Church on the southern side of Ayr on Thursday 26th September, 1901, with the trams having been built by Messrs Hurst, Nelson & Co. Ltd at its railway carriage and wagon works in Motherwell. On Tuesday 20th May, 1902, the tramway extension, of 1¾ miles was brought into use from St Leonard's Church to Burns' Monument for traffic on a limited service before the official opening on Thursday 29th May. Remarkably, there was now an electric tramway along the quiet road to Alloway, passing through the pastoral and wooded countryside between the estates of Rozelle and Belleisle; and the famous village at the heart of the Burns Country was now served by a new transport system of rails that most large towns and even cities in Britain did not possess. Soon, another more familiar medium of rails would be in process of construction to serve the village and the Carrick coast, in the form of the Maidens & Dunure Light Railway and its steam trains.

Meanwhile, during the late spring of 1902, another golfing development concerning Turnberry had begun to take shape, when on 24th April, 'a meeting of gentlemen in favour of forming a golf club for Maybole and district' was held in Maybole Town Hall. Because there was no golf course in the capital of Carrick, the aim of the proposal was to have the use of the course at Turnberry, and Thomas Smith stated that the golf course at Turnberry had been made entirely at the Marquis of Ailsa's expense and that when the new light railway from Ayr to Girvan was completed, the G&SWR would take over the course. He explained that the guests in the railway company's proposed hotel and people travelling by the trains who were given authorization to use the course would have preference; but the local clubs and the public would be entitled to use the course on terms to be agreed with the Marquis. The situation was acceptable to the meeting, and it was resolved that a golf club be formed under the name of the Turnberry Golf Club, and that the Marquis of Ailsa and his eldest son of the same name, the Earl of Cassillis, be proposed as Honorary President and Vice-President.

At a committee meeting of Turnberry Golf Club at Maybole Castle on 7th August, 1902, the subject of a clubhouse was discussed, and Thomas Smith informed the members that the G&SWR, instead of agreeing to erect a temporary building, as had been discussed with the Marquis, now proposed a permanent structure for the clubhouse and refreshment room. The same meeting agreed to a formal opening of the golf club, and, in the presence of the Marquis of Ailsa, this took place on Saturday, 6th September. John Marshall, Captain of the club, opened the proceedings:

We are met today on a historic occasion in connection with the very ancient game of golf. We are here to inaugurate the latest addition to the list of golfing, and which we are proud to name 'The Turnberry Golf Course'. The Turnberry Club has sprung into life with great rapidity, and has already attained a roll of membership that gives evidence that the 'Turnberry' will soon rival the most famous clubs in Scotland.

Turnberry golf course and club had thus become firmly established during the summers of 1901 and 1902, to bring recreational activity to the scenic coastal locality between Maybole and Girvan. Nevertheless, for the proper enterprising development of Turnberry as a golfing resort - isolated seven miles from Maybole and five miles from Girvan - the establishment of the M&DLR was necessary and eagerly awaited; but patience would be required for the Turnberry project of hotel and railway to materialize.

During the summer and autumn of 1902, the first signs of the constructional work on the M&DLR were in evidence, though much of the activity, with the arrival of some of the navvies to the locality, involved the preliminary requirements of bringing in equipment and materials. In mid-August, William Melville was concerned in supervising light work on the Culzean estate, as 'Lord Ailsa particularly stipulated for unclimbable fencing on both sides of the railway, from the point where it enters the grounds [on the northern side, near Whiteston] till it leaves them at Morriston approach'. By the late summer of 1902, heavier work had begun on the tunnel at Alloway that was to be constructed under the Ayr-Alloway road and immediately on the north-eastern side of the old kirkyard. The tunnel was to be of a square-cut and flat-roof design, instead of the conventional tubular and arched shape, because of limited room that was available between the rail level and the ground above and adjacent, which included the Auld Alloway Kirkyard, situated almost directly above the tunnel roof. It was expected to be in the spring of 1903 that the line overall would be substantially under construction.

Diverging from the main Ayr-Maybole-Girvan line 1¼ miles south of Ayr station and winding its way along the beautiful Carrick coast and its luxuriant countryside, below the Carrick Hills that were dominated by the 940 ft-high Brown Carrick Hill and the 920 ft-high Knoweside Hill, the 19½ miles of the line would run through cuttings of solid rock, over embankments and across two large viaducts and many other bridges, to rejoin the main line half a mile north of Girvan station. In so doing, it would present travellers with some of the most magnificent and breathtaking sea vistas that a railway in the British Isles could ever offer. But irrespective of the line's scenic value, there was no doubt of its necessity, and, in early April 1903, the *Ayr Observer* - never hesitant in supporting any line to and beyond Alloway - provided information about the route and the progress of the work. Included was an explanation that, owing to the wet and stormy weather for much of the previous four months, the contractors had been terribly handicapped with the progress on the line, but that, with genial weather then reasonably expected, the work would be pushed forward with renewed vigour, with the whole undertaking completed within the anticipated time, which was 1st March, 1906.

References were made by the *Ayr Observer* to the more significant features of the line's construction, including the Alloway tunnel or covered way and the adjacent Doon viaduct in their early stages of construction:

The making of this covered way is a very difficult piece of work, the concrete side-walls being founded on mud and running sand, and it is only by almost superhuman exertions on the part of the contractors and their men that some parts of the work can be completed. On emerging from the covered way the railway immediately begins to cross the River Doon on a very fine two-span arched bridge. The arch and the ornamental work on this bridge are constructed of concrete blocks, while all the rest of the work will be done in red-face freestone in low courses. The bridge will present a handsome appearance, and its design will be in harmony with the beautiful surroundings.

Between Dunure and Culzean were the two longest and highest viaducts on the route, supported on concrete piers, at the Craigencroy or Croy Glen and at the Rancleugh Glen (pronounced '*Ran*cloo'), known colloquially known as the 'Rancor' Glen. Both viaducts were steel truss or framework structures, but only in part, across their central decks, in combination with approach girder spans on either side of the trusses. The Croy crossing, the second largest, was summarized first by the paper:

Here the contractors have erected a temporary wooden structure to further the progress of the works. The permanent structure will be a 3-span steel girder bridge, with the piers built of concrete blocks, the centre span [being the truss] 100 feet, approach spans 34 feet. The rail level here is 90 feet above the bottom of the glen.

Then there was the largest crossing:

The railway now enters a long and deep earth cutting and curving round crosses over Rancleugh Glen on a steel girder viaduct of 8 spans, two central spans [being two trusses] of 120 feet, and three approach spans on either side of 56 feet. The piers will be built of concrete blocks. The rail level here is 125 feet above the glen. The viaduct is on a 25 chain curve, and with its tall piers should present an imposing appearance.

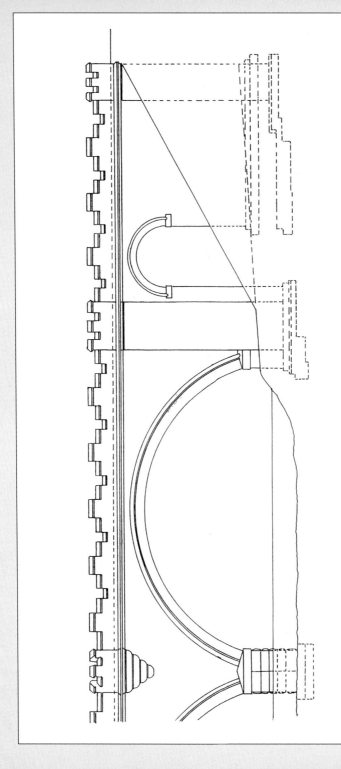

A representation of half the length of the symmetrical Doon viaduct, outlining its ornate appearance that blended with the scenic river setting.
Drawn by S. Rankin

The 'Three Brigs o' Doon' at Alloway, looking east. The M&DLR viaduct is nearest, presenting its large northern arch and the castellated parapet with a railwaymen's refuge. Beyond is the 'new' road bridge, built in 1816, and, in the distance, the 15th-century Auld Brig o' Doon, of Robert Burns fame.   *G&SWR Association*

An impression, looking north across Ayr Bay to the northern Ayrshire coast, of the excavation of the precipitous 40 ft-deep rock cutting south of Dunure in 1906, in the presence of a few remaining navvies and two G&SWR inspecting representatives. It was nicknamed 'Linkentom's Cutting' by the navvies, in honour of their 'gaffer'.

Drawn by D. McConnell

Meanwhile, during February and March 1903, arrangements and special meetings by Turnberry Golf Club and Girvan Golf Club had resulted in an amalgamation of the two clubs, with the Girvan members having become Turnberry members. The Annual General Meeting of Turnberry Golf Club was held at Maybole Town Hall on 23rd April, 1903, being a year since the formation of the club, and the committee's report for 1902-03 referred to the intended construction of the clubhouse:

> Your committee has not lost sight of the necessity of having a suitable clubhouse. As has been seen from the minutes of the last annual meeting, Lord Ailsa promised to erect a house. In the month of August last plans were laid before a meeting of Directors of the Glasgow & SW Railway. According to an agreement between Lord Ailsa and the railway company, any buildings erected on the golf course by Lord Ailsa must be taken over by the railway company when they enter into possession of the course. These plans did not meet with the approval of the Directors, the accommodation being too small to meet their requirements. Instead, the company propose to build a house [a substantial clubhouse]. Your committee understand that the plans for this house are ready, and that the work will be commenced immediately.

The long-awaited clubhouse was built during the late summer and early autumn of 1903, and the following letter, dated 17th September, from the Marquis to Robert Nisbet, the secretary and treasurer of Turnberry Golf Club, was read at the Turnberry committee's meeting at Maybole Town Hall on 25th September:

Dear Sir
    I have a letter from Mr Cooper, asking me to intimate to you in answer to yours of last week the pleasure of the Chairman and Directors of the G&SW Railway that the Turnberry Golf Club should take possession of the clubhouse at Turnberry on its completion, on the terms already arranged, and that the club should have an opening ceremony as proposed in your letter.
    I am,
        Yours faithfully,
          Ailsa

On 6th October, Mr Nisbet issued invitations for a ceremonial opening of the clubhouse by the Marchioness of Ailsa on Saturday 17th October, with the further information that public conveyances would meet trains arriving at Maybole at 10.10 and 11.10 am, and that the 9.35 am 'Golfers' Train' - which ran from St Enoch to Ayr - would run to Maybole for the occasion, to arrive at 11.10 am. For the opening, in delightful weather, a large crowd attended the picturesque coastal setting of the golf course. Among the many invited guests were the Marquis and Marchioness of Ailsa; their first son Archibald Kennedy as the Earl of Cassillis, and their third son Lord Angus Kennedy. Ex-Provost John Marshall of Maybole, as captain of Turnberry Golf Club, presented a gold key to the Marchioness, with which she performed the ceremony of unlocking the clubhouse door.
    With the work on the construction of the railway well in progress during the summer of 1903, what must the people of this quiet stretch of Ayrshire have wondered about the upheaval, as their peaceful coastal and pastoral countryside, steeped in romantic and sacred history, was being ripped through by the railway builders? In early June, an *Ayrshire Post* correspondent declared, with passive disapproval: 'There are navvies now, gangs of them, defacing the fair surface of Carrick along a route where Carrick looks across to Arran, to Ailsa Craig, to the outer gates of Clyde.' Considerable difficulty of excavation would be experienced on account of the heavy cuttings of rock and earth, most substantially as follows: south-west of the striking 250 ft-high Heads of Ayr cliffs beside Bracken Bay; north of Dunure village, at the station and under the Fisherton-Dunure road; west of Dunure Mains farm; in the northern part of the Culzean estate; and in the central part of the Culzean estate. Not only was the rock of solid whinstone, but the material in the earth cuttings, although generally of a clayey nature, was extremely hard, and would need to be dislodged by dynamite. Fortunately, as was often the case in railway building, the material from the cuttings would be able to be used in the formation of embankments elsewhere along the route. Also at this early stage of construction, a large quantity of hard, white freestone had been taken from a quarry on the land of Spring Garden farm, east of the Heads of Ayr cliffs, with the intention of being used for the bridges on Section No. 1; and, similarly, the material of the rock cuttings at Bracken Bay on section No. 1 and west of Dunure Mains farm on Section No. 2 was composed of very hard whinstone - described as 'hard blue whin' - which, when broken, made very fine metal for the concrete in the bridges.
    The railway was to run through the Culzean estate mostly in a cutting for two miles, with all the avenues there, ultimately leading to the castle, to be carried over the line. The Pennyglen Avenue, or Main Avenue, to the castle was the small road that made its way from the Maybole-Girvan road at Pennyglen Lodge, ¾ mile east of the railway, and this was to pass over the line west of the cottages of Whiteston on a skew of about 45 degrees, where a short contrived concrete tunnel, or covered

James Miller's ground-floor plan of Turnberry Hotel, 1903.

way, to be of a greater length than necessary, would screen the view of the line from the avenue. The bridge at Glenside Avenue into Culzean Castle was to be of girder construction, with extended wingwalls of concrete, and the Thomaston Avenue bridge would have a masonry arch, while the Morriston Avenue bridge would be an extended square-faced bridge or covered way, having the same purpose as the arched covered way at the Pennyglen Avenue.

One other principal and essential structure of the whole railway and golfing project was the hotel at Turnberry, and during the spring of 1903, discussions between the G&SWR and the Marquis were initiated regarding the excavations for the 15 acres of site for the building. To design the grand Turnberry Hotel, the G&SWR commissioned the renowned architect James Miller from Perthshire, who, in 1888, had become an architect for the Caledonian Railway and, in 1893, had established his own architectural business. The choice of James Miller for the design of both the hotel and the adjacent station at Turnberry was appropriate because much of his work by this time had involved the designs of many new and rebuilt railway station buildings. These included some in Renfrewshire, being, most famously, the CR stations of Gourock in 1889 and Wemyss Bay in 1903, and the G&SWR station of Greenock Princes Pier in 1893; and some in Ayrshire for the G&SWR, as with Troon in 1892, West Kilbride in 1900, and Mauchline, Prestwick and Stevenston in 1901. He had also designed the building for the Glasgow St Enoch electric subway station in 1896 and - in conjunction with his Perthshire tutor Donald Matheson, Engineer-in-Chief of the CR - for the Glasgow Central Station Hotel extension as part of the massive enlargement of the station itself that had begun in 1899 and was still in progress during 1904. Moreover, from having won an architectural competition in 1898, he had gained much acclaim for designing the buildings for the Glasgow International Exhibition of 1901.

At a Board meeting of the G&SWR on 9th July, 1903, the plans by James Miller of the proposed new Turnberry Hotel, which he had estimated to cost £50,250, were submitted and approved, with tenders requested to be obtained. On 1st September, the tenders were opened and remitted to William Melville to report on them; and on 27th October, the G&SWR decided to accept an amended offer by Messrs Morrison & Mason of £37,751, 4s. 11d., which could have represented the Directors favouring this firm to build the hotel.

More than a year later, towards the end of 1904, two Ayrshire newspapers, containing the same report, summarised the hotel's appearance and its intended physical connection to the proposed station for Turnberry. One of the newspapers was the weekly *Carrick Courier*, which had begun publication in Girvan in May of that year under the name of the *Girvan Courier*, and the other was the *Ayr Observer*:

The new hotel at Turnberry is making rapid progress. The south-east wing is slated and the internal arrangements are being gone on with. The plasterers will soon make a start. The north-east portion is being slated, while the main or front building is covered in and ready for the slates. Work is being pushed on with every possible speed; about 100 men are engaged. The

Right: James Miller, the architect of Turnberry Hotel.
Mitchell Library, Glasgow

This poor quality image from the *Ayrshire Post* in June 1905, looking north, shows the railway works and navvy huts at Knoweside, the curved embankment of the line to the Croy viaduct, and the 'mysterious' Croy Brae, as indicated by the hedgerow running from the superimposed letter 'T' truly uphill across the top right. The newspaper's caption read: 'The above is from a photograph of the queer Croy Brae. Where the letter 'T' is, most people presume, is the top of the hill; while in reality the reverse is the case'. The road to Croy shore is shown by the hedgerow across the lower part of the view.

D. McConnell

hotel stands on rising ground facing the Turnberry Golf Course, with a wide expanse of sea beyond. It is a handsome structure of great size; the view is magnificent on a clear day, while the air is balmy and bracing; as a health resort it will be second to none. As for convenience, the Carrick Light Railway is to have a station at the rear, from which a covered entrance will connect the hotel. A portion of it may be ready in the early summer.

A visual indication of the state of the railway construction at Knoweside in one part of the route appeared as a photograph in the *Ayrshire Post* in June 1905. The purpose of the photograph was to demonstrate a 'mysterious phenomenon' - in reality, an optical illusion - on a specific stretch of the Dunure-Pennyglen road at Croy. The illusion was that the road appeared to run uphill or downhill when the opposite was the case; and, long familiar to the local people, the effect was a natural part of the district (*see Appendix Six*). Fortunately, the expansive photographic view, facing north and taken from south of the small road from Knoweside that led steeply to Croy shore was advantageous in also portraying the railway works and navvy huts at Knoweside, and the Croy viaduct.

For a relatively-short railway that did not run through mountainous country, progress was slow, because of the heavy works, but the G&SWR Directors had not acknowledged a slower-than-expected advancement. Thus, at the Half-Yearly General Meeting of the G&SWR shareholders in Glasgow back on 15th March, 1904, the Board had simply reported, without elaboration, that 'the Maidens & Dunure Light Railway is making satisfactory progress'. A year and a half later, the *Ayrshire Post* correspondent 'Oculus' appeared to be certain of the line's completion when stating, in August 1905, that 'it may interest my readers to learn that the new light railway between Ayr and Girvan is to be opened in March of next year'. Nevertheless, by early October 1905, some anxiety was expressed, in combination with optimism, about whether the railway works would be finished on schedule, as recorded by the *Ayrshire Post*:

The date provisionally fixed the opening of the new Carrick railway is March 1st. When one goes over the line and notes how incomplete it is, how much of the permanent way yet remains to be laid, how unfinished the road is in a score of directions, and the entire absence of station buildings en route, it is not easy to believe that the undertaking will be completed by the appointed time; but many hands make light work, and much energy can overcome many apparent difficulties, and whether the line is opened or not on March 1st, it may be taken for granted that it will be in full swing next season, and that trains will be running every lawful day along the picturesque coastline of nearer Carrick.

The work on the stations followed soon, and at a meeting on 31st October, 1905, the G&SWR Directors began to concern themselves with the station buildings and other structures and requirements, when

> ... authority was given to erect stations at Alloway, Glenayes [Heads of Ayr], Dunure, Maidens and Turnberry; goods depots at Burton [Greenan], Knoweside, Glenside and Dowhill [Dipple]; gatekeepers' cottages at level crossings at Knoweside and Balchriston; and water supply for locomotives at Alloway, Knoweside and Turnberry - at an estimated cost for the whole of £6,460.

Houses for 'station masters, etc' were also considered and the estimated cost was to be found for these; while for Turnberry station, a plan for a loop line had been submitted and the work was ordered to be carried out at an estimated cost of £300. 'A petition for a passenger station at Knoweside goods depot' had also been submitted - with no indication recorded of where this petition had come from - but the Directors 'resolved not to erect a passenger platform', though David Cooper 'was instructed to see what can be done in the way of providing facilities for passengers.'

At the next Board meeting on 28th November, 1905, the plans and estimates were discussed for the station masters' houses at Alloway, Dunure, Maidens and Turnberry and for the workmen's houses - meaning for the other station employees - at Alloway, Burton, Heads of Ayr, Dunure, Maidens, Turnberry and Dipple. The plans were approved at a total cost not exceeding £6,042, and the same meeting authorized an amended plan of the station buildings at Alloway, increasing the accommodation there, at an estimated cost of £666. On 26th December, for Alloway station, 'an application for two additional carriages sidings [goods sidings] and headshunt siding' was approved at an estimate of £1,128; and on 23rd January, 1906, 'an application for loops for rounding trains [goods trains in the proposed yards] at Heads of Ayr station and at Burton, Knoweside, Glenside and Dipple depots' was authorized at an estimate of £774. At the same meeting, the expenditures for signalling the line, at £4,041, and for work to be done by the Telegraph Department, at £2,365, were authorized, as was an extension of the station platform at Alloway, estimated at £215 - possibly again implying, but not with definite indication, that the platform was already there. Then, by 20th February, the circumstances had evidently been changed regarding passenger accommodation at Knoweside and at Glenside, as 'the application for a platform and shelter for dealing with coaching traffic at Knoweside goods depot' was approved at an estimate of £175, as was a 'proposed passenger station at Glenside' at an estimate of £607.

The station at Glenside was originally planned as a goods depot for the traffic of Culzean Castle, with only a private platform for the use of the Marquis and his family and guests; and this had still been the case as recently as mid-November 1905 when David Cooper, in a letter dated the 18th, sent a plan, dated the 16th, of the

Front and side elevations of the typical chalet-style, with canopies, of an M&DLR island-platform station of two rooms, in representing Dunure and Maidens specifically. At Alloway was a longer island-platform version, comprising three rooms; while at Heads of Ayr and Glenside were 'single-platform' equivalents, even after Heads of Ayr became an island platform, but with Glenside also consisting of three rooms that included the private waiting room for the Marquis of Ailsa.   *Drawn by S. Rankin*

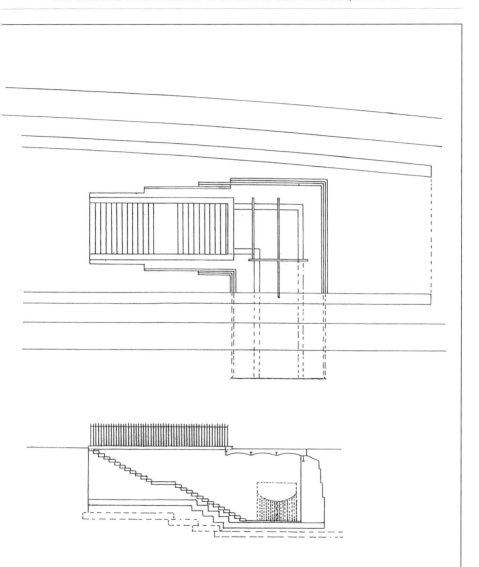

Maidens was the only M&DLR station to possess a subway, shown here as a plan and front elevation cross-section. There were safety railings at the top of the stairs at platform level, and the road-level entrance consisted of two symmetrical half-width open-framework iron gates that were curved on the top and did not extend the full height of the entrance. The exterior splayed wingwalls are not shown (*see the photograph on page 286*).   *Drawn by S. Rankin*

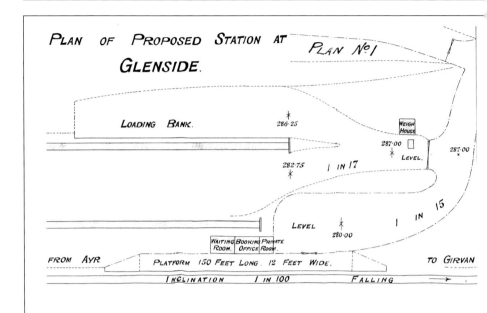

Two of the three proposed G&SWR plans, drawn by William Melville, for Glenside station. The directions are reversed compared with a conventional map, and a proper indication of the orientation is obtained by viewing the plans upside down. 'Plan No. 1' was accepted (*above*). 'Plan No. 2' was rejected (*below*).   (*Both*) *Cassillis & Culzean Estates, Maybole, and Ayrshire Archives, Ayr*

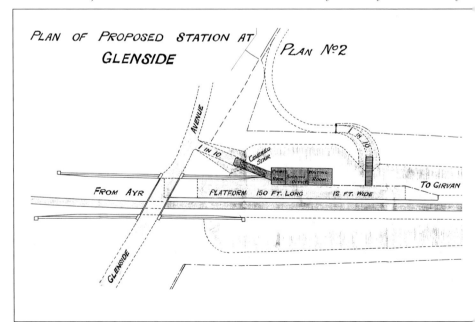

proposed Glenside station to the Marquis. This plan showed the station on the southern side of the Glenside Avenue bridge and on the western side of the railway, with a 'stair' leading down from the avenue. By early January 1906, a change of position for the station had been suggested - this by the Marquis and not the G&SWR - and a letter, dated the 8th, from William Melville to Thomas Smith referred to the change:

> I have arranged to go over a portion of the Maidens & Dunure Light Railway on Thursday, 11th curt, and Mr Cooper has asked me to see you with regard to the altered position of the private station at Glenside. I am anxious to have this matter settled as soon as possible. There is no time to lose in getting the work commenced. I should be obliged if you could meet me where the railway crosses the Main Avenue [near Whiteston] about 11.15 am. From that point I intend to walk down to Glenside.

By early February 1906, it had been decided that not only was there to be this change of position for the station but that the station would now be for the use of the public - however few such passengers would be - as was confirmed in a letter, dated the 6th, from David Cooper to Thomas Smith:

> Referring to my conversation with you the other day. I send you herewith alternative plans for a passenger station at Glenside. For convenience of working the company would prefer to adopt the plan marked No. 1.

There was also a plan marked 'No. 2'. This showed the newly-designed platform, 150 feet in length, still on the southern side of Glenside Avenue bridge but now on the eastern side of the railway and with a station building consisting of a 'private room' for the Marquis, a 'booking office' and a 'waiting room', arranged in the order north-to-south along the platform. For the Marquis, an entrance with a 'covered stair' led down from Glenside Avenue near the northern end of the platform, directly to the private room; while for the public, another entrance, from the Maybole-Girvan road, curved twice to an uncovered stairway that led to the southern end of the platform. However, plan No. 2 was rejected in favour of plan No. 1, which placed the station on the northern side of Glenside Avenue bridge and on the eastern side of the railway. The private room, booking office and waiting room were now arranged south-to-north along the platform, meaning that the private room was nearest to the station entrance in accommodating the Marquis, and a stairway to the station was no longer required because the ground was shallower for this position of the station, such that a path was sufficient. The adoption of plan No. 1 meant that not only would the Marquis and the public use the same entrance but the Marquis would have to cross Glenside Avenue bridge, continue to the Maybole-Girvan road, and then turn back by a path that would lead to the station. The reason for the change from a private to a public station for Glenside was not stated, but perhaps the Marquis simply decided that it would be inappropriate to have a station there which the local people were not allowed to use. At last, the matter of Glenside station had been decided, and David Cooper acknowledged this as being acceptable to the Marquis in a letter of 10th February to Thomas Smith:

> I have your letter of 7th instant and note that Lord Ailsa approves of the plan marked No. 1 which accompanied my letter to you of the 6th instant, and I have given Mr Melville the necessary instructions to carry out the work.

During the second half of 1905, the M&DLR had been the only line in south-western Scotland in process of construction, and the G&SWR Directors recorded at the Half-Yearly General Meeting of the shareholders on 19th September that the only work in hand involving heavy expenditure for the company was on this 'light railway'. That the M&DLR did not appear to be a light railway in its construction and intended operation had been declared - but nevertheless with appreciation of its value - by the *Ayr Observer* of 26th January, 1906:

> Why it should be called a light railway is a mystery, as it seems as substantial as any railway in existence, and the engines and carriages to be run on it are to be the same as are presently running between Ayr and Glasgow. Sufficient unto us, however, it is a railway fully equipped for comfortable travelling, and through a district remarkable for its beauty, and taking us to resorts we have hitherto thought we would require to travel hundreds of miles to get a sight of.

The same issue of the paper had provided some detail about how James Miller's luxury Turnberry Hotel was now looking, and what it contained, outside and inside, for the future guests and the golfers:

> The hotel, which stands on the hillside overlooking the links, and is without doubt the finest hotel outside of a city in the kingdom, is built in the Georgian period of architecture. The building consists of the front or main building with wings at each extremity, forming a large courtyard, down the centre of which is a commodious conservatory and lounge which is continued in a covered way right up to the station buildings, while the ends of the north and south wings are connected by a pergola over which rose and clinging plants grow. The entrance hall is handsomely panelled in oak with a dull wax finish, while the monotony is relieved by marble columns of noble proportions supporting the ceiling. The lounge immediately adjoining is also finished in oak wainscot, while it is floored in common with the hall and the main corridor with black and white marble slabs. The main entrance of marble rises from the hall, and there is also an electric passenger elevator. The billiard room to the south contains three tables and is very efficiently warmed and ventilated by steam so that the tables are always in good order. Next to the billiard room is the writing room, all done in white, as is also the drawing room. To the north of the hall is the dining room, a charming apartment finished in white enamel with French windows to the seafront going on to a verandah which runs almost the full length of the building. The kitchen offices [kitchen rooms], also on this floor, take up the greater part of the north wing and are much superior to those often found in houses four times the size of this, everything being on a most complete scale and designed in such a manner that there is no place that dirt can lodge.
>
> A passage leading off from the south end of the main building brings us to the golfers' quarters, where special provision has been made for golfers coming in from the course. Here are half a dozen bathrooms with large baths and sprays with either salt or fresh water, and a large plunge bath, besides a hairdresser's room, and drying room for wet clothes. There are also a number of bedrooms in this wing, and a lounge and bar with a separate entrance for golfers. On the first floor to which access may be had by several stairs are a large number of bedrooms, while in the main building suites of almost any size can be made up. The second floor is entirely taken up with bedrooms, all finished in white and with plenty of light. A feature of the hotel is the completeness of the bathrooms, there being no less than 18 of them all fitted up in the most modern style. All corridors and public rooms, besides a number of bedrooms, are heated by a most complete system of steam radiators, while the house is lighted throughout by electricity. Facing the shore road [north-west of the hotel and by the Maybole-Girvan road] are all

the office buildings of the hotel, including houses for all workmen about the place, while there are commodious stables and motor car sheds with pit and workshop for those who wish to keep their vehicles here, while directly in front of the hotel [on the lower frontage west of the hotel by the Maybole-Girvan road] are tennis lawns (2), croquet greens and bowling green.

In connection with the railway works at the Alloway tunnel, a curious pair of occurrences - 3½ years apart and with a Robert Burns 'ghostly' association in 'Tam o' Shanter' regarding the haunted kirkyard and graveyard being disturbed - deservedly received publicity in the local press. Back in early September 1902, soon after the start of construction of the tunnel almost below the old kirkyard, the *Ayr Advertiser* had referred to the first of these occurrences in this manner:

> Burns enthusiasts will regret to learn that as the result of the operations now in progress at Alloway in connection with the construction of the Carrick Light Railway the historic Mungo's Well mentioned by Burns in *Tam o'Shanter* has been drained of water, and is at present dry. The well is situated on the lands of Doonbrae, between Alloway's 'auld haunted kirk' and the River Doon.
> Formerly the public were admitted to the well on payment of a small charge admission, but a number of years ago this privilege was withdrawn. It is understood that the draining of the well has been caused by the excavating of the foundations for the walls of the covered way through Cambusdoon policy field, and the hope is entertained that after the walls are built and the land covered over again the water may come back.

Then, in early 1906, towards the completion of the building of the tunnel, and for the second of the two newspaper references to the well, there was a happy postscript from 'Oculeus' in the *Ayrshire Post* of 9th February:

> And when I am out at Alloway, I should like to know if the railway contractors have succeeded in fishing back the spring which supplied Mungo's well, for it is again brimming with limpid water. It will be remembered that, during the progress of cutting through the tunnel behind auld Alloway Kirkyaird, the well suddenly dried up, and the supply spring took its departure to - nobody knew where. Now it is back to its old haunt. I am all of a wonder how it returned, and when it returned, and if it is really the old spring back again, or if it is another spring that has taken up the abode of the departed one? Can anyone enlighten me?

Unfortunately, no enlightening was forthcoming.

The apprehension of those who, during the previous few years through the promotion and construction of the railway in having predicted detrimental effects at Alloway, had generally been allayed by the close of 1905; but a different opinion had been voiced a few weeks later in one of the Ayr newspapers. Here was the episode of the 'great ugly, black-stained, wooden, goods shed' that had been given first attention in the issue of 9th February, 1906 of the *Ayrshire Post* by 'Oculeus', who, in directly following the story of the returning water at Mungo's Well, presented this description and judgement of the unsightly scenario beside Alloway station:

> We'll linger a little longer near the classic spot of famed beauty and fond memories. In a few months, the excursion trains will be landing their thousands upon the cunningly-contrived sunk station platform in the lee of the Burns Monument. The railway company were most considerate in this respect when exploiting their railway scheme

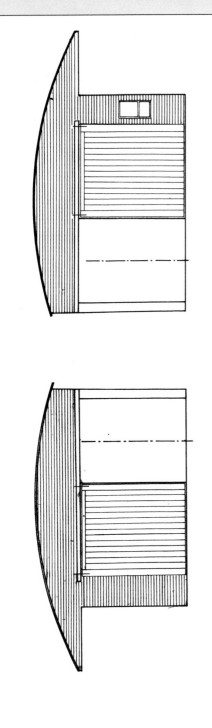

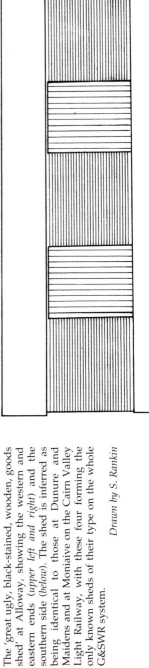

The 'great ugly, black-stained, wooden, goods shed' at Alloway, showing the western and eastern ends (*upper left and right*) and the southern side (*below*). The shed is inferred as being identical to those at Dunure and Maidens and at Moniaive on the Cairn Valley Light Railway, with these four forming the only known sheds of their type on the whole G&SWR system.

Drawn by S. Rankin

A poor quality *Ayrshire Post* photograph from February 1906, looking east, showing the 'great ugly, black-stained, wooden, goods shed' at Alloway that was quickly dismantled and not replaced because it was said to spoil the sacred Robert Burns environs. The shed lay on the northern side of the goods yard, beside the station footbridge (*left*) and its right-angled southern continuation as a walkway (*centre*) that is in construction to the main road behind the camera. The newspaper's caption read: 'The goods shed on the classic banks of the Doon - within a stone-throw of the Burns Monument, and a short throw from the Auld Kirk Yaird. This is from a photo taken from the road where the tram cars run'.

D. McConnell

and asking parliamentary powers. Now, I regret to have to say, they have departed from that give-no-offence attitude, for, right on level with the Monument and within 200 yards of it, the railway company have reared a great ugly, black-stained, wooden, goods shed - just about as ugly a structure as could be planted on any landscape, but hideous when sitting mid such hallowed surroundings and in proximity to grounds famed far and near for their beauty, and the taste displayed in the landscape gardening. I could hardly believe my eyes when I saw the structure, and it took a good deal of persuasion to convince me that it not meant as a temporary affair.

Not everyone felt aggrieved by the structure. A representative of the *Carrick Courier* provided an account, entitled 'Alloway Attractions', for the issue of 21st February, and this included a reference to the goods shed, though not as an attraction. The representative confessed to having been 'somewhat alarmed' on hearing about the goods shed but that he had seen no difficulty with the structure being there. However, the subject continued in the issue of the *Ayrshire Post* of 23rd February, which included a photograph of the shed and a further determined protest from 'Oculeus'.

It soon transpired that the G&SWR had commendably taken notice of the complaint, and 'Oculeus' was satisfied with the outcome, as stated in the *Ayrshire Post* of 9th March:

I must thank the Glasgow & South Western Railway Company for so promptly considering my request against the ugly goods shed, which they had erected at Alloway, on the Carrick Light Railway. I understand it is to be reconstructed and kept more in keeping with the classic and sacred surroundings, and to that end, workmen are presently taking the structure down. The company have shown a grand spirit in this connection, which will not be forgotten by the public. Again I thank them.

That ended the episode of the great ugly, black-stained, wooden, goods shed, to the satisfaction of the devotees of Robert Burns. The G&SWR decided not to erect a replacement shed.

Of the final stages of the building of the whole M&DLR project, the shareholders were informed at the Half-Yearly General Meeting of the G&SWR on 20th March, 1906 that the railway and the hotel 'are almost completed, and will shortly be opened'. At a Board meeting on 17th April, the Directors resolved, with the constructional work virtually finished and only refinements to be carried out, that the line would be opened to the public a month later, on 17th May. The M&DLR was of single track except at the station loops as passing places and at the two junctions with the Ayr-Maybole-Girvan railway.

The M&DLR, in weaving and undulating along the beautiful sandy and rocky Carrick coast, did not traverse high ground, but because of the nature of the terrain in forcing the route steeply beside the sea at certain locations, the impression was given that the height was greater than was the case in reality, which meant that the panoramas were indeed breathtaking. Thus, west of Heads of Ayr, the line curved north-westwards on a ledge, dramatically overlooking Bracken Bay and the Heads of Ayr cliffs, to circumvent a 300 ft-high hill jutting close to the sea, and then it curved south-westwards through a rock cutting on the hillside and emerged to present another sea view. From the cutting all the way to the Croy viaduct, the route, overall, closely followed the 200 ft contour, in only gradually ascending through this distance, but a wonderful sensation of great height was produced when only 200 ft above the sea. The effect of running over stretches of embankments also accentuated the 'illusion', which was the case with the line running 250 ft above sea level on the stretch between the Croy and Rancleugh viaducts. South of Dipple, another vivid, though short, example occurred along the short stretch between the farms of Dunnymuck and Curragh, where the railway ran firstly on an embankment about 20 ft above the adjacent road immediately south of Dunnymuck and then it was able to be squeezed along the side of a steep hill on a ledge immediately north of Curragh. The line was only 80 ft above sea level on the ledge, but the height was impressive because of the 30 ft difference of the adjacent road.

In the whole construction of the heavy works of the line, especially for a light railway, a million tons of cubic yards of earth and rock had to be removed from the cuttings and added to the embankments; and, of this quantity, 90,000 cubic yards - a high ratio of nearly one-tenth - consisted of mainly hard whinstone rock. The lengths and maximum depths of the principal cuttings were: on the jutting curve at Bracken Bay, 200 yards and 30 ft through rock; at Dunure station and south-west of the road, 400 yards and 25 ft through rock; west of Dunure Mains farm, 250 yards and 40 ft curving through rock; on the Culzean estate from Balchriston to south of Whiteston, 1,100 yards and 25 ft through earth; and on the Culzean estate south of Glenside, 450 yards and 30 ft through rock.

The bridges on the line were many, varied and substantial - again, particularly so in the case of a relatively short railway of 20 miles. The large official total of 73 principal structures, producing a high average of one bridge for every 470 yards of the route, comprised two large viaducts, 65 other bridges from 10 to 70 ft in girder span or arch span, and six culverts at least five feet in span. The possibility of future doubling of the line seems to have been taken into account in the construction of some of the bridges. However, unusually and inexplicably, only the public overbridges - where main roads crossed the railway - were built for a double line; while all the underbridges - where the railway crossed roads, tracks, and streams -

and all the accommodation or minor-road overbridges, were built for a single line. The abutments of the bridges were constructed of masonry or concrete, with the superstructure, or deck, of the public-road overbridges of cast-iron girders and arch plates, and the superstructure of the underbridges, with a few exceptions, of steel, while the accommodation overbridges, being mainly for farms, were constructed of timber that was coated with creosote. Nevertheless, while the double-width overbridges would have readily allowed the doubling of the line, this would not have been possible on the single-width underbridges - at least, not without destroying them or part of them; and presumably, it was accepted that there would always be a single track across the underbridges.

The two largest viaducts, with their abutments and piers consisting of concrete, were situated halfway along the length of the line and only a mile apart, in elegantly curving and striding, by their total spans, 171 ft across the Craigencroy Glen on two piers, and 588 ft across the Rancleugh Glen on seven piers, at heights of 90 ft and 125 ft above the respective burns. The viaducts were of an unusual construction along the spans, because there was both a single-track and a double-track width on each bridge. On the Croy viaduct over the full centre span of length of 100 ft above the truss, there was a double-track width but with the single rails running on the western side, while over the two approach girder spans of 35½ ft, only a single width existed. The truss, having a depth of 15 ft, was supported on two piers at a level below the height of the abutments, or below the rail level, but without the need for a central pier over the relatively short width of the glen. Similarly, for single and double extent on the Rancleugh viaduct, which was a grander version of the Croy structure and built in the same way, the centre spans of length 123 ft, containing two trusses, were of a double-track width that also contained the rails on the western side; while along the three approach girder spans of length 57 ft, there was a single width. The two trusses, having a depth of 17½ ft, were supported on three concrete piers - one of them as a central pier - at a level below the piers of the neighbouring approach spans, or below the rail level, though these three piers extended lower into the glen than the two piers on either side that supported the approach girder spans.

North-east of Dunure, across the ravine of the Dunduff Burn was the location of the third highest and the fourth longest bridge on the line. It was also a steel truss bridge, containing a single span of steel lattice parapets, having a criss-cross pattern, of 70 ft span, and the height above the burn was 55 ft, which was particularly impressive in relation to the length of the lattice span.

The Croy and Rancleugh viaducts and the Dunduff bridge were of the 'deck-truss' configuration, where the deck was supported by the framework underneath, as opposed to a 'through truss', with the framework support being above the deck. The trusses of the Croy and Rancleugh viaducts were of a design known as the 'Whipple trapezoidal', which was named after its originator, the 19th-century American civil engineer Squire Whipple, and the essence of the construction was that the diagonal members of the truss extended across two lattice segments or 'panels', rather than one, which produced extra strength for long spans. The truss of the Dunduff bridge was of the 'Warren' truss design, which, in originating from the 19th century English civil engineer James Warren, was based on diagonals that formed equilateral triangles and was used more often in shorter spans.

Most unusual of all the structures was the intriguing and specially-constructed concrete covered way at Alloway, immediately south-west of the station, effectively being a 140 yards-long, double-width tunnel of rectangular cross-section that curved under the Ayr-Alloway road and was offset only a few yards below, and north-west of, the historic and sacred graveyard and the surrounding square of land of the Auld Alloway Kirk.

The difficulty with the construction of the tunnel had arisen because of the limited depth or height that was available between the level of the railway and the level of the kirk and the road, but, also, importantly, the level of the adjacent lands of Cambusdoon and Doonbrae. Therefore, a conventional arched tunnel, conveniently spreading the weight downwards and outwards from the arch, to be absorbed by the abutments, would have extended a greater height above the railway along the whole of the tunnel's length and a greater distance to each side of the tunnel, in supporting additional but unwanted material in this particular case of tunnelling; and the only solution was a square cut with a flat roof that allowed the lowest possible height and was not detrimental to any of the ground above.

This alternative was by the 'cut and cover' or 'digging' method, which, in being suitable for shallow tunnels, entailed excavating an open trench from above, which would form the tunnel bore after the walls and roof had been constructed and after some of the excavated material had been replaced to the original surface level and landscaping. However, in the case of the Alloway tunnel, great care was also needed along the south-eastern side of the cut because of the immediate presence of the kirkyard with its graveyard, where no part of the foundations could be disturbed, which would otherwise have caused partial collapse. Consequently, with no angular space and leverage available, the cut on that side had to be dug vertically or nearly so, unlike in tunnels by this method generally, where a shallow-angled cut - such as 45 degrees or less in relation to the horizontal - facilitated the excavation. The Alloway cut was slow and expensive, because the process of forming the tunnel walls and the roof in the form of girders and arches could only be advanced in small horizontal distances or stages, in acting to support the 'sacred' outside material on the south-eastern side in each gradual stage of construction.

The tunnel walls, being effectively long abutments, were required to be built of reinforced concrete, so that their thickness was able to be kept to a minimum, with the concrete reinforced internally by steel bars in the form of a mesh. The abutments were supported across the tunnel width by a series of cast-iron girders, which were spaced along the tunnel length, and by a series of transverse shallow concrete arches, each of 3 ft 4 in. span between the girders and supported by them. The girders were of an inverted T-shape in cross-section, with flanges on either side of the vertical component, and it was these flanges that supported the arches, in alternating with the girders. It was advantageous that there was only shallow ground above the tunnel - the road and the kirkyard - such that the method of construction of the roof, comprising girders and arches, was sufficiently strong in supporting the weight of the material above, in addition to helping to retain the side material by horizontal pressure across the top of the tunnel walls. Over its 140 yards, the tunnel roof comprised 84 concrete arches that were supported between 85 cast-iron girders. The 25 ft width of the tunnel was able to accommodate a potential double track, but it contained only a single line that ran along its western side, with the double width ending at the Doon viaduct, as the single line of rails proceeded across the river.

From the double width of the tunnel mouth and, after only 20 yards, the railway ran onto the single width of the adjacent ornate Doon viaduct. Built principally of red-face freestone, the viaduct comprised four arches - two main centre spans of 46½ ft span and an outer span of 10 ft on either side - at a height of 28 ft above the river. It was an elegant structure, of castellated parapets of masonry and concrete coping blocks, and it was aesthetically appropriate for crossing the Doon. The arches were essentially of brick but enhanced with concrete blocks around the edge and a concrete arch-ring around the face of each arch.

Then, from the double width and full height of the tunnel mouth, retaining walls of concrete extended on either side of the line, and, from halfway along the 20 yards' distance, were stepped-down steeply to meet the freestone and concrete parapets of the viaduct. The high retaining walls were used to conceal the tunnel mouth from the grounds of Cambusdoon and Doonbrae, respectively on the north-western and south-eastern sides, and also from the picturesque banks of the river, though it was difficult to see the retaining walls from below because of the considerable height of the tunnel above the river. The Doon viaduct was the third most substantial and the third longest underbridge of the line, after Rancleugh and Croy, and also the fourth highest, after Dunduff.

The necessity of additionally concealing the railway through the two miles of the Culzean estate meant that, for most of this distance, the route was constructed in cuttings, while three of the four principal avenue overbridges were of wider construction, longitudinally along the track, than was required of them in crossing the line.

The principal crossing of the line through the Culzean estate was on the Pennyglen Avenue, resulting in the Culzean tunnel or covered way over the line. Consisting of a concrete arched roof, and with the estate road running above it and set on a skew of about 45 degrees to the railway, the tunnel was 42 yards long and of double width, with the single line on the western side. South of Glenside station was the Glenside Avenue bridge, of a girder construction and augmented by retaining walls of concrete that were extended a short distance along the railway more than was necessary for the width of the avenue, but with a much shorter concealment of the line than at the Pennyglen Avenue tunnel. South-west of Glenside was the Culzean Nursery bridge, which was substantially constructed of timber, supported by concrete abutments, and angled from the horizontal, with the higher side west of the railway. Before the end of the rock cutting south-west of Glenside, the line ran under the Thomaston Avenue bridge, built of masonry with a brick-lined arch, though not extended wider than was necessary. However, the final bridge was the extended structure at Morriston Avenue on the south-eastern part of the estate, south of the Balvaird Glen; and, like the Alloway tunnel, this bridge, with the aim of concealing the railway, consisted of reinforced concrete abutments and a flat-roof of transverse girders alternating with transverse concrete arches, and having the single line on the western side. The length of the bridge was 22 yards, and it was built on a descent along its length into the estate and on a skew of about 60 degrees to the railway, or about 30 degrees from the square.

The route of the M&DLR from Ayr to Girvan produced the following distances, simplified to the quarter-mile: from Ayr station to Alloway Junction, 1¾ miles; from Alloway Junction to Girvan No. 1 Junction at the main line north-east of Girvan, in representing the full extent of the M&DLR, 19½ miles; from Girvan No. 1 Junction to Girvan station, ½ mile; and from Ayr station to Girvan station, 21¾ miles (*see Appendix Two*). The line attained a summit of 305 feet at the northern entrance of the Culzean tunnel, and the heaviest series of gradients on the line extended for a significant total distance of 2½ miles from the Glenside rock cutting to Shanter farm, comprising a mile at 1 in 66, a mile at 1 in 70, and half a mile at mostly 1 in 70 (*see Appendix One*).

Chapter Eight

The Ceremonial Opening of the Railway and Turnberry Hotel, 1906

The M&DLR was virtually ready for opening by early May 1906, in particular to serve what had become - if not intended initially - its principal reason for being: the new golfing hotel and resort of Turnberry. As such, Turnberry's station was, by far, the grandest on the line, in contrast to the other basic, but still neat-looking, colourful - and indeed charming - chalet-style station buildings of brick and timber that were commensurate with the project being a light railway. Turnberry station was situated about 100 yards south-east of the hotel, on the western side of the railway, and at the northern end of the single platform, where the covered walkway of timber and glass led to the hotel. The attractive station building, also of brick and timber, was augmented by a glass-roofed canopy with cast-iron lattice ironwork, enhanced by wide, shallow lattice arches, and supported by six pillars along its length, with the glass providing a bright and airy feel. In appearance and facilities, the building was like the station of a sizeable town instead of one that represented hardly a hamlet, though the luxury nature of the Turnberry Hotel, in effectively forming a concentrated and specialized 'village', readily justified the G&SWR deciding upon the substantial nature of the building.

The G&SWR Directors had originally intended that the M&DLR and Turnberry Hotel - officially to be called the Station Hotel - would be opened on 1st March, 1906, which was ultimately not attainable. The opening was to be 11 weeks later, and announcements finally appeared in the Girvan-published *Carrick Courier* of 9th May and in the three Ayr-published newspapers of 10th and 11th May; and, placed on the front page of each, the announcements read:

> *Glasgow & South Western Railway.* The Maidens & Dunure Railway will be opened on Thursday, 17th May, for passenger and merchandise traffic. Simultaneously the Turnberry Station Hotel will be ready for the reception of visitors. Turnberry golf links are in excellent condition, and will be open to hotel visitors. David Cooper, General Manager.

The date of 17th May was to be the public opening for passenger and goods traffic, but a ceremonial private opening for a large number of invited guests, to travel by the new railway and see the new hotel and golfing facilities at Turnberry, had been arranged to take place on the previous day. However, the first-ever passenger train to run over the line did so on the evening of Tuesday, 15th, when a party of the G&SWR Directors and officials travelled by a special train from St Enoch station to Turnberry, where they stayed the night in the hotel. On Wednesday, 16th, the ceremonial train left St Enoch at 10.15 am to convey some of the guests and the remainder of the G&SWR representatives who were to be present at the grand opening, and it made a stop only at Ayr at 11.10 to be augmented by more guests, before heading directly for Turnberry. The train was decorated with flags and streamers, as were the stations along the new line; and the station staff welcomed the first passenger train that proceeded over the M&DLR, while local people turned out to witness the spectacle and novelty of the train as it weaved its way through their coastal district. On arrival at Turnberry before midday on a beautiful day that highlighted the magnificent sea scenery of the route, the guests had two hours before they would partake in a luncheon in the hotel, and they were courteously conducted through the grand building and its surroundings, which included a stroll on part of the beautiful golf course. Everyone was impressed with the scale of magnificence on which the hotel had been designed and furnished, and also with the excellence of the course, with some of the visitors taking the opportunity to play some golf on the exceptionally good turf.

At two o'clock, luncheon was served in the spacious dining room. Four of the G&SWR Directors were in attendance: Chairman Patrick Caird of Greenock; Deputy-Chairman Sir James Bell of Montgreenan, Ayrshire; Sir Herbert Maxwell of Monreith, Wigtownshire; and Sir Matthew Arthur of Glasgow. General Manager David Cooper and other officials of the G&SWR were also present; and among the many guests were: John Dalrymple, who was the Earl of Stair of Lochinch Castle, near Stranraer, and who was also the provost of Stranraer; James Miller, architect of Turnberry Hotel; Robert Millar, General Manager of the Caledonian Railway; G&SWR shareholder Hugh Mayberry of Glasgow; Provost Allan of Ayr; Provost Telfer of Girvan; Provost Ramsay of Maybole; ex-Provost Ferguson of Ayr; ex-Provost Marshall of Maybole; and a number of local council members, local church ministers, prominent officials of golf clubs in south-western Scotland, and representatives of the press from various parts of Scotland, England and Ireland.

Ex-Provost John Marshall of Maybole, who had been Captain of Turnberry Golf Club since 1902 but who was now relinquishing this position, proposed the principal toast of 'Success to the Maidens & Dunure Light Railway and Turnberry Hotel'. However, there also was something about the railway that he questioned:

I don't know that the Directors of the company have been altogether happy in their selection of the official name for this, their latest enterprise. 'Maidens & Dunure' sounds prosaic, whereas to my mind the 'Carrick Coast Railway' is at least more suggestive and has a better ring about it.

In acknowledging the general advantages of the railway, Mr Marshall could not resist mentioning the hope for a branch to Maybole:

May this route be a source of perennial joy and pleasure to the tourist and the traveller, and the result be increasing dividends to the shareholders of the Glasgow & South Western Railway, and such as will, at no distant date, warrant the Directors in making their next extension a branch between Turnberry and Maybole, the capital of Carrick. Gentlemen, I give you the toast of the Maidens & Dunure Railway and Turnberry Hotel, coupled with the name of Mr Caird, the worthy Chairman of the company.

Patrick Caird, who had been the G&SWR's Chairman since 1900, briefly outlined the reasons behind the establishment of the railway and the facilities at Turnberry:

When the Directors of the company were considering the question of the promotion of this line, they learned that there was a piece of land at Turnberry that would make one of the finest golf courses in the west of Scotland - and I do not forget that I am addressing many golfing experts. Recognising that the golf course would be a source of revenue to the company, they resolved to acquire the land and also to build a hotel - there being no accommodation in the district for visitors.

The third speaker was the most senior member of the G&SWR Board and one of the most scholarly individuals not only in the British Isles but worldwide, for he was deeply knowledgeable in many different fields of study and was the author of several books on diverse subjects as topography, history, biography and fiction. He was Sir Herbert Maxwell of Monreith House, near the village of Port William on the eastern shore of Luce Bay in Galloway, and he proposed the health of James Miller and of John Morrison and Thomas Mason, and complimented 'the three Ms', as he described them. However, Sir Herbert missed the opportunity to add to the novelty in his description of 'the three Ms' when he omitted a fourth, in William Melville, the Engineer of the railway and the hotel.

Not far from the ruins of the castle of Robert the Bruce now stood a new Turnberry 'castle' in the form of the luxury hotel that adjoined the railway immediately to the east. It was connected to the station, to the south-east, by a long, rectangular conservatory and lounge as part of the hotel, and by the covered walkway and its red-tiled roof from the conservatory to the station building and its canopy, allowing passengers to walk the whole length and be enclosed from inclement weather. The railway side of the hotel, although not facing the sea, was officially classed as the 'front' or main entrance, while the 'back' commanded the panoramic sea view. From the station direction, the covered way ran northwards and parallel to the railway and then turned westwards to the hotel, leading into a large rectangular courtyard that was effectively formed by the front or railway entrance of the hotel and two winged extensions projecting eastwards from, and at right angles to, the front entrance. Although the foliage of the whole approach area from the railway side was only in its very early stages of growth, the short route from the station through the covered walkway and the conservatory directly to the hotel door conveyed a wonderful first impression of the grandeur of the new Turnberry resort and of a particularly delightful setting in the near future when the foliage would attain its luxuriant development and full-permeating fragrances.

The hotel building was designed in the Georgian style of architecture and had a frontage of 300 feet, being the extent of the courtyard, west to east, from the hotel entrance. The external walls were of roughcast, coloured a light cream, and the roof was constructed of red tiles that imparted a warmth to the whole setting, being most striking when seen against a blue sky. There were 100 bedrooms, with the principal ones situated so that they overlooked the sea. The entire building was lit by electricity, with electric lifts connecting the three floors, and there were electric clocks throughout the hotel. Golfers were well accommodated by the suite of bathrooms of plunge baths fitted with shower and wave sprays, and supplied with hot, cold, fresh and salt water; and there were other salt-water baths throughout the hotel, with the salt water able to be brought from the sea by an electric pump.

The essential association between Turnberry's golfing resort and railway had been appropriately summarized by the Glasgow-published *Daily Record and Mail* newspaper of 17th May, 1906, under the heading of 'Golfers' New Mecca':

Half a century ago a golfer was a source of surmise and rude remarks among the rustics, and he was commonly mistaken for a dismounted polo player. But today almost everyone with a healthy pleasure in living is versed in the philosophy of tees and bunkers.

For the 'royal game' railways are now made, and yesterday a palace was opened at Turnberry where golfers may sleep the sleep of the tired enthusiast on the site of King Robert the Bruce's birthplace.

It is not a long railway, the new branch to the Maidens and Dunure; indeed, it extends under 20 miles from Ayr to Girvan, but few stretches even of greater length are so full of natural beauty. From the carriage windows are seen the shores, now rugged and bold, now sandy and undulating, which delight the city man on his Saturday afternoons.

The palace of Turnberry Hotel stood prominently on a terraced eminence about 100 feet above sea level, and it was nearly the same height above the low and extensive ground of the golf course, west and north-west. With the contrasting cream-coloured walls of the building and the red tiles of the roof, the grand structure was conspicuous from several miles out to sea. Conversely, the view from the hotel's elevation produced a glorious panorama from north to south of the golf course and the great highway of the outer Firth of Clyde, with, to the north-west, the mountainous isle of Arran, most vivid on account of its expanse, and, to the south of west, the prominent rock of Ailsa Craig, distinctive in terms of its nearness and its isolated position in the wide firth. More directly west, beyond the southern end of Arran, stretched the southern extremity of Kintyre, and, on the clearest days, to the south-west beyond Ailsa Craig, the coast of Ireland was readily visible, over 60 miles distant.

At the ceremonial opening of the railway and the hotel, Turnberry was in possession of two golf courses, since a nine-hole ladies' course, to the south of the main course, had been constructed during the preceding winter under the supervision of the club's new professional golfer who had been appointed by the G&SWR. He was Alex Weir, formerly of Cruden Bay Golf Club, south of Peterhead in Aberdeenshire, and he had also carried out recent considerable improvements and alterations to the original 18-hole course that had been designed by Willie Fernie in 1901. The full extent of the main course was 6,248 yards, or 3½ miles, making it one of the longest in Europe, but by the time that the players had negotiated the various natural and artificial hazards, the trek was nearly four miles.

Ironically, at the opening, there was the one surprising - and even puzzling - absence of a G&SWR Director, in that the Marquis of Ailsa did not see the inauguration of the grand project that he had initiated, and that his absence was not formally acknowledged at the luncheon. While he had been appropriately credited by John Marshall as the 'moving spirit' of the whole enterprise, there was no explanation of why he had not been able to attend. Perhaps, as was most likely, the Marquis and the Marchioness were on holiday, or perhaps other important unavoidable business was more pressing than his need to commemorate the enterprise; but the guests at the luncheon seem not to have been informed. No one explained; no one provided apologies for non-attendance on his behalf; no one toasted the Marquis; no members of the Kennedy family attended the celebrations; and no employees from the estate were officially present. The absentees also included Thomas Smith, who had explained to David Cooper by a letter of 11th May that he would be in Edinburgh on the ceremonial day to give evidence in the Court of Session.

Another puzzling aspect of the ceremonial opening of the railway and the hotel was that no newspaper or journal contained a photograph of the special train arriving at Turnberry station. This was in an era when photographs had begun to make appearances in publications - more so in the national press and especially in journals, but also in local newspapers. However, it was unfortunate that there was not a photograph of the ceremonial train and its passengers at Turnberry station; for, the arrival of the train was, by its nature, a unique occasion that should have been recorded photographically for posterity. The eminent weekly magazine *The Illustrated London News*, which might have been expected to publicize the splendours of Turnberry, contained no feature on the opening of the enterprise, while the Glasgow and Edinburgh newspapers and the national railway magazines, in describing the opening, featured no photographs either.

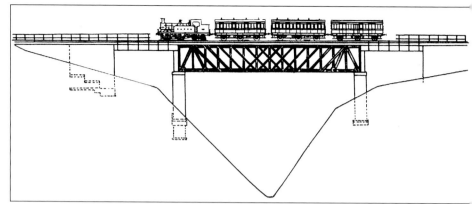

A representation of the 90 ft-high Croy viaduct, with, superimposed on the deck to the same scale, a rebuilt G&SWR '1' class 0-4-4T hauling a first class coach of four compartmants, a third class coach of five compartments and a passenger brake van. *Drawn by S. Rankin*

An impression, looking west, of the 125-ft-high Rancleugh viaduct, as a G&SWR Ayr-Girvan train of four passenger coaches and a passenger brake van, hauled by a '221' class locomotive, crosses the glen, in the early era of the M&DLR. The viaduct was built on a gentle curve that was concave on its western side and convex on its eastern side. *Drawn by D. McConnell*

The Rancleugh viaduct, looking south-west, reproduced from G&SWR's *Carrick Coast Tourist Guide*. *S. Rankin*

Chapter Nine

Early Period Train Services, 1906-1913

With the station masters and all the other station and signalling staff in place along the line, and with the signalling having been inspected by Major J.W. Pringle on behalf of the Board of Trade on 11th May, the M&DLR was opened to the public on Thursday 17th May, 1906 as intended, and the timetable, on a Monday-Saturday service, became effective from that date, as the contrasting dark-green G&SWR locomotives and the dark-red, or 'Midland-red', G&SWR coaches made their way along the highly scenic route. Notices and timetables proclaimed the following services in association with Turnberry: that the railway was open for passenger and merchandise traffic; that the hotel was ready for visitors; that the golf links, which were open to hotel visitors, were in excellent condition; that a Saturdays-only, dining-car express train for golfers left St Enoch at 1.00 pm for Turnberry; and that a tea car ran from Girvan to Ayr by the 4.30 pm train on Saturdays.

There were two principal criteria for the conveyance of passenger traffic on the line: an adequate number of trains to serve Turnberry for the adjacent hotel and the golf courses, which would be the busiest station along the route; and a less frequent service for the other stations on the line, where local rural passengers would be fewer. Golfers were expected to form the majority of the passengers for the railway and the luxury hotel but it was hoped by the G&SWR Directors that non-golfing tourists would arrive in sizeable numbers and stay at the hotel; while day-trippers, specially to see the beautiful scenery along the Carrick coast and to feel the clean fresh Carrick sea air, would also be attracted. Two other important factors in the operation of the line for passenger and goods traffic were the speed limit being restricted by the Light Railways Act to 25 miles per hour and the route being of single line, with passing places, or loops, which necessarily governed the times between stations.

The G&SWR, like most of the other railway companies, had abandoned the provision of second-class travel in the late 19th century, and, consequently, the M&DLR would be served by first-class and third-class coaches. With golf being mainly a sport of the affluent and leisure-orientated citizens, the establishment of the M&DLR - in primarily having the aim of catering for the clientele of Turnberry Hotel and Turnberry Golf Club and in secondarily serving the local farming and fishing population - provided the obvious potential and medium for maintaining a clear separation of two 'classes' of travellers along the Carrick coast. There was indeed an adequate service of trains to accommodate golfers and the holiday interests of the hotel, and, therefore, Turnberry was the only station between Ayr and Girvan which was given an express service and at which all the trains on the line stopped.

There were four crossing places, or loops, on the single-track line - at Alloway, Dunure, Maidens and Turnberry. However, unlike at the island platforms of Alloway, Dunure and Maidens, passenger trains were not allowed to cross each other at Turnberry station because the platform, as a single structure, served only one running line, with the loop formed mainly to the north of the platform; but two goods trains could cross, as could a passenger train at the station with a goods train in the loop. The line's signal boxes were located at Alloway, Heads of Ayr, Dunure, Glenside, Maidens and Turnberry stations, and at the line's junctions with the main Ayr-Girvan route - Alloway Junction and Girvan No. 1 Junction - where no signal boxes had existed until the establishment of the M&DLR.

OPENING OF THE NEW MAIDENS AND DUNURE RAILWAY.

YESTERDAY the official opening of the new railway from Ayr to Girvan via Dunure and the Maidens was taken part in by a large company, comprising the directors of the Glasgow and South-Western Railway Co's., and invited guests. A party of the directors proceeded by special train to Turnberry on Tuesday evening, and the remainder of the company were conveyed by special train yesterday. The day was fine, and a splendid view was obtained of the scenery en route. Arrived at Turnberry, the party had a couple of hours during which to inspect the hotel and surroundings, and everyone was greatly impressed with the scale of magnificence on which the hotel has been designed and furnished, and with the undoubted excellence of the golf links. Mr Patrick T. Caird, chairman of the directors, presided at a luncheon, and, after the usual loyal toast had been honoured, ex-Provost Marshall, Maybole, in an eloquent speech, proposed "Success to the Maidens and Dunure Railway, Turnberry Hotel and Golf Links." The Chairman, in replying, expressed a hope that the efforts of the Company to cater for golfers and holiday makers generally, and to provide facilities for the agricultural traffic of the district, would be appreciated. Sir Herbert Maxwell afterwards proposed the health of the architect (Mr Miller, Glasgow), and the contractors (Messrs Morrison & Mason, Glasgow), to which Mr Millar replied, and the proceedings terminated with the health of the Chairman being toasted on the call of Mr Mayberry, Glasgow.

THE RAILWAY.

The course of the new railway is very well known to the majority of the inhabitants of this district, but the beauties of the country it opens up can hitherto have been familiar only to a limited and favoured few, and the opportunity afforded by the new railway to become better acquainted with a country-side historically import-

CARRICK COAST RAILWAY.

THE OFFICIAL OPENING.

LAND OF POETRY, ROMANCE, AND BEAUTY.

EXCELLENT RAILWAY FACILITIES PROVIDED.

TURNBERRY AS A HEALTH AND PLEASURE RESORT.

GOOD EXPECTATIONS FOR FUTURE.

On the invitation of the Chairman and Directors of the Glasgow and South-Western Railway Company, a large and representative party of gentlemen took part in the formal opening of the Maidens and Dunure Railway on Wednesday. It has been constructed by a railway company which is one of the most enterprising railroad organisations in the kingdom. A full description of the new line appeared in our last week's issue, so it is unnecessary to again enter into details; suffice it to say that the railway is about twenty miles in length, that it passes through a land of poetry, romance, and beauty, and that it will open up a district in Ayrshire that has suffered from the absence of such facilities. The party journeyed to and from Turnberry in a magnificently decorated special train, and at the stations on the route and elsewhere there was a good deal of bunting displayed, while people turned out here and there to view the spectacle. Happily, the weather, though cold near the sea, was dry during the greater part of the day. On arrival at Turnberry, an inspection of the hotel and grounds was made, and an opportunity afforded of strolling on the beautiful golf links, which are among the best in the south-west of Scotland, and which were laid out in 1901 by Willie Fernie, Troon. The directors of the Railway Company; Mr David Cooper, the general manager, and a worthy Ayrshire man; Mr Thomas, the hotels manager, and other officials.

THE MAIDENS AND DUNURE RAILWAY

TURNBERRY HOTEL

In our last issue we gave a description of the new railway to Turnberry. Any notice of this great undertaking would be very incomplete without special mention of the magnificent hotel which has been erected, and which will form the great attraction of the line.

The new hotel adjoins the railway, and is connected to the station by a covered way that leads through a large Conservatory to the entrance lounge. It is situated on an undulating slope of ground at a height of about 100 feet above sea level, an elevation which commands an extensive view not only of the golf links but of the Irish Channel. On a clear day the coast of Ireland is distinctly visible from the terrace in front of the hotel. The building has a frontage of 300 feet, and the whole of the principal rooms are situated so that their windows overlook the sea.

The entrance lounge is a magnificent apartment, 81 feet by 30 feet. It is paved in Italian marble, the walls are panelled with oak, and the ceiling is of richly decorated plaster. In front of the lounge, extending its whole length, and also in front of the dining-room, is a wide balcony with French casements opening down to the floor level, so that teas or dinners can be served on the balconies in fine weather.

The dining, drawing, and visiting rooms adjoin the lounge and are decorated in the Georgian style, with panelled walls and ceilings finished in pure white.

The billiard-room is a handsome apartment with alcoves at either end for smoking accommodation. Three billiard tables are provided.

On the first floor are a series of suite rooms, comprising sitting-room, bath-room, and two or three or more bedrooms, as may be required, the rooms being made communicating, so that any size

The opening of the Maidens & Dunure Light Railway and Turnberry Hotel, as reported in the three Ayr-published newspapers, *from left to right, Ayr Advertiser - 17th May, Ayrshire Post - 18th May, Ayr Observer 18th May, 1906.*

D. McConnell

OPENING OF
MAIDENS AND DUNURE LIGHT RAILWAY

This Light Railway between Ayr and Girvan will be opened on Thursday, 17th May, when the following Passenger Train Service will come into operation:

STATIONS.	a.m.	a.m.	a.m. (Tues., Thurs., & Sats.)	a.m. (Sats. only)	p.m. (Not on Sats.)	p.m. (Sats. only)	p.m. (Sats. only)	p.m. (Not on Sats.)	p.m. (Sats. only)	p.m.	p.m. (Not on Sats.)	p.m. (Sats. only)
Glasgow (St. Enoch) dep.	5†25	8.40	9.35	11.5	12.30	1.0	1.7	2.15	2.15	5.10	6.15	6.15
Ayr arr.	6†58	9.47	10.25	11.55	1.25	1.50	2.12	3.39	3.47	6.0	7.35	7.35
Ayr dep.	7.25	10.0	10.30	12.0	1.35	1.55	2.25	3.50	4.0	6.10	7.45	8.5
Alloway	7.35	10.10			1.45		2.35	4.0	4.10		7.55	8.15
Heads of Ayr	7.45	10.20			1.55		2.45	4.10	4.20		8.5	8.25
Dunure	7.53	10.28			2.3	Luncheon Train	2.59	4.18	4.28		8.13	8.33
Knoweside	*	*			*		*	*	*		*	*
Glenside	*	*			*		*	*	*		*	*
Maidens	8.12	10.48		12.38	2.23		3.19	4.36	4.47		8.33	8.53
Turnberry	8.18	10.54	11.10	12.44	2.33	2.35	3.25	4.42	4.55	6.51	8.39	8.59
Girvan arr.	8.30	11.5	11.22	12.55	2.45	2.46	3.36	4.55	5.6	7.3	8.50	9.10

STATIONS.	a.m.	a.m.	p.m. (Sats. only)	p.m. (Not on Sats.)	p.m. (Tues., Thurs., & Sats.)	p.m. (Not on Sats.)	p.m.	p.m. (Sats. only)
Girvan dep.	7.15	8.33	12.30	2.20	4.30	5.24	5.50	7.15
Turnberry	7.28	8.50	12.44	2.33	4.42	5.36	6.3	7.28
Maidens	7.34		12.50	2.39	Tea Car – Girvan to Ayr on Saturdays		6.9	7.34
Glenside	*		*	*			*	*
Knoweside	*		*	*			*	*
Dunure	7.54		1.11	2.59			6.30	7.55
Heads of Ayr	8.1		1.19	3.7			6.38	8.3
Alloway	8.10		1.28	3.16			6.47	8.15
Ayr arr.	8.18	9.30	1.36	3.25	5.22	6.16	6.55	8.23
Ayr dep.	8.25	9.35	1.50	3.40	5.25	6.25	7.0	8.30
Glasgow (St. Enoch) arr.	9.15	10.40	2.55	5.10	6.20	7.28	8.30	9.40

* Knoweside and Glenside Stations – Trains marked thus will call at these Stations, when required, to pick up and set down Passengers on notice being given.

† On Mondays leave Glasgow 6. 0 a.m. and arrive Ayr 7. 5 a.m.

S. Rankin and D. McConnell

The first-ever timetable of the M&DLR - a reconstructed reproduction, owing to difficulties with direct copying.

It was probable that the M&DLR's Ayr-Girvan local trains, in addition to the
Dalmellington trains, usually departed from Ayr station's fifth platform - a dock or
bay platform, with no through line - that had been built in 1902, immediately south
of the road bridge at the station, and entered on foot by the main southbound
platform and under the bridge. South of the station, there were loop lines on both
sides of the southbound main line, and the fifth platform materialized from an
existing extension track from the loop almost to the road bridge. Through trains
from Glasgow for Turnberry used the station's main southbound platform.

Especially for golfers - though not restricted to them - were several express
services, or 'golfers' trains', from Glasgow to Turnberry, calling only at Ayr and
Turnberry before continuing to Girvan. As 'express' services, in a relative sense over
the 25 mph speed limit, they consisted of the following: the 9.35 am ex-Glasgow
(10.30 ex-Ayr) running on Tuesdays, Thursdays and Saturdays only; the 11.05 am ex-
Glasgow (12 noon ex-Ayr) running on Saturdays; the 1.00 pm ex-Glasgow (1.55 ex-
Ayr) running on Saturdays; and the 5.10 pm ex-Glasgow (6.10 ex-Ayr) running on
Mondays to Saturdays, containing a through portion for Girvan via Turnberry and
calling only at Turnberry after Ayr. The Saturdays-only 1.00 pm ex-Glasgow was
referred to in the timetable as a 'luncheon train', and it reached Turnberry at 2.35, to
give a fast run from the city in a little over an hour and a half. From Girvan, the
through trains via Turnberry to Glasgow were: the 8.33 am on Mondays to
Saturdays; the 4.30 pm on Tuesdays, Thursdays and Saturdays; and the 5.24 pm on
Mondays to Saturdays. The 4.30 pm ex-Girvan service included, on Saturdays only,
the return working of the dining car of the southbound luncheon train as the tea car
from Girvan to Ayr, departing from Turnberry at 4.42.

Because all the trains on the M&DLR stopped at Turnberry, golfers could travel
by any service, but the G&SWR naturally encouraged the use of the golfers' trains.
The 9.35 am ex-Glasgow through service on Tuesdays, Thursdays and Saturdays,
which reached Turnberry at 11.10, allowed the golfers several hours for their sport
and then relaxation in the golf club or hotel if they wanted to return on the 4.30 pm
through service to Glasgow, with the bonus on Saturdays of the tea car; and
similarly, on Saturdays, the 11.05 am ex-Glasgow through service provided
sufficient time for a game, allowing a return by the 4.30 pm ex-Girvan tea-car
service. It was also possible for golfers to use the 1.00 pm ex-Glasgow on Saturdays,
which was the luncheon train, and return by the 4.30 pm tea car, but their time on
the golf course was then limited to well under two hours, though some passengers
may have used both trains for a short day-trip. There was an imbalance of services,
with more trains to than from Turnberry. Perhaps the southbound difference
resulted from the priority that the G&SWR envisaged in taking golfers to Turnberry,
in allowing them more trains in that direction without the need to give too much of
a choice in returning them too early from the hotel and golfing facilities. With the
services separated into Mondays to Fridays and Saturdays, the more complex
southbound timetable, as a summary for Turnberry, read more clearly as follows:

Mondays to Fridays	†		TT				
	am	am	am	pm	pm	pm	pm
Glasgow	5.25	8.40	9.35	12.30	2.15	5.10	6.15
Ayr	7.25	10.00	10.30	1.35	3.50	6.10	7.45
Turnberry	8.18	10.51	11.10	2.33	4.42	6.51	8.39

Notes:
† - Dep. 6.00 am Mondays, other station times unaltered. TT - Tuesdays and Thursdays.

Saturdays	am	am	am	am	pm	pm	pm	pm	pm
Glasgow	5.25	8.40	9.35	11.05	1.00	1.07	2.15	5.10	6.15
Ayr	7.25	10.00	10.30	2.00	1.55	2.25	4.00	6.10	8.05
Turnberry	8.18	10.51	11.10	12.44	2.35	3.25	4.55	6.51	8.59

It was indeed prestigious for Turnberry's clientele to have the facility every Saturday of the dining car that was the only catering vehicle in the entire G&SWR coaching fleet, having been built only in 1905. Based at Carlisle, it performed a 'breakfast-car' run over the G&SWR's principal route on the 6.28 am Carlisle-St Enoch service on Mondays to Fridays and normally returned on the 5.30 pm St Enoch-Carlisle service as a tea car. However, on Saturdays, in additionally operating as the Turnberry tea car from Girvan to Ayr, it was not able to return from Ayr to Glasgow in time to be attached to the 5.30 pm to Carlisle. The dining car's schedule was therefore as follows: Mondays to Saturdays, as a breakfast car from Carlisle to Glasgow; Mondays to Fridays, as a tea car from Glasgow to Carlisle; Saturdays, as a dining car from Glasgow to Girvan; and Saturdays, as a tea car from Girvan to Ayr. The method of returning empty from Ayr to Carlisle in readiness for the Monday breakfast run from Carlisle to Glasgow was possibly by the dining car being attached to the Saturday evening Ayr-Carlisle Post Office sorting train, via Annbank and Mauchline.

Nevertheless, excluding the elite Turnberry, and as was evident from a study of the opening M&DLR timetable by anyone at the time, there were excessive periods, extending from five to six hours, between trains in the same direction in 'accommodating' the intermediate stations of the line. An illustration of this was provided by the interval between the first two northbound trains of the day, Mondays to Saturdays, that called at Maidens, Glenside by request, Knoweside by request, Dunure, Heads of Ayr and Alloway. The first of the two, the 7.15 am ex-Girvan, called at, for example, Maidens at 7.34 am but the next one to call there was at 12.50 pm, with the other intermediate stations, apart from Turnberry, having the same interval. However, even with the additional 8.33 am ex-Girvan train, Turnberry was left with an interval of nearly four hours between its second and third northbound trains of the day, from 8.50 am to 12.44 pm. Similarly, in the southbound direction, there was a long interval for the intermediate stations, apart from Turnberry. Thus, after an interval of 2½ hours from the first southbound train, which was the 7.25 ex-Ayr, the 10.00 am ex-Ayr called at, for example, Alloway at 10.10; but on Mondays to Fridays, there was no other stopping train in that direction until the 1.35 ex-Ayr that called at Alloway at 1.45 pm, 3½ hours after the previous train to call there. The same applied to the other intermediate stations, with Turnberry excepted, but, this time, also with Maidens excepted on Saturdays, because the 12 noon train called there at 12.38. Moreover, the situation was much worse on Saturdays for the intermediate stations, because there was no southbound train for them, apart from Turnberry, between the 10.00 am and the 4.00 pm ex-Ayr, which was also the last southbound Saturday train of the day for the intermediate stations, except for Turnberry, where the 6.10 pm ex-Ayr, which was the 5.10 pm through service from Glasgow, called at 6.51.

The timetable for June 1906 was, in essence, similar to the one at the start of the service on 17th May, with the exception of adjustments of five to 15 minutes in a few timings. However, the timetable was sufficiently unchanged for the local people still to disapprove of the long intervals between the intermediate stations. The complaints were vividly explained by a letter in the *Ayrshire Post* of 8th June, 1906

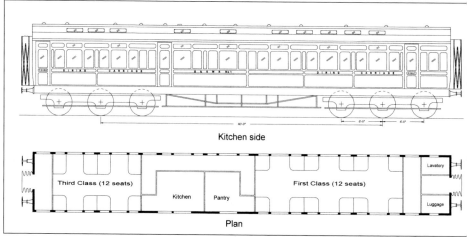

Kitchen side

Plan

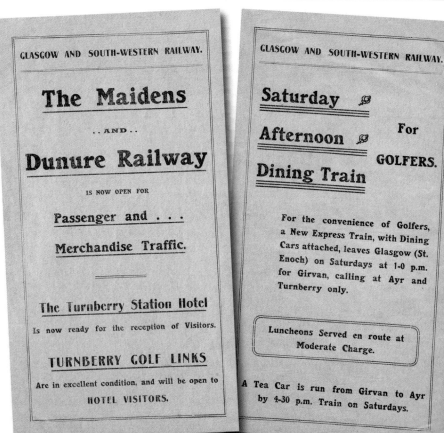

Left: The first G&SWR and Turnberry line dining car, which was designed by James Manson, the company's locomotive superintendent, and built in 1905. It was used on the M&DLR on Saturdays from July to September 1906.   *Drawn by J. Easthope*

Bottom left: Both sides of a G&SWR leaflet issued for the opening of the M&DLR.   *R.H. Smillie*

Turnberry Hotel, soon after, or even before, its opening in 1906. At the extreme left are the Turnberry Cottages, and, to their right, the hotel's garage and stables.   *Carnegie Library, Ayr*

A compact M&DLR timetable for July 1906, from *Bradshaw's General Railway and Steam Navigation Guide*.   *G&SWR Association*

AYR, DUNURE, and GIRVAN.—Glasgow and South Western.

Miles	St. Enoch Station	mrn	mrn	mrn		mrn	aft	aft	aft	aft	aft	aft	aft	aft
	802 GLASGOW ......dep.	5b25	8 40	9 35		11 5	12½e	1 8 0	1 8 5	2 15	4 10	5 10	6e15	6815
	Ayr ....dep.	7 25	10 0	1030		12 0	1e35	1855	2s25	3 55	5 25	6 10	7e40	8 8 5
3	Alloway	7 35	1010				1c45		2s35	4 5			7e50	8s15
6¼	Heads of Ayr	7 45	1020				1e55		2s45	4 15			8 e 0	8s25
8	Dunure	7 53	1028				2 e 3		2s53	4 25	5 48		8 e 8	8s33
11	Knoweside	Sig.	Sig.				Sig.		Sig.	Sig.			Sig.	Sig.
13	Glenside............	Sig.	Sig.				2e18		3 8 8	Sig.			Sig.	Sig.
15¼	Maidens	8 12	1048			1238	2e23		3813	4 47			8e28	8s53
16¾	Turnberry............	8 18	1054	1110		1244	2e33	2835	3819	4 55,6	9 6 51		8e34	8s59
21¼	**Girvan** 802 ....arr.	8 30	11 5	1122		1255	2e45	2846	3s30	5 6	6 21	7 3	8e45	9s10

Mls		mrn	mrn	aft	aft	aft	aft		aft	aft	aft	aft	
—	**Girvan** ......dep.	7 10	8 33	1230	2 e 5	2s10	4 30		5 15	5s50	7s15	7e25	
5	Turnberry............	7 23	8 50	1232	2e17	2s22	4 42		5 27	6 s 3	7s28	7e37	
6¼	Maidens	7 29		1240	2e33	2s35				6 8 9	7s34	7e43	
8¼	Glenside............	7 35		Sig.	Sig.	Sig.				Sig.	Sig.	Sig.	
10¼	Knoweside	Sig.		Sig.	Sig.	Sig.				Sig.	Sig.	Sig.	
13¼	Dunure	7 54		1 0	2e44	2s52			5 50	6s30	7s55	8 e 6	
15¼	Heads of Ayr	8 1		1 9	2e52	3 8 1				6s38	8 s 3	8e13	
18¼	Alloway	8 10		1 18	3 e 1	3s10				6s47	8s15	8e22	
21¼	**Ayr** 805 ....arr.	8 18	9 30	1 30	3e10	3s20	5 22		6 10	6s55	8s23	8e30	
63¼	805 GLASGOW (St Enoch) ar	9 15	1040	2 55	5e10	5s10	6 20		7 28	8s40	9s40	10e0	

b Leaves at 6 mrn. on Mondays.   *e* Except Saturdays.   *s* Saturdays only.
For **OTHER TRAINS** between Ayr and Girvan, see pages **802 to 807**.

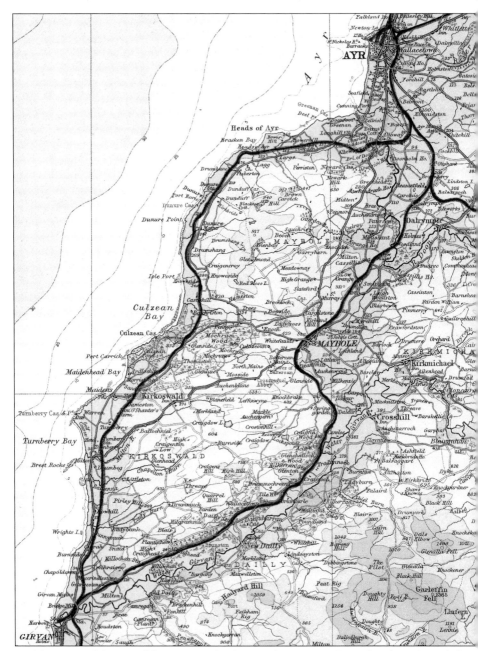

The route and districts of the M&DLR, also showing the main Ayr-Girvan line through Maybole. From Bartholemew's *Survey Atlas of Scotland, 1912*, half-inch to the mile, reproduced slightly smallet than actual size.
                                                                    Carnegie Library, Ayr

from a local representative 'A. Farmer', in declaring that 'the Glasgow & South Western Railway Company will have to make more efforts to suit the convenience of people in the district, especially those who live in the vicinity of the railway, if they wish good financial results':

As was to be expected, at the start the service was unsatisfactory; and even after our grievances were laid before the company, we are to have the same timetable for June. I am one of those who live about halfway between Ayr and Girvan, and I think I voice the sentiments of farmers and others who are interested in the new railway. The first train for Ayr leaves Girvan at 7.10 am and the next at 12.20 pm. Now, one is too early and the other too late for the market, so we farmers have to drive to town as before. There is a train which leaves Girvan at 8.30 am and calls at Turnberry only. Its rate of speed is 25 miles an hour and its passengers are few and far between. This will be the most serviceable train of the day to all parties, but here the company close the door to their own interests. In the afternoon there are no local trains from Ayr between 3.55 pm and 7.40 pm, and between these are two expresses, apparently to suit the Turnberry Hotel people. I don't think there should be so many express trains. Passengers to a certain station have to drive a matter of four or five miles to their home, through the company refusing to stop their 25 miles an hour trains.

The G&SWR Directors, in surprisingly ignoring part of the accommodation of the local people too much in favour of the Turnberry passengers, seemed to have forgotten that the original purpose of a line along the Carrick coast was to serve the rural population. Would the Directors take heed of what 'A. Farmer' had said, validly, on behalf of the people of the district? For July 1906, which represented the whole summer timetable until the end of September, a minor change was the addition of the 5.25 pm Ayr-Turnberry express service on Mondays to Saturdays, which called at Dunure at 5.48. However, this stop was not introduced for the particular benefit of Dunure passengers but because of the running of the 5.15 pm Girvan-Turnberry express on Mondays to Saturdays, which was re-timed from 5.24 pm. The two expresses needed to cross at a convenient location and the solution was to schedule them to stop at Dunure, such that the 5.15 northbound called at Dunure at 5.50. By this time, Glenside also had a definite stop of one train in each direction per day: at 7.35 am Mondays to Saturdays, from the 7.10 am ex-Girvan; and at 2.18 pm Mondays to Fridays, and 3.08 pm on Saturdays, from the 1.35 and 2.25 pm ex-Ayr, respectively. The G&SWR Directors, in therefore having implemented several changes for July, had sadly not implemented the sensible recommendation by 'A. Farmer'.

Between July and October, the passenger train services remained generally similar, and from October, when the winter timetable began, there were still only minor changes overall but with two important services withdrawn. One was the 5.25 pm Ayr-Turnberry express on Mondays to Saturdays, which had called at Dunure, though the 6.10 pm Ayr-Turnberry express on Mondays to Saturdays continued. The other - more significantly - was the Saturday luncheon train for golfers, the 1.00 pm Glasgow-Turnberry express. The 4.30 pm ex-Girvan service, as the 4.42 ex-Turnberry, still operated on Tuesdays, Thursdays and Saturdays, but it no longer conveyed the Saturday tea car.

From the opening of the line, through the summer and winter of 1906, there had been one goods train per day in each direction between Ayr Falkland yard and Girvan goods station on Mondays to Saturdays, with no change in the timings during that period. It left Ayr in the morning and returned from Girvan in the afternoon, with the following schedule of departure times:

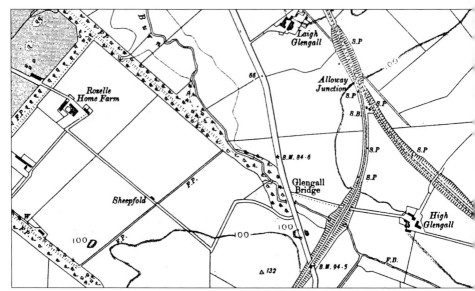

Alloway Junction. Ordnance Survey 6 inch to the mile map of 1908, reproduced actual size.
NLS Map Library, Edinburgh

Alloway station, tunnel and village and the Burns tourist attractions OS 6 inch to the mile map of 1909, reproduced actual size.   *NLS Map Library, Edinburgh*

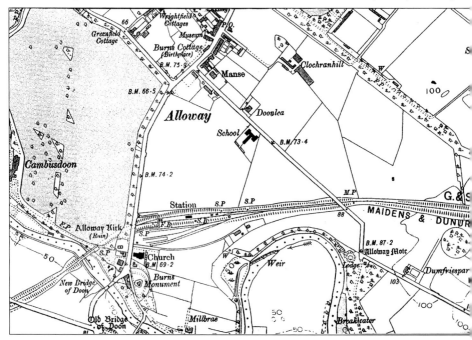

A postcard view of Alloway station, looking east towards the Doonholm Road bridge, in the early era of the M&DLR. The overall attractiveness of the station, with chalet building and platform flower beds, is enhanced by the shallow cutting. On the upper right is the higher-level goods yard that was entered from the Ayr direction by trailing points, a headshunt and trailing points again, resulting in a zigzag ascent from the main line.   *G&SWR Association*

The south-western end of Alloway tunnel, showing the end elevation of the tunnel mouth and the side elevation of the adjoining south-eastern retaining wall that was stepped down to the castellated parapet of the Doon viaduct. Centre left is a larger-scale cross-section of one of 84 transverse shallow concrete arches of 3 ft 4 in. span, spaced between 85 inverted T-shaped cast-iron girders on the underside of the roof along the tunnel's length.
Drawn by S. Rankin

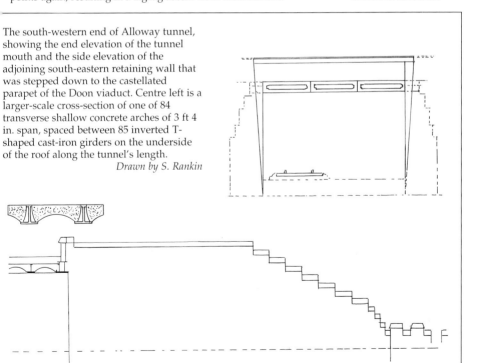

Alloway was also reached by the Ayr Corporation Tramway along the tree-lined country road between the Rozelle and Bellisle estates. The reason for the tramway extension to Alloway is represented by a tram passing Robert Burns' Cottage in the main street of the village, looking north, and the trams continued for nearly half a mile further south, to terminate beside the Burns Arms Hotel and close to the Burns Monument. *Carnegie Library, Ayr*

Alloway tunnel, station footbridge and adjacent Doonside, also showing the single-track rails and passing loop of the Ayr Corporation Tramway to the Burns Arms Hotel. Ordnance Survey 25 in. to the mile map of 1909, reproduced actual size. *NLS Map Library, Edinburgh*

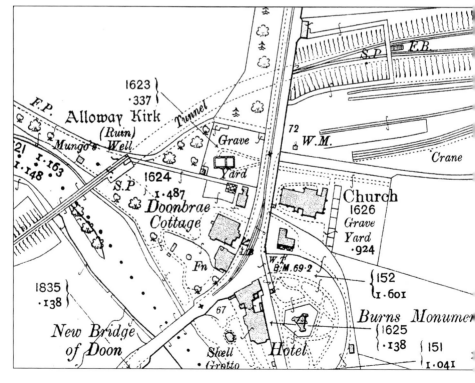

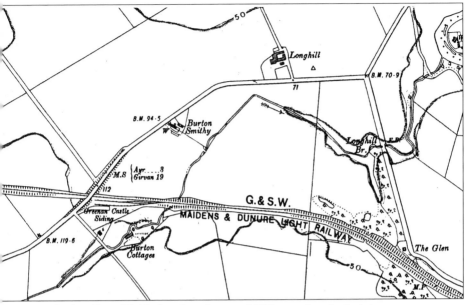

Greenan Castle sidings. OS 6 inch to the mile map of 1908, reproduced actual size.
NLS Map Library, Edinburgh

Heads of Ayr station and the Bracken Bay curve. OS 6 inch to the mile map of 1908, reproduced
actual size.   *NLS Map Library, Edinburgh*

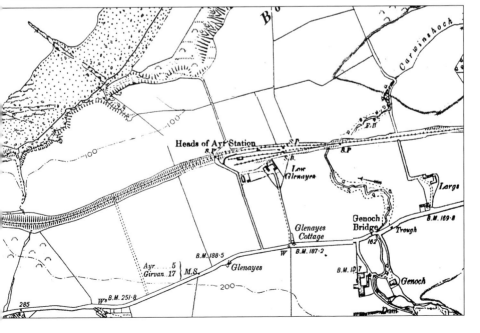

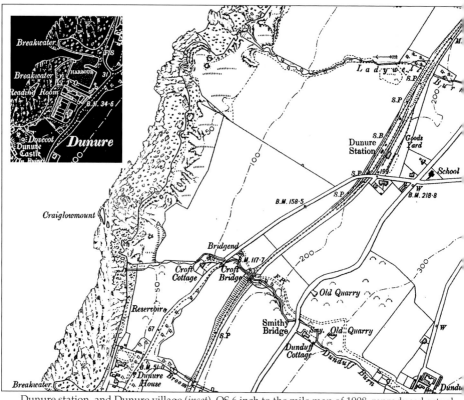

Dunure station, and Dunure village (*inset*). OS 6 inch to the mile map of 1908, reproduced actual size.

NLS Map Library, Edinburgh

Knoweside station and Croy viaduct. OS 6 inch to the mile map of 1908, reproduced actual size.

NLS Map Library, Edinburgh

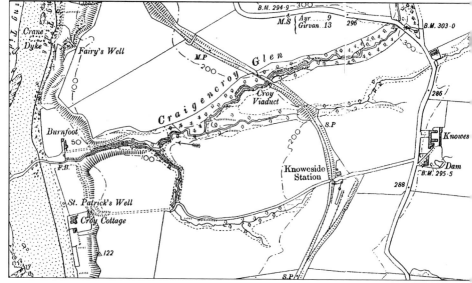

The M&DLR goods service, 1906

Ayr	dep.	8.40	am	Girvan	dep.	3.00	pm
Alloway Jn		8.50		Dipple		*	
Alloway		9.25		Turnberry		3.30	
Greenan Castle				Maidens		3.50	
Heads of Ayr		9.50		Glenside		*	
Dunure		10.50		Knoweside		*	
Knoweside		*		Dunure		4.45	
Glenside		*		Heads of Ayr		5.16	
Maidens		11.30		Greenan Castle			
Turnberry		12.00	noon	Alloway		5.46	
Dipple		*		Alloway Jn		5.51	
Girvan	arr.	12.15	pm	Ayr	arr.	6.00	

* Calls when required.

The departure times allowed for the necessary shunting at the various yards and sidings. Greenan Castle siding was shown in the timetable but without times and without a note, and it is possible that the initial traffic there was much more infrequent than at Knoweside, Glenside and Dipple.

The goods train carried mainly agricultural produce to and from the farms of the Carrick coast and inland in the vicinity of the line. This included animal feeding, fertiliser, farm machinery, milk, and crops, including the early Carrick potatoes of June and July that were so important to, and so dependent on, the new line which had opened at an ideal time for their picking or 'howking', largely by the Irish itinerant and industrious workers; while livestock were also conveyed, particularly in connection with the Tuesday market at Ayr. However, it is probable that, in addition to the daily goods train, extra non-timetabled trains were run irregularly, and possibly on most days, during June and July to transport the large amount of early potatoes. Livestock were also conveyed, particularly in connection with the Tuesday market in Ayr; while coal for the villages, hamlets, cottages and farms was delivered in one or two mineral wagons to each station or siding, weekly or as required, and a local coal merchant would deliver it. Supplies for Turnberry Hotel by the goods train included all food and beverages, and coal for the boiler house to drive the electricity generator and provide hot water for the whole building; while the hotel's refuse was taken away by the train for disposal. In essence, and as applied to railways generally, the M&DLR carried anything that required to be shifted, for the line became the common carrier for most commodities in the district. This was in an era when road transport that conveyed goods consisted almost entirely of horse-drawn vehicles, though motor vehicles in the form of wagonettes and charabancs, or small motor buses, had also begun to make their appearance, albeit occasional and of little significance in relation to the railways.

In January 1907 - at long last, more of consequence for the local people, and in seemingly partial response to the letter from 'A. Farmer' - a Tuesdays-only 'market train' was introduced to run from Maidens to Ayr. It left Maidens at 9.30 am, calling at all the stations to Ayr, including Glenside and Knoweside as standard stops without request, to arrive in Ayr at 10.20; and it addressed the problem on market day that, with too much emphasis on the Turnberry expresses, there was too long a gap in the local service through the morning for the people at the intermediate localities all the way from Maidens to Alloway. Presumably, the G&SWR Directors considered that there was no requirement both for this train to start from Girvan or Turnberry and to be run on the other days of the week. As empty coaching stock, the market train ran outbound from Ayr at 7.45 am in working to Maidens, and it effectively became a special service for the local communities north of Turnberry on market day.

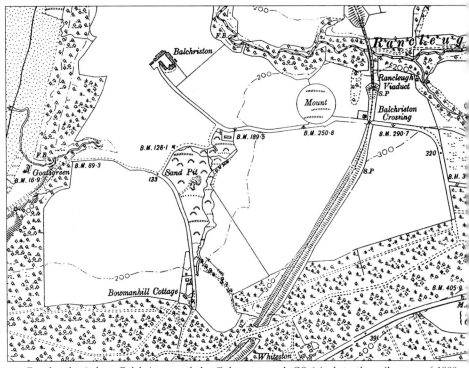

Rancleugh viaduct, Balchriston and the Culzean tunnel. OS 6 inch to the mile map of 1908, reproduced actual size.   *NLS Map Library, Edinburgh*

An impression, looking north-east, of a G&SWR '8' class locomotive hauling an Ayr-Girvan passenger train through the 42-yards-long and single track, but double width, of the skewed Culzean tunnel, in the early era of the M&DLR.   *Drawn by D. McConnell*

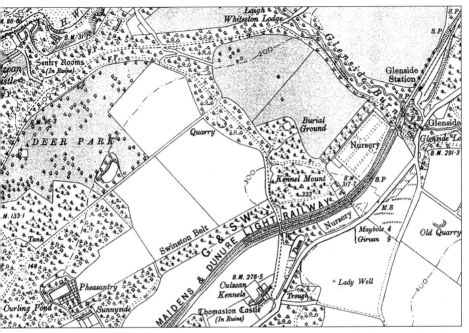

Glenside station and cutting, and Culzean Castle. OS 6 inch to the mile map of 1908, reproduced actual size.   *NLS Map Library, Edinburgh*

Maidens station and village. OS 6 inch to the mile map of 1908, reproduced actual size.
                                                              NLS Map Library, Edinburgh

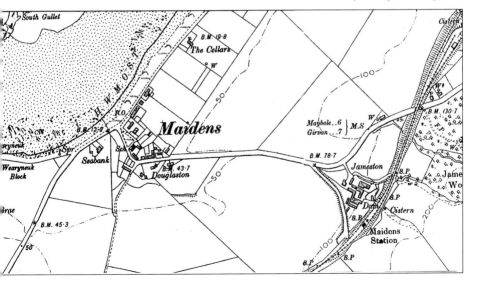

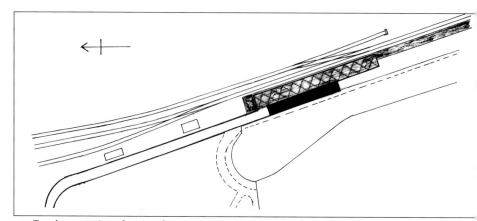

Turnberry station, showing the entrance via the covered walkway from the hotel to the platform. The glass canopy roof, which extended to the platform edge, is represented by hatching, with the station building solid black and the platform shaded. Projecting beyond the southern end of the station building is the curtain wall that supported the remainder of the canopy on its western side, while the rectangle of shading outside the canopy's gable is the platform's northern ramp.

Drawn by S. Rankin

Turnberry station and hotel. OS 6 inch to the mile map of 1908, reproduced actual size.

NLS Map Library, Edinburgh

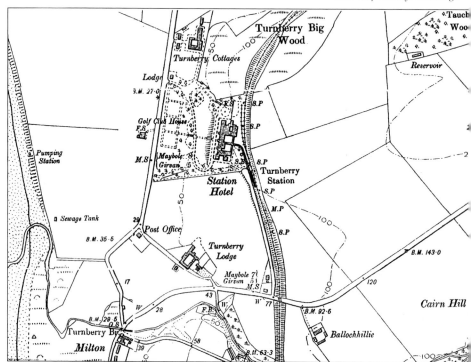

Turnberry Hotel soon after, or even before, its opening in 1906, looking north-west to the front entrance on the railway side of the building. The new appearance is evident in the view, which shows the southern pergola, the conservatory behind it, and the covered walkway to the station.
RCAHMS, Edinburgh: Bedford Leisure Collection

Turnberry station, the M&DLR loop, the hotel siding, the covered walkway and the hotel building and grounds. OS 25 in. to the mile map of 1909, reproduced actual size.
NLS Map Library, Edinburgh

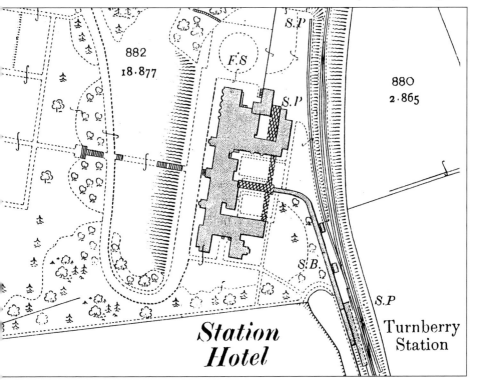

The southern end of the Turnberry Hotel and the station, showing (*left to right*) the covered walkway, the roof of the signal box, the station building, the curtain wall support and the platform fence. *Carnegie Library, Ayr*

Also in January 1907, there was the commencement of an early- morning fish train from Dunure to Ayr or even Glasgow. A note in the working timetable recorded that:

> A fish train will be run, when necessary, from Dunure to Ayr to connect with the 7.00 am train ex-Ayr, and may be run through to Glasgow. Station master at Dunure to advise the station master at Ayr when train is wanted, and latter will make necessary arrangements.

The fish train from Dunure was operated by a light engine - meaning an engine on its own or with a guard's van attached - that left Ayr at 5 am for a 6.30 departure from Dunure, in time for 7 am at Ayr, but there was no indication of how the fish vans reached Dunure. On the arrival of the engine at Dunure, the crew would load the fish boxes between 5.30 and 6.30 am, to send the train on its way quickly because fish, being perishable, was high priority and ran at passenger-train speeds, with much of it destined for Billingsgate fish market in London. Alternatively, the fish vans may have been conveyed previously by the daily goods train and detached at Dunure, such that there were always enough of them when required for the fish train. In each case, the train had to be arranged, or marshalled, in the correct order, with the vans placed at the tail-end on leaving Dunure to return to Ayr. The preference where there was no turntable at a branch station or anywhere *en route* - and, therefore, when the engine had to run backwards in one direction on an out-and-back trip - was to have the engine facing forwards on hauling the loaded train.

The introduction of the Dunure fish train may have superseded an idea of a different nature involving the fish from the village. On 6th July, 1906, a G&SWR drawing had been drafted by William Melville for a proposed short fish-loading platform by the road bridge at the south-western end of Dunure station; and consisting of a plan and cross-section, it showed that the platform was to be 50 feet long and 15 feet wide and connected to the bridge by a narrow access on a 1 in 12 gradient. The cross-section indicated the necessity of some rock excavation through the smaller cutting on the western side of the station, with the fish platform to be squeezed between the cutting and the northbound line of the station platform loop. The estimated cost was £107, but a plausible reason for its abandonment was that the fish platform would only have been long enough for two vans, especially in consideration of the expense of excavation and building, whereas the fish train could contain several vans positioned at the station platform, at no extra cost.

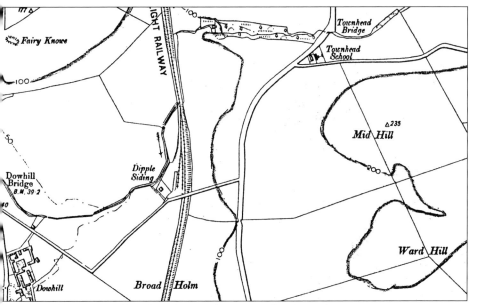

Dipple sidings. OS 6 inch to the mile map of 1908, reproduced actual size.

NLS Map Library, Edinburgh

Girvan No. 1 Junction (*top right*) and Girvan (No. 2) Junction (*bottom centre*). OS 6 inch to the mile map of 1908, reproduced actual size. *NLS Map Library, Edinburgh*

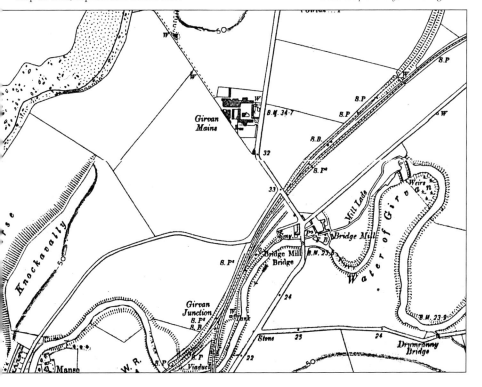

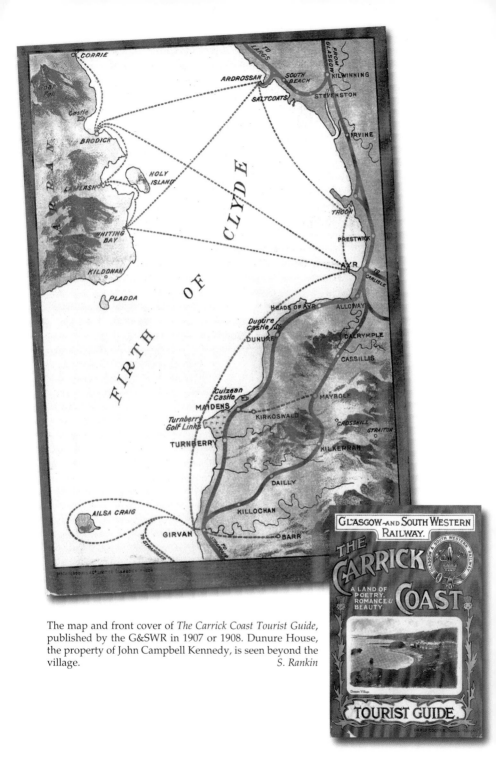

The map and front cover of *The Carrick Coast Tourist Guide*,
published by the G&SWR in 1907 or 1908. Dunure House,
the property of John Campbell Kennedy, is seen beyond the
village.   *S. Rankin*

A minor change in January 1907 was the retiming of the passenger service on Tuesdays, Thursdays and Saturdays from 10.30 to 10.45 am ex-Ayr and from 4.30 to 3.40 pm ex-Girvan, but these trains were discontinued in April. From March, the 6.10 pm from Ayr, with its through portion from Glasgow to Turnberry, became a stopping train, departing from Ayr at 6.08 pm and calling at all the intermediate stations, with Knoweside and Glenside as request stops. From June, in covering the summer period until the end of September, new services were introduced over the five miles between Girvan and Turnberry, with five trains in each direction, Mondays to Saturdays, to augment the trains that ran over the whole line. These Turnberry 'shuttle' services, having a 10 minute running time, provided connections to and from the Ayr-Stranraer line at Girvan and allowed passengers the alternative means of travelling to and from Turnberry by the Maybole route, though a changing of train was always required at Girvan. The combination of the shuttle trains and the through trains resulted in Turnberry being commendably served in the summer of 1907, particularly to and from Girvan; and the summarized times read:

Through services			TE		TE			
			Sa		Sa			Sa
	am	am	pm	pm	pm	pm	pm	pm
Ayr	7.25	11.00	12.10	1.35	2.25	3.55	6.08	8.05
Turnberry	8.18	11.54	12.54	2.33	3.05	4.55	6.57	8.59
Girvan	8.30	12.05	1.05	2.45	3.16	5.06	7.10	9.10

	†	TE					
			Sa			Sa	Sa
	am	am	pm	pm	pm	pm	pm
Girvan	7.10	8.30	12.30	2.05	5.05	5.50	7.15
Turnberry	7.23	8.50	12.42	2.17	5.18	6.03	7.28
Ayr	8.18	9.30	1.37	3.10	6.10	6.55	8.23

Notes
TE - Turnberry express, non-stop Ayr-Turnberry or vice versa.
† - Dep. 7.05 am Mondays, other station times unaltered. Sa - Saturdays.

Shuttle services	am	am	pm	pm	pm
Turnberry	10.00	11.10	1.40	6.30	8.10
Girvan	10.10	11.20	1.50	6.40	8.20

	am	am	pm	pm	pm
Girvan	9.05	10.40	1.15	6.00	7.15 *
Turnberry	9.15	10.50	1.25	6.10	7.25 *

* 10 minutes later on Saturdays

In the spring of 1907, a new dock platform had been installed at Girvan station, along the southern half of the original platform length on the eastern side and terminating at the southbound station building near the middle of the platform - therefore with the track facing south - for until then, there had been only the two platforms from 1893. Major J.W. Pringle of the Board of Trade inspected the new platform, the lengthening of the station loop and other track alterations on 9th May, 1907, and these additions may have resulted from the increased use of the station from the opening of the M&DLR. Although it is unlikely that the M&DLR trains

GLASGOW AND SOUTH-WESTERN RAILWAY.

MAIDENS & DUNURE LIGHT RAILWAY

DEPARTURES
from
TURNBERRY

JULY AND AUGUST 1909

Week Days only.

a.m

7 23 Maidens, Glenside, Knoweside, Dunure, Heads of Ayr, Alloway, Ayr, Glasgow (St Enoch). Also connection at Ayr for stations to Kilmarnock and Express to Dumfries, Carlisle, and Midland Line to London (St Pancras) arr 6 30.pm.

8 18 Girvan.

8 38 Stations to Ayr, Prestwick, Paisley (Canal), Glasgow (St Enoch) Also (Tuesdays Excepted) connection at Ayr for stations to Kilmarnock and Express to Dumfries, Carlisle, and Midland Line to London(St Pancras) arr 8 15.pm. Also connection at Kilmarnock for through Express to Manchester (Victoria) and Liverpool (Exchange) arr 5 0.pm.

9 25 Market Train – Tuesdays Only. Stations to Ayr for stations to Kilmarnock and Express to Dumfries, Carlisle and Midland line to London (St Pancras) arr 8 15.pm. Also connection at Kilmarnock for through Express to Manchester (Victoria) and Liverpool (Exchange) arr 5 0.pm.

10 54 Mondays, Wednesdays and Fridays Only. Girvan.

11 10 Girvan – for stations to Ayr (Via Maybole) Newton on Ayr, Prestwick, Troon, Irvine, Kilwinning, Johnstone, Paisley (Gilmore Street), Shields Road, Eglinton Street, Glasgow(St Enoch) Also connection at Ayr for stations to Kilmarnock and Express to Dumfries, Carlisle and Midland Line to London (St Pancras) arr 10 25.pm.

11 54 Tuesdays, Thursdays and Saturdays Only. Girvan.

p.m

12 42 Saturdays Only. Stations to Ayr, Paisley (Gilmore Street) Shields Road, Glasgow (St Enoch).

12 50 Saturdays Excepted. Girvan, for Maybole, Ayr, Paisley(Gilmore Street), Shields Road, Glasgow (St Enoch).

12 54 Saturdays Only. Girvan.

2 22 Stations to Ayr, Newton on Ayr, Prestwick, Troon, Irvine, Kilwinning, Johnstone, Paisley(Gilmore Street), Shields Road, Eglinton Street, Glasgow (St Enoch). Also connection at Ayr for Kilmarnock and Express to Dumfries and Carlisle for Midland Line.

2 38 Girvan.

3 21 Saturdays Only. Girvan.

4 55 Girvan.

5 18 Stations to Ayr, Paisley (Gilmore Street). Shields Road, Eglinton Street, Glasgow (St Enoch).

6 30 Girvan. for Pinmore, Pinwherry, Barrhill, Glenwhilly, New Luce, Dunragit, Castle Kennedy, Stranraer.–Connection for Newton Stewart.

6 57 Girvan.

7 28 Saturdays Only. Stations to Ayr, Paisley (Gilmore Street). Shields Road, Eglinton Street, Glasgow (St Enoch). Also connection at Ayr for Prestwick, Troon, Kilmarnock and First Class Sleeping Saloon and Through Carriages to Dumfries, Carlisle. and Midland Line to Leeds, Sheffield, Derby and London (St Pancras). arr 7 30.am.

8 0 Saturdays Excepted. Girvan. for Stations to Ayr (Via Maybole). Stations to Troon, Irvine, Kilwinning, Dalry, Johnstone, Paisley (Gilmore Street), Shields Road, Eglinton Street, Glasgow (St Enoch). Also Connection at Ayr for Kilmarnock and First Class Sleeping Saloon and Through Carriages to Dumfries, Carlisle. and Midland Line to Leeds, Sheffield, Derby and London (St Pancras). arr. 7 30.am.

9 9 Saturdays Only. Girvan.

Turnberry Hotel, Ayrshire.

A 1909 Turnberry summer timetable that was produced by Turnberry Hotel to list the train times from Turnberry station, while highlighting the connecting services at Ayr and Kilmarnock for stations in England and the services that did not operate every day. *Turnberry Hotel* departed from and arrived at this new platform, because it was south-facing, they were probably stabled there between services, in being kept free of the main northbound and southbound lines at the station.

During the summer of 1907, there were fewer Turnberry expresses than in 1906, suggesting less need for the previous number or more consideration for local passengers. Unfortunately, the dining-car and tea-car services were not repeated in 1907, either because they had been not sufficiently patronized in 1906 or their operation had incurred too long a day for the crew. There was also the 9.30 am market train from Maidens to Ayr on Tuesdays, which continued to fill the gap in the morning services by calling at the intermediate stations and adequately serving the local farming people on that one day. The timetable for June 1907 indicated two instances when two trains ran 10 minutes apart from Girvan to Turnberry on Saturday evenings. The first was the 5.50 pm ex-Girvan on Saturdays that ran to Ayr and was followed by the 6.00 pm ex-Girvan that ran on Mondays to Saturdays to Turnberry only. Then the 7.15pm ex-Girvan, which ran to Turnberry on Mondays to Fridays, continued to Ayr on Saturdays and was followed by the 7.25 on Saturdays to Turnberry only.

The shuttle services between Girvan and Turnberry ceased with the start of the winter timetable in October 1907; and one other notable variation occurred in relation to the 11.00 am ex-Ayr Mondays-to-Saturdays service. The 11.00 am now ran only on Tuesdays, Thursdays and Saturdays and was replaced by a 10.00 am on Mondays, Wednesdays and Fridays.

Irrespective of significant and minor changes since the opening of the line, a discernible pattern in the overall M&DLR timetables had emerged for both summer and winter. The June 1908 and the combined July and August 1908 timetables, with all three months being identical, maintained the summer pattern of the previous years and reintroduced the shuttle services, but with four trains in each direction instead of the five in the previous summer. From June, one change that benefited the Turnberry locality was the commencement of the Tuesdays-only market train from the principal and grandest station on the line at 9.25 am, calling, as previously, at Maidens at 9.30 and all the other intermediate stations, and retaining the arrival time in Ayr of 10.20. Perhaps the G&SWR Directors had received requests or complaints from the local farmers south and east of Turnberry that the whole farming district further south than Maidens needed to be accommodated with an intermediate morning train. Moreover, Turnberry guests could use the service if they so desired, as the train, like all others on the line, was composed of first- and third-class compartments.

The G&SWR Directors had been compelled to adjust their thinking towards the value of the local passengers who had no interest in the golf or the hotel. While many golfers and other travellers and guests were indeed patronizing the railway and the hotel, the numbers of them throughout the year were likely to have been significantly fewer than had been anticipated by the G&SWR Directors. Thus, most of the services on the M&DLR by the summer of 1908 were calling at most of the stations, and there were now only two trains that could be termed Turnberry expresses. They were both Saturdays-only southbound services, being the 12.10 pm ex-Ayr, which also called at Maidens, and the 2.25 pm ex-Ayr, which ran directly to Turnberry.

As an indication of the need to encourage more golfers to Turnberry, another compromise, which originated from a repeated request, was eventually granted by the G&SWR Directors. At a meeting of the committee of Turnberry Golf Club back on 26th May, 1906, nine days after the opening of the railway, the recommendation

G&SWR '22' class 0-6-0, No. 84, on the loop at Turnberry, immediately north of the station platform, with a short goods train from Ayr to Girvan, *c*. 1910. The train consists of a 6-ton outside-framed van for sundries, an 8-ton mineral wagon containing bags and a 10-ton brake van. The '22' class engines were first built in 1881 but No. 84 was built in 1886. The covered walkway between the station and the hotel is behind the engine. *I. Middleditch*

G&SWR '361' class 0-6-0, No. 371, on the hotel siding, immediately north of Turnberry station, *c*. 1910, looking north. The M&DLR is discerned behind the engine, in line with the upper part of the faraway buffer and a few feet higher than the siding level. The first wagon is an old James Stirling brake van of the 1870s with a 'birdcage' guard's lookout on the roof, and it is likely that it functioned as a 'sundry van' for the M&DLR. *NAS, Edinburgh*

had been made 'that the railway [company was] to be approached with a view of members getting cheaper golfing fares all round'. The essence of the suggestion lay in the displeasure of golfers from Girvan and Maybole who felt that the train fares from their towns to Turnberry were too high in relation to the fares from Pinwherry, south of Girvan, to Turnberry and from Ayr to Turnberry, which were given as examples. The reply from the G&SWR's General Manager, David Cooper, to the Turnberry Golf Club's secretary, Robert McConnell, was read at the next Turnberry committee meeting on 28th June, 1906:

> *Railway Fares for Golfers.* What you say with regard to the fare from Girvan to Turnberry being so high compared with Pinwherry or Ayr to Turnberry is brought about by the rule under which return tickets are issued from stations to Turnberry at single fare for the double journey, minimum one shilling. It is usual in all cases of cheap fares to have a minimum of one shilling, but in the case of Girvan and Turnberry, I am arranging to give a cheap fare of one shilling first-class and sixpence third-class, and this I trust will meet the case. We do not propose to introduce fares between Maybole and Turnberry.

This meant that no cheap through fares would be issued from Maybole to Turnberry and that the Maybole golfers would have to continue to pay separate fares from Maybole to Girvan and from Girvan to Turnberry. Did the Maybole golfers then happen to reflect, with regret, the illogical and spiteful decision in 1898 by the Maybole Town Council and townspeople to oppose the M&DLR and the proposed short branch from Maybole to Maidens that would have allowed them directly to reach their sporting haven at Turnberry?

After the rejection by the G&SWR of a cheap fare for the Maybole golfers to Turnberry, it was nearly two years before the subject was reintroduced, and success for the resolute golfers occurred this time because of a petition that had been signed by them and sent to the G&SWR. At a Special Meeting of the Turnberry committee on 11th April, 1908, a discussion took place about the large number of resignations that had been received from members during the previous two years, and it was agreed that a letter was to be submitted to David Cooper, 'pointing out the reasons given for such resignations, and asking him to meet a deputation from the committee to discuss matters'. No doubt, many of the resignations had already come from the club's large Maybole membership, and would continue, because of the lack of cheap train fares being provided for them. Fortunately, the G&SWR Directors now understood the seriousness of the resignations and, at last, they responded positively, with the outcome announced at another Special Meeting of the Turnberry committee on 25th April, 1908:

> The secretary read letter from Mr David Cooper enclosing petition re golfers' fare from Maybole to Turnberry, enquiring if a fare at one shilling and eight pence return from Maybole to Turnberry would increase the traffic between these places and keep the Maybole members from retiring. The secretary was instructed to reply that it was the committee's opinion that a fare such as proposed, provided it was available via Ayr or Girvan, would have the desired result.

Not only did the golfers obtain the cheap fare through their determination but, later that year, the club managed to persuade David Cooper to operate a Saturdays-only morning train from Girvan to Turnberry in the winter timetable, and, as was recorded at a meeting of the committee on 3rd October: 'It was agreed that the secretary should bring under the notice of Mr Cooper his promise to consider the question of running

M&DLR Passenger Services, June 1910

Ayr → Girvan

Station		am	M-F am	am	Sa am	Sa pm	Sa pm	Sa pm	Sa pm	C pm	pm	pm	M-F pm	Sa pm
Ayr	dep.	7.25	10.00		11.00		12.10	1.35	2.25	3.55		6.08		8.15
Alloway	arr.													8.23
Heads of Ayr	arr.	7.35	10.10		11.10			1.45	2.34	4.05		6.14		8.25
	dep.	7.45	10.20		11.20			1.55	2.44	4.15		6.24		8.35
Dunure		7.51/7.53	10.28		11.28		A	2.03	2.52	4.23		6.31		8.43
Knoweside	dep.	*	*		*			*	*	*		*		*
Glenside	dep.	8.07	10.40†		*			2.20	*	4.37		6.45		*
Maidens	arr.						12.46	2.26		4.45				
	dep.						12.48	2.28		4.47				
Turnberry	arr.	8.12	10.50		11.48				3.15			6.51		9.03
	dep.	8.18	10.56	11.10	11.54	12.50	12.54	2.38	3.21	4.55	6.30	6.57	8.00	9.09
Girvan	arr.	8.30	11.07	11.20	12.05	1.00	1.05	2.50	3.31	5.06	6.40	7.10	8.10	9.20

Girvan → Ayr

Station		am	C am	Tu am	Sa am	Sa pm	M-F pm	pm	Sa pm	C pm	M-F pm	Sa pm
Girvan	dep.	7.10	8.25	9.10	10.40	12.30	12.30	2.10	5.05	6.00	7.15	7.11
Turnberry	dep.	7.23	8.38	9.25	10.48	12.42	12.40	2.22	5.18	6.10	7.25	7.28
Maidens	dep.	7.29				12.47		2.26				
Glenside	dep.	7.35	8.44	9.30		12.50		2.28	5.24			7.34
Knoweside	dep.	*	8.50	9.36		*		*	5.30			*
Dunure		7.52	8.56	9.42		*		2.46/2.49‡	*			7.55
Heads of Ayr	arr.	7.54	9.06	9.52		1.10			5.45			8.03
	dep.	8.01	9.13	10.00		1.19		2.57	5.52			8.11
Alloway	arr.	8.10	9.22	10.10		1.28		3.06	6.01			8.15
Ayr	arr.	8.18	9.30	10.20		1.37		3.15	6.10			8.23

Notes

* - Request stop. † - Calls at Glenside on Thursdays. On other days calls only when required. A - Calls at Dunure when required, to set down passengers. ‡ - On Saturdays leaves Dunure 2.52 pm. C - Calls at Balchriston Level Crossing Mondays to Fridays. M-F – Mondays to Fridays. Sa - Saturdays. Tu - Tuesdays.

STATION HOTEL, TURNBERRY.

THIS Hotel is connected by covered way with Turnberry Station, on the new Light Railway between Ayr and Girvan. Express Trains by Midland Railway from London (St. Pancras), Leeds, Manchester, &c. It contains over 200 Apartments, and will be found comfortable and complete in its arrangements Perfect Heating, Ventilation, and Sanitation. Electric Light. Lift. Lounge. Hairdressing Saloon. Billiard Room (3 Tables). Conservatory. Garage and Stables.

Magnificent Suites of Rooms, comprising Sitting Room, Bed, Dressing, and Bath Rooms.

Special Suites of Baths for Golfers—hot and cold—fresh and sea water—also Plunge Bath, Drying Rooms, &c. The walls, partitions, and principal floors of the building are fire-proof throughout.

During the Autumn, Winter, and Spring months the climate is mild, pleasant, and recuperative, fog and snow being practically unknown.

The railway distances from the following towns to TURNBERRY STATION are:—Birmingham 296, Bradford 212, Edinburgh 92, Glasgow 56, Leeds 219, London 399, Liverpool 227, Manchester 229, Newcastle 168.

FINE CENTRE FOR MOTOR AND CYCLE TOURS.

TURNBERRY GOLF COURSES.

Both the No. 1 Course (6,115 yards) and the No. 2 Course (5,115 yards) are in fine condition for play.

CHARGE FOR HOTEL VISITORS, 1s. per day; 5s. per week.

COMBINED HOTEL AND RAILWAY COUPONS

are issued at St. Enoch Station Booking Office, to include the following:—

First Class Return Fare between Glasgow and Turnberry, and Board and

		Lodging from Monday to Wednesday morning,					
Do.	do.	Tuesday to Thursday	do.	-	-	-	£1 7s. 0d.
Do.	do.	Wednesday to Friday	do.	-	-	-	
Do.	do.	Thursday to Saturday	do.	-	-	-	
Do.	do.	Friday to Monday	do.	-	-	-	£1 17s. 0d.
Do.	do.	Saturday to Monday	do.	-	-	-	£1 8s. 0d.
Do.	do.	for One Week, -	-	-	-	-	£3 14s. 0d.

NOTE.—The Company reserve the right to suspend these Bookings at certain seasons of the year, information regarding which may be had at the BOOKING OFFICE, ST. ENOCH STATION.

For Tariff and further particulars apply

Chief Office :   J. H. THOMAS, Manager,

St. Enoch Station Hotel, Glasgow.   G. & S.-W. Ry. Coy.'s Hotels.

HOTELS UNDER SAME MANAGEMENT:

ST. ENOCH STATION, Glasgow; STATION, Ayr; STATION, Turnberry; STATION, Dumfries.

Telegrams—"Souwestern."   Telephone—20 Girvan.

JUNE 1911

Advertisement for Turnberry Hotel from the G&SWR passenger timetable for June 1911.
G&SWR Association

a forenoon train during the winter months.' In consequence, a meeting on 7th December, 1908 indicated the granting of the request by way of the reintroduction of the 10.40 am from Girvan and a return working from Turnberry at 11.10.

Also in the winter timetable for 1908-09, the 12.10 pm ex-Ayr, Saturdays-only now called at Dunure, 'when required, to set down passengers', in addition to still calling at Maidens. This time, the implication was that the Dunure stop, which did not result from trains having to pass there, was for the benefit of the village. More significantly, the 2.25 pm Ayr-Turnberry express on Saturdays, which had run since the opening of the line, became a local service, calling additionally at Alloway, Heads of Ayr, Dunure and Maidens, and there were now no non-stop services over the line for Turnberry passengers.

In June 1909, with the goods train still running at exactly the same times as had been the case from the opening of the line, a 9.25 am livestock train from Girvan to Ayr on Tuesdays also appeared in the working timetable and made only three stops: departing from Dipple at 9.39, Maidens at 9.55, and Glenside at 10.05, with an arrival time in Ayr of 10.40. A note in the working timetable referred to the three intermediate locations: 'Will call where necessary to attach livestock traffic.' Cattle were farmed in the more immediate vicinity of the line and sheep were farmed in the hillier districts but also in the vicinity of the line, and the existence of the livestock train confirmed that cattle wagons were in use on the line, but, unlike the Highland Railway having double-deck sheep wagons, the G&SWR did not have special wagons for sheep, and they had to be conveyed in the cattle wagons. The livestock train followed soon after the Tuesday passenger market train that, in June 1909, now traversed the whole line and departed from Girvan at 9.10 am, with the same timings for the other stations as in the previous year, retaining the arrival time in Ayr of 10.20.

The main difference of the summer passenger timetable of 1910 from those of the previous years since 1907 was the simplification of the alternating 10 am and 11 am ex-Ayr services, and from June 1910, the times were changed to 10 am on Mondays to Fridays and 11 am on Saturdays - thereby eliminating confusion to passengers. Another minor but novel change was the appearance in the working timetable, but not the public timetable, of a new stop for one service in each direction, with a note that referred to the 8.25 am ex-Girvan and the 3.55 pm ex-Ayr calling at 'Balchriston Level Crossing' daily except on Saturdays. The stop was not shown as request-only, implying that there was sufficient justification for both the stop and it not being conditional - primarily for the railway family who operated the level-crossing gates. However, it is possible that people who lived in the sparsely-populated locality, such as the tenants and workers at Balchriston farm and at isolated cottages, were unofficially allowed to use the two trains because there was no other transport.

During the three years from 1910 to 1913, the passenger services were stabilized, with fewer small variations and with a pattern similar to what had occurred previously. The most significant change appeared in 1913, with the introduction, on 2nd June, of two through coaches in each direction between Turnberry and Kilmarnock, in connection with services to and from England, via Leeds and the Midland route, 'thus affording facilities for golfers and tourists from Carlisle and the South', as was stated in the Ayr and Glasgow newspapers. The four services were: the 8.05 am from Turnberry via Girvan and Maybole; the 9.20 am ex-Girvan, as the 9.35 ex-Turnberry, via the M&DLR, calling at all the stations on the line; the 2.55 pm from Kilmarnock via the M&DLR, calling at all the stations on the line, but at Knoweside by request on Saturdays; and the 6.12 pm from Kilmarnock via Maybole and Girvan. The through coaches ceased from the winter timetable in October 1913.

Chapter Ten

Mid-Period Train Services, 1914-1922

Behind the scene of the visible timetable workings of the M&DLR, delays to trains during the period from July to September 1913 had caused David Cooper, the G&SWR's General Manager, to consider that the situation had approached crisis point, such that a series of communications, beginning in early April 1914, took place between Mr Cooper and Charles Cockburn, who was the superintendent of the line, or head of operations, and the senior manager after the General Manager. Having succeeded Mr Cooper in that position in 1895, and having previously been employed for 17 years in various capacities with the London, Chatham & Dover Railway, the experienced Mr Cockburn had already provided Mr Cooper with information about the delays, in terms of 'minutes lost' along the route, of all the goods trains during July, August and September 1913. The train-register books of the signalmen were the source of the recorded timings and delays for the trains, such that if the times between a train being offered to and accepted by a signalman to proceed along the line were not the same to the minute, then there was officially a delay by the difference in minutes.

Signal box	Minutes lost			
	July	*August*	*September*	
Alloway	593	302	5	
Heads of Ayr	734	271	38	
Dunure	958	604	971	
Glenside	617	428	30	
Maidens	907	185	102	
Turnberry	846	308	50	
Girvan No. 1	625	186	103	
Total minutes	5,280	2,284	1,299	
Total hours	*88*	*38*	*21½*	*147½*

The considerable individual differences of the three months' delays - 5,280, 2,284 and 1,299 minutes in totalling 147½ hours - were largely attributable to the potato trains at the peak traffic season, particularly in July and early August and particularly at Dipple (between Girvan and Turnberry). Furthermore, as Mr Cockburn had informed Mr Cooper, trains conveying passengers from England to Turnberry - being the only station on the line that mattered in terms of passenger revenue - could be held back for as much as half an hour at Maidens, only five minutes before Turnberry, and it was readily acknowledged that delays to the trains that conveyed the Turnberry clientele were unacceptable, irrespective of the other traffic. Mr Cockburn explained that an improved service between Turnberry and Glasgow would be achieved better via Girvan because there would only be a short mileage between Turnberry and Girvan at the restricted maximum of 25 mph, whereas 60 mph could be attained from Girvan to Ayr; and he showed that the delays principally occurred to southbound trains at Alloway and Turnberry and to northbound trains at Girvan No. 1 and Dunure, resulting from the lack of loops at Heads of Ayr and Dipple.

To reduce the delays, Mr Cockburn, in consultation with William Melville, the Engineer-in-Chief, had an obvious solution in mind - to install loops for the use of

M&DLR Passenger Services, July 1914

Ayr to Girvan

Station		C TK	TK	TK	M	Sa	C M-F	Sa	TK M-F	TK Sa	C		TK	Sa
		am	am	am	am	pm	pm	pm	pm	pm	pm	pm	pm	pm
Ayr	dep.	7.30	9.35	10.10	7.40	12.15	1.35	1.55	3.50	4.00	4.35	6.08	7.15	9.15
Alloway	arr.	7.38		10.18			1.45	2.05						7.25	9.25
Alloway	dep.	7.39		10.20			1.55	2.15						7.35	9.35
Heads of Ayr	dep.	7.47		10.30								H		7.43	
Dunure	arr.	7A51												7.45	
Dunure	dep.	7A53		10.37		D	2.03	2.23				5.04			9.43
Knoweside	dep.	*		*		*	*	*				*		*	*
Glenside	dep.	8.07		10.51		*	2.20	*				*		*	*
Maidens	arr.					12.51	2.26	2.42			4.36	5.21			
Maidens	dep.	8.12		10.56		12.53	2.28	2.43			4.38	5.22			
Turnberry	arr.													8.05	10.03
Turnberry	dep.	8.18	10.25	11.02		12.59	2.38	2.49	4.40	4.48	5.29	6.46	8.10	10.09
Girvan	arr.	8.30	10.40	11.12		1.10	2.50	3.00	4.50	5.00	5.40	6.56	8.20	10.20

Girvan to Ayr

Station		C M	C Tu-Sa	M	TK	TK	C Sa	M-F	Sa	CK Sa	C	
		am	am	am	am	am	pm	pm	pm	pm	pm	pm
Girvan	dep.	6.45	7.10		9.25	11.50	12.35	2.10	2.25	4.20	5.00	7.05
Turnberry	dep.	6.58	7.23	7.40	9.35	12.03	12.45	2.22	2.35	4.30	5.12	7.15
Maidens	dep.	7.04	7.29		9.40	12.10	12.50	2.27	2.41	4.35	5.18	
Glenside	dep.	7.10	7.35		9.46		12.52	2.28	2.42	4.37	5.22	7.22
Knoweside	dep.	7.16	7.41		9.52		*	*	*	*	*	*
Dunure	dep.	7.25	7.52		10.00	12.30	*	*	*	*	*	*
Heads of Ayr	dep.	7.31	7.54		10.02	12.33	1.12	2.49	3.01	4.55	5.41	7.42
Alloway	arr.	7.36	8.01		10.10	12.38	1.21	2.57	3.09		5.48	7.45
Alloway	dep.	7.40	8.10			12.47	1.30	3.06	3.18		5.56	7.58
Ayr	arr.	7.50	8.20		10.30	12.55	1.39	3.16	3.27	5.20	6.05	

Notes

* Request stop. † - Calls at Glenside on Thursdays and on other days calls only when required. A - On Mondays waits the crossing of 7.40 am from Turnberry. C - Calls at Balchriston Level Crossing. D - Calls at Dunure when required to set down passengers. H - On Saturdays waits the crossing of 4.20pm from Girvan. TK - Through-coach Turnberry-Kilmarnock or vice versa. CK - Connection at Ayr for Kilmarnock and the South via Leeds. Sa - Saturdays. M-F - Monday to Friday. M - Mondays. Tu-Sa - Tuesday to Saturday.

passenger trains at Heads of Ayr and Dipple - which had also been suggested several times and as far back in 1907. His plan would therefore shorten the distances between crossing places because the existing single-line sections were too long for a line that was limited to only 25 mph, whereby lost time could hardly be made up on the long sections at such a low restricted speed. Unfortunately, Mr Cooper was displeased at the revived idea of new loops, and, on 9th April, he expressed this feeling, seemingly through sarcasm, to Mr Cockburn by asking, in reference to Heads of Ayr, 'whether a plan of alterations proposed so many years ago is still the "last word" on the changes which you thought necessary at this place to meet the case'. Mr Cooper wanted changes only to the timetable to eliminate the delays, by making Alloway and Heads of Ayr conditional stops, like Glenside and Knoweside, and, on 6th May, he asked Mr Cockburn for a new timetable that would show an improved service and conditional stops at Heads of Ayr and Alloway.

Ironically, in view of Alloway station's platform being the longest on the line - at 550 feet, to accommodate excursion traffic - the scant regard that was shown to it by Mr Cooper in the correspondence, in wanting it to be reduced to conditional or 'halt' status, implied that the light railway had not attracted as many day-trippers to the Burns environs as had been expected, either by the assessments of the G&SWR or the objectors at the promotional stage of the railway. While many passengers by train from the Glasgow and Kilmarnock directions conveniently continued by train from Ayr to Alloway, there were other travellers who, having already arrived in Ayr to spend the day, proceeded to Alloway by Ayr Corporation's electric tramway - thereby depriving the railway of a significant number of passengers.

In response on 14th May, Mr Cockburn disagreed with the proposal of a conditional stop at Alloway because it would not be effective enough, with an estimated saving of only 30 minutes per month when there was a need to save 50 hours. The saving was negligible because the trains either required to stop or had to reduce speed in preparation for possibly stopping - even if only for one passenger leaving or joining the train in each case - thereby defeating the aim of saving time.

Consideration - if quickly dismissed - had also been given to another proposal by Mr Cooper to the use of a steam railmotor, or 'steam motor carriage', on the line for economy of working. A railmotor, of the type that was suggested for the M&DLR, was a combined small locomotive and passenger coach, or a coach with a small locomotive 'built into it', which comprised the engine and coach constructed as one vehicle on the same frame. They had been fashionable on the lines of various railway companies in different designs in England around 1900, from the competition from electric trams in cities and towns and to serve rural areas; and a few years later on the G&SWR and the Aberdeen-based Great North of Scotland Railway. The G&SWR had produced three railmotors in 1904-05, with each coach seating a total of 50 passengers in the two sections of third class-only accommodation, and they worked principally on the Cairn Valley Light Railway to Moniaive from Dumfries, the Catrine branch from Mauchline, and to Kilwinning and Largs from Ardrossan, with their aim to counter some competition from the large motor charabancs and small motor buses that had gradually appeared in some towns and districts during the first decade of the 20th century. The railmotors could haul another coach or two and they were capable of being driven from either end. However, Mr Cockburn opposed the use of railmotors on the M&DLR, and, in his reply of 14th May, he informed Mr Cooper of this:

I have considered the question of running the railmotor on the Turnberry line but, on looking to the gradients, I am afraid it would not produce the economic results you desire, and therefore I would not recommend it. Our experience of these carriages at Catrine and Dumfries is that being only one class the first-class passengers do not like them and they are scarcely suited to haul any additional vehicles over the steep gradients.

Mr Cockburn had been supported in his view by the G&SWR's locomotive superintendent, Peter Drummond, which Mr Cooper accepted, if with reluctance, in a communication of 29th May, 1914 to Mr Cockburn: 'If the steam car is as stated by Mr Drummond unsuitable for working over the Turnberry line, that is an end to it, and the steam car may be left out in the further consideration of this matter.' Additionally, Mr Cooper had obtained proposals and estimates from Mr Melville for the cost of constructing the loops, and, on the condition of Mr Cockburn producing a new timetable that was appropriately based on their installation, Mr Cooper agreed to consider these plans. Unfortunately, the estimated cost by Mr Melville for the new loops and the calculated additional mileage by Mr Cockburn for a new timetable were not to Mr Cooper's satisfaction, and he continued his reply tersely to Mr Cockburn in the letter of 29th May:

> You are aware that the estimated cost of the alterations which are suggested to permit of the more expeditious working of the Turnberry line is put at £2,372 by the engineer. You are also aware that the latest proposal by you for the 'improvement' of the service involves an additional weekly mileage of 664 miles.

Mr Cooper wanted more justification for the spending of £2,372 on constructing the loops - £1,257 for Heads of Ayr and £1,115 for Dipple - but, nevertheless, he agreed to take the proposal to the G&SWR Board. The matter was resolved on 1st June, 1914, with the Board having decided in favour of proceeding with the loop lines - though, strangely, Mr Cooper did not inform Mr Cockburn of the outcome, such that he had to be told by Mr Melville.

The installations of the new loops were very speedily carried out during early and mid-June 1914 because they were essential for the new timetable of the summer passenger traffic. Heads of Ayr station was widened and became an island platform, while the original signal box was replaced by a larger box to accommodate the extra levers, and a signal box was built at Dipple to control the new loop there. The loops at Heads of Ayr and Dipple were brought into use on Monday 15th June, 1914, when the first trains used them for crossing. Records of the new train movements were also begun a week later by Charles Cockburn - no doubt to justify to David Cooper the installation of the loops, which did indeed reduce delays, by greatly improving the flexibility of working. For the six days of the second week of operation, from Monday 22nd to Saturday 27th June, Mr Cockburn sent a report to Mr Cooper, showing that 25 trains had used the Heads of Ayr loop and eight had used the Dipple loop. The total saving was 385 minutes, or virtually 6½ hours, which was equivalent to about 27 hours when taken over a month. Therefore, a saving of more than half the aim of 50 hours had been attained from this one improvement procedure on its own; but while the outcome of the loops was admirable for the working of the railway, the episode indicated the strained relationship between David Cooper and Charles Cockburn.

In conjunction with the new loop facilities, and from Mr Cooper's earlier request, Mr Cockburn had additionally provided a summer timetable of an 'augmented and improved train service between Glasgow, Ayr, Turnberry and Girvan', to commence on 1st July, 1914 and continue through August. The principal features of the new timetable were the re-introduction of Turnberry expresses for the first time since 1908 and the increase of through coaches between Turnberry and Kilmarnock in connection with the South. The expresses, in being non-stop between Ayr and

Turnberry, amounted to three per day southbound, and one northbound that started from Turnberry instead of Girvan. The 6.08 pm Turnberry express from Ayr for Girvan was the long-established through service that formed part of the 5.10 service from Glasgow, and it divided at Ayr, departing at 6.05 pm for Girvan via Maybole. Over the whole of the M&DLR, there were five through coaches from Kilmarnock and two through coaches to Kilmarnock, and one other service that provided a direct connection at Ayr for Kilmarnock. The through coaches connected at Kilmarnock with the daytime and overnight services to and from London St Pancras via Leeds and the Midland route. The 6.58 am first train of the day from Turnberry, as the 6.45 am from Girvan, had the purpose of serving passengers who had spent the weekend at Turnberry but who had to return to their employment on that day.

However, in addition to the trains over the whole line, there were services to and from Turnberry, either as a through coach from Turnberry via Girvan and Maybole to Ayr or as a shuttle between Girvan and Turnberry only:

Dep. Turnberry for Girvan and Ayr: 8.05 am TK, 11.10*, 12.50 pm* M-F, 6.30*, 8.10† TK.
Dep. Girvan for Turnberry: 10.40 am,, 12.30 pm* M-F, 6.05.

Notes: TK - Through coach Turnberry-Kilmarnock. * - Shuttle. M-F - Mondays to Fridays. † - 7.15pm ex-Ayr via M&DLR returning to Ayr via Maybole.

Another timetable was produced that was headed 'London, Liverpool & Manchester & Turnberry via Midland Railway' that showed the through coach connections between Turnberry and the South via Kilmarnock. With no services on the M&DLR on Sundays, the times of the through coaches in connection with the St Pancras daytime and overnight services were:

		GM	D	D	GM SL M-Sa				
		am	am	am	pm	SL			
Turnberry	dep.	8.05			8.10				
Girvan	dep.	8.18	9.25	11.50	8.30	*Additional Services**			
Turnberry	dep.		9.35	12.03		pm		pm	
Ayr	dep.	9.07	10.45	1.05	9.30	10.40	W	10.40	Sa
Kilmarnock	dep.	9.58	11.38	2.06	10.08	11.36	M-F	11.51	Sa
London St Pancras	arr.	6.30	8.15	10.25	7.35	8.05	M-F	8.20	Sa

				D	NSL	SL	SL
		M-F	Sa	M-Sa	Su-F	Su-F	M-Sa
		am	am	am	pm	pm	
London St Pancras	dep.	4.50	4.50	9.45	8.15	9.30	12.00 *midnight*
Kilmarnock	dep.	2.20	2.20	6.12	5.28	6.45	8.47
Ayr	dep.	3.50	4.00	7.15	7.30	7.30	9.35
Turnberry	dep.	4.40	4.48	8.18	8.18	8.18	10.25
Girvan	arr.	4.50	5.00	8.30	8.30	8.30	10.40

Notes: GM - Via Girvan and Maybole. D - Dining car, Kilmarnock-London or vice versa. SL - Sleeper, Kilmarnock-London or vice versa. NSL - Non-sleeper, London-Kilmarnock. M-F - Mondays to Fridays. M-Sa - Mondays to Saturdays. Su-F - Sundays to Fridays. W - Wednesdays. Sa - Saturdays. * - 10.40 pm ex-Ayr on Wednesdays and Saturdays, in addition to 9.30 pm ex-Ayr on Mondays to Saturdays, connects with later Glasgow-London train, dep. Kilmarnock 11.36 pm on Mondays to Fridays and 11.51 on Saturdays, providing connections to more English cities than 10.08 pm ex-Kilmarnock, running on Mondays to Saturdays.

From the opening of the M&DLR in 1906, the schedule of the daily goods train had remained constant from and to Ayr, Girvan and the intermediate station yards or sidings; and thus, by 1914, the times were still the following: Ayr, depart 8.40 am; Girvan, arrive 12.15 pm; Girvan, depart 3.00 pm; and Ayr, arrive 6 pm. Additionally, the train called at Dipple Tile Works siding when required. This siding, within the existing Dipple sidings as the westernmost line there, had been in use since its construction three years previously, and a G&SWR Board-meeting minute of 18th April, 1911 had recorded the its origin:

Turnberry [Dipple] Tile Works Siding. An application by Mr James Gilmour for a siding into a tile work between Turnberry and Girvan recommended by Traffic Committee of 4th inst was submitted and the work ordered to be carried out at an estimated cost of £202. Mr Gilmour has agreed to pay 5 per cent per annum on the cost of the siding and to allow the company the partial use thereof. In the event of him taking entire possession he has agreed to pay the cost of construction and will thereafter maintain the siding.

Horses were among the livestock traffic that was conveyed by the G&SWR, and this had been mentioned by Charles Cockburn in his correspondence to David Cooper about the train delays and the unsuitable solution of railmotors:

Of course if we confine them [railmotors] simply to the journey between Girvan and Turnberry they would be kept in steam to perform at the most two or three trips per day which, of course, is expensive working to the locomotive department. If they were to be made use of between Ayr and Turnberry then they would not be capable of hauling the horse-box traffic we have between Ayr and Dunure.

In most cases, the railway horse box included a small compartment for the groom at the opposite end to the fodder compartment, with the horse or horses in the middle, and the largest horse boxes could accommodate six horses, though a smaller vehicle for two horses was more usual. Although horses were able to be conveyed to and from Alloway, Heads of Ayr, Dunure and Maidens stations by special arrangement, the principal traffic originated at Dunure from the large-scale breeding of Clydesdales by William Dunlop of Dunure Mains farm, who was a renowned breeder. His most famous horse was a magnificent and world-famous stallion named Baron of Buchlyvie, having cost him £9,500 for sole ownership by way of an auction at Ayr market in 1911 after a legal dispute, and with the previous world record sale for a Clydesdale stallion having been £3,000. Mr Dunlop's enterprise at Dunure Mains resulted in Clydesdales being brought from, and sent to, places all over Britain by railway and they were loaded and unloaded at Dunure goods yard, with many home and foreign buyers visiting the farm regularly. Unfortunately, in late June 1914, the Baron was accidentally kicked by a mare and he suffered a broken leg that resulted, sadly, in Mr Dunlop having no option but to have his valuable animal destroyed.

It was left open to speculation how long the improved service of the summer of 1914 would have lasted if the world events of the summer of 1914 had not intervened. The timetable was intended to have continued through August and September, but the impact of Britain's declaration of war on Germany on 4th August ended further recorded discussion on the merits of the additional train services. The Regulation of the Forces Act of 1871, which was passed in consequence of the Franco-Prussian War of 1870-71, authorized the Liberal government, led by Prime Minister Herbert Asquith, to take possession of the railways at the outset of war, and this control was implemented for the first time in 1914, immediately under the national overseeing direction of a Railway Executive Committee, consisting of representatives of the major railway companies, on behalf of the government. However, the routine management and operation by the companies remained unaltered - except for the priority of the government facilitating the movement of rolling stock and troops along the lines of different companies as a convenient and imperative national system. Restrictions were therefore placed on the travelling public, with timetables and trains subject to change or cancellation and lines subject to sudden closure for indeterminate periods, but passenger and goods trains still ran to the timetables whenever possible.

On 28th August, 1914, David Cooper issued the following information about the G&SWR timetables:

From 1st September, 1914, until further notice. All previous timetables are hereby cancelled. The Glasgow & South Western Railway Company intimate that in consequence of the European war crisis their ordinary passenger and goods train services will be subject to material alteration or discontinuance without further notice.

However, it is likely that there was little or no change to the trains on the M&DLR, and the summer timetable may have operated largely as scheduled. A winter timetable, similar to what had been issued in previous winters, was brought into effect on 1st October, but there were no Turnberry expresses, with the fastest being the Saturdays-only 12.20 pm ex-Ayr that called at Maidens and at Dunure by request. The timetable for July and August 1915 was, in essence, similar to that of October 1914, with slight differences in timings, and with the summer and winter timetables having the same overall appearance from then through 1915 and 1916. A sample summer timetable for June 1916, of the departures from Ayr and Girvan for services over the whole line and of the Turnberry-Girvan shuttle services, consisted of the following trains:

Through services
Dep. Ayr: 7.40 am B, 10.20, 1.35 pm B, 4.00 TK B, 6.08, and 8.15 Sa.
Dep. Girvan: 7.10 am B, 9.25 TK, 2.10 pm, 5.05 B, and 7.15 Sa.

Shuttle services
Dep. Turnberry: 11.05 am, 12.50 pm, and 8.10.
Dep. Girvan: 10.48 am, 12.30 pm, 6.05.

Notes: TK - Through coach Turnberry-Kilmarnock or vice versa. B - Calls at Balchriston Level Crossing. Sa - Saturdays.

The timetable included one Saturdays-only train in each direction, but by October, all the trains ran on Mondays to Saturdays, such that 1916 became the first year that there were no Saturdays-only trains.

Herbert Asquith had remained Prime Minister in a National or Coalition government from May 1915 until he was replaced by fellow Liberal David Lloyd George in December 1916; and with no sign of the cessation of the war, circumstances had necessarily changed throughout the United Kingdom, with modifications constantly in process. This was the case in the district of Turnberry because a military transformation was already in progress during late 1916. In

A pre-World War I postcard view of Maidens station, but with a postmark on the back of Glasgow, 1915, looking north-east along the island platform and showing the station staff beside the large 'Maidens for Kirkoswald' nameboard that had replaced the original of 'Maidens'. The tall signal box on the platform allowed the signalman to see over the roof of the station building; and part of Jameston farm is seen at the left. *M. Chadwick*

A scene during the annual British Ladies' Open Amateur Championship at Turnberry in 1921, overlooked by the hotel, with the station to the right. The June final was played in beautiful weather before nearly 5,000 spectators, with many having travelled by the M&DLR. *Ladies' Golf Union, St Andrews*

December, the War Office informed the G&SWR that a decision had been made 'to establish a temporary training school for the Royal Flying Corps (RFC) at Turnberry and that, in connection therewith, it is essential that the company's hotel, garage and also the golf links should be placed at the disposal of the War Office at the earliest possible date'. Of necessity, the G&SWR had already been aware of the requisitioning that would convert the area between Maidens and Turnberry into an aerodrome, with a grass airstrip, for the training of pilots in aerial combat. Although it was only 13 years previously, in 1903, that the American brothers Orville and Wilbur Wright had made the first very short powered flights in an aeroplane, which they and others proceeded to improve, the revolutionary new form of transport had developed so rapidly in the intervening period that it was soon adopted for military use.

The area around Turnberry, including the golf courses, was taken over by the War Office on 13th January, 1917, with the formation of the Royal Flying Corps' No. 2 (Auxiliary) School of Aerial Gunnery at the new grass-strip aerodrome and with Turnberry Hotel as the unit's headquarters and accommodation for the officers and staff. From this time, the RFC at Turnberry brought considerable passenger and freight traffic to the generally-quiet M&DLR, and also much bustle to the locality of Turnberry and Maidens, for, in spite of early motor transport, the railway was the prime means of moving men and materials, though road vehicles facilitated movements within and around the aerodrome, presenting a contrasting animation to the previous less populated golf courses and the relaxed golfers.

By January 1917, further restrictions upon national railway services to passengers had been implemented, with a drastic curtailment of facilities on main line and branch line routes, to discourage the public from travelling - particularly for reasons of pleasure - because the object of the restrictions was to provide engines, rolling-stock and manpower for the fluent running of the national wartime operations. Thus, from 1st January, 1917, with the establishment of the aerodrome at Turnberry, the M&DLR passenger service was reduced to just two southbound and three northbound trains daily, departing as follows: from Ayr at 9.15 am and 6.25 pm; and from Girvan at 7.25 am, 1.40 pm and 5.00 pm. All the trains called at all the stations, including Balchriston Level Crossing; and there was also the goods train, still timed to leave Ayr at 8.40 am and leave Girvan at 3.00 pm, calling at Dipple Tile Works siding when required.

The scattered buildings at the aerodrome included four 'aeroplane sheds', 16 'canvas hangars' and many other structures, such as sheds, technical stores, workshops and offices, and they were built immediately north of Turnberry farm and to the west and south-west of it, extending beyond the Maidens-Turnberry road, with the grass airstrip situated on the northern side of the aerodrome. During early 1917, the presence of the RFC troops and personnel and civilian construction workers for the aerodrome buildings had resulted in the M&DLR being used also on Sundays for one train in each direction between Girvan and Turnberry. The two trains were listed in the February 1917 G&SWR Working Timetable under the heading of 'Alterations already in force', implying that they had commenced in January, with the timetable introduction to them as follows:

Train Service for Troops between Girvan and Turnberry. The following service is in operation daily, Sundays included, for troops (about 100 men) travelling between Girvan and Turnberry.

The departure from Girvan was at 7.25 am and from Turnberry at 6.00 pm, and the timetable notes for the two services, listed as No. 1 and No. 2 respectively, explained for the benefit of the train crews:

> No. 1 - Additional train on Sundays only; on other days is 7.25 am ordinary [public service] to Ayr. On Sundays engine leaves carriages at Turnberry to form No. 2 and returns light to Girvan. No. 2 - Additional train daily, Sundays included. Carriages to form train are sent to Turnberry by 3.00 pm goods from Girvan; engine of 4.00 pm from Stranraer to Girvan runs forward to Turnberry to make this run. On Sundays light engine leaves Girvan for Turnberry at 5.30 pm.

An extra Saturday troop train was added by March 1917, leaving Turnberry at 2.00 pm, after running empty from Girvan at 1.30, but the 6.00 pm did not then run on Saturdays. By May, the only difference in these trains was that the 6.00 pm was retimed to 6.30; while by November, there was one train in each direction on Sundays only: at 7.00 am from Girvan and 6.00 pm from Turnberry, and each was listed as a passenger train. However, in the alterations to the December working timetable but likely having commenced on 1st November - and with no indication of troop trains - three other special services appeared as No. 1, No. 2 and No. 3, under the heading of 'Conveyance of Workmen between Ayr and Turnberry'. The times were: No. 1 - Ayr, depart 6.00 am, and arrive Turnberry 6.45; No. 2 - Turnberry, depart 1.15 pm, and arrive 2.00; and Turnberry, depart 5.05 pm, and arrive 5.58. The timetable notes explained:

> No. 1 - Additional train. Engine and empty carriages proceed to Girvan, engine thereafter returning to Ayr as instructed, and carriages being kept to return off 4.55 pm ordinary [public service] Girvan to Ayr, except on Saturdays; on Saturdays engine and carriages form No. 2. No. 3 - Is 4.55 pm ordinary Girvan to Ayr.

The 6.00 am ex-Ayr ran Mondays to Saturdays; the 1.15 pm ex-Turnberry ran on Saturdays only and called at Alloway at 1.53; and the 5.05 pm ran Mondays to Fridays. The reason for the workmen's trains was not stated in the timetable, but they were probably associated with the construction of the aerodrome.

During the summer of 1918, a branch railway for goods traffic was built from the M&DLR westwards to the aerodrome. An undated military report of that year for No. 1 Fighting School and the aerodrome at Turnberry in 1918 noted that there was a railway siding under construction to the site, but this report was certainly from sometime after May of that year because it was then that No. 1 (Auxiliary) School of Aerial Gunnery at Turnberry was renamed No. 1 Fighting School. An undated accompanying military map of the aerodrome, superimposed on an Ordnance Survey map, illustrated the branch, five-eighths of a mile in length, that diverged 30 degrees south-westwards from the M&DLR immediately south of the railway overbridge for the small road that ran to the east of Turnberry farm past Turnberry Wood and Turnberry Hill Cottage. The branch proceeded south-westwards for about ¼ mile, to the south of Turnberry farm, and turned sharply westwards for a similar distance, to cross the Maidens-Turnberry road on the level, curve sharply northwards and terminate a short distance beyond the road crossing. A G&SWR Board-meeting on 11th June recorded the approval stage for the branch and the sidings:

Turnberry - Auxiliary School of Aerial Gunnery. The recommendation of the traffic committee of 28th ultimo to construct sidings at the request of the government, in connection with a branch line [to the aerodrome] between Maidens and Turnberry was approved, and the work authorized to be carried out at an estimated cost of £3,015 to be paid for by the government.

A more detailed plan of the branch and the sidings, accompanied by a gradient-profile drawing of the branch, dated 22nd April, 1918 and on behalf of Messrs Robert McAlpine & Sons, contractors, of Clydebank, had indicated the precise nature of the railway communication to the aerodrome. Immediately on the western side of the M&DLR, at the junction for the airfield branch, there was a main loop and an attached secondary loop to the side; and extending north and south of the junction were two sets of sidings - known as 'head sidings' on the plan, or headshunts - that were connected to the main line on either side of the junction, by way of the main loop. The plan also indicated 'marshalling sidings', forming a double loop that was aligned east-west, on the southern side of the branch, immediately before the branch crossed the Maidens-Turnberry road.

Previously, a bridge carried the M&DLR over the small road to Turnberry Hill Cottage, but, for the construction of the branch, the bridge was infilled and the road ramped-up to reach the level of the railway and form a level crossing for the now-greater width of the two lines together of the M&DLR and the branch. From the junction immediately east of the level crossing, the aerodrome branch proceeded on the western side of, and parallel to, the M&DLR, with both lines ascending at 1 in 200 across the level crossing. The M&DLR continued, more southerly, on this gradient, but the branch, in diverging more south-westerly, descended very steeply, at 1 in 20 for 275 yards and at 1 in 30 for 220 yards, while curving sharply westwards about 400 yards from the M&DLR junction. After 600 yards, the gradient suddenly changed from 1 in 30 to a very shallow 1 in 246 for 330 yards, towards the Maidens-Turnberry road, and then the branch curved sharply northwards, to terminate after a distance of 280 yards, beside a shed within the aerodrome boundary (*see Appendix One*). Whatever traffic the aerodrome branch conveyed for the war effort was short-lived, encompassing only a few months, for the Great War ended in November 1918, but during the dire situation of hostilities, the branch had latterly formed another important part of the wartime scene of the area.

From the amalgamation of the Royal Flying Corps and the Royal Naval Air Service, which had been established in 1914, the Royal Air Force (RAF) had formed in April 1918 to develop co-ordination in the air, with Turnberry incorporated within the RAF and with the unit having been renamed in September 1917 to No. 1 School of Aerial Fighting and then renamed twice more in May 1918 to No. 1 School of Aerial Fighting and Gunnery and No. 1 Fighting School. Between January 1917, when the RFC formed at Turnberry, and February 1919, when the RAF vacated Turnberry, 5,000 officers, non-commissioned officers and other ranks of the Imperial, Colonial and American Air services had been trained for their part in the hostilities, with 39 of them having sacrificed their lives in the immediate vicinity.

Meanwhile, during 1918, the limited train service over the M&DLR during 1918 had been represented by two periods. In the timetable from 1st January 'until further notice', the departures from Ayr were 10.35 am and 5.45 pm, and from Girvan 7.00 am and 4.50 pm. The Turnberry departure times by these services were 11.20 am and 6.40 pm for Girvan, and 7.18 am and 5.01 pm for Ayr, with the trains calling at all the stations. From 1st October, 1918 'until further notice', the only changes were the

The short branch from the M&DLR to Turnberry aerodrome, between Maidens and Turnberry, in 1918, with a separate enlargement of the junction sidings, which included two loops. Four 'aeroplane sheds' lie south of the grass landing strip and 16 'canvas hangars' are situated west and east of the strip; while other aerodrome buildings are spread west and south of the level crossing at the Turnberry-Maidens road. *Drawn by D. McConnell*

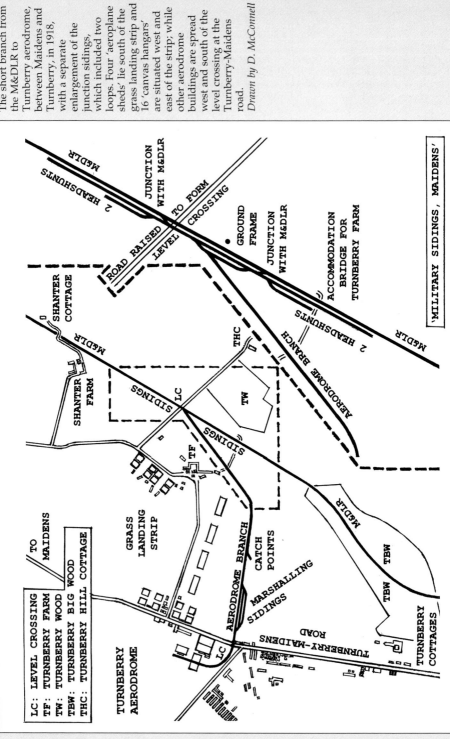

'MILITARY SIDINGS, MAIDENS'

LC: LEVEL CROSSING
TF: TURNBERRY FARM
TW: TURNBERRY WOOD
TBW: TURNBERRY BIG WOOD
THC: TURNBERRY HILL COTTAGE

departures from Ayr being 10.30 am and 5.55 pm, producing corresponding time differences southbound at all the stations.

In February 1919, with Turnberry Hotel having been returned to the G&SWR, the committee of Turnberry Golf Club held their first meeting since June 1917, and it was their immediate intention to restore the two golf courses - these being No. 1 Course and No. 2 Course that had been established back in 1909 by Alex Weir - for the damage to them was not substantial. The club regained possession of the courses in April, and the more coastal No. 1 Course was opened for play that month, with the more inland No. 2 Course intended to be ready soon afterwards.

Gradually during mid-1919, the M&DLR passenger timetable attained a post-war revival and an increase of train services. In February, there had still been only two trains southbound and three northbound: the 10.30 am and 5.45 pm from Ayr, and the 7.05 am, 12.55 pm on Saturdays only and the 4.50 pm from Girvan. The 12.55 pm was listed in the working timetable as a 'Workers' Train' - probably in operation because of the dismantling of the airfield buildings - but it was also listed in the public timetable without this specification, and except for the 12.55, the trains called at all the stations, including Balchriston Level Crossing. There was also a 9.15 pm service from Girvan to Turnberry that was not listed to return with passengers, presumably solely for conveying passengers only to, and not from, Turnberry hotel. However, by June 1919, the post-war revival and increase of train services on the M&DLR had begun, with domestic holidays and pleasure journeys having resumed. The timetable included a train that was referred to as a 12.10 pm 'express passenger' on Saturdays, though it called at Dunure and Maidens as well as Turnberry. A Saturdays-only 'workers' train' also operated from Turnberry at 12.10 pm for Girvan, but an amendment to the working timetable, dated 7th June, recorded that this train had been discontinued, while the 9.15pm Girvan-Turnberry service ran on Saturdays only, and, when necessary, for passengers from the South.

From July, two new Turnberry express services were provided - one in each direction - with the running of a breakfast and tea car. These were the 7.40 am that started service from Turnberry for Glasgow, and the 5.10 pm from Glasgow, being the 6.05 from Ayr, that terminated at Turnberry at 6.40 pm. For the 7.40 am ex-Turnberry on its arrival at Ayr, a note in the working timetable stated: 'Will arrive outside down [northbound] platform at 8.17 am, and be propelled to rear of 8.25 am, Ayr to Glasgow'. The 5.10 pm from Glasgow, as the return-direction service, reached Ayr at 6.00 and divided to form the 6.05 to Turnberry and the 6.10 to Girvan via Maybole. The July 1919 M&DLR timetable read:

Dep. Ayr: 10.10 am, 12.10 pm Sa, 1.35 M-F, 1.55 Sa, 5.25, 6.05 TE T, 7.15

Dep. Girvan: 6.30 am, 12.30 pm, 4.50, 7.00 Sa.
Dep. Turnberry: 7.40 am TE B.

Notes: TE - Turnberry express, non-stop Ayr-Turnberry or vice versa. T - Tea car. B - Breakfast car. M-F - Mondays to Fridays. Sa - Saturdays.

The tea and breakfast car was not the same coach that had been used on the short-lived luncheon and tea service on Saturdays back in 1906 but was a 1916 rebuild, with a new body, of a former Midland Scotch Joint Stock (MSJS) main line restaurant car of 1894.

Back in February 1919, the goods train had still departed from Ayr at 8.40 am and departed from Girvan at 3.00 pm, but from June, the times had become 10.30 am and 2.30 pm respectively - thereby making 1919 the first year of change for the timings

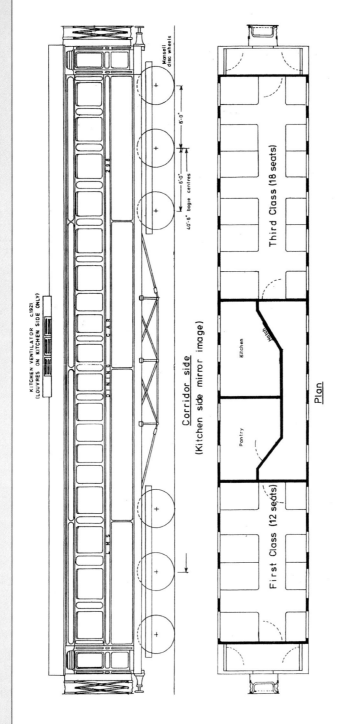

KITCHEN VENTILATOR c.1921
(LOUVRES ON KITCHEN SIDE ONLY)

Mansell
disc wheels

6'-0"

6'-0"

40'-6" bogie centres

Corridor side
(Kitchen side mirror image)

First Class (12 seats)

Pantry

Kitchen

Third Class (18 seats)

Plan

The second G&SWR dining car of the M&DLR, as a rebuild of a Midland Scotch Joint Stock restaurant car of 1894 that was transferred from the Midland Railway to the G&SWR in 1909 and used on the M&DLR on Mondays to Saturdays from July to September 1919 to 1923 as a breakfast and tea car. Its body was destroyed by fire in 1915 and a new body, designed by Peter Drummond, was built onto the Midland 12-wheeled underframe in 1916. The car was stabled overnight at Girvan, in working the early-morning express to Glasgow and the early-evening express back, both via Turnberry.

Drawn by S. Rankin

G&SWR '119' class 4-4-0, ex-No. 133, showing its new 1919 number 710, at Turnberry station, *c.* 1920, hauling a Girvan-Ayr train, consisting of, in order behind the tender, a seven-coapartment third, a six-compartment first, another third, and a four-wheeled brake van. The covered walkway to the hotel is on the right, with the station nameboard unusually situated on the platform ramp, and the station building is the original, with the glazed gable-end canopy that was destroyed by fire in 1926. *GNSR Association: Barclay-Harvey Collection*

G&SWR '1' class 0-4-4T, ex-No. 2, as modified in 1920 with new cab, bigger coal bunker, shorter chimney and new number 729, at Turnberry station, *c.* 1920, hauling a Girvan-Ayr train. The leading coach is a four-compartment brake third of Hugh Smellie design, with a guard's lookout, though it is the driver and fireman who look out, with curiosity, towards the camera, but not realising the posterity value of the snapshot of the line. *GNSR Association: Barclay-Harvey Collection*

of the train. Unlike the February working timetable that erroneously listed the train as calling at Dipple Tile Works siding, the June working timetable made no mention of this. Indeed, the train had no longer called there from early 1918, or possibly even before that year, as was evident from a G&SWR Board-meeting minute of 16th April, 1918 having recorded that the tile works company had been placed in liquidation and the whole of the plant had been dismantled. The June 1919 timetable had also contained a note that the train called at Greenan Castle and at the 'Military Sidings, Maidens', when required, which meant the sidings by the junction with the aerodrome branch and not to any additional sidings. The reference to Maidens instead of Turnberry may have been to avoid confusion between the junction sidings and Turnberry's siding and loop which were adjacent to the hotel and station and which were also used during the war.

A summary of the times in composite form for June 1920, July 1921 and June 1922 portrays the pattern of the passenger traffic on the M&DLR services during the last three summer workings of passenger traffic on the M&DLR under the ownership of the G&SWR - for the reorganization of Britain's railway system, which had been planned during the war, was forthcoming from 1st January, 1923:

Through services via Maidens

Dep. Ayr for Girvan			*Dep. Girvan for Ayr*		
June 1920	*July 1921*	*June 1922*	*June 1920*	*July 1921*	*June 1922*
am	*am*	*am*	*am*	*am*	*am*
8.15	8.15	8.15	7.30	7.25 TE B	7.25 TE B
9.35 TE			(7.40 TE B)*	7.30	7.30
10.05	10.05	10.05	9.50	9.50	9.50
pm	*pm*	*pm*	*pm*	*pm*	*pm*
12.10 Sa	12.10 Sa	12.10 Sa	12.30	12.30	12.30
1.35	1.35	1.35	2.05	2.05	2.05
3.50	3.50	3.55	4.55	4.55	5.00
6.05 TE T	6.05 TE T	6.05 TE T	6.50	6.50	6.50
6.15	6.15	6.15			
7.25	7.55	7.55			

Through services to or from Ayr via Maybole

Dep. Turnberry for Girvan			*Dep. Girvan for Turnberry*		
June 1920	*July 1921*	*June 1922*	*June 1920*	*July 1921*	*June 1922*
am	*am*	*am*	*am*	*am*	*am*
		8.50 TG	9.50	9.50	8.25 Sh
11.00	11.00				
pm	*pm*	*pm*	*pm*	*pm*	*pm*
			2.05	2.05	
12.52 Sa	12.52 Sa		6.00	6.00	6.00 TG
2.30 Sa	2.30 Sa				
6.20	6.40	6.20 Sh			

Notes:
* - Passenger service starts from Turnberry. TE - Turnberry express, non-stop Ayr-Turnberry or vice versa. B - Breakfast car on Turnberry express. T - Tea car on Turnberry express. TG - Through coach, Turnberry-Glasgow or vice versa. Sh - Shuttle service, Turnberry-Girvan only. Sa - Saturdays.

Three maidens at Maidens in the late G&SWR era. In 1920-22, three girls, who would become the mother and aunts of co-author Stuart Rankin, spent family holidays at Maidens, and two of them and a friend, sitting on a railway barrow, appear in a photograph at Maidens station. *Left to right*, they are Jean Borland (b. 1913), Elizabeth Borland (b. 1911) and their unknown friend. Jean and Elizabeth's older sister Margaret (b. 1909), who became Stuart's mother, may have photographed the three visible maidens, in therefore being a fourth invisible maiden. All three sisters lived long, with the last survivor being Jean, in attaining the age of 91; and it was Stuart's attendance at Jean's funeral in 2005 that led to the disclosure of the poignant and evocative photograph to him by Kathryn Holderness, who is Jean's niece, Elizabeth's daughter and Stuart's cousin. In the captured moment of a long-departed and nostalgic era, perhaps Jean heard a train approaching from the north, as she chose the wrong time to look away, but the other two girls smile serenely at the camera.   *K. Holderness*

In May 1920, the first train of the day had departed from Turnberry at 7.40 am, being the 7.30 stopping ex-Girvan train to Ayr. However, from June, this train, still running as the 7.30 ex-Girvan and timed from Turnberry at 7.44, was preceded by the 7.40 am breakfast-car express that started from Turnberry and ran non-stop to Ayr and Glasgow, and, therefore, two northbound trains left Turnberry station only four minutes apart. Also from June, the 5.10 pm express from Glasgow that divided at Ayr to form the 6.05, with the tea car, to Turnberry and the 6.10 to Girvan via Maybole, was followed at Ayr by a new 6.15 pm ex-Ayr stopping train via Turnberry. The 7.40 am ran as empty coaching stock from Girvan to Turnberry and the 6.05 pm ran similarly from Turnberry to Girvan, but in September 1920 - possibly resulting from complaints - the trains started and terminated as passenger trains at Girvan, with the departure and arrival time, respectively, of 7.25 am and 6.53 pm. Presumably, why the G&SWR did not do so previously was to offer exclusivity for Turnberry passengers, but it was only logical to reconsider and include the Girvan-Turnberry section for public traffic.

While June 1919 had been the first year of change in the timings of the daily goods train, the second notable change in regard to it had occurred by June 1922 - possibly having begun in 1921 - when it was now operating only southbound on the M&DLR, with the return trip via Maybole. This change of route back to Ayr enabled the same goods train to cater for the yards on the main line, principally Kilkerran and Maybole, as well as those on the M&DLR, by the one round trip.

Right: Alloway station and its platform flower beds, looking east from the footbridge, in a poor quality image from a 1926 issue of the *LMS Railway Magazine.*
G&SWR Association

Below: A reasoned speculative impression of Balchriston halt in the mid- to late-1920s, with a solitary passenger awaiting his train, in a view looking south, as the line proceeds through the earth cutting in the northern Culzean estate. The building on the right consists of the two cottages for the crossing-keepers' families.
Drawn by D. McConnell

Chapter Eleven

Late Period Train Services, 1923-1930

It had been agreed during the war by the government and the railway companies that state control of the railways would continue for an interim period after the cessation of hostilities because of the ravages to Britain's railway system, locomotives and rolling stock. This meant that the redevelopment of the network nationally could not be achieved by returning to the situation of the many independent and rival companies that had existed before the start of the war; and with them so badly equipped to serve the nation, it was accepted that the only way that a recovery could occur was by a reorganization of the country's railways, and even by their nationalization. After the war, state control continued for the interim period under the Railway Executive Committee because the advantages of a unified national system would be maintained. The reorganization of the railways had begun with the formation of a new governmental department called the Ministry of Transport, which was established by an Act of Parliament in August 1919, under the Liberal-Conservative National government of Liberal Prime Minster David Lloyd George.

The railways were eventually returned from state control to the original companies on 15th August, 1921, and four days later the Railways Act of 1921 authorized an amlgamation of the railways into what would be a small number of large companies. Ultimately, after much discussion, there were to be only four new and separate groups or companies for the railways of Great Britain, with Scotland encompassed by two 'longitudinal' forms of amalgamation in conjunction with England and Wales, in being contained within two of the four new companies. Only one of the company names had been decided on the passing of the Act, which was the Great Western Railway (GWR), as the only one of the four to retain its original name, in covering south-western England and most of southern and central Wales; and it was in late 1922 that the other three company names were designated. The area of eastern England and eastern Scotland formed part of the London & North Eastern Railway (LNER), while the area of south-eastern and most of southern England formed the Southern Railway (SR). For the remaining amalgamation, covering central and western England, northern Wales, parts of southern and eastern Wales, and western and northern Scotland, the name was to have been the London, Midland & Northern Railway, but this was soon changed to the London, Midland & Scottish Railway Company (LMS), which assured a Scottish identity in the name, in spite of not encompassing all of Scotland.

In essence but not in exactness, the five principal Scottish companies were incorporated into the western or LMS amalgamation of the Caledonian Railway, Glasgow & South Western Railway and the Inverness-based Highland Railway, and the eastern or LNER amalgamation of the North British Railway and the Aberdeen-based Great North of Scotland Railway. Indeed, the inconsistency was such that the western-orientated LMS would reach eastern Scotland at Aberdeen by the Caledonian Railway from Glasgow and at Thurso and Wick by the Highland Railway from Inverness, while the eastern-orientated LNER would reach western Scotland at Fort William and Mallaig by the North British Railway from Glasgow. Additionally, the north-south amalgamations allowed the three main Anglo-Scottish trunk routes to be operated by the one company throughout, which were: London to Glasgow and Edinburgh by the western route of the LMS, via Carlisle; London to Glasgow and Edinburgh by the Midland route of the LMS, via Carlisle; and London to Edinburgh by the eastern route of the LNER, via Newcastle. The large railway amalgamations, involving the whole country and 123 railway companies being incorporated into four, had been a complex operation from its beginning in 1921, with the 'Grouping', as the reorganization was known, to take effect officially on 1st January, 1923.

Overall control of the former G&SWR system was now based on London, but regional administration for Scotland - under the LMS Northern Division - was still implemented from Glasgow. However, no significant changes to the Maidens & Dunure Light Railway's timetable were introduced under the LMS compared with the G&SWR, for there was no reason to make any. Within the principal summer timetable of the LMS, in operating from 9th July, 1923 until further notice, the train services for July were:

Through services
Dep. Ayr: 8.20 am, 10.08 TE, 10.15, 12.10 pm Sa, 1.35, 3.55, 5.20 TG, 6.05 TE T, 6.15, 7.55.
Dep. Girvan: 7.25 am TE B, 7.32, 8.50 TG, 9.45, 12.30 pm, 2.05, 4.45 TE, 5.00, 6.50.

Shuttle services
Dep. Turnberry: 8.25 am, 6.00 pm.
Dep. Girvan: No shuttle services.

Notes
TE - Turnberry express, non-stop Ayr-Turnberry or vice versa. TG - Glasgow-Turnberry through coach via Maybole and Girvan or vice versa. T - Pullman tea car, Glasgow-Turnberry-Girvan. B - Pullman breakfast car, Girvan-Turnberry-Glasgow. Sa - Saturdays.

From 1st May, 1923, the tea-car and breakfast-car services had operated on the 5.10 pm from Glasgow to Turnberry and Girvan and on the 7.25 am from Girvan to Turnberry and Glasgow, but a Pullman coach had replaced the 1916 rebuilt MSJS coach, with the LMS having abandoned the G&SWR terminology of 'tea car' and 'breakfast car' by referring to the coach as a 'Pullman Restaurant Car'. Having the name *Mary Carmichael*, after one of Mary Queen of Scots' ladies-in-waiting, this 1914-built coach was originally operated by the Caledonian Railway, as the first, or one of the first, vehicles to have been transferred by the LMS from the former CR system to the former G&SWR system.

From 1st June and for the rest of the summer of 1923, there were three services from Ayr to Girvan on the arrival of the 5.10 pm from Glasgow. They were the 6.05 Turnberry express and the 6.10 via Maybole, as the dividing portions of the 5.10, and a separate 6.15 M&DLR stopping train. The same set of three services applied to the 9.00 am train from Glasgow on its arrival at Ayr, where the departures were 10.03 via Maybole, 10.08 non-stop to Turnberry, and 10.15 on the M&DLR stopping train. However, in October 1923 - as had also been the case back in May - there was a reversal of the two evening departure times from Ayr. Thus, during the summer, the 6.05 via the coast had been non-stop to Turnberry, followed at 6.10 by the Maybole portion; but in winter, with less traffic to Turnberry, the Turnberry portion became the 6.10 as a stopping train, while the Maybole portion was the 6.05. The same principle of three services at Ayr from the 9.00 am and 5.10 pm ex-Glasgow services that had occurred in the summer of 1923 was in evidence on the corresponding trains for the summer of 1925; but the latter timetable also contained a Saturdays-only Turnberry shuttle service that terminated at Maidens instead of Turnberry. It departed from Girvan at 9.00 pm and from Turnberry at 9.12, with an arrival time at Maidens of 9.17, and then leaving at 9.25 for a 9.42 arrival at Girvan as empty coaching stock.

In the early evening of Monday, 11th October, 1926, Turnberry station was destroyed by a fire. When it was first discovered shortly after seven o'clock, the flames were issuing through the roof of the station master's office. For a time, there were fears that the hotel was in danger because it was connected to the station by the covered walkway, but, fortunately, the hotel was equipped with modern fire apparatus, and the small Turnberry Fire Brigade that was attached to the hotel prevented the fire from reaching the hotel. The situation was helped by the presence of a wild north-westerly wind directing the flames away from the hotel, but by the time that the Ayr Fire Brigade had arrived within an hour, the fire had attained too much of a hold on the station building, which could not be saved. The station was closed, with the last train having left at 7.12 pm, and while the cause of the fire was unknown, it was thought that it may have originated by a spark from the engine or by the fusing of an electric wire for the lighting. The reconstruction of the station building and the canopy was carried out on the basis of the original plans, such that it was almost identical to its predecessor, and the work was treated as a routine matter by the LMS Scottish Local Committee in Glasgow because the details were not recorded. However, one difference between the original and replacement structures was that the gables of the canopy on the original contained windows while the replacement did not.

In the June 1927 working timetable, the following trains called at Balchriston on request: the 10.10 am, 1.35 pm, 3.55 and 6.15 from Ayr; and the 7.45 am, 12.40 pm on Mondays to Fridays, 1.04 on Saturdays, and 5.00 from Girvan. An accompanying note explained the reason:

These trains may be stopped at Balchriston Level Crossing between Glenside and Knoweside, to set down or pick up schoolchildren and other passengers, or the crossing-keeper, for which time has been allowed. The stops must be arranged through the station master and he must arrange for attendance at the crossing.

After the war, until 1922 under the G&SWR and from 1923 under the LMS, the most important trains in connection with Turnberry were the 8.25 am from Ayr to St Enoch and the return at 5.10 pm from St Enoch to Ayr, with both of these 50 minute Glasgow-Ayr non-stop expresses containing portions from and to Girvan and with part of the 5.10 continuing as the 6.10 ex-Ayr and the 7.05 ex-Girvan to Stranraer. In July 1927, the compositions of the 8.25 am ex-Ayr and the 5.10 pm ex-Glasgow trains, from the engine backwards, were:

8.25 am from Ayr, arr. Glasgow 9.15, of 7 vehicles, composed of:
(a) Coaches via-Maybole, as 7.20 am ex-Girvan, arr. Ayr 8.10, with
first, Girvan-Glasgow,
third, Girvan-Glasgow,
brake third, Girvan-Glasgow,
brake third; Girvan-Glasgow.
(b) Coaches via Turnberry, as 7.25 am ex-Girvan, arr. Ayr 8.20, with
brake third, Girvan-Glasgow,
Pullman dining, Girvan-Glasgow,
brake composite, Girvan-Glasgow.

5.10 pm from Glasgow, arr. Ayr 6.00, of 10 vehicles, composed of:
(a) Coaches via-Turnberry, as 6.05 pm ex-Ayr, with
brake composite, Glasgow-Girvan,
Pullman dining, Glasgow-Girvan,
brake third, Glasgow-Girvan.
(b) Coaches via Maybole, as 6.10 pm ex-Ayr, with
third, Glasgow-Girvan,
third, Glasgow-Stranraer,
first, Glasgow-Stranraer,
third, Glasgow-Stranraer,
brake van,
first, Glasgow-Ayr,
third, Glasgow-Ayr.

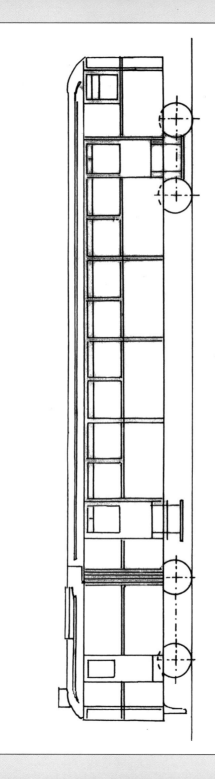

LMS Sentinel steam railcar, as used on the M&DLR, showing, *left to right*, the engine and driving compartment, the third class passenger compartment and the driving-only compartment.

Drawn by S. Rankin

A new steam-powered and self-propelled coach for passenger traffic was introduced on the M&DLR in the September 1927 timetable. The *Ayr Observer* of 26th July, 1927 had described the coach and the reason for its emergence in a neighbouring county, before its arrival in Ayrshire:

The railway companies have been a little late in the day in awakening to the menace of the bus companies' activities, but they appear now to be entering into the competition for traffic with energy and resource. The latest departure by the LMS Company is the introduction in the Lanarkshire area of a new light steam carriage for short distance traffic. The new coach is luxuriously fitted after the manner of the deluxe omnibuses, and the seats can be made to face either way, just as on tramcars. Curtains, not blinds, are fitted on the windows, and the carriage is electrically lighted and steam heated. Forty-four passengers can be seated comfortably, and a maximum speed of 45 miles per hour can be reached. The coach can be driven from either end, and as an ordinary train, the guard's services being dispensed with. It is stated that the new conveyance can be run at about one-third of the cost of the ordinary steam train. The lowest cost should enable the railway company to run a good service of vehicles on routes where traffic is light and on which it would not be economical to increase the present ordinary train service. The experiment is stated to have met with considerable success, and its introduction to other suitable areas may be anticipated.

Then, on 26th August, the *Ayrshire Post* had provided further information, under the heading 'Railway Steam Coach to Compete with Buses', explaining that the new coach was proving successful in service from Ayr to Dalmellington and Rankinston on Sundays. The paper added that it would probably run from Ayr to Maybole on Saturday afternoons and that there was a probability within a few weeks of services by it commencing from Ayr to Turnberry and Girvan, to Kilmarnock, and to Mauchline and Catrine; and a brief depiction of the railmotor followed:

The interior of the coach is not unlike that of a road omnibus, and the seats are most comfortable, the running, naturally, being much smoother on rails. There is seating accommodation for fully 50 persons. At the front is a compartment which contains the steam engine whereby the coach is driven, and at the rear is another compartment for the accommodation of the guard.

This coach was the Sentinel steam railcar that was manufactured by the Sentinel Waggon Works in Shrewsbury, Shropshire, and purchased firstly by the LNER and then the LMS, with 13 of the 14 LMS vehicles being used in Scotland. It was, in effect, a revived attempt at establishing the principle of the railmotor of the early 1900s to counter the increasing bus popularity. Ayr locomotive shed received an allocation of two LMS Sentinel steam railcars and one of them was introduced on the M&DLR in September 1927, operated by the driver and fireman but without the need for a guard. The railcar consisted of third-class accommodation only, and the times of the workings on the M&DLR in the September 1927 timetable were: 10.10 am, 1.38 pm and 4.00 from Ayr; and 7.40 am, 12.20 pm on Saturdays, 12.35 on Mondays to Fridays, 2.45 and 5.07 from Girvan. Balchriston was included in the places served by the railcar, with stops by request on the 10.10 am, 1.38 pm and 4.00 services from Ayr and on the 7.40 am, 12.35 pm on Mondays to Fridays, and the 5.07 from Girvan. The railcar service was continued in the public timetables from 26th September through the winter months of late 1927, but a note in the working timetable from 2nd January, 1928 informed the railway staff that the 10.10 am ex-Ayr and 7.40 am ex-Girvan services were 'being worked by ordinary engine and carriages instead of railmotor on Saturdays and Mondays until

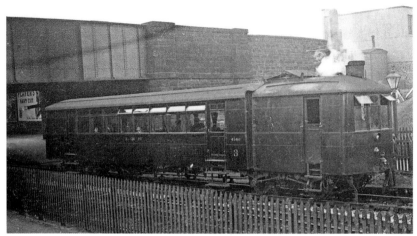

LMS Sentinel steam railcar No. 4146 departs from Ayr station with passengers on board. The passenger section appears clean and new, and the railcar could be working via Turnberry to Girvan, or, if not, to Dalmellington. Nos. 4146 and 4147, allocated to Ayr, were two of four LMS Sentinels, all built in 1927, that worked in Ayrshire. The '3' indicates the sole third class accommodation.   *D. Stirling*

further notice'. Then, from 1st April, these services reverted to the railcar daily, to provide the same four timings in each direction as originally. The railcar ceased operating on the M&DLR at the end of April 1928, in not being shown thereafter, and its short-lived services had been verified in the winter public timetables, from 26th September to 30th April, 1928, by the revealing note 'Third Class Only'.

It is likely that the railcar was 'sub-shedded' to Girvan when it operated the M&DLR services, for it is unlikely to have run empty daily from Ayr to Girvan early in the morning to be in place at Girvan for the 7.40 am run. Although there was no 'balanced' working for the railcar back to Girvan in the evening along the M&DLR, there was an unusual 'third-class only' 6.40 pm Saturdays only and 7.10 pm Saturdays excepted from Ayr to Maybole, and the car probably operated this turn and then continued empty to Girvan. The Sentinels were unable to haul additional vehicles, supposedly because of having insufficient power but, in more basic terms, because they contained no couplings and buffers, in therefore being consigned to work alone, instead of coupled to other rolling stock. However, the major problem of the Sentinels on the M&DLR, like the earlier G&SWR railmotors, was that they were of third-class accommodation only, in an open saloon, and they were unlikely to have been popular with the Turnberry clientele who expected the privacy and comfort of first-class compartments, such that this was probably the decisive reason for their withdrawal from the route. Nevertheless, they continued on the other routes in Ayrshire as had been planned, and additionally worked Ayr-Kilmarnock Sunday services.

From 1st May, 1928, the trains that had been worked by the railcar reverted to the orthodox locomotive-hauled trains, but another change occurred and continued until the end of September, as denoted in the working timetables by the letters 'R' and 'V' for the following services:

	R	V	V	R		R	R	R	V	V
							Sa	M-F		
	am	*pm*	*pm*	*pm*		*am*	*pm*	*pm*	*pm*	*pm*
Ayr	10.10	1.38	4.00	7.55	Girvan	7.40	12.20	12.35	2.45	5.07
Girvan	11.07	2.36	4.57	8.53	Ayr	8.43	1.25	1.33	3.39	6.05

Notes: R - Brake composite with no guard Mondays to Saturdays. V - Brake composite with no guard Mondays to Fridays but usual locomotive-hauled train on Saturdays with guard.

Unusually, these services consisted only of a locomotive and a single brake composite coach, for it was usual for locomotive-hauled trains to possess a guard, who authorized the driver to depart from each station. However, with the Sentinel railcars not having carried a guard, there was the belief that the same principle could be tried with a one-coach train at times of light traffic, as the driver could easily see when everyone was aboard. The services that were shown with a 'V' may have been noticeably busier on Saturdays, requiring more than one coach and a guard. The two sets of brake-composite services - and the trial, if that had been the intention - ended with the September 1928 timetable.

The introduction of the Sentinel railcars was nearly responsible for the village of Dunure obtaining another station, for, in October 1927, the LMS had considered the provision of a passenger halt nearer the village than the existing station at Fisherton. This was coincident with the appearance of the Sentinels on the line, and the proposed halt was intended to encourage local passenger patronage in counteraction to a bus service that had reached Dunure from Ayr and was operated by Ayr & District Motor Services. A draft plan of the location of the halt on the south-eastern side of the village had been produced, also showing a 5 ft-wide, ash-covered footpath, with self-closing gates at each end, that was to extend from the road that passed through Dunure, opposite the castle, eastwards for 220 yards in a straight line towards the railway. The platform was to be built on the western side of the line and immediately south of an arched bridge that carried the line over a small burn. The proposal had depended on the success of the Sentinels on the line, but, ultimately, they appear to have been found unsuitable in working the line. The halt had not materialized for that reason alone, but another difficulty would have been the difference in height between the path at the road and at rail levels, being 100 and 200 feet respectively, with the path therefore having to surmount 100 feet along the length of the footpath, producing a steep 1 in 7 average gradient, which did not seem to have been considered at the draft stage but which may later have been assessed as impracticable.

Unconnected with the passenger operations of the line, a special notice, which was issued in June 1929 under the authority of Charles Byrom, the chief general superintendent of the LMS, indicated the workings of the trains for the Carrick new potatoes as a sample season of this traffic at the end of the 1920s. By this period in the line's history, regular freight train workings of a branch or local nature had been given 'trip' numbers and the times were not shown in the working timetables. They were treated separately by being supervised directly from Kilmarnock as the control centre, such that they were classified by 'K' numbers, designating Kilmarnock, in booklets entitled *Train Trip and Shunting Engine Notice, Ayr District*. The M&DLR all-year-round daily goods train was 'K156', based at Ayr, and the seasonal potato trains were 'K140', 'K153', 'K169', also based at Ayr, and 'K178', based at Girvan. The potato 'trip workings' operated to timings that were listed in the 'trip notice', and

Rebuilt G&SWR '6' class 4-4-0, ex-G&SWR No. 197, as '191' class LMS No. 14234, at Heads of Ayr station with a Girvan-Ayr passenger train, photographed by railway enthusiast Jim Aird in September 1930. Happily, for nostalgia and posterity, the scene still reflects the G&SWR era, almost eight years after the start of LMS ownership.   *G&SWR Association*

Rebuilt unidentified G&SWR former '22' class 0-6-0, as '135' class, ascends the steep gradient, changing from 1 in 80 to 1 in 70 at the gradient post in the foreground, on the curve from Heads of Ayr to the Bracken Bay cutting with the daily southbound-only Turnberry goods train, *c.* 1930, when the few survivors of the class were still active around Ayr. The view shows the embankment stretching back to Heads of Ayr station in the middle distance.   *I. Middleditch*

they would be readily altered or suspended when not required, on certain days - usually when there was heavy rain that prevented the potatoes being picked or loaded - and the day's operation was more easily arranged under the trip system than by the working timetables.

	K140	K153	K153	K169		K178
	Ayr	Ayr	Ayr	Ayr		Girvan
Outward journeys		M-F	Sa			M-F
Ayr Falkland Jn	8.30 *am*	10.20 *am*	10.20 *am*	2.45 *pm*	Girvan	4.00 *pm*
Alloway		11.00	11.00	3.08	Maidens	7.24
Greenan Castle				3.22	Dunure	7.48
Heads of Ayr		11.30	11.30	3.34	Heads of Ayr	8.08
Dunure		11.48	11.48	3.50	Ayr	8.50
Knoweside		12.03 *pm*	12.03 *pm*	4.04		
Glenside	9.50	12.24	12.22	4.12		Sa
Maidens	11.23	1.30	12.28		Girvan	2.35 *pm*
Turnberry		1.50			Killochan	3.25
Dipple	12.20 *pm*	2.15			Maybole	4.50
Girvan Goods	12.30	2.27			Ayr	5.27

Return Journeys
K140 - M-F Girvan dep. 1.50 pm via Maybole to Ayr arr. 2.35 M-F, but Sa Girvan dep. 1.55 pm, Ayr arr. 2.40. K153 - M-F Girvan dep. 3.35 pm via Maybole, Ayr arr. 5.10; but Sa terminates Maidens arr.12.28 pm and dep. 3.12 via M&DLR, Alloway dep. 4.05, to Ayr arr. 4.15. K169 - Glenside arr. 4.12 pm and dep. 5.45, Knoweside 6.08, Dunure 6.39, Heads of Ayr 7.05, Greenan Castle 7.20, Alloway 7.50, Ayr arr. 8.05. K178 - M-F Ayr dep. 9.40 pm via Maybole to Girvan arr. 10.40, but Sa Ayr dep. 6.15 pm via Maybole to Girvan arr. 7.15.

Meanwhile, a prestigious new first class sleeper service to and from London had been bestowed on Turnberry in the summer of 1928, within the timetable period of 9th July to 23rd September, and it was continued in 1929 for the corresponding timetable from 8th July to 22nd September. A former LNWR first class sleeper coach with a clerestory roof was attached to the overnight Euston-Dumfries-Stranraer Harbour* train in both directions between Stranraer and Turnberry. While the Stranraer service ran seven nights a week, the Turnberry coach ran six, in leaving Euston on Sunday-to-Friday evenings and Turnberry on Monday-to-Saturday evenings. The Turnberry schedule was the same for 1928 and 1929: departing Euston at 8.00 pm, except on Saturdays, but 8.30 pm on Sundays, and arriving at Turnberry at 8.45 am, except on Sundays; and leaving Turnberry at 6.42 pm, except on Sundays, and arriving at Euston at 7.30 am. Northbound, after being transferred from the Euston-Stranraer Harbour service, the coach was shunted to Stranraer Town† and attached to the 7.05 am, the first train of the day, to Glasgow. At Girvan, it was attached to the 8.34 am local service to Turnberry only, and immediately after the passengers had detrained at Turnberry, it returned empty on the 8.50 am service back to Girvan, to be conveyed later that day, also running empty, as part of another local service from Girvan to Ayr via the M&DLR.

The reason for the sleeper coach proceeding to Ayr was because the 'housekeeping' duties of cleaning and bed-making were carried out by the Station Hotel staff there, in preparation for the overnight service from Turnberry via Stranraer to Euston. The southbound coach was attached to the rear of the 6.05 pm from Ayr after this had divided from the 5.10 pm ex-Glasgow express, and it called

* Also known as Stranraer Pier.
† Conveniently called Stranraer Town in this book but officially named Stranraer until 1953, when it received the suffix Town.

GLASGOW AND AYR TO TURNBERRY AND GIRVAN.

WEEK DAYS.

		J			K						A							N
Glasgow (St. Enoch)	dep.	5E 5		7 0	9 0		10 15	10 45		11 10	12 30		12 33	1 0	1 3	2 10		
	arr.	6 54		8 43	10 2		11 21	11 55		12 40	1 28		1 43		1 53	2 40	3 39	3 53
Ayr	dep.	7 3		8 48	10 5	10 12	11 26	12 2	12 2	12 50	1 33	1 38	1 46	1 58	2 45	3 45	3 55	5 2
Alloway	,,					10 20						1 45					4 3	
Heads of Ayr	,,					10 28			12 22			1 55					4 11	
Dunure	,,					10 34						2 2					4 16	
Knoweside	,,					10 45						2 12					4 24	
Glenside	,,					10 49						2 18					4 31	
Maidens	arr.					10 55			12 39			2 24					4 37	
Turnberry	dep.		8 50			10 59			12 43			2 28					4 42	
	arr.	7G44	9 2	9 37	10 40	11 0	11 11		12 44			2 29					4 43	
Girvan	dep.	8 34		9 55				12 52	12 55	1 40	2 8	2 39		2 23	2 50	3 37	4 35	4 55	5 37
Turnberry	arr.	3 45		10 6														4 42	

WEEK DAYS—Continued. | SUNDAYS.

		P			H											
Glasgow (St. Enoch)	dep.	4 10	5 10		5 52	6 20	6 25	7 30		9 15	10C30	10C40	11C40	4C 0	
	arr.	5 16	6 3	H	7 11	7 37	7 41	8 55	H	10 28	11 36	11 56	12 49	5 13	
Ayr	dep.	5 21	6 5	6 10	6 18	7 16	7 50	7 50	9 0	9 5	9 5	10 35	11 40	12 2	12 55	5 18	
Alloway	,,				6 26						9 15						
Heads of Ayr	,,				6 34						9 24						
Dunure	,,			6 38	6 40	7 35				9 31						
Knoweside	,,				6 49					9 40						
Glenside	,,				6 55	7 49				9 47						
Maidens	,,			6D41	7 1	7 55				9 53						
Turnberry	dep.			6D42	7 5	7 59				9 59						
	arr.					8 0				9 59						
Girvan	arr.	5 56		6D53	7 0	7 20	8 12	8 39	8 39	9 51	9 56	10 11	11 26	12 15	12 37	1 30	5 53
Turnberry	dep.																
	arr.																

A—Pullman Restaurant Car—Glasgow to Ayr.
C—Glasgow (Central Station).
D—First Class Sleeping Accommodation—Turnberry to London (Euston), via Stranraer.
E—On Monday (except July 21st) leave Glasgow at 5.53 a.m.
G—Passengers for Turnberry change at Girvan.
H—Passengers to the Turnberry Line by these Trains change at Ayr.

J—Restaurant Car—Ayr to Stranraer.
K—Restaurant Car—Glasgow to Stranraer.
N—Restaurant Car—Glasgow to Stranraer (Saturdays excepted) and Ayr to Stranraer (Saturdays only).
P—Pullman Restaurant Car—Glasgow to Girvan (via Turnberry).

WEEK DAYS.

				P				G	H	G	H			GJ			K			
Turnberry	dep.						8 50		11 0			12*44				2 29			
Girvan	arr.						9 2		11 30			12*55				2 39			
	dep.	6 5	7B18	7 22	7 47	8 34	8 38	9 55	11 30	12 35	12 53	11 11	12 57	1 42	2 45	3 55	4 40
Turnberry	arr.		7 36	7 57		8 45		10 6		12 46			1 7					
	dep.		7 37	8 2				10 7		12 49			1 8					
Maidens	,,		7 41	8 13				10 18		12 57			1 13					
Glenside	,,			8 19				10 25		1 3			1 19					
Knoweside	,,			8 28	D			10 41		1 12			1 25					
Dunure	,,			8 33				10 49		1 17			1 34					
Heads of Ayr	,,			8 41				10 59		1 22			1 39					
Alloway	,,			8 50		9 15		9 58	12 20		1 33		1 48					
Ayr	arr.	6 40	8 10	8 17									1 36	1 48	1 58	2 18	3 39	4 36	5 31
	dep.	6 45		8 22	9 0		9 20	10 5	11 32	12 28		1 54		2 23	3 48	4 46	5 37
Glasgow (St. Enoch)	arr.	8 0		9 15	10 11		10 22	11 32	11 32	1 54		2 55		3 29	5 23	6 28	6 45

WEEK DAYS—continued. | SUNDAYS.

		N		H	K						H									
Turnberry	dep.										7 59			5*59					
Girvan	arr.								7 20			10*11						
	dep.	5 12	5 7	5 36	6 0	6 1	6 35		7 35	9 25	9 32	10 40	1 30	6 45	7 35	8 50
Turnberry	arr.		5 17														
	dep.		5 18					7 15									
Maidens	,,		5 28					7 21									
Glenside	,,		5 35					7 27									
Knoweside	,,		5 39					7 37									
Dunure	,,		5 44					7 42									
Heads of Ayr	,,		5 50					7 50									
Alloway	,,		5 56					7 59									
Ayr	arr.	5 51	6 4	6 13					8 30	10 0	10 25	11 10	2 5	7 22	8 5	9 23
	dep.	5 55	6 20		7 0	6 58	7 10		8 22	8 40	10 5	10 30	11 15	2 12	7 30	8 10	9 30
Glasgow (St. Enoch)	arr.	7 28	7 28		8 15	8 38	8 12		9 38	10r12	11 15	11 51	12 13	3 30	8 44	9 18	10 44

B—On Mondays (except July 21st), leaves Ayr at 8.15 a.m. and runs through to Glasgow separate from Turnberry portion.
C—Glasgow (Central Station).
D—Calls at Dunure at 7.57 a.m. when required to take up Passengers for Glasgow on notice being given to the Station Master the previous evening.
d—On Wednesdays leaves Ayr at 8.40 p.m. and arrives Glasgow (St. Enoch) at 10.12 p.m.
G—Passengers from Turnberry change at Girvan.

H—Passengers from Turnberry Line by these Trains change at Ayr.
J—Pullman Restaurant Car—Ayr to Glasgow.
K—Restaurant Car—Stranraer to Glasgow.
W—Will not run after August 30th.
P—Pullman Restaurant Car—Girvan to Glasgow, via Turnberry.
r—On Saturdays till August 30th, leaves Ayr at 8.35 p.m. and arrives Glasgow (St. Enoch) at 9.48 p.m. *—Saturdays only.

The last-ever M&DLR summer timetable before the withdrawal of passenger services between Alloway Junction and Turnberry, but with the Ayr-Turnberry services via Maybole retained, from the LMS timetable 7th July to 21st September, 1930.   *G&SWR Association* at Maidens at 6.38, with arrival and departure times of 6.41 and 6.42 from Turnberry, allowing the sleeper passengers to board at Turnberry. Arrival at Girvan was 6.53, and the sleeper coach departed as part of the 7.05 pm ex-Girvan service to Stranraer Town, which had been the 6.10 pm from Ayr via Maybole. The sleeper was detached at Stranraer Town and shunted to Stranraer Harbour for attaching to the Euston service. The essence of the Turnberry-Stranraer sleeper service, in both directions, was:

London Euston	*dep.*	8.00 *pm**	Turnberry	*dep.*	6.42 *pm*
Stranraer Harbour	*arr.*	5.57 *am**	Girvan	*arr.*	6.53
Stranraer Town	*dep.*	7.05	Girvan	*dep.*	7.05
Girvan	*arr.*	8.32	Stranraer Town	*arr.*	8.30
Girvan	*dep.*	8.34	Stranraer Harbour	*dep.*	9.42
Turnberry	*arr.*	8.45	London Euston	*arr.*	7.30 *am*

Notes: * – Depart Euston 8.30 pm on Saturdays and Sundays, arrive Stranraer 5.10 am on Sundays and Mondays, but no sleeper to Turnberry on Sunday mornings. No sleeper from Turnberry on Sunday evenings.

From the introduction of the sleeper service in 1928, the composition of the 6.05 pm train, from the engine backwards, became: a brake composite coach; the *Mary Carmichael* Pullman dining coach; a brake third-class coach; and the sleeper coach. For this train in 1929, the LMS passenger timetable from 8th July to 22nd September indicated the dining coach as 'Pullman Restaurant Car - Glasgow to Girvan (via Turnberry)' and the sleeper coach as 'First Class Sleeping Accommodation - Turnberry to London (Euston), via Stranraer'.

The 1929 sleeper service operated until the end of the summer timetable period on 22nd September; but, unfortunately, patronage had been far short of expectations, and as early as February 1930, there was correspondence from the LMS headquarters at Euston on the matter. On 25th February, John Henry Follows, as the LMS Vice-President in London, informed Sir Edwin Stockton, who was resident in Manchester as the Chairman of the LMS Northern Division - or Scottish - Hotels Committee, of the improved services between London and Turnberry that were to commence on 1st June, 1930. Attention was drawn that passengers from the 9.50 am train from St Pancras would be able to arrive at Turnberry at 8.00 pm, which was 42 minutes quicker than that of the summer of 1929, while passengers leaving Turnberry on the 8.02 am train would have a connection time at Ayr of only 13 minutes compared with 20 minutes in 1929. The night services, with through sleeping cars, were considered satisfactory - these being Euston, depart 8.00 pm, and Turnberry, arrive 8.45 am; and Turnberry, depart 6.42 pm, and Euston, arrive 7.30 am. However, Mr Follows pointed out that there was an average of only one through passenger in each direction each night, and that there was the necessity of running 58 miles between Stranraer and Turnberry for that average of one person. He added that the Euston-Turnberry service, in being continued during the summer of 1930, was provided purely for the accommodation of passengers for Turnberry Hotel and that the circumstances did not justify the running of the services if considered only on the basis of traffic receipts; while he also mentioned that there were proposals for providing Turnberry Hotel with a road motor service, but no details were stated.

Nevertheless, the Turnberry sleeper coach was continued during the corresponding timetable period for 1930 - 7th July to 21st September - and with the same schedule as in 1928 and 1929.

Chapter Twelve

Closures, Retentions and New Services, 1930-1942

It was unfortunate for the railways - though the people could not have realised it at the time - that the beginning of the 20th century, which still witnessed largely horse-drawn vehicles on the roads, heralded another new medium and era in transport, even if there would not be a competitive threat to the railways for many years. The new form of transport was not the electric tram that had been installed mainly in some of the cities and larger towns throughout Britain during the late 1890s and early 1900s. The trams did not generally represent a threat to the trains, for they usually served more local areas within the cities and towns, and they were often complementary to the trains that carried people over greater distances, far beyond the trams' limited extent of operation.

The new transport was the motor car, which had made its appearance even before the end of the 19th century, but its effect on rail transport - both on trains and trams - was negligible during the early 20th century, and, with the trains continuing to reign overall, the subsequent threat of road to rail transport was gradual and subtle, requiring fully two-to-three decades to become noticeable. As had been the case with the trams, the early motor vehicles, in the form of wagonettes, were also complementary to the trains, such that it was not surprising that the eventual damaging more distant future for the railways from motorized transport could not have been foreseen by anyone. In Ayrshire, as in other areas throughout Britain, the gradual improvement and increase in motor transport through the first two decades of the 20th century led to several services of large motor charabancs and small motor buses that were operated by individuals and small companies, but these vehicles still offered only limited competition to the trams and the trains, and only in some towns and districts. Trams were still the most popular and convenient method of transport for large numbers of people over local distances in cities and towns, which was why, as in Ayr and also in Kilmarnock, they continued to survive beside the motor buses. However, further developments occurred in motor transport and buses gradually became bigger and could travel further, into country areas, but, while eminently suitable for local distances, they were not able to rival the train for speed and comfort over longer expanses.

During the early- to mid-1920s, new and larger amalgamated bus companies began to operate in Ayrshire, with longer-distance services, including: Ayr & District Motor Services, extending to New Cumnock in eastern Ayrshire; the Scottish General Transport Company, having transferred its headquarters from Bothwell in Lanarkshire to Kilmarnock, with services connecting Kilmarnock, Troon, Ayr and Dalmellington; the Ardrossan-based amalgamated Ayrshire Bus Owners Association, with its principal route from Ardrossan to Kilmarnock, and having been established for the protection of the constituent companies from the competition of the larger Scottish General, also known as Scottish Transport. Bus competition had already begun to make a detrimental impact on the Kilmarnock tramway system, such that the service to Hurlford closed in 1924 and was replaced by buses, and the remainder of the system closed in 1926.

Bus services were next operated into Ayrshire from places and companies outside the county during the mid-to-late 1920s. In particular, three rival Glasgow-Kilmarnock-Ayr services via Fenwick Moor, over Ayrshire's busiest long route, were provided by Midland Bus Services of Airdrie in Lanarkshire, by Southern Bus Services of Newton Mearns in Renfrewshire, and by Scottish General Transport in Kilmarnock; but three became two when the Midland purchased the Southern in 1929. During the same period, other new companies had appeared, including: Ayrshire Pullman Motor Services, based in Ayr, in running services to Maybole, Girvan, Ballantrae and Newton Stewart; A.A. Motor Services also in Ayr, connecting the county town and Ardrossan; and Clyde Coast Services, running between its Saltcoats headquarters and Largs. Various smaller bus companies also existed in the county, connecting the villages with the towns.

One other advantage for motorized transport that had become evident from the second decade of the 20th century was a double facility that was offered through the interchangeable charabanc, whereby, with the temporary removal of the seats, a sizeable passenger bus could become a vehicle for carrying goods, including farm produce and animals, and it could be changed back again as required. These goods vehicles, known as vans and lorries, were convenient for shorter or local distances as they began to replace horses for haulage; and, while initially working in conjunction with the trains, they would later, like the buses, become a rival to the railways, but the repercussions of this could not have been realised early in the century, and distances that were classed as beyond local became more easily attainable by lorries only after World War I.

Thus, by the end of the 1920s, buses, vans and lorries had become more widespread means of conveyance for people, goods and animals, if still mainly on a local scale, and the impact was increasingly felt by the railway industry, as was in evidence from a few railway closures having first occurred by then nationally. Further closures were implemented during 1930, though then and previously, they applied mostly to passenger traffic, as goods traffic continued, with the implication that passenger traffic was detrimentally affected more than goods traffic. Naturally, small rural branches with sparse traffic were at the greatest risk of closure, and, sadly, this included the scenic Maidens & Dunure Light Railway as an obvious target. The first railway closure in Ayrshire by the LMS as a result of bus competition was the former branch of the Lanarkshire & Ayrshire Railway and Caledonian Railway from Kilwinning to Irvine, when passenger services were withdrawn on 28th July, 1930, as the introduction of cheap fares on the branch had failed to improve the situation.

By at least as early as the summer of 1930 - and possibly well before - there had been contemplation by the LMS of closing the M&DLR to passengers, as was in evidence from the financial involvement of the railway company in an Ayrshire bus company; and, by then, such participation was customary not only for the LMS but for the other three of the 'big four' railway companies of the Grouping. In response to concerns from the railway companies as far back as 1921 about increasing bus competition, this association had resulted directly from the appointment of a royal commission on transport in 1928 by Prime Minister Stanley Baldwin's Conservative government and from the subsequent passing of four Acts of Parliament that year - one each for the LMS, the LNER, the GWR and the SR. This allowed them to become part-operators of the local motor buses within the railway 'territory', and, in effect, to work in conjunction with the competition from the buses and promote the development of the two forms of transport together.

Accordingly a bus service for the coastal road between Ayr and Girvan was initiated during 1930, following the acquisition by the LMS of a shareholding in Ayrshire Pullman Motor Services (APMS) of Ayr back on 1st February of that year. By way of the buses of APMS, a local service had firstly and quickly been introduced to some of the local districts south of Ayr, such as Doonfoot, Alloway, Culroy and Maybole, to provide a direct bus connection with Ayr station 'in furtherance of the road and rail co-ordination policy'. The policy was extended by late July, with the service continued into the districts of the M&DLR, when a new half-hourly bus service, as a 'circular tour' between Ayr and Girvan, operated from the alliance of the LMS and APMS. The outward journey from Ayr station was usually by Doonfoot, Heads of Ayr, Dunure, Croy, Culzean, Maidens and Turnberry, with the return journey by Maidens, Kirkoswald, Maybole, Culroy, Alloway and Doonfoot; but, conveniently for the public, the route could be reversed when circumstances required this, and return tickets between Ayr and Maidens, Turnberry and Girvan were available by either route. The APMS buses were painted in the LMS livery of crimson lake, with the coat of arms on the sides.

The new and frequent Carrick coast bus service encompassed the whole route of the M&DLR, while also connecting the coast with Maybole, and the bus service was ominous for the future of the railway for passenger traffic, though the LMS was not concerned about the competition because of its financial interest in the bus company for serving the coastal area. LMS passenger services of trains and buses were now running side-by-side along the Carrick coast from July 1930, and with the train still providing a restaurant service between Glasgow and Turnberry in both directions. Naturally, there seemed no point, and no financial logic, in the LMS retaining a train and a bus service over the same route, and through the summer and autumn of 1930, deliberation had been given to the withdrawal of the railway services, which meant passenger traffic between Alloway Junction and Turnberry, with the line south of Turnberry remaining open for passengers. These thoughts of closure were reinforced at a meeting of the Traffic & Works Sub-Committee of the LMS Northern Division's Scottish Local Committee in Glasgow on 21st October, 1930, under the matter of 'Maidens & Dunure Light Railway: Proposed Withdrawal of the Passenger Train Service between Ayr and Turnberry':

The Chief General Superintendent [Charles Byrom] reported that notwithstanding the granting of cheap fare facilities, the passenger traffic originating on the Maidens & Dunure Light Railway has rapidly diminished as a result of motor bus competition and he recommended, as the company has acquired an interest in the road transport in the area:

(1) That the passenger train service between Ayr and Turnberry should be withdrawn, leaving the passenger traffic to be dealt with by omnibuses of an associated road undertaking.

(2) That, as from 1st December, 1930, Alloway, Heads of Ayr, Dunure, Knoweside, Glenside and Maidens stations should be closed for passenger traffic and the halt at Balchriston level crossing should be closed entirely.

(3) That the stations concerned should continue to deal with and account for parcels, miscellaneous and livestock traffics, such traffics to be conveyed by freight train.

(4) That an augmented rail service should be provided between Girvan and Turnberry which would ensure a connection to and from Turnberry with most main line trains at Girvan.

The LMS representatives at the meeting heard that the withdrawal of the passenger train service would enable an estimated saving of £1,272 per annum to be effected and that the leasing of certain accommodation at the stations and the making of alterations in the permanent way and signalling was being considered to effect further economy.

It was not surprising that such measures were thought necessary. The line, in traversing through a sparsely-populated farming and fishing district, could not provide a large passenger-traffic revenue, and, although there had been realistic hopes by the G&SWR that an increase in population would take place over the years, no newcomers in significant numbers arrived, and the line remained largely patronized by a limited number of the more affluent passengers in the form of golfers. Certainly, the local people used the line as they needed it, but there were too few of them to make it profitable. Furthermore, aside from the golfing resort of Turnberry, the stretch of coast between Ayr and Girvan, in spite of its rugged and invigorating nature and its magnificent sea views, had never been developed to the required extent to induce sufficient holiday visitors, with the quaint but unexpanded villages of Maidens and Dunure being the largest intermediate settlements. Perhaps the name 'Maidens & Dunure' for the railway had been an attempt to publicize the villages and boost them into larger resorts; but this did not happen, and the settlement of Turnberry, the principal place of attraction, increased only from a hamlet to a village. Ultimately, Turnberry Hotel and its golfers could not justify the trains continuing to serve the district in an era of changing transport circumstances.

Turnberry Hotel and the former Caledonian Railway golfing hotel of the LMS at Gleneagles in Perthshire had also suffered a recent diminished patronage, as had been explained at a meeting of the Hotels Sub-Committee of the LMS Scottish Local Committee in Glasgow on 9th September, 1930:

> The Controller [of LMS Hotels, Arthur Towle] reported that from experience gained during the last few months in the company's hotels, as well as from information he had obtained from other hotels both in this country and in western Europe generally, hotel business on a considerably lower level than last year must be expected for a time.
>
> He further reported that during the winter months, Gleneagles Hotel and Turnberry Hotel were largely dependent on guests coming from Glasgow and the vicinity and that as there was barely sufficient business even in normal winter times for both these hotels he asked [for] instructions with regard to the closing of one or both of them after the New Year until Easter.

The closing of Gleneagles for the winter was then recommended, with Turnberry to remain open, at a time when there was an unexpected decline in the hotel business.

This decline was simply one of many consequences of an economic industrial crisis on a global scale, which had begun in America with the financial disintegration of the New York stock exchange in 1929, to spread quickly to Europe and elsewhere, causing an ongoing reduction in industrial output and an increase in unemployment (and which later became known as the 'Great Depression' after the effects of its severity and duration were fully realized). Britain and Scotland - especially industrial cities, including Glasgow - were adversely affected by unemployment and poverty, and businesses, transport, holidays and related sports and pastimes were in a dispirited state.

From the start of the APMS-LMS bus service in the summer of 1930 along the route of the M&DLR, there had naturally been rumours of the impending withdrawal of the passenger train traffic. However, the train service was still indicated in the recently-issued 1930-31 winter timetable, having commenced from 22nd September; and with no foreknowledge or experience of the strategies that would be adopted by railway companies for passenger closures, the public - including railway enthusiasts - thought that the appearance of the M&DLR service in the forthcoming timetable meant a reprieve from closure. There had been no reason to think that the service would cease during the timetable period, because the winter timetable for the M&DLR was accompanied by the statement that the services were to be 'altered and amplified' from 1st June, 1931, and the timetable read as follows:

		am	am	Sa pm	pm	pm	pm	Sa pm
Ayr	dep.		10.12	12.02	1.38	3.55	6.13	9.05
Alloway			10.20		1.46	4.03	6.21	9.15
Heads of Ayr			10.28		1.55	4.11	6.29	9.24
Dunure			10.33	12.22	2.00	4.16	6.34	9.31
Knoweside			10.42		2.09	4.25	6.43	9.40
Glenside			10.48		2.15	4.31	6.49	9.47
Maidens			10.54	12.38	2.21	4.37	6.55	9.53
Turnberry	arr.		10.58	12.43	2.25	4.42	6.59	9.58
Turnberry	dep.	8.50	10.59	12.44	2.26	4.43	7.02	9.59
Girvan	arr.	9.02	11.10	12.55	2.36	4.55	7.13	10.11

		M am	am	am	M-F pm	Sa pm	pm	pm
Girvan	dep.	7.22	7.40	8.25	12.35	12.57	5.07	8.44 A
Turnberry	arr.	7.33	7.50	8.37	12.45	1.07	5.17	8.55 A
Turnberry	dep.	7.37	7.55		12.46	1.08	5.18	
Maidens		7.41	8.00		12.51	1.13	5.23	
Glenside			8.06		12.57	1.19	5.29	
Knoweside			8.12		1.03	1.25	5.35	
Dunure		7.57 D	8.21		1.12	1.34	5.44	
Heads of Ayr			8.26		1.17	1.39	5.49	
Alloway			8.35		1.25	1.48	5.56	
Ayr	arr.	8.17	8.43		1.33	1.58	6.04	

Notes: A - Will only run when there are passengers for Turnberry by 9.50 am from London St Pancras. D - Calls at Dunure when required to take up passengers for Glasgow St Enoch on notice being given to the station master the previous evening. Sa - Saturdays. M - Mondays. M-F - Mondays to Fridays.

Unfortunately, that was to be the last timetable for the whole of the route of M&DLR, because the decision about the line's future from LMS headquarters at Euston was made public - if hardly prominent - only two months after the starting date of the timetable that was supposedly to operate through and beyond the winter. The dreaded pronouncement was that the line would to be closed to all passenger trains north of Turnberry but that Turnberry station would remain open for passenger services to and from Girvan. Thus, in the issue of the *Ayrshire Post* of 21st November, 1930 - but placed inconspicuously under a section called 'Jottings' on page 9 - there was the following notification:

From the beginning of December further reductions are being made in the London, Midland & Scottish services in Scotland. Passenger traffic to Turnberry will be worked via Girvan, and the line from Ayr to Turnberry which serves the Heads of Ayr, Dunure and other small towns will be closed to passengers.

The end of the service north of Turnberry was also briefly announced in the nationally-published *Railway Gazette* of London on 28th November, which was only three days before the official closure date of 1st December:

Further Scottish Stations to Be Closed. It is understood that, commencing December 1st, LMS passenger traffic to Turnberry will be worked via Girvan, and the line from Ayr to Turnberry closed to passengers.

Such scant publicity vividly signified the lack of consideration from the LMS to the closure, and the subsequent apparent lack of concern, locally and nationally, with no protests, resulted from the fact that there was no concept as to a procedure for complaints or appeals, at a time when railway companies could remove trains without having to consult the public and the local authorities who depended on the services. The sudden closure had come as a surprise to the local people, and even to the line's employees, in having been unaware of the internal railway discussions during the previous months.

Someone who was aware of the possibility of the withdrawal of the whole passenger service was Jim Aird of Prestwick, as an enthusiast of railways and transport in general, and who had been 'assured' at Heads of Ayr station in September 1930 that the service was not being withdrawn, because it was shown in the winter timetable. His visit then was on a warm and sunny day, when, in resting on a grassy slope beside the line and eating brambles near Bracken Bay, he witnessed a train from Girvan coming round the cliff edge and conveying the Turnberry sleeper coach to Ayr for cleaning; and soon afterwards, a southbound goods train passed.

Jim was determined that he would travel on the last train, which was the 9.05 pm Saturdays-only service from Ayr to Girvan on 29th November, and with no Sunday service on the line, this was two days before the official closure date of Monday 1st December, when no trains would run. His journey was on a crisp and clear moonlit night, which allowed the route to be seen better in the darkness. The last train, of two unheated passenger coaches and a brake van, was crowded from Ayr, but gradually it emptied, and Jim observed a stout elderly lady alight at the tiny platform of Balchriston halt and slip and slide down the frosty platform's ramp, with the contents of her shopping scattering in all directions. After Maidens, he was left with a solitary companion who turned out to be one of the Turnberry signalmen and who expressed his anger at the finish of the passenger service. Girvan station was not ready to receive the train and it remained at the No. 1 signal box in the moonlight, until, finally, it and its last two travellers reached the platform. Jim then clambered down, half-frozen, as the train's only official passenger, and therefore he laid claim to closing the Turnberry road's passenger service; but he was apparently not expected because there was no one to collect his ticket! A battery of fog-signals had heralded the arrival and departure of the train at each intermediate station.

That ended the passenger service over most of the extent of the M&DLR, leaving only the passenger service between Girvan and Turnberry and the goods and seasonal potato trains over the whole line, such that it was no doubt eerily strange and sad for the local people no longer to see and hear passenger trains trundling over the route between Alloway and Turnberry.

After the 1930 withdrawal, a local timetable was arranged for a shuttle service between Girvan and Turnberry, providing for several through workings to and from Glasgow and other good connections at Girvan, with the journey time being no greater for Turnberry than previously via the light railway northwards. The 1931 timetables, in declaring that the local stations from Alloway to Maidens were now closed for passenger traffic, advertised the replacement bus service of Messrs Ayrshire Pullman Motor Co., though the bus times were not published in the

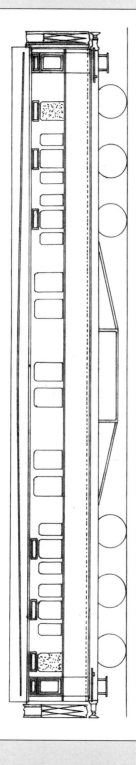

The LMS 12-wheeled, 68 ft composite sleeping coach that was used on the Turnberry–Euston services during the 1930s, accommodating six first class and 16 second class passengers. There were six separate single-berth first class compartments (middle section, with larger windows), containing a fully made-up bed, and two third class compartments (on either side, with three smaller windows), containing four berths in two-tier bunks, comprising only a pillow and blanket. At each end of the coach was a lavatory (with a window of frosted or opaque glass, as indicated by the stippling), and between one lavatory and the passenger door (right) was the sleeping-car attendant's compartment. Six coaches were built in 1930 and six in 1931, and they were therefore available by the time of the decision to widen the scope of the Turnberry sleeper service to include third class. They were the first composite sleeping coaches in Britain, in providing both first and third class accommodation in one vehicle, and the third class compartments were also convertible to seating for day use by folding away the top bunks. This coach was not the same type that inaugurated the Turnberry sleeper service in 1928, which was an LNWR first class, 12-wheeled clerestory coach, 65 ft long and built for the LNWR and Caledonian West Coast Joint Stock routes. The decision in 1932 by the LMS Northern Division to augment the Turnberry sleeper service, instead of possibly withdrawing it, and to add third class accommodation meant that two coaches were needed when justified by traffic; or, alternatively, for lighter traffic, the use of the LMS sleeper composite needed only a single coach. In effect, the composite sleeper could have been 'tailor-made' for the Turnberry service.

Drawn by S. Rankin

railway timetable. In the summer timetable from 6th July to 13th September, 1931, there was a frequent service between Girvan and Turnberry - in part, hourly and with Turnberry receiving more trains than previously by the whole line - including six through Glasgow-Turnberry workings in each direction per day, to produce a total of 12 trains per day to Turnberry and 13 from Turnberry. The London Euston-Turnberry first-class sleeper coach via Stranraer continued to run during the summer of 1931, still arriving at Turnberry as the 8.34 am from Girvan, proceeding back via Girvan before travelling empty - now via Maybole - to Ayr for cleaning and day-stabling. On returning to Turnberry from Ayr via Maybole to Girvan - and probably attached to the 5.02 pm ex-Ayr - the sleeper coach departed from Turnberry as part of the 6.25 pm local service to Girvan and then from Girvan at 6.50 for Stranraer Town, which was still the 5.10 pm ex-Glasgow that ran faster by cutting out nearly all the stops between Ayr and Girvan. In 1929 and 1930, the main-line portion via Maybole had been purposely slowed between Ayr and Girvan, having called at all the stations, allowing the M&DLR portion - running 'express', although at only 25 mph - to reach Girvan first; but by 1931, with no coastal portion, the slower service on the main line was no longer necessary, and the main-line portion called only at Maybole.

The Turnberry-Girvan timetable, with Glasgow and London through coaches, from 6th July to 13th September, 1931, read:

Dep. Turnberry for Girvan: 7.25 am G, 8.00 G, 8.50, 10.15, 11.15 G, 12.50 pm G M-F, 12.54 G Sa, 2.26 G Sa, 2.30 G M-F, 5.15 G, 6.25 L, 7.09, 7.40, 9.15 Sa, and 10.20 Sa.
Dep. Girvan for Turnberry: 7.33 am, 8.34 L, 9.50, 10.48 G, 12.30 pm M-F, 12.40 G Sa, 2.13 G, 4.45G, 5.45, 6.46 G, 7.18 G, 8.39 Sa, and 10.05 Sa.

Notes: L - Through sleeper London Euston-Turnberry or vice versa via Stranraer. G - Through coach Glasgow St Enoch-Turnberry or vice versa. M-F - Mondays to Fridays. Sa - Saturdays.

The withdrawal of passenger trains between Alloway Junction and Turnberry was followed by another 'rail' closure nearby, when the whole of the Ayr tramway system from Prestwick to Alloway ceased to operate at the end of 1931, after 30 years of largely profitable existence but with serious financial losses latterly because of the competition from buses. From the purchase in November 1931 of the Scottish General Transport Company by the Scottish Motor Traction Company of Edinburgh, the latter company had also purchased the Ayr tramway, with the last trams having run late on Thursday 31st December, 1931 and the bus service having commenced on New Year's Day. In June 1932, Western Scottish Motor Traction (Western SMT) was formed, with its headquarters in Kilmarnock, as the subsidiary for south-western Scotland of the parent company in Edinburgh, and purchase of some local bus companies in Ayrshire by SMT soon proceeded, including the takeover of Ayr & District Motor Services and Ayrshire Pullman Motor Services.

A year and a half after the cessation of the Alloway Junction-Turnberry passenger service, consideration was given by the LMS to a new limited passenger service over the whole line, with two trains only in the northbound direction and for the benefit of Turnberry Hotel. As the provision of a train service was intricately connected with the success of the hotel, the question of better communication with Turnberry was raised by the Hotels Sub-Committee of the Scottish Local Committee, especially in view of a drastic alternative that had been suggested of withdrawing the passenger service between Girvan and Turnberry and, therefore, the entire passenger service on the line. At a meeting on 17th May, 1932 in Glasgow, the Hotels Sub-Committee 'were of the opinion that no time should be lost in deciding on proper communication either by train or suitable hotel omnibus running to and from Kilmarnock, Mauchline or Ayr'. However, at a meeting on 14th June, the Hotels Sub-Committee ultimately decided that 'it was not considered that the institution of an omnibus service between Turnberry Hotel and Ayr, Mauchline or Kilmarnock, as required, would result in attracting more business to Turnberry Hotel'. The outcome was the following services between London and Turnberry during the summer of 1932, including the introduction over the whole of the M&DLR of two new 'experimental' trains, as they were referred to by the LMS:

From London to Turnberry:
9.50 am from St Pancras - with a change at Mauchline only.
8.00 pm from Euston - with first class sleeping accommodation through to Turnberry. (Consideration is being given to third class sleeping accommodation being also provided.) The question of continuing the above service during the winter months was under consideration by the Chief General Superintendent [Charles Byrom].

From Turnberry to London:
8.30 am (New experimental train) - to run via the Maidens line and to connect at Kilmarnock with the 9.20 am train from Glasgow (St Enoch) to London (St Pancras).
6.25 pm - with sleeping car accommodation via Stranraer (as last year).
8.30 pm Saturdays excepted (New experimental train) - to run via the Maidens line and to connect at Kilmarnock with the 9.15 pm train from Glasgow (St Enoch) to London (St Pancras).

The 8.30 am and 8.30 pm experimental trains from Turnberry were the 8.15 am and 8.15 pm from Girvan to Kilmarnock, operating Mondays to Saturdays and calling only at Turnberry on the M&DLR, to provide connection at Kilmarnock with the morning and night expresses from St Enoch to St Pancras and thereby reducing the number of changes required for Turnberry passengers elsewhere through England. The services also contained a through coach from Turnberry to Glasgow, via Kilwinning and Paisley, and this was attached at Ayr to the Glasgow train. The experimental trains began on Monday 4th July, 1932, in appearing in the timetable from 4th July to 11th September, 1932, becoming, in effect, Ayr-Kilmarnock local services that were extended backwards to start at Girvan. The morning train called at Newton-on-Ayr, Prestwick, Monkton, Troon, Barassie and Drybridge, which meant all stations except Gatehead, while the evening train called at the same stations, except Monkton and Gatehead.

For Turnberry-bound passengers by the 9.50 am service from St Pancras - as had been intended by the LMS for the experimental services - there was only one change of train at Mauchline, and this was because a evening connecting train, which also commenced on 4th July, 1932, operated from Mauchline directly to Ayr and Turnberry on Mondays to Saturdays. It was the continuation of the Mauchline-Ayr connecting service that had been introduced in 1929, and the stations and times for 1932 were: Mauchline, depart 6.10 pm; Ayr, arrive 6.25, and depart 6.27; Maybole, depart 6.45; Girvan, arrive 7.02, and depart 7.04; and Turnberry, arrive 7.15 pm.

Additionally on 4th July, 1932, a sleeper composite coach, of first-class and third-class accommodation, in place of the first-class sleeper, was introduced on the service between Turnberry and Euston in both directions. The aim was to try to widen the appeal of the sleeper service, which was augmented by a brake composite coach, of first-class and third-class seated accommodation; and, therefore, in 1932, two coaches operated between Turnberry and Euston via Stranraer.

On 1st August, 1932, an engine failure occurred on one of the experimental services, as had been noted soon afterwards by David L. Smith, a railway enthusiast from Dalmellington. While hauling the 8.15 pm from Girvan to Kilmarnock via Turnberry, it developed a problem with the boiler and came to a stop on the single line at Knoweside, where there was no telegraphic communication. The train was uncoupled from the engine and sleepers were placed into the firebox, such that sufficient steam was raised in the boiler to move the engine alone to Heads of Ayr, where assistance was summoned. The service train ultimately reached Ayr at 10.20 pm, with passengers for the London train conveyed via Annbank to Mauchline by a replacement engine. The London express was scheduled to pass Mauchline at 10.09 pm where the signalman had been instructed to stop the express to allow the connection. On the shorter route of 11½ miles from Ayr to Mauchline via Annbank, and with no stops, compared with 25¼ miles via Kilmarnock and with several stops, the train reached Mauchline at about 10.40 pm, allowing the express to depart possibly at about 10.45, only half an hour late.

For the winter timetable from 12th September, 1932 until further notice, the morning train was adjusted to run 15 minutes earlier, with departures of 8.00 am from Girvan and 8.15 am from Turnberry, calling at the same stations as previously, and still containing the through coach for Glasgow; but the evening service no longer provided the through coach from that date, before it ceased, with the last train running on Friday 30th September. In the opposite direction, the evening Mauchline-Ayr-Turnberry service that connected with the morning train from St Pancras, departed at 6.05 pm, to run unconditionally to Ayr, but it became conditional from Ayr to Turnberry, with a footnote stating: 'Will be run only for passengers from stations south of Carlisle'. Therefore, when there were such passengers - even just one - the train proceeded to Turnberry, with an arrival time of 7.10 pm, and when there was none, there was no service.

The experimental service was affected by another occurrence in December 1932, in the form of flooding on the line, for during the weekend before the Christmas weekend, unusually prolonged and heavy rainfall, partly accompanied by strong winds, had fallen in Ayrshire and throughout south-western Scotland. The weather station at Turnberry Hotel, which was officially recognised by the Air Ministry Meteorological Office and where the readings were taken by the hotel staff, recorded high rainfall from Friday 16th to Monday 19th December. This coastal rainfall was augmented by even heavier rainfall over the Carrick hills immediately to the east, resulting in the saturation of the high ground, such that the water tumbled down the steep hillsides and submerged much of the flatter coastal strips. By Tuesday, 20th, when the rain had significantly eased but with the water having accumulated over the past few days, there was still heavy flooding along the coast; and it was on this day that the 8.00 am train from Girvan via Turnberry to Ayr and Kilmarnock was stopped at Dunure station by a depth of five feet of water and was compelled to return to Girvan and run to Ayr via Maybole.

Unfortunately, the experimental service appeared not to have been a success, with, firstly, the last evening train having run on Friday 30th September, 1932 and then the last morning train running on Friday 31st March, 1933; but it is probable that the service was originally provided only as an appeasement to Turnberry Hotel and was not expected to last long by the LMS railway authorities. The train possibly consisted of two or three coaches to carry a few passengers, and the extent of the timetable for the service during its full period of 1932-33 was:

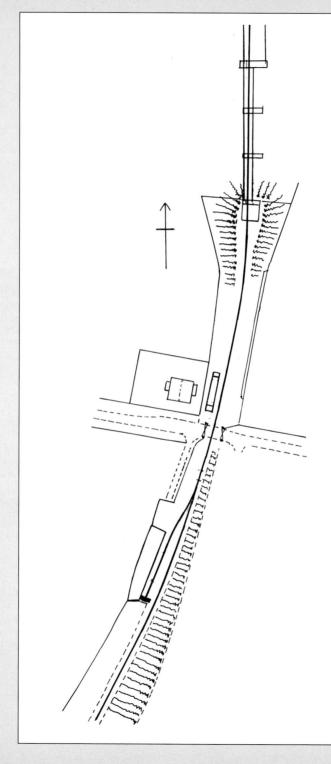

Balchriston in the mid-1930s, showing the level crossing, the railway cottages and the inferred position and size of the halt north of the crossing, with the Rancleugh viaduct further north and the position and size of the siding and loading bank south of the crossing. The halt and siding were not in use during the same years. Also depicted are the embankment at the southern end of the viaduct and the start of the cutting through Culzean estate.

Drawn by S. Rankin

		A TG	B TG	A TG	C
		am	am	pm	pm
Girvan	dep.	8.15	8.00	8.15	8.15
Turnberry	arr.	8.26	8.11	8.26	8.26
Turnberry	dep.	8.30	8.15	8.30	8.30
Ayr	arr.	9.07	8.55	9.07	9.07
Ayr	dep.	9.09	9.09	9.09	9.09
Kilmarnock	arr.	9.50	9.45	9.44	9.44

Connection for London St Pancras

Kilmarnock	dep.	9.55	10.04	9.50	9.50

Notes: A - 4th July to 11th September, 1932. B - From 12th September, 1932 but ceased (last train ran) 31st March, 1933. C - From 12th September but ceased (last train ran) 30th September, 1932. TG - Through coach Turnberry-Glasgow St Enoch via Kilwinning and Paisley.

During the period of the experimental service, the line north of Turnberry had still been officially regarded as closed to passengers, with none of the intermediate stations reopened and the public timetables repeated that Ayrshire Pullman Motor Services provided buses. However, by this time APMS had been incorporated into Western SMT, but it is likely that the company name and livery of the buses had not yet been changed.

A summarized indication of winter running of through coaches between Glasgow and Turnberry via Girvan after the 1930 withdrawal was provided by the timetable commencing 12th September, 1932 until further notice:

		am	pm	pm	pm
Glasgow St Enoch	dep.	8.45	12.30*	2.15	5.10*
Turnberry	arr.	10.45	2.24 Sa	4.49	6.54

		am	pm	pm	pm
Turnberry	dep.	11.20	2.34 Sa	5.26	8.27 Sa
Glasgow St Enoch	arr.	1.52 pm	5.20	7.25*	10.25*

Notes: * Stranraer train, otherwise Turnberry train terminating or starting Girvan. Sa - Through coach Saturdays on Turnberry branch.

Goods traffic continued on the line, much as in the past, and the famous Carrick early potatoes still formed an important staple traffic every year between May and August. Balchriston was one farm where the potatoes were grown in large quantities, and a siding was considered for the location in 1933. At a meeting of the Traffic Sub-Committee of the LMS Northern Division in Glasgow on 16th May, 1933, it was reported that Mr J. Lyburn of Balchriston farm had made an application to the company for 'a siding connection and loading bank accommodation' for his farm and that the cost of the work was estimated at £695. However, Mr Lyburn had stated that he was not prepared to pay this sum but that he had applied to pay the company £50 per annum for a period of 19 years, which was the unexpired period of his lease at Balchriston farm; and it was recommended at the meeting that the work should be carried out and that Mr Lyburn's offer should be accepted. It was further explained that the provision of the siding would secure Mr Lyburn's potato traffic and manure traffic to the railway, with the conveyance charges amounting to £600 per annum. It is probable that the siding and loading bank were quickly constructed in late May or early June to allow Mr Lyburn's potatoes to be transported from the siding during the imminent season. Presumably, Mr Lyburn would previously have had to take the potatoes to Glenside, possibly by horse and cart even then, for conveyance by rail, which seemed inappropriate when the line passed near Balchriston farm and his potatoes crossed the line at Balchriston to head for Glenside.

Through the mid-to-late 1930s, a frequent and consistent set of timings for the Girvan-Turnberry service was maintained, with only slight changes between different years, as represented by July in 1935, 1937 and 1939:

Depart Girvan for Turnberry			*Depart Turnberry for Girvan*		
July 1935	*July 1937*	*July 1939*	*July 1935*	*July 1937*	*July 1939*
am	*am*	*am*	*am*	*am*	*am*
7.08 M	7.08 M	7.08 M	7.30 M R	7.32 M R	7.33 M R
7.40	7.44	7.44	8.00	8.00	8.00
8.43L	8.55 L	8.55 L	9.00	9.24	9.20
9.40	9.40	9.40		9.59	9.59
10.40	10.40	10.40	10.00		
			11.23	11.21	11.22
pm	*pm*	*pm*			
12.30 M-F	12.25 Sa	12.25 Sa	*pm*	*pm*	*pm*
12.35 Sa	12.30 M-F	12.30 M-F	12.55	12.53	12.51
	12.36 Sa	12.38 Sa	2.39 Sa	2.45 Sa	2.46 Sa
2.04 M-F	2.14 Sa	2.11Sa			4.57
4.31	4.30	4.27	5.05	5.05	
5.57	5.54	5.53	6.15 L	6.15 L	6.15 L
6.37 R	6.35 R	6.35 R			6.53 Sa
7.24 M-F*	7.14 Sa*	7.15Sa*	7.00	7.00 M-F	7.00 M-F
7.25 Sa	7.23 M-F*	7.24 M-F	7.40 Sa	7.01 Sa	7.30 Sa
			8.05 M-F	7.35 Sa	8.07 M-F
				8.05 M-F	

Notes: R - Restaurant car, Glasgow-Turnberry or vice versa. L - Through coach, and sleeper when demand required, London Euston-Turnberry or vice versa via Stranraer. M - Mondays. M-F - Mondays to Fridays. Sa - Saturdays. * - M-F or Sa as indicated, connections Mauchline-Turnberry, dep. Mauchline 6.05 pm in 1935 and 1937 and 6.10 pm in 1939, with passengers changing at Ayr and Girvan.

The first train of the day, on Mondays only as the 7.08 am from Girvan to Turnberry, had the purpose of being positioned to form the first service from Turnberry in serving passengers who had spent the weekend at Turnberry but who had to return to their employment on that day. The train, conveying the *Mary Carmichael* Pullman restaurant car, returned from Turnberry to Girvan to join the express service to Glasgow, although the LMS, having purchased the Pullman cars on 4th December, 1933, had incorporated them into their own stock and livery and had discontinued the Pullman name by applying running numbers instead.

Consistency of timings had also applied to the Turnberry sleeper during the summers of the 1930s. From the timetable that had commenced on 12th September, 1932 and until further notice, the sleeper service was extended beyond the summer, and it appeared in the timetable for April 1933, implying that the passenger patronage had increased sufficiently. On occasions from 1932, when there was greater than the usual demand - possibly rare and during specific summer-holiday periods and at Christmas and New Year - the sleeper composite was replaced by a first-class sleeper coach and a third-class sleeper coach, such that, including the brake composite coach that still operated, there were then three coaches serving Turnberry from and to Stranraer.

Also, during 1933, the sleeper coach or coaches began terminating at and departing from Stranraer when there were no passengers to or from Turnberry, but the brake composite coach still ran between Stranraer and Turnberry. If there were no northbound passengers to Turnberry, the sleeper remained at Stranraer; and if there were southbound passengers from Turnberry the next evening, they were directed to board the brake composite at Turnberry, which was attached at Girvan to the Stranraer train, and then to board the sleeper at Stranraer.

		July 1931	July 1932	July 1933	July 1935	July 1937	July 1939
Turnberry	dep.	6.25 pm	6.25 pm	6.20 pm	6.15 pm	6.15 pm	6.15 pm
Girvan	arr.	6.37	6.36	6.31	6.26	6.26	6.26
Girvan	dep.	6.50	6.48	6.47	6.45	6.39	6.39
Stranraer Town	arr.	8.16	8.16	8.08	8.05	8.00	8.00
Stranraer Hbr	dep.	9.42	9.42	9.42	9.42	9.55	9.37
London Euston	arr.	7.30 am	7.30 am	7.30 am	7.30 am	7.30 am	7.30 am
London Euston	dep.	8.00 pm	8.00 pm	7.30 pm	8.00 pm	8.00 pm	8.00 pm
Stranraer Hbr	arr.	5.10 am	5.10 am	5.10 am	5.10 am	5.10 am	5.08 am
Stranraer Town	dep.	7.05	7.05	7.15	7.15	7.25	7.25
Girvan	arr.	8.32	8.32	8.36	8.35	8.46	8.46
Girvan	dep.	8.34	8.34	8.37	8.43	8.55	8.55
Turnberry	arr.	8.45	8.45	8.48	8.54	9.06	9.06

Coach classes	SLF	SLC & BCK
for both directions		but with SLF and SLT replacing SLC when required by sufficient demand

Notes: No sleeper from Turnberry on Sunday evenings. No sleeper to Turnberry on Sunday mornings. Standard abbreviations for coach types: SLF - sleeper first class; SLC - sleeper composite first and third class; SLT - sleeper third class; BCK - brake-van composite, seating first class and third class, in addition to conveying guard, luggage and parcels. The SLC was introduced on 4th July, 1932, but in July 1934, the SLC, or an SLF and an SLT as two coaches, ran between London and Stranraer, with a BCK between Stranraer and Turnberry.

While the Turnberry-Girvan, the Turnberry-Glasgow and the Turnberry-London services had kept the southernmost five miles of the branch in passenger use during the 1930s, a spectacular international occasion in Glasgow, in the early summer of 1938, had provided the rare opportunity for a one-day special passenger train to run over the whole of the M&DLR for the benefit of the local people of Carrick. The large-scale event, having been scheduled to last six months from the beginning of May until the end of October, was the British Empire Exhibition that was being held in promotion of the revival and promotion of Glasgow's industry, culture and heritage within the British Empire in the gradual economic recovery in the aftermath of the Great Depression. Special excursion trains were operated by the LMS to convey people to the exhibition at Bellahouston Park, south-west of the city centre,

Sometime between 1936 and 1939, the stations of the M&DLR were photographed by a Latin professor at Glasgow University, Christian James Fordyce, and, thanks to his interest as a likely railway enthusiast, the next seven photographs illustrate how the buildings and platforms appeared long into the LMS period. Alloway station, looking east, mid- to late-1930s, with the platform's flower beds no longer flourishing. The northern line is in place though it may not have been used for through traffic, and by the late 1930s, it had become a siding with buffers housing two railway camping coaches for holidaymakers.   *G&SWR Association*

Heads of Ayr station, looking east, mid- to late-1930s. Only the southern line is in use at the opposite side of the island platform, with a solitary wagon visible in the goods yard and with the nameboard still present several years after the station's closure to passengers.
G&SWR Association

Dunure station, looking north-east, mid-to-late 1930s. The eastern line has been removed, though the goods yard was still in use via the Ayr-facing points beyond the platform. There is a different goods shed, further from the station, than at the time of the line's opening and the stairway was the public entrance that led from the Fisherton-Dunure road. *G&SWR Association*

Knoweside station, looking south, mid- to late-1930s . There was no station building - just a small shelter - but the short curved platform managed to accommodate two nameboards, even though the station served no village. The timber trestle supports the water tank.

G&SWR Association

Glenside station, looking south-west, mid- to late-1930s, with the station nameboard built on the platform ramp, as at Turnberry. The station building at its southern end contained the private waiting room for the Marquis of Ailsa and in the distance is the Glenside Avenue bridge.
G&SWR Association

Maidens station, looking north-east, mid- to late-1930s, with both lines through the island platform remaining in use for goods trains. *G&SWR Association*

Turnberry station and hotel, looking north, mid- to late-1930s, with the station still in use for the Girvan-Turnberry passenger shuttle. The loop and its short siding to the buffers are seen in the middle distance as the line and loop curve to the right in the distance towards Turnberry Big Wood, while the points and the start of the siding for the hotel are discernible immediately beyond the platform.   *G&SWR Association*

and one of those trains was arranged to traverse the coastal route from Girvan to Ayr. The date was Friday 20th May, 1938, when two locomotives were positioned at Girvan station to haul a train of what was said to consist of seven or eight LMS non-corridor coaches. The majority of the passengers boarded at Girvan, in taking advantage of a run, as a novelty, over the scenic coastal line that was otherwise closed to them; and the train departed at 8.40 am, to call at all the original passenger stations except Heads of Ayr, with the service terminating at Ibrox station, a short walking distance north of Bellahouston Park. Unfortunately, the passengers were denied an intended return trip over the line because, after concerns by the signalman at Girvan station, information had reached Glasgow headquarters that the two locomotives were too heavy for the coastal line, which was untrue, and the train was forced to proceed to Girvan via Maybole, with passengers for the intermediate stations between Ayr and Girvan conveyed by bus.

Another new Turnberry service had been initiated from the timetable of 4th June, 1938. In addition to the 6.15 pm through sleeper from Turnberry to London Euston, a train left Turnberry at 8.07 pm to run via Girvan to Kilmarnock, arriving there at 9.36 and connecting with the 9.15 pm sleeper service from St Enoch, except on Saturdays, departing Kilmarnock at 9.52 to London St Pancras. The arrangement therefore involved only the one change of train - at Kilmarnock - for passengers from Turnberry, and the service was continued during 1939. A less convenient connecting service for Turnberry operated in the reverse direction, from the St Pancras-St Enoch sleeper, but with changes at Ayr and Girvan, as follows: St Pancras, depart 9.30 pm; Kilmarnock, arrive 6.47 am, and depart 7.05; Ayr, arrive 7.37, and depart 8.39; Girvan, arrive 9.33, and depart 9.40; and Turnberry arrive 9.51 am.

LONDON, MIDLAND AND SCOTTISH
RAILWAY.

EMPIRE
EXHIBITION,
1938. SCOTLAND. 1938.
Bellahouston Park, Glasgow.

SPECIAL EXCURSIONS
On WEDNESDAY, 18th MAY,

		a.m.	Return Fares. s. d.
New Luce, ... leave		9.26	8 3
Glenwhilly, ... ,,		9.38	8 3
Pinwherry, ... ,,		10.4	7 3
Pinmore, ... ,,		10.12	7 3
Girvan, ... ,,		10.25	6 9
Maybole, ... ,,		10.50	5 1
Ibrox, ... arrive		12.0	
Glasgow (St. Enoch), ... ,,		12.10	

Returning from Glasgow (St. Enoch) at 7.45, and Ibrox at 7.50 p.m.

	a.m.	Return Fares. s. d.
Girvan, ... leave	10.55	5 9
Maybole, ... ,,	11.15	4 9
Bellahouston Park, ... arr.	12.42p	

Returning from Bellahouston Park by any afternoon or evening train.

On FRIDAY, 20th MAY.

	a.m.	s. d.
Girvan, ... leave	8.40	6 3
Turnberry, ... ,,	8.50	5 9
Maidens, ... ,,	8.59	5 9
Glenside, ... ,,	9. 8	5 9
Knowside, ... ,,	9.15	5 3
Dunure, ... ,,	9.27	5 3
Alloway, ... ,,	9.30	4 9
Ibrox, ... arrive	10.37	

Returning from Ibrox at 7.20 p.m.

Advertisement with timetable that appeared in the Girvan-published *Carrick Herald* for the Empire Exhibition special train via the M&DLR in 1938. *D. McConnell*

Glenside station, looking north-east, in the LMS goods-only era, but still generally representative of G&SWR years.   *G&SWR Association*

The new modern futuristic world that had been portrayed to, and thoroughly enjoyed by, the Empire Exhibition's vast number of visitors, totalling 12½ million, was subdued by the threat of another war with Germany; and, ultimately, on 3rd September, 1939, the Conservative Prime Minister Neville Chamberlain, leading the National or Coalition government, declared that Britain was at war. As in the previous war with Germany, Britain's railways again were brought under the managing responsibility of a Railway Executive Committee, under the overall control of the government, to ensure the unification of railway operations amid the circumstances of war and the priority use for the transport of troops, equipment and supplies. Passenger services, especially holiday specials and dining-car facilities were subject to long delays or reduced in frequency or withdrawn, as the people were discouraged from travelling on inconsequential journeys.

Sadly, in the autumn of 1939, services were significantly curtailed on the short Girvan-Turnberry line. The Turnberry sleeper service was discontinued a week after the day of declaration of the war, commensurate with other sleeper services, which meant that the last train in each direction possibly ran northbound on Friday 8th, into Saturday 9th September, and southbound on Saturday 9th, into Sunday 10th. Railway and other large hotels were requisitioned by the government for use as hospitals under the Emergency Hospital Scheme that allowed them to be used for war-related purposes. Turnberry Hotel was closed at the end of October 1939 and was taken over by the Department of Health for Scotland. The local railway service between Girvan and Turnberry was reduced to only three or four trains in each direction per day, as was indicated in the timetable for January 1940 that continued through the summer and autumn with an extra train from Girvan producing a balance during the summer of 1941:

A 1935 aerial view of Turnberry Hotel and the station, showing the covered walkway between them. In 1927-28, the hotel was modernized and enlarged, to include two new wing extensions for the southern and south-eastern ends of the building and a verandah extension to the front of the dining room. The introduction of the London (Euston)-Turnberry sleeper service in 1928 was in conjunction with the changes, and a further improvement to the hotel was the installation of central heating in 1937. *Carnegie Library, Ayr*

Turnberry station platform below the canopy, looking north, possibly in the mid- to late-1930s when still used for passenger traffic to and from Girvan. The sign on the canopy gable points through the covered walkway 'To the Hotel and Golf Courses', with posters present on the notice board. This view represents the bright and airy appearance of the station at any time during its use. *RCAHMS, Edinburgh: Rokeby Collection*

	June 1940				*June 1941*			
		Sa					Sa	
	am	*pm*	*pm*		*am*	*am*	*pm*	*pm*
Depart Girvan for Turnberry	10.30	2.07	4.30		8.05	10.30	2.07	4.45

			Sa				Sa	
	am	*am*	*pm*	*pm*	*am*	*am*	*pm*	*pm*
Depart Turnberry for Girvan	8.05	11.20	2.39	5.17	8.25	11.10	2.30	5.17

Note: Sa - Saturdays.

By the spring of 1941, Girvan engine shed had sadly been closed. On 4th February, 1940, the shed, which was latterly seen as unnecessary as part of a policy of economy by the LMS in London, was reduced in importance, becoming a subsidiary to Ayr and having little work; and on 1st March, 1941, it was ultimately closed, with most of the men being transferred to Ayr, and the engine for the Girvan-Turnberry passenger service travelling daily to and from Ayr, where it was stabled overnight.

In essence, the same timetable of 1941 struggled into 1942 but, not surprisingly, with the service sadly destined for a demise that was additionally induced by the large-scale military presence in the area, announcements about the closure to passenger traffic appeared in the *Ayr Advertiser* and the *Ayrshire Post* of 26th and 27th February, 1942. The almost-identical notifications were insignificantly displayed: that in the *Ayrshire Post* was especially so, on the bottom left of page 3, under the vague heading of 'LMS Train Services', in solely referring to the Turnberry line; but the version in the *Ayr Advertiser* was overall more prominent on the middle of page 9 and headed in bold type 'Girvan-Turnberry Trains':

> *To be withdrawn from Monday.* The LMS Railway Company intimate that from Monday, March 2, the passenger train service between Girvan and Turnberry will be temporarily withdrawn. Local bus services will be in operation between Maybole, Turnberry and Girvan.

Since there were no Sunday trains, the last Turnberry passenger train ran on Saturday 28th February, 1942, and the official date of the so-called 'temporary' closure was Monday 2nd March, though the goods service remained. The LMS's March 1942 timetable indicated the withdrawal of the passenger service and that: 'The Western SMT Company Ltd operate a service of omnibuses on the Turnberry, Girvan and Maybole route, which afford connections with trains at Girvan and Maybole stations.'

David L. Smith, who had noted the 'temporary' nature of the closure, travelled on the last train to and from Turnberry - the 4.45 pm and 5.17 pm - and recorded that there were four coaches and a fish van for Mallaig, the terminus of the West Highland Railway Extension from Fort William. The fish van was trailed from Girvan to Turnberry and back to Girvan because all the vehicles were to be ready for immediate coupling at Girvan to the 4.20 pm ex-Stranraer service to Glasgow. While surprise was expressed by David about the inclusion of a fish van, because Mallaig was a renowned and busy fishing port, the reason for the van heading there was that Mallaig possessed kippering factories, to where was sent the herring from Loch Fyne and from the Firth of Clyde that had been landed at Girvan by the town's fishermen. David had been able to travel back from Turnberry on the footplate, as he was well known over the G&SWR system and was friendly with the train crews.

The next three photographs show the sad and overgrown appearance of three M&DLR stations in the late-LMS goods-only era. Heads of Ayr station, 1945, looking east, with the nameboard and posts removed.   *RCAHMS, Edinburgh: Rokeby Collection*

Knoweside station, 1945, looking north, showing the water tank, the level crossing, the crossing-keepers' cottages and a hut that may have been used as the shelter on the platform.
                                        RCAHMS, Edinburgh: Rokeby Collection

Glenside station, 1945, looking south-west.   *RCAHMS, Edinburgh: Rokeby Collection*

Meanwhile, intense activity had been occurring elsewhere at Turnberry during the previous year to the closure because of a decision by the Air Ministry to build a Royal Air Force aerodrome across the golf course. In early 1941, the large firm of contractors George Wimpey and Company of London had arrived to begin the work of construction of the new aerodrome of three concrete runways, hangars and other buildings; and in the spring of 1941, the members of Turnberry Golf Club were informed that the golf courses were to be requisitioned by the Air Ministry. The playing of golf ceased at the end of October, but the club resolved to continue in name for the duration of the war. With the golf course destroyed, the aerodrome was opened at the beginning of February 1942, and by then, the Turnberry Hotel was in use both as a military hospital for convalescent patients and as a mess for RAF officers. The establishment of the RAF airfield was the reason for the closure of the passenger service, to make way for troop trains - hence, accounting for the intended temporary closure - though the public passenger traffic to Turnberry had also, not surprisingly, diminished during wartime, and secrecy in the area was reinforced by the closure to the public of the Maidens-Turnberry road.

During 1942, the airfield was the base of RAF No. 5 (Coastal) Operational Training Unit ((C) OTU), previously located temporarily at Chivenor in Devon, for the training of the crews of Bristol Beaufort torpedo-bomber aircraft. With the beginning of the era of the troop trains, the Operations Record Book of RAF Turnberry had recorded in 1942 for 5th May, 6.20 am - 'Special train from Chivenor arrived Turnberry station with 5 officers, 500 other ranks, 19 WAAF and 8 civilians'. A few days earlier, on an unspecified date, an advance party of officers and 50 other ranks had also reached Turnberry from Chivenor, after a 28 hour train journey that experienced air-raid delays at Exeter and Carlisle. No. 5 (C) OTU departed from Turnberry for Long Kesh in Northern Ireland at the end of December 1942, to be replaced by RAF No. 1 Torpedo Training Unit and their Beaufort and Handley Page Hampden aircraft; and two entries in the Operations Record Book registered two train departures in 1943: for 4th January, 'Main party of No. 5 (C) OTU, ie 2 officers, 340 men, left Maidens station at 6.40 for Long Kesh'; and for 7th January, '2nd

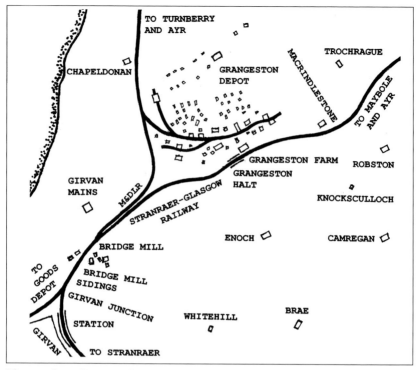

The area from Girvan to Grangeston munitions depot, showing the M&DLR, the Ayr-Maybole-Girvan line and the neighbouring countryside of farms and houses. The standard-gauge sidings of the depot were entered by a trailing junction, 1¼ miles from the M&DLR junction near the former Girvan No. 1 box that was closed in 1935. Within the sidings, there were 2 ft 6 in. narrow gauge lines for internal traffic, while sections of the standard gauge sidings were also multiple, in presenting a more complex system than is represented on the map.   *Drawn by D. McConnell*

section of main party for Long Kesh left Maidens station at 7.15′. It is probable that the trains from Chivenor consisted of Southern Railway stock - a novel sight along the Turnberry line - but hauled by an LMS locomotive.

The year 1942 had indeed been eventful for the railway and its vicinity. At the onset of the war, the government had decided to increase the production of explosives and armaments, with six factories having been built between 1939 and 1941 in southern Scotland for the Ministry of Supply, to provide equipment for the armed forces. One of these factories, to manufacture munitions, was established at Grangeston, 1½ miles north-east of Girvan in the wide segment of ground beyond the vee of the M&DLR and the main line, and in 1942 - certainly by October - a private siding, by a junction facing Turnberry, was in use to serve the factory that was operated by Imperial Chemical Industries on behalf of the Ministry of Supply for the secretive work. As an outstation of ICI's Nobel Industries Ltd at Ardeer, in northern Ayrshire, which produced dynamite that had been invented by the Swedish chemist and industrialist Alfred Nobel in 1866, the Grangeston site also possessed its own standard gauge and 2 ft 6 in. narrow-gauge railway system for internal traffic, accounting for a multiplicity of sidings within the substantial establishment. Additionally, there was a double platform, called Grangeston Halt, on the Maybole-Girvan railway for the use of the employees.

Chapter Thirteen

The Locomotives of the Turnberry Road

The pre-Grouping G&SWR and CR locomotive classes, where the class numbers preceded the word 'class', were referred to by their 'running' numbers that originated from the first built of the particular classes - meaning that the first-built of the class was given the same number as the class number. For example, the first locomotive of the G&SWR '22' class was numbered 22 and the first of the '8' class was numbered 8, but some classes were numbered randomly, such that this didn't preclude later numbers being given a lower number than the first-built locomotive. However, the LMS locomotives, with the class numbers following the word 'class', were referred to by their 'power' numbers, in that they were established by the power of the locomotives, with a class '5' locomotive being more powerful than a class '2'. The LMS used blocks of numbers for their locomotives, such that, with a few exceptions, all the locomotives of the same class formed a consecutive block, based on their date of construction.

The forerunners of the Glasgow & South Western Railway Company were the Glasgow, Paisley, Kilmarnock & Ayr Railway Company and the Glasgow, Dumfries & Carlisle Railway Company, and it was their amalgamation in 1850 that resulted in the formation of the G&SWR in 1850. The GPK&AR Board had realised the need for repairs to the locomotives and rolling stock, and this resulted in the establishment in 1840 of the company's Cook Street works, south-west of Bridge Street station, in Glasgow. The wheel arrangements of the early GPK&AR engines from 1839 through the 1840s were 2-2-0 and 2-2-2 for passenger traffic and 0-4-0 for goods traffic, as more engines were ordered for the working of the lines to Ayr and Kilmarnock and the proposed extension to Carlisle. The majority were built by independent manufacturers, but some were later built by the G&SWR at Cook Street.

By early 1853, Peter Robertson had been the locomotive superintendent of the GPK&AR and G&SWR in succession for fully 12 years, having bravely managed with meagre financial and engineering resources; but the G&SWR Board then decided that they needed a new man, and they appointed the young and knowledgeable Patrick Stirling of Kilmarnock, after forcing the resignation of Mr Robertson. The gifted family of engineers comprised his father, Robert; his younger brother, James; and his son, Matthew. Patrick's father was the inventor of the Stirling heat engine that converted hot air into motion, and he was also a prominent Church of Scotland minister in Galston, Ayrshire. One of Patrick's early considerations for the G&SWR resulted from his natural enthusiasm to the Board's recommendation that the locomotive works should be transferred from the cramped Cook Street, where eight locomotives had been built from 1845 to 1851, to his home town of Kilmarnock, and he selected the site. Appropriately, Kilmarnock was located in a central position in relation to the company's railway system, and the new works were brought into use in 1856, with the first locomotive produced there by Patrick in 1857, and he developed 2-2-2, 0-4-2 and 0-6-0 designs. For the G&SWR, his express passenger engines were 2-2-2 'singles' - so called because they consisted of single-axle driving wheels, which he favoured for passenger locomotives; and after a few experimental designs, his 0-4-2 inside-cylinder tender engine, in progressively more powerful versions, became the mainstay of most secondary passenger and goods trains, with 0-6-0s for mineral trains and heavily-graded lines. Patrick left the G&SWR in 1866 to head for Doncaster in becoming the locomotive superintendent of the Great Northern Railway (GNR).

It was during the 1860s, in Patrick Stirling's era at the G&SWR, that locomotives had begun to be provided with some protection for the driver and fireman from the wind and inclement weather, for until then, inexplicably, there had been initially no cab at all and then only a 'weatherboard' at the front of the footplate and across most of its width, but without containing any form of roof. It was said that a lady member of the Stirling family drew attention to the crews being exposed to all kinds of weather and that there should be some shelter for them. Patrick responded but only in a limited way, in providing a short-length cab with circular portholes at the front - known as 'the spectacle plate' - and with a curved roof that was little better than a weatherboard for forward travel, while offering no shelter for backward running. Nevertheless, such developments formed a beginning for some degree of protection for the engine crews.

James Stirling, born in Galston, partly trained under his brother at Kilmarnock where he had become the works manager before Patrick departed for the GNR. After discovering that a 2-4-0 could haul more than a 2-2-2, because of greater tractive weight, James upgraded the hauling power of new passenger engines from 2-2-2 to 2-4-0, producing two new classes that had 6 ft 7 in. driving wheels for main lines and 6 ft 1 in. for more steeply-graded lines, with the additional driving wheels achieving a substantial increase in adhesion weight. On most railways, driving wheels of about 5 ft diameter became established for goods and mineral work; 5 ft 6 in. for mixed traffic; and 6 ft and greater for express passenger trains. For the two new classes, he designed a steam-powered reversing gear that was an alternative to the manual reversing gear in the cab, and the power made reversal operation easier. While Patrick had also included circular portholes in the upper sides of some of his short-length cabs, James introduced 'cutaway' or lower sides on the cab to waist height, and these allowed the crew a ledge on which they could conveniently lean, sideways and backwards.

During the early-to-mid 1870s, James designed 0-4-2 and 0-6-0 classes for heavily-graded lines - all of which worked into the 1920s - and two 0-4-2s of the same class were recorded as having worked on the Maidens & Dunure Light Railway during the period 1906-10. On the public opening of the line in 1906, Nos. 258 and 276 of the '221' class, mixed-traffic engines, with 5 ft 7 in. driving wheels, were sent to Girvan, to become based there, for the branch operation, and they continued to work the line during that period, for both passenger and goods traffic. They had been rebuilt - No. 276 in 1901 and No. 258 in 1902 - by the later G&SWR locomotive superintendent James Manson.

In 1873, James Stirling produced the G&SWR's first 4-4-0, which, as a prototype, was No. 6 of the '6' class, with driving wheels of 7 ft 1 in., for express work, and it was the first 4-4-0 in Britain that was built in a significant quantity, with a few earlier 4-4-0s on other lines being only experimental. This new 4-4-0 was built by the G&SWR in time for the opening of the Settle & Carlisle Railway in 1876, providing the G&SWR with a route to London and incorporating Glasgow-London through services of the G&SWR and the Midland Railway in conjunction.

In 1878, James left the G&SWR, in moving to Ashford in Kent to become the locomotive superintendent of the South Eastern Railway. His successor, Hugh Smellie, was born in Ayr but trained at the Kilmarnock works, and he continued a tradition of the Stirling brothers in having domeless boilers, while also retaining the limited shelter of the cabs; but larger boilers were produced, as were smoother-running tenders of greater capacity. Hugh designed a 2-4-0 class - '157' - and two 4-4-0 classes - '119' and '153' - and engines of all three classes were recorded in later years on the M&DLR. The 12 2-4-0 engines of '157' class were of similar power to a 4-4-0 but were capable of being used on the smaller and earlier turntables that could not accept a 4-4-0. His other significant production was numerically the '22' class 0-6-0, which was the largest single class of the G&SWR, comprising 64 engines. Under the management of Hugh, there appeared the first four tank engines for passenger traffic - the '1' class 0-4-4Ts of 1879 - although they were designed by James Stirling, and they operated on local trains between Glasgow and Renfrew and between Glasgow and Barrhead via Paisley. Two of the class - Nos. 2 and 21, renumbered later to 729 and 731 - worked on either or both the M&DLR and the Ayr and Cumnock branches at the end of their careers. No. 729 was photographed at Turnberry station *circa* 1920, and it is probable that No. 731 also worked on the branch. Hugh Smellie moved to the CR in 1890 but he died seven months later in 1891 at the age of only 50, and, thus, the career of a gifted engineer was sadly cut short.

James Manson, born in Saltcoats, succeeded Hugh Smellie in 1890 and spent most of his career with the G&SWR in different periods. He had become the works manager at Kilmarnock under Hugh, but, in 1883, he left the company to be appointed locomotive superintendent of the Aberdeen-based Great North of Scotland Railway (GNSR), and he returned in 1890 to that position with the G&SWR. James rebuilt 30 of the '221' class, which included Nos. 258 and 276 that were used on the M&DLR from the opening, and improvements from the rebuilding were new domed boilers and new cabs that gave better shelter, in having a roof with longer side sheets and 'cutaways' that extended further back along the footplate. The bigger and more sheltered cab was part of the natural evolution of locomotives, for James Manson's era was more than 30 years after that of Patrick Stirling. The improvements for the G&SWR applied to other locomotives generally, based on James' 4-4-0 designs for the GNSR, and they commenced with the G&SWR '8' class 4-4-0 design of 1892.

James continued the use of 6 ft 9 in. driving wheels that Hugh had introduced on his '153' class of 1886 and '8' class of 1892, with both of these classes having worked on the M&DLR; and for goods traffic, he developed the 0-6-0 in four successive classes - '306', '160', '361' and '17'. At the time of the line's opening, the '266' class 0-4-4T, of six engines Nos. 266 to 271, had just been built in 1906 for harbour and general goods work, but the final two, Nos. 270 and 271, were initially allocated to the M&DLR passenger trains, and they were the only two locomotives of the post-1900 period that had a direct connection with the light railway and were specifically allocated to it. A G&SWR '361' class 0-6-0 locomotive - No. 371 - was photographed on the hotel siding at Turnberry, with a goods train, about 1910. The 34 engines of the '361' class were built in 1900, 1907 and 1910 by Neilson Reid of Glasgow and by the North British Locomotive Company at the same works. They formed the principal goods engines of James Mason's design, which operated all over the system on main line and branch line duties, and they were vacuum-braked, enabling them also to work passenger trains.

It was during James Manson's era that the G&SWR decided to introduce railmotors and he was instructed to build this 'steam motor and carriage combined' that comprised the engine and coach constructed as one vehicle on the one frame. Three railmotors were produced at the Kilmarnock works in 1904 and 1905, as 0-4-0 tank engines, and although they were used in public service on sections of the G&SWR system, this did not include the M&DLR. David Cooper, the General Manager, suggested their use on the M&DLR in 1914 but they were not authorized because their third-class accommodation would not have been to the liking of the Turnberry first-class passengers, but also supposedly because they were 'scarcely suited to haul any additional vehicles over the steep gradients' of the M&DLR, according to Charles Cockburn, the superintendent of the line, with the support of Peter Drummond, the next locomotive superintendent from James Manson's retirement in 1911. The second reason was not true, as the railmotor did haul additional coaches on steep gradients, with the engine, in effect, in the 'middle' of the configuration when one or two extra coaches or goods vehicles were attached. The rear

G&SWR '221' class 0-4-2, No. 229, built in 1874 and rebuilt in 1903 with a domed boiler and a more commodious cab shelter, and with vacuum brakes, in allowing passenger working. Of this mixed-traffic class of 60 engines that were found throughout the G&SWR system, Nos. 258 and 276 were allocated to Girvan in 1906 to work passenger and goods trains on the M&DLR.

G&SWR Association

Former G&SWR '266' class 0-4-4T, No. 270, as LMS No. 16084, at Ayr shed in the late 1920s. Like No. 271, it was built in 1906 and used for passenger trains on the M&DLR, but it returned to local goods working and shunting at Ayr, for which it was designed.   *G&SWR Association*

of the coach was occupied by the guard in a small compartment when the railmotor ran forwards, which was ideal, but when it ran backwards, the driver also travelled in the guard's compartment and operated the vacuum brake, with the fireman remaining on the footplate, operating the regulator and reverser. Such awkwardness, even in combination with their third-class accommodation, seemed not to have been sufficient for their rejection to working on the M&DLR, and hence the 'reason' of them not being able to haul extra vehicles on a steep gradient had been added to the objections.

Peter Drummond, born at Polmont, east of Falkirk in Stirlingshire, had been the locomotive superintendent of the Inverness-based Highland Railway since 1896. He was the younger brother of the Ardrossan-born Dugald Drummond, who had been the locomotive superintendent of the Caledonian Railway from 1882 to 1890. Peter was heavily influenced by Dugald and was scornful of the locomotives of his G&SWR predecessors, James Manson and Hugh Smellie. Peter produced six classes of engine, including 0-6-0, 4-4-0, 2-6-0 and 0-6-2T. During the General Strike of May 1926, which was called in support of the coalminers and included the railway workers, a replacement supervisor, possibly at Kilmarnock as the control location and with scant knowledge of the railway operations, sent a Peter Drummond '279' class 0-6-0 - thought to be LMS No. 17756 and ex-G&SWR original No. 297 (not 279) - along the Turnberry road on a goods train. This engine had a maximum axle load of 19 tons 17 cwt, which was one of the heaviest types on the G&SWR system, and its jaunt broke 11 rails on the line - a fitting epitaph for the 0-6-0 on the 16-ton axle-load limit that still needed to be observed at that time. To many staff without local knowledge, the route seemed only a line on a map. Yet, there was documentation specifically prohibiting the large and heavy Drummond engines from the light railway, which, particularly in the emergency circumstances of the strike, was unknown or overlooked.

The 1910-18 period provided two identifications of locomotives that worked on the M&DLR. An example of the branch goods train was hauled by a Hugh Smellie '22' class 0-6-0, No. 84, which was photographed at Turnberry station, *circa* 1910, and consisted only of three vehicles: an elderly 6 ton goods van for sundries of small loads; an 8-ton mineral wagon containing bags; and a 10 ton brake van. A former express engine of the Hugh Smellie '157' class 2-4-0, No. 186A appeared on the southern end of the line from 1911-14, working out its time after being ousted from main line work. The 'A' after its number denoted that it had been replaced by another newer engine, No. 186. It hauled a stopping passenger train from Glasgow to Girvan and back, with two trips to Turnberry from Girvan, entailing a total distance of 140 miles on two tons of coal.

Peter Drummond was succeeded in 1918 by Robert Whitelegg, formerly locomotive superintendent of the London, Tilbury & Southend Railway, which had been acquired by the Midland Railway in 1912, and on arrival at Kilmarnock, Robert completed 10 Peter Drummond 0-6-2Ts, already on order, but with slight modifications. Unfortunately, he had come to the G&SWR at a time when four years of war had sorely depleted the company in men, materials and maintenance facilities. In 1919, he made administrative changes in his department, with all locomotives renumbered in an entirely new scheme that was intended to bring classes together, instead of using the part-random numbering that had developed since 1850, but these new numbers would only last four years until the Grouping. Robert was best known for his 4-6-4T 'Baltic' engines, comprising six massive tank engines built by the North British Locomotive Company, Glasgow, in 1922 for express passenger work. The 'Baltics' - known to the railwaymen as the 'Big Pugs', with the term 'pug' being a frequently-used Scottish nickname for any size of tank engine - were the most powerful of all the G&SWR locomotives. He resigned from railway service at the Grouping of 1923, for

G&SWR '13' class 0-6-0, No. 563 and built in 1877 originally as No. 13, as the first of its class of 12 engines that were designed for heavily-graded lines. It was another engine of this class, No. 577 and ex-No. 49, that worked on the M&DLR potato traffic in 1923 when it was sent at the age of 45 to Girvan. *G&SWR Association*

G&SWR '8' class 4-4-0, No. 103. This engine, built in 1894, was one of the class total of 57 that were found throughout the G&SWR system, with some of them running on the M&DLR as service passenger trains and as Turnberry specials', in being within the line's axle-load limit. However, No. 103 was one of five of the class to have been rebuilt in 1910 with a bigger boiler that debarred it from light-railway use. *G&SWR Association*

he did not want to become a subservient officer in a larger company, and he became the General Manager of Beyer, Peacock & Co, locomotive builders in Manchester.

During World War I, any engines that were spare at Girvan or Ayr and were not larger than an '8' class 4-4-0, which was the largest and heaviest that was allowed for passenger traffic on the M&DLR, would suffice for working the line; and between 1914 and 1916, James Stirling '6' class 4-4-0 No. 205, rebuilt in 1901, was used, in spite of the engine needing an overhaul. This was one of 16 '6' class engines, from a total of 22, that were rebuilt from 1899 to 1901 and re-classed as '191'.

Towards the end of World War I during the second half of 1918, locomotives began working on the aerodrome branch for goods traffic, which was constructed that summer on a very steep descent at 1 in 20 and 1 in 30 from east to west. They were 0-6-0s of any of the classes usually found on the M&DLR at the time, which were designed by Hugh Smellie or James Manson, of the '22', '306', '160' and '361' class. An 0-6-0, rather than an older and smaller 0-4-2, was necessary for adhesion and braking power for six wagons, and to avoid the risk of wagon runaways, the engine, whichever direction it was heading, was always on the aerodrome end of the train on the 1 in 20 and 1 in 30 gradients between the M&DLR junction and the marshalling sidings, using these essential sidings as a run-round loop facility, where the descent was very shallow, at 1 in 246. The need for two loops at the marshalling sidings enabled the rounding of a train and the temporary storage of a second train, whether its wagons were loaded or empty.

From 1920 to 1924, two of the James Stirling '1' class 0-4-4Ts of 1879 were in allocation at Ayr. They had been modified by Robert Whitelegg to contain larger side tanks and bunkers, and they had become, from their original numbers of 2 and 21, Nos. 729 and 731 under his renumbering scheme of 1919. No. 729 certainly worked on the M&DLR passenger service, as it was photographed at Turnberry *circa* 1920, and No. 731 probably worked on the line. At 40 years old, they were virtually worn out and withdrawn in 1925. Also photographed at Turnberry *circa* 1920, when it was based at Ayr, was Hugh Smellie '119' class 4-4-0, No. 710 - originally G&SWR No. 133 - which, from 1921 or 1922, was based at Stranraer before also being withdrawn in 1925. The 24 engines of the '119' class were built between 1882 and 1885 and were known as the 'Wee Bogies', which was a nickname to distinguish them from the later-built Hugh Smellie '153' class main line 4-4-0s that were known as the 'Big Bogies'. At Ayr, the 'Wee Bogies' were the principal express engines when new, and they worked to Glasgow. Apart from two engines that were withdrawn at about 30 years of age, the class lasted well over 40 years in service.

An example of a '153' class, or 'Big Bogie', working later on the M&DLR was the engine that failed on the Girvan-Kilmarnock evening experimental service on 1st August, 1932. The engine was LMS No. 14144 of Hurlford shed, formerly G&SWR No. 55 and rebuilt by Robert Whitelegg in 1922. It developed leaking tubes in the boiler, causing it to come to a stop at Knoweside, and sleepers were pushed into the firebox to raise sufficient steam to take the engine to Heads of Ayr, where assistance from Ayr was summoned.

Potato traffic and the railway were crucial to each other throughout most of the line's operation, with the transport of the crop by the trains being vastly more beneficial to the farmers than the previous inconvenient and slow horse-drawn carting by road to Ayr, as was also the case with fish, and these trains did not appear in the working timetable. The tattie trains were seasonal 'trip workings' that were subject to variations, dependent on the weather and the loadings of the crop on different days, and sometimes there was more than one train in a day. The engine could have been a seasonal transfer. For example, a James Stirling '13' class 0-6-0,

No. 577, as ex-No. 49, which was to become the last survivor of its class, was sent to Girvan at the age of 45 for the summer of 1923 and possibly afterwards, as it was withdrawn in 1928, as LMS No. 17109. In 1929, there was allowance for four daily workings in each direction, and three of these were based, for engine allocation and working, on Ayr and one at Girvan. In 1930, the Hugh Smellie '22' class 0-6-0 LMS No. 17141, ex-G&SWR No. 296, and rebuilt as '135' class by Robert Whitelegg, worked the potato trains, as had been noted by David L. Smith; and an unidentified '22' rebuild on a goods train was also photographed, *circa* 1930, to the west of Heads of Ayr station on the ascending curve of the line by Bracken Bay.

A Sentinel railcar service operated on the M&DLR from January to April 1928, when cars Nos. 4146 and 4147 were allocated to Ayr, and either or both appeared on the line. With the exception of one car, all the Sentinels were sent to Scotland and operated in various areas from September 1927 until the early 1930s, with the cars at Ayr working on the Ayr-Kilmarnock, the Dalmellington-Rankinston-Ayr and the Ayr-Mauchline-Catrine services. The combined engine and coach was powered by a small high-pressure boiler and engine that was produced by the Sentinel Waggon Works in Shrewsbury - being also builders of road steam-powered vehicles and railway shunting engines - and the boiler and engine were enclosed inside one end of the articulated vehicle, driving the bogie at that end by chains. The coach body was built by Cammell Laird & Co. of Nottingham, a famous name in shipbuilding at Birkenhead in Cheshire. Development of the Sentinels occurred between 1925 and 1930, in several batches totalling 80 cars for the LNER, and the subsequent version at each stage was an improved design from its predecessors. Unfortunately, the LMS, having purchased 14 in 1926 and 1927 at a relatively early phase of their development, did not possess the best model and did not purchase any more, which contributed to their short life of about eight years under the LMS, though they lasted twice as long under the LNER. Problem features included the chains becoming detached from the drives, poor riding of the early articulated coaches, and fickle boiler injectors and pumps. Unreliability was such that most depots that had two or three Sentinels used one of them only as a spare, to allow for breakdowns and repairs.

The recollections of railway enthusiast Jim Aird of Prestwick allowed confirmation of several locomotive classes on the line, and it was fortunate for the history and posterity of the line that he had taken note of its engines. In September 1930, near Bracken Bay by Heads of Ayr, he witnessed a train from Girvan that was hauled by a James Manson '8' class 4-4-0, with the Turnberry sleeping car, next to the tender, on its way to Ayr for cleaning. This was possibly LMS No. 14161, as ex-G&SWR No. 73, but uncertainty exists about the photograph. Soon afterwards, a southbound goods train appeared with a rebuilt Hugh Smellie '22' class 0-6-0, though it is not known whether he photographed this train. However, he did photograph, at Heads of Ayr station, and probably on the same day, a Girvan-Ayr passenger train, hauled by a James Manson '191' class 4-4-0, LMS No. 14234, which was a rebuild of the James Stirling '6' class, as ex-G&SWR No. 197. It was withdrawn on 31st December, 1930, a month after the closure of the Alloway Junction-Turnberry section for passenger traffic, as probably having been in use on the line during the final months, such that it then had nothing more to do. Jim travelled on the last passenger train of the regular service over the whole line, on Saturday 29th November, 1930, which consisted of two coaches and a brake van, hauled by a James Manson '361' class 0-6-0, as LMS No. 17475, built by Neilson Reid of Glasgow in 1900 as G&SWR No. 363, originally for main line goods but subsequently, by the mid-1920s, relegated to branch workings. Because the engine was a goods type, there was no steam heating for the two non-corridor bogie coaches of G&SWR and CR ancestry and the Midland Railway six-wheeled van.

Jim also noted that the passenger trains were invariably hauled by James Manson '8' class 4-4-0s or James Stirling '6' class 4-4-0s or Hugh Smellie rebuilt '119' and '153' class 4-4-0s; while goods trains were worked by the James Stirling lighter types of 0-6-0s, meaning James Stirling '13' class and Hugh Smellie '22' class. He also remembered seeing a James Stirling 0-4-4T working at Dunure, which meant a '1' class - and perhaps it was No. 729 or 731 - before 1925, as this class had finished by then. Of further interest, he travelled on a train hauled by Manson '8' class bogie and remembered 'clocking' 50 mph near Greenan Castle on the line's 25 mph limit! Indeed, a study of the M&DLR timetables revealed that the fastest trains, stopping only at Turnberry or at Maidens and Turnberry, meant that speeds between 25 and 40 mph, or even higher, were sometimes necessary on parts of the line to keep to the timetables. If officialdom recognised this, nothing was said, but if an accident had occurred where excessive speed was judged to be a factor, then the matter would have been treated seriously.

It was probably a highly-polished Manson '8' class locomotive from the G&SWR's Corkerhill shed, in south-western Glasgow, that conveyed the train from Glasgow to Turnberry for the ceremonial opening of the M&DLR on 16th May, 1906 and that the train and coaches were similar in appearance and length to the train of four coaches that opened the Catrine branch of 1¼ miles from Brackenhill Junction, south-east of Mauchline, on 1st September, 1903. Certainly, for the Catrine opening and for the opening of the 15¾-miles of the Cairn Valley Light Railway to Moniaive on 1st March, 1905, the engine was a Manson '8', which was the largest type that was allowed on the two branches. The Turnberry train, which was hauled by the most impressive of the G&SWR's locomotives classes, may have comprised five or six coaches, but probably not more, to keep the load below the maximum of about 150 tons, in the circumstances of accommodating guests for a special occasion over a new line that had not yet carried the public.

There were occasionally Directors' 'VIP' specials to Turnberry and these, almost certainly, were hauled by an '8' class engine. An early instance, probably before 1910, was when the Directors' and Officers' Saloon was attached to the rear of the 5.10 pm non-stop Glasgow-Ayr express because the 'top brass' were travelling to Turnberry, which was no doubt for a salubrious evening of wining and dining. At that time, the 5.10 was routed via the G&SWR's Paisley Canal line, to avoid loss of revenue on the Glasgow & Paisley Joint Railway that was shared with the CR, but the lively tail-swing of the saloon on the frequent curves of the Canal line caused discomfort to the occupants of the saloon. The outcome was that the 5.10 pm was changed, soon thereafter, to run on the straight line to Paisley Gilmour Street and to permit a more comfortable ride for future evenings of the 'top brass' in heading to Turnberry; and, thus, in a sense, the M&DLR accounted for the re-routing of a principal G&SWR express. The bogie saloon, No. 174, was built by the G&SWR at Kilmarnock in 1895 on a standard 43 ft underframe that was extended with observation balconies at each end, making its overall length 46 ft 6in.

For the M&DLR goods and potato services during the 1930s, there were generally three types of locomotive, but principally two from the former Caledonian Railway.

John Farquharson McIntosh had become the locomotive superintendent of the CR in 1895, and he had initially ordered a final batch of 0-6-0 locomotives that were of the standard design of Dugald Drummond, the CR's locomotive superintendent from 1882 to 1890. Built in the early 1880s with 5 ft driving wheels and 18 in. diameter cylinders, these engines, of the CR '294' class, had been continued and slightly modified between 1891 and 1895 by John Lambie as the locomotive superintendent after Dugald Drummond, and then by John McIntosh, with the number of engines of the class having ultimately increased to 244 under the latter's leadership. From 1899, John

Ex-CR '294' class as ex-LMS class '3F' 0-6-0 'Jumbo', and as BR No. 57279, hauls the daily southbound-only Turnberry goods train across the Doon viaduct in March 1950.   *D. Cross*

Ex-CR '812' class as ex-LMS class '3F', and as BR No. 57617, runs tender-first in hauling a southbound early-potato special, with tarpaulins on the wagons, south of Dunure and north of the deepest cutting on the line in July 1950. The coast of northern Ayrshire is discernible through the haze.   *D. Cross*

McIntosh had produced a new larger design of 0-6-0, based on the successful CR express passenger 'Dunalastair' classes of 4-4-0s of 1896 and 1898, containing various new standard boiler and cab details, and still comprising 5 ft driving wheels but with the cylinder size increased to 18½ in. These larger 0-6-0s, totalling 96, were designated CR '812' and '652' classes, which were very similar but with different detail fittings. Under the LMS, the '294s' were classified as '2Fs', while the '812s' and '652s' were classified as '3Fs' - with 'F' indicating 'freight'. However, unlike some of the '812s', which worked passenger trains, the '652s' were goods-only engines and it was this class as '3Fs' and the '294s' as '2Fs' that most frequently worked the goods and potato trains of the Turnberry road during most of the 1930s.

A relaxation of the weight restrictions of the axle-load limit allowed the third type of engine to work the trains of the Turnberry road - mainly the Girvan-Turnberry passenger service - during the 1930s, and this was by virtue of the London, Midland & Scottish (Maidens & Dunure Light Railway Amendment) Order of February 1931. For the first 25 years of the line's existence, the locomotive power was restricted by the G&SWR (Maidens & Dunure Light Railway) Order of 1899 to a maximum of 16 tons on any axle, or above any one pair of locomotive wheels, and this was the major difference between the M&DLR and a standard railway. The 1931 Order reduced the distinction, by allowing a maximum weight of 20 tons per axle to be used on the M&DLR, in conjunction with the laying of heavier rails. From the new legislation, the LMS class '2P' 4-4-0, which was essentially a Midland Railway engine that had been designed under Henry Fowler, the chief mechanical engineer of the MR and then the LMS, began working on the Turnberry road, mainly on the Girvan-Turnberry passenger service, for it was most suitable for light passenger traffic - with 'P' indicating 'passenger'. Comprising 6 ft 9 in. driving wheels, they had been used in 1928, the first year of their introduction by the LMS, on the former G&SWR system generally, with much success. A great affection developed from the crews for the '2Ps' because of their reliability, versatility, 'free-steaming' or good steam-producing design, ascending ability, and power to haul loads beyond their intended maximum.

After the closure of the Alloway Junction-Turnberry section to passengers in 1930, the most likely locomotive to work on the Turnberry shuttle was James Manson '8' No. 14195, as ex-G&SWR No. 111, based at Girvan, until its withdrawal in December 1932. Another possibility from Girvan was the rebuilt '22', LMS No. 17155, as ex-G&SWR No. 100, but this was more likely to have worked the goods and potato trains, until its withdrawal in October 1932. Afterwards, from the authority of the 1931 legislation, the usual motive power for the shuttle were the '2Ps', in possibly also working some of the experimental services of 1932 and 1933 between Girvan and Kilmarnock via Turnberry. By October 1932, there had been six '2Ps' at Girvan - most of them being used on the main Ayr-Girvan-Stranraer line, with one available for Turnberry - but, with few observations of them on the Turnberry service during the 1930s, the shed allocations provided the best inference of their use. The other engines that worked the experimental service were of the '153' class, as in No. 14144 which suffered leaking tubes on 1st August, 1932. They were from Hurlford shed, and it is reasonable to deduce that they were regular turns on the service, especially on the evening run, such that, having arrived at Kilmarnock, the engine returned to the shed. For the morning service, the regular engine was almost certainly a Girvan-shed working, with the '8' class No. 14195 eligible for it until its withdrawal, when a '2P' would take over.

Also of significance, it was a double-headed '2P' arrangement that had hauled the 1938 special passenger train of seven or eight coaches northbound over the whole line for the Empire Exhibition in Glasgow on Friday 20th May, 1938. A single '2P' would have been limited to hauling a maximum of five coaches on the M&DLR, because of the steep gradients, and a double-headed train was therefore necessary for more than five coaches. The Girvan signalman wrongly believed that the two '2P' engines were too heavy for the Turnberry road, and his concern resulted in the train returning from Glasgow via Maybole to Girvan. In reality, this was unwarranted because the '2P' engine, in addition to all engines of class '5' and downwards, was allowed by the 1931 legislation, whereby heavier engines than previously were allowed to be operated in conjunction with the laying of heavier rails. However, the fact that the relaxation had been consented to by the Ministry of Transport in February 1931, so soon after the closure in December 1930 of the Alloway Junction-Turnberry section for passenger traffic, possibly accounted for the Girvan signalman and the LMS authorities in Glasgow being unaware of the new situation, with their apprehension reinforced by the 'sudden' appearance of a double-headed passenger train, which may have been the first and only instance in public service on the line, though the longest RAF troop trains of World War II may also have been double-headed.

Of further significance, the last passenger train on the service between Girvan and Turnberry on Saturday 28th February, 1942 was hauled by a '2P', and David L. Smith travelled on the train to Turnberry and on the footplate back to Girvan. He recorded that No. 610 hauled four coaches and a fish van in both directions, so that all the vehicles would be ready on the return to Girvan for fast coupling to the Stranraer-Glasgow service.

Six CR class '3F' 0-6-0s and three CR class '2F' 0-6-0s had replaced withdrawn G&SWR 0-6-0 and 0-4-2 engines at Ayr in 1932; and, with variations in the number of locomotives over the succeeding years because of transfers, the numbers increased significantly to 11 '3Fs' and 14 '2Fs' at Ayr in 1946, and they worked regularly on the Turnberry road during and after the war. For most of the line's workings, the '2Fs' were used alternately with the '3Fs' when the load was within their lesser capacity, and with their sturdiness and high power in relation to their smaller size, the '2Fs' were given the nickname of 'Jumbos' - probably after the name of a famous African elephant at London zoo. An allocation of four '2Ps' at Ayr in 1932 increased to 10 in 1946, and the class worked on the Turnberry road, occasionally instead of the regular '3Fs' and the '2Fs'.

No information appears about which specific '2Fs', '3Fs' and '2Ps' regularly worked the Turnberry road, and only the allocation numbers at Ayr and Girvan could indicate the possibilities for each locomotive class at each location. Thus, for example, the numbers of the three types of locomotives at each of the two sheds were:

Ayr - '2F': 3 in 1932; 7 in 1933; 14 in 1946; and 11 in 1950. '3F': 6 in 1932 and 1933; 11 in 1946; and 9 in 1950. '2P': 4 in 1932; and 10 in 1946 and 1950.
Girvan - '2F': 1 in 1932. '3F': 2 in 1932. '2P': 6 in 1932.

Three locomotives of two other classes at Girvan in 1932 could have been used on the M&DLR occasionally: one former CR 'Dunalastair II' or '766' class 4-4-0, LMS No. 14335 and ex-CR No. 779; and two LMS class '4F' 0-6-0s. The 'Dunalastair II' was a development in 1899, with a larger boiler, of the very successful original 'Dunalastair' or '721' class of 1896 - named after the estate, near Loch Rannoch in Perthshire, of the CR's Chairman, James Bunten - with both of these powerful express classes having been designed by John McIntosh. The LMS '4F' 0-6-0 was a main line goods engine that, designed by Henry Fowler, was first built by the Midland Railway from 1911 and then by the LMS until 1941, with the total number of them built being 580, but there were relatively few in Scotland, divided among the G&SWR, CR and Highland Railway territories.

A summarizing table portrays details of locomotive classes that were known to have worked on the whole of the original M&DLR during its lifetime or on the Girvan-Turnberry section from the 1930s to the 1950s. However, there were more locomotives of the same or similar classes, simply to maintain the services, and, thus, No. 205, as mentioned for the 1914-16 period, could not sustain the services by itself.

Origin	Loco. Supt	Class	Type	First built	Where built	Period on M&DLR	Examples on M&DLR
G&SWR	JS	221	0-4-2	1874	Glasgow (D)	1906-c.30	258 (R)
G&SWR	JS	221	0-4-2	1874	Glasgow (N)	1906-c.30	276 (R)
G&SWR	JM	191	4-4-0	1899	Kilmarnock	1914-28	205* (R)
G&SWR	JM	191	4-4-0	1899	Kilmarnock	1914-1928	14234* (P)
G&SWR	JS	1	0-4-4T	1879	Kilmarnock	1920-24	729 (P)
G&SWR	JS	13	0-6-0	1877	Kilmarnock	incl. 1923	577 (R)
G&SWR	HS	22	0-6-0	1881	Kilmarnock	1910-30	84 (P)
G&SWR	HS	157	2-4-0	1879	Kilmarnock	1911-14	186A (R)
G&SWR	HS	119	4-4-0	1882	Kilmarnock	c.1920	710 (P)
G&SWR	HS	153	4-4-0	1886	Kilmarnock	incl. 1932	14144 (R)
G&SWR	JM	266	0-4-4T	1906	Kilmarnock	incl. 1906	270 (R)
G&SWR	JM	266	0-4-4T	1906	Kilmarnock	incl. 1906	271 (R)
G&SWR	JM	8	4-4-0	1892	Kilmarnock	1906-c.30	Unidentified (R)
G&SWR	JM	361	0-6-0	1900	Glasgow (NR)	1910-30	371 (P)
G&SWR	JM	361	0-6-0	1900	Glasgow (NR)	1910-30	17475 (R)
G&SWR	RW	135	0-6-0	1920	Kilmarnock	1910-30	17141† (R)
G&SWR	RW	135	0-6-0	1920	Kilmarnock	1910-30	Unidentified† (P)
CR	DD	2F	0-6-0	1883	Glasgow (SR)	1930s-40s	Unidentified (R)
CR	JMc	3F	0-6-0	1899	Glasgow (D)	1940s-55	Unidentified (R)
CR	JMc	3F	0-6-0	1908	Glasgow (SR)	1940s-55	17633 (P)#
CR	JMc	3F	0-6-0	1899	Glasgow (SR)	1940s-55	57617 (P)#
CR	JMc	2F	0-6-0	1883	Glasgow (SR)	1940s-55	57279 (P)#
LMS	HF	2P	4-4-0	1928	Crewe/Derby	1931-42	610 (R)

Notes

Locomotive Superintendent, as designer: JS - James Stirling; HS - Hugh Smellie; JM - James Manson; RW - Robert Whitelegg; DD - Dugald Drummond; JMc - John McIntosh; HF - Henry Fowler.

First built: This is the year when the first of the class was built and not necessarily the year of building of the particular examples for each class.

Where built: Kilmarnock - G&SWR works; Glasgow (D) - Dübs & Co; Glasgow (N) - Neilson; Glasgow (NR) - Neilson Reid and later North British Locomotive Co; Glasgow (SR) CR works, St Rollox; Crewe/Derby - LMS works.

Period on M&DLR: This is imprecise for each locomotive class, and the listing of a single inclusive year or a range of years does not preclude the locomotive number or class working on the line in other years.

Examples: (R) - recorded, (P) - photographed.

* - Rebuild by James Manson of James Stirling '6' class of 1873, to become '191' class of 1899. † - Rebuild by Robert Whitelegg of Hugh Smellie '22' class of 1881, to become '135' c;ass of 1920. # - Examples photographed only post-WWII, still showing LMS No. as 17633 or with replacement BR No. as 57617 and 57279.

Some of the locomotive classes in the table - '22', '8', '221', and '191' - were also recorded as entries in the Signalman's Report Book for Maidens during the years from 1917 to 1928; but, additionally, a few other locomotives were able to be noted on the line only by means of this source, including the James Manson '336' class. A '336' class engine - original G&SWR No. 351 - in hauling a passenger train from Ayr to Girvan in 1920, failed and was attached to the engine of the next passenger train to complete the journey to Girvan. The '336' class 4-4-0, which was designed in 1895 and built in 1895 and 1899 at Kilmarnock works with 6 ft 1 in. driving wheels for more steeply graded lines, was similar to the 6 ft 9 in. '8' class. The Maidens signalwoman who recorded the incident was Jeannie McCallum. In 1922, there was a delay of two minutes to an officers' special in 1922, hauled by an '8' class - ex G&SWR original No. 36 - and, embarrassingly, the fireman dropped the tablet in the presence of the 'top brass'. Other G&SWR classes that were noted in the Maidens book were: '160' in 1917 and 1928; '306' in 1919 and 1920; and '361' in 1919. While the Maidens book represented only a sample of the locomotives that were recorded on the line, it was nevertheless important in listing and confirming examples of locomotives classes and numbers that worked on the M&DLR.

The M&DLR locomotives, as part of the G&SWR colour scheme, were green, with the shade originally dark green. The principal variation occurred under Peter Drummond, who, from the appearance of his locomotives in 1913, introduced the lighter or medium olive green appeared in 1913 and this colour was continued by Robert Whitelegg until the end of the G&SWR era. During the LMS era, the locomotives were painted black.

Regular Passenger Train Stock on M&DLR

G&SWR first, third and composite coaches, 31 ft long, six wheels, used on Ayr-Girvan local services.

G&SWR first, third and composite coaches, 43 ft long, eight wheels, used on Glasgow-Turnberry through services.

G&SWR passenger brake van coaches, 31 ft long, six wheels.

Ex-MR passenger brake van, 25 ft long, four wheels, one vehicle only.

G&SWR Manson breakfast & tea car, 60 ft long, 12 wheels, used only in 1906.

G&SWR Drummond breakfast and tea car, 60 ft long, 12 wheels, used 1919-23.

Ex-CR Pullman restaurant car *Mary Carmichael*, 60 ft long, eight wheels, used 1923-39.

Ex-LNWR first sleeper coach, 65 ft long, 12 wheels, used from 1928.

LMS 3rd sleeper coach, 60 ft, eight wheels, used from 1932.

LMS first and third composite sleeper coach, 68 ft long, 12 wheels, from 1932.

All vehicles in similar colours of G&SWR dark red or MR red or LMS crimson lake.

Regular Non-Passenger-Train Stock on M&DLR (all four-wheeled)

Eight and 10 ton mineral wagons, for coal.

Eight and 10 ton goods wagons, for potatoes and manure.

Six ton covered wagons, for stores, small packages and hotel supplies.

Low-sided or 'cart' wagons for occasional horse-drawn carriages and farm implements.

Cattle trucks.

Fish vans.

Horse boxes, from various railway companies.

10-ton goods brake vans.

Chapter Fourteen

The Signalling of the Turnberry Road

The signalling system of the Maidens & Dunure Light Railway was inspected by Major J.W. Pringle of the Royal Engineers on behalf of the Board of Trade on 11th May, 1906, six days before the commencement of public traffic. From its opening, the M&DLR, being of single track with passing loops, was operated by the 'electric train tablet' system of signalling, with the line divided into 'tablet sections', or stretches of track, where, in accordance with safety, only one train at a time was allowed on the section of the line that was controlled by each signal box. The 'tablet' for single-line operation in general was effectively a safety token, or authority, for entry to a section, in the form of a flat and usually disc-shaped slab of metal that was placed and slid into a 'token instrument' or 'block instrument'. This was an electro-mechanical machine inside each signal box for controlling the insertion and removal of the tablet, with adjacent instruments linked by telegraph wires along the route of the line. The type of electric train tablet and block instruments on the M&DLR was Tyer's No. 6, from the design of the pioneering railway-signalling engineer Edward Tyer of London, who had established Tyer & Company in 1851 for the manufacture of signalling equipment. The possession of the tablet allowed a train to proceed into a section, and, in essence, the electrical circuits of the machine prevented more than one tablet for a section of line being out of the instruments simultaneously. The points were mechanically interlocked with the signals, such that the appropriate signal could not be released against an incorrect point setting that would lead to derailment. Thus, before a train could proceed into a section, the conditions had to be satisfied of the line occupancy, as authorized by the tablet, and of the interlocking setting of the correct points and the corresponding signal.

The instrument in a signal box at one end of the section for issuing a tablet was electrically interlocked with another instrument at the opposite end, so that only one tablet could be in use at a time, and the procedure also meant that a section of line could not contain two trains that were travelling in the opposite or the same direction. The electric connection between the block instruments was accomplished by a current that ran through the telegraph wires between the successive signal boxes to produce electric impulses and communicate relevant information, in the form of a bell code, about a train being able to enter or leave a section. The tablet, which was engraved with the names of the locations at each end of the section and a serial number, varied in size, shape or configuration, so that it could not be placed into the instrument for the adjacent section. The tablet was held in a pouch with a metal hoop for its convenient hand exchange, and the fireman usually carried out the exchange with the signalman on behalf of the driver.

At the opening of the M&DLR, there were seven block sections, beginning and ending at the signal boxes at these locations: Alloway Junction, Alloway station, Heads of Ayr station, Dunure station, Glenside station, Maidens station, Turnberry station and Girvan No. 1 Junction. Alloway Junction box was situated in the vee between the M&DLR and the main line to Girvan; Alloway station box lay beside the southern crossing loop through the station, within the shallow cutting and almost directly opposite the station building; all the other station boxes were built on the platforms; and Girvan No. 1 box was located between the M&DLR and the main line where they ran parallel, 160 yards north of the junction. Island platforms, where all types of trains

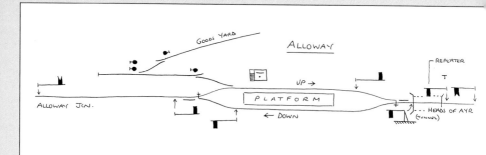

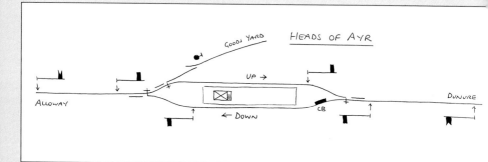

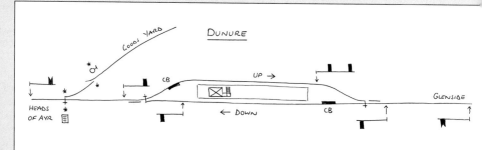

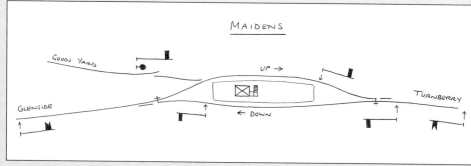

Signalling diagrams for Alloway, Heads of Ayr, Dunure and Maidens stations and yards, 1923, indicating signal boxes on the island platforms at Heads of Ayr, Dunure and Maidens, and the signal box on the southern side of the southbound platform line at the eastern end of the station at Alloway. The 1914 loop line for Heads of Ayr was built on the southern side of the original line and station platform.

could cross, were provided initially at Alloway, Dunure and Maidens. At Alloway and Maidens, the signal box controlled the entry to the yard, but at Dunure, the access was by a ground frame within the single-line section, north of the station loop, and it was operated by the section tablet. Heads of Ayr and Glenside were tablet stations without having a crossing loop, though Heads of Ayr later acquired a loop, an island platform and a new signal box, and all three were brought into use on 15th June, 1914. North of Turnberry station's single platform, there was a loop which did not permit two passenger trains to cross, because of the single platform, but which permitted a passenger train and a goods or potato train to cross, with the passenger train always running on the platform or western side of the loop and the goods train on the eastern side. Goods and potato trains were able to cross here, and a light engine could round a passenger train at the platform. Single-line platforms were provided at Knoweside and Glenside, with Knoweside having no signal box and only a ground frame for access to the small yard but with Glenside, as a block post, having a signal box that enabled goods or potato trains to be shut into the yard, out of the way of a passenger train. Greenan Castle siding was controlled by a ground frame, as was Dipple siding but with the latter only until the replacement by a signal box and a loop that were used from 15th June, 1914.

From the opening and through the early years of the operation of the line, the G&SWR working timetables contained the following note that referred to the one goods train in each direction, which were the 8.40 am ex-Ayr and the 3.00 pm ex-Girvan: 'A telegraph lineman will travel with one or other of these trains, when required, to redistribute tablets between Alloway Junction and Girvan, and the train he travels with must stop at all tablet stations to allow him to put the tablets into their places and rejoin the train.' This instruction was to allow the lineman to transfer tablets from one end of the section to the other and then back to their block instruments because the train service was 'unbalanced', with more trains in the one direction than in the other, such that the tablets accumulated at one end. As indicated in the Signalman's Report Book for Maidens during 1906, the lineman's visit took place at approximately four-weekly intervals.

On other occasions, for the working of the M&DLR signal boxes outside normal working hours, the tablets were withdrawn in advance and left in an agreed place inside the signal box, and these were exchanged by the guard, who, in being called the pilotman, acted like a travelling signalman, by exchanging tablets and authorizing the train to pass the signals at danger. This applied, for example, on the early-morning fish train that commenced in 1907, whereby, to save calling out a signalman for this one train, the tablets for the sections to Alloway, to Heads of Ayr and to Dunure were withdrawn from the block instruments by each signalman at Alloway Junction, Alloway and Heads of Ayr signal boxes the previous night and left in the signal boxes for the pilotman to take through the relevant block section. With the signals left at 'danger', the train proceeded along the line and stopped at each box to let the guard collect the tablet for the section ahead and leave the tablet for the section that the train had just left, while he also left a pilotman's ticket in each box to indicate that the train had passed through the section. The process was repeated on the return journey.

The signals and signal posts, of the Stevens design, as on the G&SWR system generally, were manufactured by Stevens & Sons, signal contractors, of London and Glasgow or by the G&SWR at its own signal, telegraph and permanent way works at Irvine. When the M&DLR was opened, lower quadrant signals were in use on all railways, whereby the signal arm was positioned horizontal to indicate 'stop -

danger' and was lowered to indicate 'clear - proceed'; but gradually, from the 1920s and 1930s, the signal construction was changed to upper quadrant, with a raised arm meaning 'clear - proceed'. However, as the M&DLR was closed for passenger traffic between Alloway Junction and Turnberry in 1930, it was not altered from lower quadrant, and it was de-signalled during 1936-37, except for the Girvan-Turnberry section, which remained lower quadrant.

The signals at the M&DLR stations consisted of a home signal on each approach and a distant, or caution, signal that was placed at an appropriate distance before the train reached the home signal, while there was a starting signal at each end of the platform for trains departing. In the case of Alloway, the home signal on the station approach for Ayr-bound trains was bracketed on the retaining wall at the north-eastern end of the tunnel, and the position of the station in relation to the tunnel required another signal, known as a repeater home signal - even though it preceded the main home signal. The repeater home signal was bracketed outside the south-western end of the tunnel, and it was worked in unison with the main home signal, to display the same indication. The curve of the tunnel and the proximity of the station to the tunnel mouth meant that the driver could not see the main home signal and the points for the loop at the island platform until his train was very close to the signal, while smoke from the engine also sometimes obscured this signal; and, therefore, the repeater home signal was necessary as an safety measure. If the station was not clear to enter, an Ayr-bound train was stopped immediately before the south-western end of the tunnel and not inside it.

The signal box for Dipple sidings, which, like Heads of Ayr signal box, had opened on 15th June, 1914, was closed on 21st September, 1925, to become the first instance of a signal box closure on the line, and it was replaced by a ground frame, which was a small lever frame at ground level to allow the train crew to operate the points by the tablet, without the need of a signal box. However, Dipple box was reinstated on 20th June, 1932.

A ground frame was also used temporarily during World War I for the short branch to Turnberry aerodrome during the second half of 1918 and for an indeterminate period during 1919. The layout of the several sidings - referred to as the 'Military Sidings, Maidens' - included a double loop, side by side, with junction sidings extending northwards and southwards from the main loop. The ground frame was located on the eastern side of the M&DLR, approximately at the middle of both the length of the main loop and the whole layout from north to south, and access to the branch and the sidings was obtained by the tablet and key covering the section between Maidens and Turnberry. The branch was worked by 'one engine in steam' - meaning that only one train was allowed at any one time.

After the 1930 passenger closure of the line from Alloway Junction to Turnberry, the Girvan-Turnberry passenger section had continued to be worked by the electric-token system in association with a token instrument or machine at Turnberry signal box. The principles here were the same as for tablet instruments, but the token used was key-shaped, of the type known as Tyer's key token. Girvan No. 1 box, at the M&DLR junction, held responsibility for the Girvan-Turnberry section until the closure of the box on 23rd June, 1935, when its functions passed to Girvan No. 2, at Girvan Junction, which was renamed Girvan No. 1, with Girvan No. 3, at Girvan station, renamed Girvan No. 2. From the closure of the boxes at Alloway, Heads of Ayr, Dunure and Glenside on 16th June, 1936 - but not Maidens, Turnberry and Dipple at that time - the line for goods trains, including the potato trains, from Alloway Junction to Turnberry was worked as 'one engine in steam'. This was a basic and economical means of working, as there was only the one token for the section, in the form of a 'staff' or baton with the token key attached to it, requiring no need to maintain instruments and the associated wires. The disadvantage was that the staff had to travel alternately in each direction, requiring arrangements to return it to the end at which it would next be needed when the service was restricted to this pattern. The train crew operated the ground frames at the yards along the line by the attached token key.

During the six months from 16th June to 16th December, 1936, there were the following four block sections in operation on the M&DLR, with 'one engine in steam' for the goods trains applying over the first two sections: Alloway Junction-Maidens; Maidens-Turnberry; Turnberry-Dipple; and Dipple-Girvan, until the closure of Maidens, Turnberry and Dipple boxes on 16th December, 1936, when ground frames were installed at all three locations, but with Dipple losing its loop facility. At Turnberry, the loop was necessarily retained for the run-round of the passenger-service engine, and the passenger trains were controlled by a 13-lever ground frame in the open and by what was termed a 'no-signalman' token instrument in the station master's office, which was operated by the train crews because there was no longer a signalman there.

Thereafter, between 1936 and 1942, the single block section between Alloway Junction and Turnberry was worked as 'one engine in steam' by the train staff, while the electric-token system continued between Turnberry and Girvan because of the passenger trains. The signals at Turnberry provided protection against difficulties if trains approached the station from both directions simultaneously. The staff for the Alloway Junction-Turnberry section was held by the signalman at Alloway Junction until it was required for a goods train, and south of Turnberry, the signalling arrangement meant that all trains used the electric-token system. Because the goods service was one-way only, the Alloway-Junction staff was eventually returned to the signalman at Alloway Junction, usually by a northbound goods train via Maybole or by a potato train via Maidens during the summer season.

After 28th February, 1942, there were no more public passenger services between Turnberry and Girvan but passenger troop trains began to run over the whole line, in connection with RAF Turnberry and the conversion of the Turnberry Hotel into a military hospital that year. Later in 1942, Grangeston siding was opened to serve the munitions factory of the Ministry of Supply, under the operation of ICI, with the siding, in facing Turnberry to the north, being worked by a 2-lever ground frame that was unlocked by the token for the Girvan-Turnberry section. The troop trains, the Grangeston trains and the goods and potato trains continued during the war.

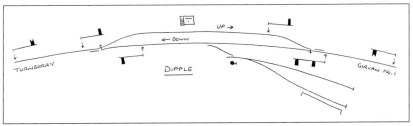

Signalling diagram for Dipple loop and sidings, 1923, indicating the signal box on the eastern side of the loop. The 1914 loop line was built on the eastern side of the original line.   *G&SWR Association*

Chapter Fifteen

The Butlin's Opening
and the Turnberry Revival, 1947-1951

At the end of the war in May 1945, the Coalition government was in the process of dissolving - having been led to victory by the Conservative Prime Minister Winston Churchill, after the resignation of Neville Chamberlain in 1940 - and the general election in July 1945 resulted in the return of a Labour government by an overwhelming margin, under Clement Attlee as Prime Minister. A policy of extensive nationalization was imminent, and, apart from its application to transport, there was to be state ownership for the large industries of coal, gas, electricity, and iron and steel, while there were also to be social reforms in what would include a nationalized health service, a national insurance scheme, large-scale housing developments and more extensive education. The Conservative Party, with complacency and naive confidence about retaining power because of Mr Churchill's wartime achievements and popularity, had not offered to introduce such essential and effective programmes for Britain's post-war reconstruction and development; and a principal part of this revival was the Labour Party's radical intention to reorganize the railways from the four Grouping components into one national concern.

Much optimism was expected from the railway reorganization nationally, but one unexpected and novel revival on a local scale - though also with a wider impact - which was independent of the proposals by Labour, was to be initiated for the northernmost section of the Carrick coast railway, from Alloway to Heads of Ayr. This was two years after the end of the war and five years after the closure of the southernmost section of the line, from Girvan to Turnberry, for public passenger traffic, and it was in response to the emergence of a revolutionary and expanded form of holidays for the mass British people. The establishment of holiday camps had already been long in existence before the 1940s, but they had been developed in the immediate pre-war years to an unprecedented level by one man. He was William Heygate Edmund Colborne Butlin, and his enterprise would bring new life and holiday activity to Heads of Ayr and to the northern part of the old and sedate Carrick coast line in the form of passenger services. The year 1947 was to be the beginning of the era of trains in accommodating the new Butlin's holiday camp at Heads of Ayr.

William or Billy Butlin was born in Cape Town, South Africa, in 1899, to English parents who had emigrated there. The marriage was not successful and Billy returned to England with his mother, who remarried and settled in Toronto, Canada, with Billy initially remaining in England but eventually joining his mother and her new husband in Toronto. Leaving school in Toronto at the age of 14, Billy worked for Toronto's largest department store, and one benefit that he obtained from this was the opportunity to partake in their summer holiday camp - an experience that, unknown to his young mind at the time, was to have a significant bearing on his future. After serving with the Canadian army during World War I, he decided to pursue the same form of business as his mother's family in Bristol, England, and he became involved in fairground stalls in Toronto, which was to be another indicator of his destiny as a natural showman. In 1921, he left Canada for England, working his way there as a ship's crewman, arriving in Bristol and finding his mother's fairground family, who helped him to set up his own stall for 'hoop-la', which was a game in which small hoops were thrown over prizes to win them. He achieved much financial success in this venture, ironically because he allowed more prizes to be won than did the other stallholders, such that the public kept returning to his stalls more often and paid more money - and thus had his inventive mind begun to play a part in his future. He learned of the circus company of Bertram Mills and their annual six-weeks' Christmas show at London's Olympia and, enterprisingly, leased a stall there, attaining success to the degree that he could afford to bring his widowed mother back to England. Billy soon expanded and glamorized his business with more stalls - and with staff in uniforms, which formed another indication of his future.

After the railways had revolutionized public transport by steam power, the arrival of other public transport by motorized means - firstly as charabancs and then as buses - brought a further revolutionary change in travelling, with people from the interior of the country now also able to enjoy a trip to the coast for a respite or holiday. This temporary migration had already been observed beyond a simple fact by Billy, and he believed that he could capitalize on it, for himself and for the people. In conversation with two other showmen, who had stalls at the small town of Skegness on the Lincolnshire coast, he learned of their financial success, and he soon moved there, leasing coastal land from the Earl of Scarborough in 1927 and built a small holiday fun or amusement park, containing hoop-la stalls, a tower slide, a haunted house ride, a little scenic railway and - from an idea that he had brought from Toronto - 'Dodgem' car rides. He opened an amusement park of stalls and funfair rides at nearby Mablethorpe, and then another two far away from there in Glasgow and Edinburgh; and, during the next few years, he established funfairs in several districts of London; while, from his success at Skegness, he installed 'Dodgems' in new amusement parks at Bognor Regis in Sussex, Hayling Island and Southsea in Hampshire, Felixstowe in Suffolk, Littlehampton in Sussex, Clacton in Essex, and Rhyl in Denbighshire.

In addition to expanding his empire of seaside funfairs, Billy had been considering the development of a much more accommodating and self-contained type of holiday camp than was available already. He had acquired the idea from his and other people's negative experiences on holiday, in that the owners of boarding houses did not want the holiday residents to occupy their rooms between meals, so that the guests were effectively ejected for most of the day; and to Billy Butlin, this was astounding and unacceptable. He particularly felt sorry for the residents with children, who were forced to leave the boarding houses at set times in wet weather, only to trek around with their children having nowhere to spend the time in the rain and having limited facilities even in sunny weather. He was determined that he would remedy the situation, and he visualized a holiday centre for the British working class families where they could have enjoyment in any weather conditions, by the provision of holiday accommodation that would allow and encourage the residents to stay on the premises for as long as they wanted during their holiday. His grand vision for a British holiday camp would also encompass other forms of entertainment, such as amusements, funfair rides, theatres, dance halls, and indoor and outdoor sports facilities and swimming pools, all conveniently situated on the premises.

It took a few years before his ambitious plan could take shape, as he searched for an ideal place to build his camp, which would be beside the sea; and it eventually turned out to be on poor - and, therefore, cheaply-bought - farming land at Skegness. Nevertheless, a new era in British holidays occurred with the opening of Butlin's Holiday Camp at Skegness in 1936, offering a week's full board, three meals per day, and the use of all entertainments and facilities for an inclusive price. The customers, or campers, were assisted by the principal staff who, from the vivid colour of their uniformed jackets, were known as 'Redcoats'.

From the start, Billy Butlin's innovative, if initially rudimentary, venture at Skegness was immensely successful, with the camp more than doubling in size in 1937, such that other similar holiday camps were contemplated for construction during the few years. Clacton opened in 1938 on a larger scale; while Billy also opened an amusement park that year at the Empire Exhibition in Glasgow. It was also opportune for Billy that, soon after his holiday-camp enterprise had begun, the Holidays with Pay Act of 1938, under the Coalition government that was led by Conservative Prime Minister Neville Chamberlain, had authorized at least one week's paid holiday to over 11 million workers. Until then, only three million people had been fortunate to have paid holidays - and, from the opening of the Clacton camp, the Butlin's slogan became: 'Holidays with pay! Holidays with play! A week's holiday for a week's pay!' The week's holiday for the week's pay included the cost of the journey by railway, as part of Billy's determined but good arrangements with the LNER, in serving Skegness and Clacton. The commendable enterprise of Billy Butlin and the passing of the Holidays with Pay Act, which Billy had actively supported, combined to lead to a large expansion of the holiday and tourist market in Britain: paid holidays for the everyday British people who would otherwise not have been able to afford them.

The building of a Butlin's camp at Filey in Yorkshire was half finished when war with Germany was declared in September 1939. The government requisitioned the camps at Skegness for the Admiralty and Clacton for the Army, to have them transformed into military bases during the war, and financial negotiations were agreed with Billy for the use of both camps - with the government paying him a rental of 25 per cent of the previous year's profits on them for the duration of the war. Furthermore, the unfinished Filey camp was requisitioned by the government, as an airbase that would be called RAF Hunmanby Moor, under an agreement that Billy would complete the work, with the cost to be paid by the government, and that he would have the opportunity at the end of the hostilities to buy back the camp for only three-fifths of the cost. Skegness and Clacton would also be given back to Billy; but, in the meantime, the Admiralty, in requiring another camp as a naval base, asked him to build another intended holiday camp on the southern coast of England. However, while he was searching for a suitable location, the plan was abandoned because of the entire northern coast of France falling under the control of Germany, and, instead, the Admiralty considered north-western Wales, with Billy choosing a site near the small town of Pwllheli on the Lleyn Peninsula in Caernarfonshire. Then, before Pwllheli was finished, Billy was requested to build yet another camp as an interim naval base, which was to be south-western Scotland, and he chose a site near Ayr. Both camps were to be built to Butlin's specifications, so that they could be used as Butlin's camps after the war; and, as with Filey, Billy would be given the opportunity to buy them for three-fifths of the cost of building them. The arrangement suited both parties: Billy would acquire three new camps much cheaper and the Admiralty would receive part of the full expenditure for bases that they would no longer need after the war. For naval purposes, with Skegness having been given the name *HMS Arthur*, Pwllheli became *HMS Glendower* and Ayr was *HMS Scotia*.

The location for the Ayr naval base was three miles south-west of the town, on the eastern side of the dramatic Heads of Ayr cliffs, where the land gently sloped to the sea, and *HMS Scotia* was opened in January 1942 as a training establishment for naval telegraph and visual signalling operators, which included detachments from the navies of The Netherlands, Belgium, France and Norway. At its maximum capacity, there were 3,200 trainees present, contributing to a total staff of all ranks of 4,000; and after the end of the war in May 1945, the Admiralty began moving out as had been agreed, though the base was still occupied in December 1946, with the decommissioning planned for early 1947. Meanwhile, with a new post-war era in holidays about to commence and with Billy Butlin hailed as the 'king of holiday camps', Butlin's Ltd confidently informed the recently-established Scottish Tourist Board, as early as December 1946, that the new camp at Ayr would be opened on 17th May, 1947 and that bookings for accommodation had already been received. During the late winter and early spring of 1947, the renovations and additions were hurriedly carried out, as a new typical Butlin's holiday village of chalets, dining hall, lounges and bars, amusement park, sports fields, games rooms, swimming pools, and many other facilities began a metamorphosis on the sloping ground between the Dunure road and the sea. The location was magnificent for a holiday camp that, when in full operation, would accommodate many thousands of guests during the summer season of five months from May to September. Beside the entrance to the camp, there was to be an extensive single-storied hotel that would be converted from its wartime use as the officers' quarters of *HMS Scotia*.

Also on the sloping ground between the proposed hotel and camp was the embankment that carried the old M&DLR and its all-year-round goods and seasonal potato trains, but with no passenger trains running along the route. However, the enterprising Butlin's Ltd, having readily noted the value of the adjacent railway, had made arrangements with the LMS to have it reinstated for passenger traffic between Alloway Junction and Heads of Ayr and to have a station built inside the camp. On 9th January, 1947, the *Ayr Advertiser* reported under the heading of 'New Railway Station?':

We understand that consideration is being given to the laying down of a railway station at the camp. This would allow special trains bringing campers from Midland cities to run direct through Ayr to the camp. Special trains would take away those leaving at the end of their holiday. It is hoped to have the station platform and signal box built in time for the forthcoming season.

As had been decided half a year previously to the day, Butlin's holiday camp opened precisely on schedule, on Saturday 17th May, 1947, and the Butlin's summer Saturdays-only train service commenced on that day, which happened to be the 41st anniversary of the opening of the Maidens & Dunure Light Railway in 1906. However, at the beginning, the service amounted to only one train in each direction per day, until a better indication had been determined about how many trains would be required. On the day previous to the opening, the *Ayrshire Post* had referred to the station and the beginning of the new train service:

Passengers travelling to and from Butlin's camp will have as from tomorrow a station right in the camp area, which will be known as the Heads of Ayr station, and part of the local section. This station, located between Greenan Castle siding and Heads of Ayr goods station, will enable passengers to step right off the train at their destination as it is in the camp area. It is a Saturdays-only service and to begin with there will be one

A pair of poor quality local newspaper photographs of the arrival of the first-ever passenger train at Heads of Ayr Butlin's station on 17th May, 1947. The engine is an LMS Stanier class '5' 4-6-0, No. 5157 *The Glasgow Highlander*. The first is from the *Ayr Advertiser*, showing a kilted member of Butlin's staff welcoming the driver and fireman.

D. McConnell, and Ayrshire Weekly Press

From the *Ayrshire Post*, showing Butlin's female Redcoats waving to the train.

D. McConnell, and Scottish Universal Newspapers

train leaving Ayr at 1.03 pm, returning at 1.50 pm. As time goes on it is expected that the service may be increased to bring special train loads from England.

No descriptions of the opening day's events appeared in the two Ayr newspapers, but, in acceptable compensation, each provided a different and valuable photograph of the historic occasion of the arrival of the first train. The *Ayr Advertiser* of 22nd May contained a close-up photograph that was headed 'First Butlin Train Arrives' and was captioned 'A kilted member of the entertainment staff greets driver and fireman of the first holiday train to arrive at Butlin's camp, near Ayr'. On 23rd May, the *Ayrshire Post* published a wider-angled but less clear photograph, headed 'Holiday Camp Opened', of the arriving train, bearing flags and a Union-Jack shield with the Butlin's name below, and being greeted by eight female 'Redcoats'.

The following week, both Ayr papers recorded that Robert Dunlop, a relief clerk at the District Goods and Passenger Manager's Office at Ayr, had been appointed station master at Heads of Ayr in connection with Butlin's camp and that he would be the railway company's principal representative in the LMS inquiry and booking office, which was not located in the building on the station platform but in a 'Nissen hut' at the railway entrance to the camp.

The new LMS Heads of Ayr station for Butlin's was situated on the higher ground of the camp near the entrance road that ran downhill from the Ayr-Dunure road and a mile east of the original M&DLR Heads of Ayr station, which was still occasionally used for goods. The station building was of a modern and utilitarian design, of basic rectangular masonry structure with a flat roof and with no platform shelter, which was typical of the wartime and post-war austerity period, and a stairway, on the west of the building, led down from the platform into the camp. The station comprised a single platform and a single line with a run-round loop on the southern side, while the platform was long enough, at more than 900 ft, for 14 LMS 60 ft-long coaches.

For the start of the Butlin's service, the line from Alloway Junction to the new Heads of Ayr Butlin's station had required the installation of new signalling, as well as the re-laying of the track with heavier rails to accommodate the regular service of new and larger passenger trains than had operated on the M&DLR many years previously. The new signals, to the standard LMS design, and a loop, had been constructed at the station, and a 15-lever frame, built by Messrs McKenzie & Holland, signal contractors, of Worcester, had been housed in a signal room at the eastern end of the station building. On summer Saturdays during the Butlin's season, the section from Alloway Junction to Heads of Ayr was worked by electric tablet with the section from Heads of Ayr to Turnberry worked as 'one engine in steam' with telephone communication for the goods and potato trains on Mondays to Saturdays. Outside the Butlin's season, the section from Alloway Junction to Turnberry used a single train staff, and each autumn until the spring, the Alloway Junction-Heads of Ayr electric tablet working was suspended, with the signal box and the loop at Heads of Ayr closed and the signal arms removed from the posts. The tablets in this case were square in shape, which suggested that the instrument had previously been used for a long section elsewhere. It is likely that the electric-token system was retained between Turnberry and Girvan after the war, even after the cessation of the military passenger trains, such that the goods and potato trains used it thereafter. That this was the case was reinforced by the station master being present at Turnberry to operate the 'no-signalman' token instrument in the station master's office.

West of Heads of Ayr Butlin's station, for trains from the Dunure direction, there was a fixed distant signal, 900 yards from the western end of the loop, and then an

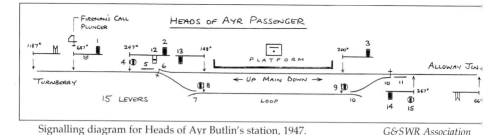

Signalling diagram for Heads of Ayr Butlin's station, 1947.   *G&SWR Association*

The simple track layout at Heads of Ayr Butlin's station, showing the run-round loop, platform, station building, stairs to the camp and the entrance road that ran from the Ayr-Dunure road and under the railway, to curve into the camp. The position of the original 1947 stairs is indicated, though the route from them to the camp is uncertain (*see the aerial photograph on page 202*). However, new stairs and a straight path (*shown in the drawing as a broken line from west of the station building*), with a roofed but open-sided walkway, were built later at an unknown date, resulting in the stairs being 40 ft nearer to the building. The railway booking office, as a Nissen hut, is indicated at the Butlin's end of the broken line. Another broken line east of the station building represents a sloping path that was also built later to accommodate luggage barrows. Higher ground lies south, and lower ground north, of the station, with a larger area of embankment extending immediately north of the platform and west of the road bridge, on both sides of it, while a smaller area of cutting is immediately south of the loop line.   *Drawn by D. McConnell*

Heads of Ayr Butlin's station, looking east, with its long platform, masonry-built utilitarian building and run-round loop, as the railway passes between the higher ground towards the Ayr-Dunure road and the lower ground towards the sea. Although the photograph is from 1955, the scene represents any year from the station's opening in 1947, and also for many years afterwards. Butlin's camp lies at the lower level to the left of the view.

Dunbartonshire Archives, Kirkintilloch: McEwan Collection

outer and an inner home signal, 400 yards and 35 yards respectively from the western end of the loop - thereby protecting the station when a Butlin's passenger train was positioned at the platform or stabled west of it for a short period. The distant signal was 'fixed' in the sense of the arm being permanently positioned horizontal for caution. The outer home signal contained a fireman's call plunger, or button, which, on being pressed by the fireman, sounded a bell or buzzer in the Heads of Ayr signal box, allowing on Saturdays an Ayr-bound potato train or a northbound goods train during the potato season to inform the signalman of 'train waiting'. This was needed because the long section without a signalman at the other end meant that there was less than the usual certainty when the goods train might arrive, and if a Butlin's passenger train was present at the platform, the potato or goods train proceeded past the station by way of the loop.

Ayr was the fifth Butlin's camp to be opened, after Skegness in 1936, Clacton in 1938, Filey in 1945, and Pwllheli in 1947 - or, as they became known in Butlin's advertisements, 'holiday villages by the sea' - and while the Ayr camp had opened on 17th May to holidaymakers, with 500 campers in residence, the official opening ceremony and luncheon occurred two and a half weeks later, on Wednesday 4th June in the presence of Billy Butlin and more than 1,000 invited guests. The inauguration was performed by the wife of the Right Hon. Thomas Johnston, who was Chairman of the Scottish Tourist Board in Edinburgh and who had been Secretary of State for Scotland from 1941 to 1945.

The establishment of a Butlin's camp in Scotland was of immense importance to Thomas Johnston, to the Scottish Tourist Board, to the nation in general, and to Ayrshire and Carrick more specifically. For his commendable concerns, actions and accomplishments for Scotland through his long career of political and non-political posts, including fighting poverty and bureaucracy, Mr Johnston was highly and widely regarded - indeed, to an exceptional degree - for integrity, patriotism and altruism, because he was enthusiastic in the development of his nation before self interest and ambition. While Secretary of State for Scotland during the hostilities, he prepared the foundations for post-war reconstruction in housing, health, agriculture, fishing and industry; and he also created one of Scotland's greatest industrial and social triumphs - the North of Scotland Hydro-Electric Board, which revolutionized the Highlands by the construction of power stations, dams, tunnels and power lines that brought electricity to the remote communities and households, while providing many thousands of new jobs.

Such was the astute, honourable and quietly charismatic but determined gentleman who was a principal participant at the official opening of Butlin's camp at Heads of Ayr, which would bring animation and enterprise to the northern Carrick coast and its railway. The railway interest was represented by Sir Robert Greig, Chairman of the Scottish Committee of the LMS, and he explained that when they were approached by Butlin's about providing a railway service to the camp, they were very glad to help, and he hoped that after the LMS had passed away, following nationalization their successors would be in a position to carry thousands to the camp. The nationalization of the railways was also to the satisfaction of the far-seeing and logic-minded Thomas Johnston, for he had long advocated it; and this new structure of the state taking control was ultimately necessary because of the ravages to the railway system from German bombing raids during the war, such that the constituents of the Grouping, with insufficient resources, could not remedy the situation by investment and modernization.

The Transport Act, 1947, which was passed in spite of strenuous opposition from the Conservatives, had the purpose of transferring public and goods transport and their affiliations under the overall state control of the new British Transport Commission (BTC). In being responsible to the Minister of Transport for general transport policy, the BTC had the ultimate aim of establishing an integrated public-transport system, by way of five independent components or 'executives' to manage specific sections of the transport industry, and these were: the Railway Executive; the Road Transport Executive; the London Transport Executive; the Docks and Inland Waterways Executive; and the Hotels Executive. From the 1947 Act had come the demise of the four large railway companies of the Grouping - LMS, LNER, GWR and SR - with their private railway enterprises being replaced, formally on 1st January, 1948, by the one state ownership under the BTC, but managed by the Railway Executive and acquiring the name of British Railways (BR), which was divided into six geographical areas. British Railways Scottish Region (BR(ScR)) encompassed all the lines north of the Border.

In that final year of 1947 for the LMS, the introductory Butlin's early-summer (May), Saturdays-only service of one train in each direction between Ayr and Heads of Ayr had not appeared in the public timetable, but the LMS *Working Timetable of Passenger Trains* for the period 16th June to 5th October, 1947 had presented what was, by then, a service of six trains in each direction between Carlisle and Heads of Ayr:

		pm	*pm*	*pm*	*pm*	*pm*	*pm*
Ayr	*arr.*	1.03	1.53	2.20	3.08	4.38	5.08
Ayr	*dep.*	1.08	1.58	2.30	3.13	4.43	5.13
Heads of Ayr	*arr.*	1.20	2.10	2.45	3.25	4.55	5.25

		am	*am*	*am*	*am*	*am*	*pm*
Heads of Ayr	*dep.*	8.00	8.20	10.40	11.10	11.50	12.50
Ayr	*arr.*	8.12	8.32	10.53	11.13	12.02	1.03
Ayr	*dep.*	8.17	8.34	10.58	11.17	12.05	1.07

All the trains were Saturdays-only expresses from or to Carlisle, running 'when required' and stopping at Ayr 'only to change engines or enginemen'. The stop at Ayr to change the engine crew was because the Carlisle crews were not familiar with the line from Ayr to Heads of Ayr and the trains had to be taken over the branch by local crews. In the 1947 passenger timetable, which stated the distance between Alloway Junction and Heads of Ayr as 3¼ miles, the Butlin's service of trains was included within the pages headed 'Ayr, Girvan and Turnberry, and Stranraer and Portpatrick', when, ironically, Turnberry station had been closed to passengers since 1942.

The popularity of Butlin's was such that a massive total of 25,000 visitors spent a holiday there from June to September during that first season of 1947, and an increased train service operated in 1948, under the new British Railways. Nine trains served Heads of Ayr in each direction, running mainly to and from Ayr, but allowing connections to and from Glasgow and the cities in England, with the remainder being direct services between Kilmarnock and Heads of Ayr and between Glasgow and Heads of Ayr. Although the M&DLR had closed for passenger traffic from Alloway to Turnberry in 1930 and from Girvan to Turnberry in 1942, there were still two sets of notes in the BR(ScR) summer timetable of 1948 to ensure that passengers - mainly those now travelling to and from the new Heads of Ayr station - were aware of no passenger trains running on the old line further south. The notes referred to buses running separately on the northern and southern halves of the route between Ayr and Girvan:

Ayr and Turnberry via Dunure. [Note 1] The passenger train service between Ayr, Alloway, Heads of Ayr, Dunure, Knoweside, Glenside and Maidens has been withdrawn. The Western SMT Co Ltd operate a service of omnibuses on the Ayr and Girvan via Dunure and Maybole routes which afford connections with trains at Ayr and Girvan stations. [Note 2] The passenger train service between Girvan and Turnberry has been withdrawn. The Western SMT Co operate a road omnibus service between Turnberry, Girvan and Maybole which affords connections with trains at Girvan and Maybole.

Another new Butlin's enterprise at Heads of Ayr began in the summer of 1948 with the opening of the company's large Heads of Ayr Hotel that was situated prominently on the higher ground inside the camp, by the gates at the Dunure road. With Billy Butlin in attendance, the inauguration took place on Monday 7th June in the presence of 400 guests, including Charles Kennedy, who was the fifth Marquis of Ailsa and Helen Ethel McDouall, the Marchioness of Ailsa - together providing an appropriate combination of surnames for this event in Carrick. The opening ceremony was performed by Mrs A.F. Gratton, who was the daughter of Thomas Johnston, Chairman of the Scottish Tourist Board; and Mr Johnston, in addressing the 400 assembled guests, paid tribute to the energy and resourcefulness of the Butlin's organization in advancing the tourist industry in Scotland. He highlighted the difference between the enterprising Heads of Ayr Hotel and the languishing railway-owned hotel further along the coast, by declaring about the new venture: 'It is in marked contrast with the lethargy shown in the large neighbouring hotel at Turnberry, where, despite the utmost pressure from the Tourist Board, nothing has been done.' The Heads of Ayr Hotel, which was formerly the officers' quarters at *HMS Scotia*, contained 74 bedrooms, a dining-room and cocktail lounge for 400 people, a ballroom for 1,000 dancers, and a conference hall for an audience of 1,200.

During the years after the war, while the goods trains had been leisurely making their way along the Carrick coast and while the Butlin's enterprise of holiday camp and hotel had become firmly established with immense success at Heads of Ayr, efforts had been proceeding to revive both the golf course and hotel at Turnberry. Perhaps even Thomas Johnston's remarks at the opening of the Heads of Ayr Hotel in 1948, in referring to the lethargy at Turnberry, had helped to create the spirit of revival there. The LMS had been displeased about the state of the whole area of Turnberry, with the airfield having obliterated the golf course to the extent that there was a general feeling by the company's Directors, and by the local golfing population, that there would never again be a golf course at Turnberry. The tearing of the course of its admirable undulating sand dunes to accommodate the airfield that stretched from Turnberry through Maidens to Ardlochan had left a glaring unsightliness by its concrete runways, taxiways, perimeter roads, hangars, transformer houses and the many other buildings that were widespread - forming a scene which, in having no aesthetic characteristics but being essential for the purposes of the war, had ruined the pastoral beauty. It had been much easier to erase the softness of the golf links by the solidity of the airfield than it would be to erase the latter's structures and return the area to the sporting greenery. With the devastation to the airfield from the 1939-45 war having been much worse than that from the 1914-18 war, a second reverse transformation sadly looked a near-impossible task to those who were hoping otherwise but who had to be realistic about their despondency.

In such pessimistic but understandable thinking, how wrong they were to be - but happily so - because, thanks to the determination of one gentleman in London, the dream of a new Turnberry would not remain a forlorn hope. This one man who was eager to resuscitate the hotel and golf courses was the appropriately-named Frank Hole, who had been employed as the LMS Hotels Accountant in 1934 and had become Controller of the LMS Hotel Services on 1st January, 1945 on the retirement of Arthur Towle. It was the energetic Frank Hole, who, with his interest in golf, persevered in the belief that Turnberry golf links could be restored from the abandoned Turnberry airfield, and he continued to strive for the reopening of the hotel. Furthermore, he was able to convince others in official positions, such that his exertions resulted in sufficient financial compensation from the government for the ruin and desolation that lay at Turnberry. It was also encouraging that Turnberry Golf Club had continued to exist - albeit in a dormant form, during and after the war years because of a few extremely dedicated and patient members who had met every year to ensure the club's preservation, should their minority optimism ever become reality.

By the time that a decision to proceed had been made, the railways and their hotels had been nationalized - under British Railways and British Transport Commission Hotels - and, thanks to Mr Hole, who continued as Controller of the Hotels Executive, it was officially announced that the hotel and the golf links at Turnberry would be derequisitioned soon. This was officially communicated in August 1948 by Philip Albert Inman as Lord Inman of Knaresborough in Yorkshire, who was Chairman of the BTC Hotels Executive and also a Labour MP who had been Chairman of the Board of Governors of the British Broadcasting Corporation, or BBC, in 1947. Work on the restoration of the hotel and links would begin immediately afterwards, though Lord Inman had to acknowledge that much exertion would be involved in bringing back the courses.

Finally, plans were able to be activated during 1949 for the establishment of a new Turnberry golfing resort, to be retrieved from the mass and mess of concrete, tarmacadam and weeds, firstly, by demolition work, and secondly, by artistry that would return the gentle green beauty to Turnberry. A campaign was planned for the 'military battle' that lay ahead, and it proceeded through the late summer and early autumn of 1949 by obliterating parts of the airfield from the land that it had usurped for several years. In addition to the demolition of the many airfield buildings, the work comprised the breaking-up, excavation and removal of the concrete and tarmacadam hard-standings of apron parking areas, taxiways and perimeter roads, using such heavy equipment as concrete-breakers, diggers, bulldozers, scrapers and compressors. However, the substance of the three runways remained because the effort and expense of removing them was too great, but, happily, the golf course would be rendered replaceable with the runways still in place. The excavated rubble amounted to many thousands of tons, resulting from four-feet deep foundations, and some of this material was replaced to fill the gaping holes that inevitably resulted from the excavations; some of it was used to form the foundations for the new course; and the sizeable remainder was carted away by lorries for the additional useful purpose of building a new sea wall at Maidens harbour.

The Hotels Executive had invited the experienced golf-course architect Philip Mackenzie Ross, appropriately from the golfing town of North Berwick, to design the new Turnberry course, and the large specialist and long-established firm of Messrs Sutton & Sons of Reading in Berkshire to assess what would be required in carrying the design into effect. Suttons were experts in seeds, including grass seeds, turfs and in constructional landscaping work for golf courses. By October 1949, significant progress had been made - especially in so short a period in proportion to the heavy operations - that the aim was then seriously considered in having nine holes of the 18-hole course ready for play by the summer of 1950, as this would be advantageous for the intended reopening of Turnberry Hotel in the spring of 1950. Towards the end of the year, the progress was still being counted as satisfactory because the principal substance of the work had been executed by the removal of most of the airfield, though much still had to be done, as in producing a satisfactory drainage system, in constructing the fairways, greens and tees, and in shaping the artificial slopes. All this needed to be carefully created and blended aesthetically with the nature of the surrounding terrain, involving the substantial task of cutting, carrying and laying of 30 acres with 290,000 sections of turf.

The new Turnberry Hotel of 147 bedrooms reopened on Thursday 1st June, 1950; for, during the previous 12 months, an 'army of tradesmen' had also been transforming the large building from its military-hospital status of the war years back into its original purpose of a luxury holiday and golfing resort. Thousands of pounds were spent in the process of refitting and re-equipping the hotel into one of the most modern in Europe; and on the last day of May, the press had been invited to see the results internally, including,

> ... a luxury indoor swimming pool; miles of new, inch-deep carpeting in every room, deadening every footfall, ranging from delicate colours for the bedrooms to the darker but attractive burgundy shades of the covering of the corridors; glittering chandeliers with clusters of electric lights overhead; every room redecorated in new furniture, or, in some cases, to utilise some of the old furniture; the American bar reconstructed, and the hair-dressing saloons and shops operating, as before the war; the ballroom, where the resident orchestra presides, with the ultra-modern lighting arrangement and colour scheme that was worked out bearing in mind that on bright days rays from the green lawns in front filter through the tall windows; and suites following the newest in decoration, by having one wall papered and a contrast of paint on the other walls.

The Ailsa Course was reopened for play over nine holes on Friday 16th June, 1950. The cost of its reconstruction was believed to be between £50,000 and £70,000, and permission to reconstruct the second course - the Arran - had just been received, with the work soon to commence. By the summer of 1951, the hotel and one 18-hole golf course at Turnberry had been restored when, only a few years before, such greenery seemed impossible to visualize, while decay and then demolition looked to be the ultimate outcome for the hotel.

Happily, Turnberry had been given a new lifeline, but it was sad that the railway would not be reopening for passengers, after informal talk about the prospect of this happening. Thus, the following letter, dated 17th May, 1950, from Mr T.H. Moffat, Deputy Regional Officer of the Railway Executive of BR(ScR) at Buchanan Street in Glasgow, on behalf of Mr T.F. Cameron, the Chief Regional Officer, had been sent to Mr Etienne Vacher the Area Superintendent of the Hotels Executive in Scotland, at Glasgow Central station:

Dear Mr Vacher:
Reopening of Turnberry Hotel
   I refer to our conversation in regard to the possibility of reinstating the passenger service between Girvan and Turnberry in connection with the reopening of Turnberry Hotel on 1st June.

Having had the matter investigated, it transpires that before the service was withdrawn, prior to the war, it was very poorly patronised and there is every reason to believe that the patronage would not be any greater under present-day conditions. For some time, we have been - and still are - withdrawing unremunerative passenger services, and in all the circumstances you will appreciate that the cost of providing a service at the present time, namely £120 per week, would not be justified.

Yours sincerely,

T. Moffat, for CRO.

Unfortunately, in spite of what seemed to have been Mr Vacher's enterprising attempt to revive the southern end of the line between Girvan and Turnberry for the benefit of the hotel, all that would remain for passengers on any part of the former M&DLR would be the bustling Butlin's services at the northern end, while the sedate goods and potato trains would continue to trundle over the whole line.

An aerial view of Butlin's Holiday camp, from the sea looking south, in the late 1940s, with Butlin's Heads of Ayr Hotel and the Ayr-Dunure road at the extreme top of the view, on the higher ground. The railway runs from left to right, or east to west, between the camp and the hotel, and encompasses the long station platform, station building, loop, platform steps to the camp and bridge over the Butlin's access road. Later, in conjunction with new platform steps nearer the station building, a roofed but open-sided walkway was constructed between the station and the camp.   *Butlin's Memories*

Chapter Sixteen

The Final Era of the Goods Services, 1946-1959

For several years after the opening of Butlin's camp in 1947, the more interested holidaymakers would have observed the old Maidens & Dunure Light Railway in operation beyond the Heads of Ayr passenger terminus station, as the daily Turnberry goods and the seasonal potato trains traversed the line; and some of the campers, especially railway enthusiasts, no doubt stood on the station platform and watched them pass. The goods and potato trains were now in the last phase of the whole line, with the '2Fs', '3Fs' and '2Ps' working the services after the war.

After World War II, the daily goods train, which operated on Mondays to Saturdays and which was known as the 'K156' trip, was the only regular service to run over the whole line throughout the year, but, it did not appear in the working timetables, and, instead, it was designated in the 'train trip and shunting engine' booklet. The routine for 'K156' was that it proceeded back to Ayr by the main line through Maybole, but that on Saturdays when required - usually only during the main potato season of June and July - it returned by the light railway. However, during the potato season, there was also a Mondays-to-Fridays train solely for the famous and eagerly-awaited early crop from the Carrick coast, immediately when ready for picking from late May or early June through July. This train left empty wagons at the yards along the line on the way south for the next day and picked up the wagons, loaded with potatoes, on the way back to Ayr. On Saturdays, when the potato train did not run and when there were sufficient potatoes to be gathered, which was dependent on the weather of Saturday and the previous few days, 'K156' acted as the potato train and returned by the coastal route instead of by Maybole.

Each yard or siding on the line had its own method of working for the various goods wagons, according to the layout and direction of the points and sidings. The foreman at Falkland yard gave the guard a daily list that detailed how many wagons were to be detached at each station, such that the wagons were placed behind the train in the appropriate order for uncoupling at the stations, as the train made its way southwards. It left Falkland yard, varying over the post-war years, between 8 and 9 am, with wagons of coal from the Ayrshire collieries for the villages and farms, manure from the Ayr cattle market and chemical fertilisers for the farms, and the sundry van containing diverse items for the farms and laundry for Turnberry Hotel, though not everything was conveyed on the same days, and coal, for example, was usually taken only once or twice per week.

In summer, during the post-war period and extending into the 1950s, the goods train consisted of a number of wagons that varied around a dozen but only about half the summer number in winter. For the various farms, cottages, hamlets and villages, the train worked its way southwards to haul fertiliser, animal feed and coal in the wagons, but they were also served by the 'sundry van'. This was placed behind the tender and conveyed such items as packages, agricultural machinery and spares - indeed any products or produce that were best able to be accommodated by the railway - and it was the sundry van that carried miscellaneous goods for Turnberry Hotel. On 15th August, 1951, the railway enthusiast David L. Smith saw the returning Turnberry goods train passing through Ayr station shortly after 6 pm with a Caley 'Jumbo' engine - BR No. 57354, as ex-LMS No. 17354, from Hurlford shed - hauling about 25 wagons, which was generally twice that of the usual summer

On 26th September, 1949, George Robin, a railway enthusiast from Glasgow, travelled over the M&DLR on the daily southbound-only Turnberry goods train, with BR permission, and he photographed the generally overgrown and deserted stations, the train and its crew, of driver Nick Armstrong, fireman Willie McMillan and guard Charlie Tyson. Of additional interest, from the content of the photographs, the train carried two illicit passengers part of the way, because one man is seen at Dunure and Knoweside and another is seen at Knoweside and Glenside. The engine was an ex-CR '3F', officially as BR No. 57633 but still in its LMS livery and number of 17633. Alloway station, 1949, in the low illumination of dawn, with the train crew, *left to right*, Charlie Tyson, Willie McMillan and Nick Armstrong. *Mitchell Library, Glasgow: Robin Collection*

Dunure station, 1949, with, *left to right*, the first illicit passenger, who is also seen at Knoweside, and the train crew, Willie McMillan, Nick Armstrong and Charlie Tyson.
Mitchell Library, Glasgow: Robin Collection

Knoweside station looking north, 1949, with the goods train at a stop over the level crossing for the engine to take water from the tank. The first illicit passenger is joined by a second, who is also seen at Glenside.   *Mitchell Library, Glasgow: Robin Collection*

The goods train on the Rancleugh viaduct, 1949, from the south-west, highlighting the truss, girder and pier constructions.   *Mitchell Library, Glasgow: Robin Collection*

The goods train, and Charlie Tyson, on the Rancleugh viaduct, 1949, from the southern end of the structure.   *Mitchell Library, Glasgow: Robin Collection*

Glenside station, 1949, with, *left to right*, Willie McMillan, Nick Armstrong, Charlie Tyson and the second illicit passenger, but with the first not present. The door nearest the camera was for the private waiting room of the Marquis of Ailsa, and the adjacent sign reads 'Public Telephone'.
Mitchell Library, Glasgow: Robin Collection

Maidens station, 1949, with Charlie Tyson beside the engine.
Mitchell Library, Glasgow: Robin Collection

Turnberry station, 1949, with Charlie Tyson and probably the Turnberry goods porter beside the engine, while two workmen are discerned on the track at the right. The building, canopy and platform - and the flower tubs, seats, signs and posters - are impressive and reinforce the light and airy feel, 7½ years after the station's closure to passengers, in a view of what looks like the station of a large town that still served the public.   *Mitchell Library, Glasgow: Robin Collection*

The goods train at Dipple, 1949, with the loop beyond the brake van.
Mitchell Library, Glasgow: Robin Collection

The train crew at Dipple, 1949, with additionally, second from left, the Dipple goods agent.
Mitchell Library, Glasgow: Robin Collection

goods train on the Turnberry road. As usual, this resulted from its return along the main line via Maybole that allowed this working to serve both lines and more goods yards, such that, by the time of reaching Ayr, the load was substantially increased by the main-line yards.

Between Girvan and Turnberry, there was a goods service to the hotel siding for the 'laundry van', which contained wicker-basket hampers of the hotel laundry and which was taken perhaps two or three times a week, or as required, to be washed at Slateford, Edinburgh, and returned clean, as part of the service for British Transport Commission Hotels. The laundry van, or sometimes two vans, proceeded to and from Glasgow via Maybole on a Girvan or Stranraer goods or passenger train, and to and from Girvan by a '2F' or '3F' or '2P'. Most of the time, the engine hauled only the laundry van and the guard's van, but every few weeks, it was augmented by one or two coal wagons or the returning empties, because coal was needed for heating the hotel. Also still in existence was the short run between the Grangeston munitions factory of ICI for the Ministry of Supply (later Ministry of Defence), operated by a '2F' or '3F' or '2P'. The services for Grangeston and Turnberry were separate, such that the one train did not serve both places because the irregular timings for each did not generally coincide.

There was also a daily list for the guard of the potato train that indicated how many wagons were to be detached at which yards and which wagons containing vacuum brakes were ultimately to be attached, loaded with potatoes, on the return journey to Glasgow and elsewhere in Scotland and England because, at their best soon after picking, they needed to reach the markets quickly, and they had priority over non-perishable goods. Thus, the wagons - with and without vacuum brakes - were left at the yards on the Turnberry line on the southbound journey for filling with potatoes and collected the next day, except if continuous heavy rain prevented the picking or loading of the crop. Although some loaded wagons could sometimes be collected by the southbound train if convenient, it was usually the northbound train that conveyed the crop to Ayr, as that was the purpose of the train heading back northwards. The train was shunted at Girvan goods yard, close to the harbour, and at Bridge Mill sidings, where potatoes were also loaded, being very convenient for Girvan Mains farm. The potato train contained somewhere between 15 and 40 wagons, depending on the specific period involved, with estimates ranging from 15 to 20 during and immediately after the war and from 20 to 40 slightly later, towards 1950, with the difference possibly explained in that there may have been more than one potato train in the former period and only one in the latter. The goods or potato trains carried other produce when required, such as cabbages from Bridge Mill, turnips from Knoweside, and whelks from Dunure for Billingsgate fish market in London.

The most complicated shunting operation for 'K156' was at Alloway, where the goods yard was adjacent to the passenger station but situated at a higher level than the main line that descended at 1 in 80 towards the station to proceed through the tunnel. The siding connection to the yard was indirect, such that entry to it from the direction of Alloway Junction was in a 'reversing zigzag' or 'back and forth' manner to ascend the gradient between the main line and the yard. This was achieved firstly by trailing points from the Ayr direction, at the eastern end of the island platform. The trailing points provided access for the engine and the wagons to be shunted to a short link-siding that ran eastwards, past another set of trailing points for entry to the yard, to proceed into a headshunt siding that led as far as the Doonholm Road bridge. Alloway yard contained no loop, which meant that for 'running-round' shunting, either the station loop or the practice of gravity shunting had to be used.

Turnberry station, with a light covering of snow. All passenger traffic had long ceased when these two photographs were taken in December 1950 of the early BR period, with the scenes partly representative of the winter appearance of the station during any era of its lifetime.

From the north, with the station building still in use for the station master and porter in connection with the daily goods train from Ayr and the sundry van from Girvan. *H. Stevenson*

From the south, a bleak-looking view of the nameboard, but not the posts, removed.

H. Stevenson

The headshunt, which was an extended section of track or a siding that could accommodate an engine and enough wagons to allow shunting into the main yard, ran immediately beside, parallel to, and on the same steep descent of 1 in 80 as the main line, while the gradient from the yard entry points was level into the yard. The gradient of the headshunt had to be sufficiently steep for the wagons to be able to run by gravity into the yard.

The wagons to be detached at the yard were placed at the front of the train - meaning between the tender and the rest of the wagons that would be detached at the other yards - and the whole train did not proceed into the yard, as its other wagons were left braked on the main line. Only those wagons for the yard were propelled up the link-siding and towards the headshunt by the engine - which was now uncoupled from them - when the wagons were then given the vigorous but judicious push that forced them into the headshunt, with the engine pausing on the link-siding, before reaching the headshunt points. The momentum of the wagons firstly carried them sufficiently far along the uphill gradient of the headshunt to be stopped by gravity or by manual-lever braking; and, on the points being changed - and the brake being released, if used in the process - the momentum of the wagons down the headshunt allowed them to run into the level yard and lose speed to come a stop before the buffers. The points were changed again twice, allowing the engine to move into the headshunt and then into the yard to place the wagons into the sidings, which would save some time.

Gravity shunting was not officially approved but its use was seemingly 'unofficially ignored', and it was also necessary when the yard contained no run-round loop, which was the case at Alloway. The advantage of gravity shunting in this respect was that it placed the engine on the correct or appropriate side of the headshunt - simply because there was no loop in the yard - such that the wagons could be pushed by the engine into the yard sidings.

Alloway originally possessed a loop at the station but not at the yard, and by the mid-to-late 1930s gravity shunting had become the only shunting method that was possible there - meaning that conventional shunting was impossible, because of the reduction to a siding of the northern line of the loop through the station's island platform. The general principle of the layouts for all the stations and yards on the M&DLR was that where a loop existed at the station, there was no loop in the yard, with the converse applying. However, the later exceptions were Heads of Ayr and Dipple, as each originally possessed a loop at the yard from the opening of the line in 1906, with no loop on the main line, and each was provided with a loop in 1914, when Heads of Ayr station consequently became an island platform. These two main-line loops had been installed because of the necessity of introducing the crossing of trains there to prevent delays to the passenger services, but by the mid-to-late 1930s, the loops at Heads of Ayr and Dunure, in addition to Alloway, had been removed. Maidens was the only other island-platform station, and, with the yard at the goods depot having no loop, the importance of the yard for goods traffic was such that the loop at the passenger station was retained for shunting back to the yard.

Alloway was the only yard that contained a headshunt and where gravity shunting was used. At Greenan Castle, Heads of Ayr, Dunure, Glenside and Dipple, where the points faced the Ayr direction, and at Knoweside, Maidens and Turnberry, where the points faced the Girvan direction, conventional shunting was the official means of operation, with the engine pushing or pulling the appropriate wagons into the yard or siding, or rounding them in the station loop or yard loop. However, in reality, unofficial 'fly shunting' was often used at the yards that were

Alloway station and its forlorn garden, *c.* 1950, with the northern line of the loop removed and the southern line used for the Butlin's trains and the goods and potato trains. The station building was demolished sometime between 1950 and 1955, as it is not present in a 1955 photograph.   *G&SWR Association*

entered by facing points from the Ayr direction, because this was more convenient and quicker for the railwaymen, who, naturally, were competent in its operation. For fly shunting, the wagons that were to be detached were placed directly behind the tender, as the train stopped a sufficient distance before arriving at the points. The guard applied the brake in his van before stepping down to walk along the track and uncouple the wagons from the rest of the train behind it. With the fireman standing by the points, the guard sanctioned the driver to move the engine slowly forward, at walking pace, and the guard, following the speed of the engine, uncoupled the wagons from the tender judiciously before the engine reached the points and while the wagons were still being pulled. Immediately after the uncoupling, the guard directed the driver to increase the speed of the engine along the 'main line' and effectively take it 'out of the way' of the points; and then, immediately after the train had cleared the points, the fireman set the points towards the siding, with the result that the wagons, by reason of their momentum, were propelled into the siding and usually to the correct distance.

The yard at Dunure, like that at Alloway, was adjacent to the station and at a higher level - more so at Dunure, but with facing points to the Ayr direction, 400 yards north of the station platform, and without the link siding and headshunt. Perhaps more traffic had been expected at Alloway, in that the layout was constructed more like a larger goods yard, or perhaps Alloway had been the first yard to be laid out and then a decision was made to lay out Dunure and the other yards simpler and cheaper. Furthermore, if expense had been a consideration, another difference between Dunure and Alloway was the deep rock cutting at Dunure station, which would have had to be excavated to a greater width to accommodate a headshunt, whereas at Alloway, the lower-height cutting had been formed through softer material.

Turnberry Hotel siding diverged from the loop of the main line at the northern end of the station platform by a junction facing the Girvan direction, and wagons from the Ayr direction were simply reversed into the siding, which was relatively long, at 160 yards. The siding terminated on the north-eastern side of the hotel, which was the most suitable place for serving it with coal. The main line was on a rising gradient northwards from the junction but was level at the station, where the junction was conveniently made. Although the siding could accommodate 20 wagons, such a number was unnecessary, and an RAF aerial photograph, *circa* 1945, of the area around the hotel and the station showed five wagons situated at the northern end of the siding. The hotel still needed to be supplied with coal during its conversion to a military hospital, and the number of wagons then was reasonably representative of any period in the hotel's history, with perhaps an average of two to five wagons at any one time.

Balchriston siding and Grangeston munitions works private sidings, with both having facing points in the Ayr direction, were still in use after the war. Balchriston was used only for the seasonal potato traffic, being worked, since its opening in 1933, by the method of shunting called 'tail roping' on southbound trains and using the same principle as fly shunting but with a rope instead of the orthodox wagon coupling. This was because an uphill gradient was against the southbound train approaching Balchriston for thrusting the wagons into the siding. Before reaching the points, the engine was stopped and uncoupled from the wagons that were to be shunted into the siding, and these wagons, at the front of the train, were uncoupled from those behind them. With the rest of the train held by the brake van at the rear, a strong hemp rope was attached to the rear of the engine and to the leading wagon for the siding. The engine moved slowly forwards and the points were changed immediately after the engine had moved past the points but before the first wagon had reached them. The wagons were then hauled into the siding by the engine continuing slowly forwards on the main line. The rope was disconnected and the points were changed back, to allow the engine to reverse to collect the other wagons that were to conveyed southwards from Balchriston. Grangeston was served not by the southbound daily goods train but by the local 'trip' engine, with the brake van behind the tender, hauling the wagons from Girvan and reversing them into the Grangeston siding, where the points trailed from the Girvan direction. The engine then proceeded to Turnberry to use the loop as a run-round facility, to place the brake van behind for the return journey to Girvan.

There were two calls at Girvan for 'K156'. The first was Bridge Mill sidings, which was convenient for several farms to the east but particularly so for Girvan Mains immediately north. Then, continuing towards the town, the train turned south-westwards from Girvan Junction towards the goods depot near the harbour. On Mondays to Fridays during the potato season, the returning northbound potato train usually left Bridge Mill, where potatoes were loaded, soon after the arrival there of the southbound 'K156'.

In the autumn of 1949, a journey over the coastal line had been accomplished by the Glasgow railway enthusiast George Robin, after his acquisition of a brake-van pass for the 'K156' goods train, and George had also been able to photograph aspects of the line. He remembered that the LMS had run an 'evening cruise train' in the mid-1930s from Glasgow to Girvan via Turnberry - the train thereby using the nominally-closed route for passengers - and returning by Maybole, but that it left St Enoch too early for him to take, such that all he had previously managed was a trip on the Girvan-Turnberry passenger section before he was called for war service. However, in compensation for missing a passenger journey over the whole line, he became a guest passenger on 'K156'; and to his even greater joy, he was unofficially invited onto the footplate for the run, having been made welcome by the crew: Nick Armstrong, driver; Willie McMillan, fireman; and Charlie Tyson, guard. The engine was a Caley '3F' - LMS No. 17633, which had become BR No. 57633 but was still in its LMS unlined black livery and number, then of Hurlford shed and formerly of Ayr shed. With thousands of locomotives to be repainted from nationalization, and with priority given to passenger engines, No. 17633 had not reached that stage, though its number was nevertheless 57633 officially under BR, where, for LMS engines, '40,000' was added to the LMS number to produce the BR number.

After loading sundries at Ayr station, No. 17633 and its train of seven wagons and brake van left at 7.15 am. Some shunting or propelling work was done at Alloway yard, Greenan, Heads of Ayr and Dunure, and then there was the obligatory stop at Knoweside, if only for water, with the wagons stopped across the public road. No work was done at Glenside, as the train then proceeded to Maidens, shunting back from the former passenger station with their goods load to the yard, where the crew took their break. At Turnberry, George saw what he thought were yards but which consisted only of the hotel siding and the run-round loop, and he was pleased that Turnberry station looked so smart, in being freshly painted and clean, though no public passenger train had called since 1942. At Dipple, he noticed the novelty of an experimental section of track there which was laid with concrete sleepers. Thanks to the crew, in kindly accommodating their guest from having the road to themselves, the train was specially stopped at the stations to let George to photograph them. Alloway, Dunure, Knoweside, Glenside, Maidens, and Turnberry stations were thus able to be captured for posterity as a representation of their post-war appearance. Not only that: at Dipple, where no official business was required, the train was stopped and George was able to photograph the crew and the goods porter, standing in front of the engine; but, most spectacularly, he had been provided with the opportunity to take two photographs of the Rancleugh viaduct. Firstly, the train was stopped on the viaduct and George took a photograph of the train along the track; and then, on returning to the engine, he was run to the southern end of the viaduct, where the train stopped again, to let George off so that he could descend the embankment, with the train backing onto the viaduct, allowing him to take an impressive photograph, from below the level of the railway, of the train crossing the viaduct, while also highlighting much of its structure.

By - and also well before - the post-war era of the goods and potato service, there had long been no passenger trains over the whole of the coastal line, but passengers had nevertheless been carried on occasions, unofficially. They were local people who had no other means of transport. Since there was no single bus that covered the whole route of the line - the Western SMT bus running from Ayr to Dunure and Knoweside, and the same company's Ayr-Maidens-Girvan bus running via Maybole - the daily goods train, for many years, had obligingly conveyed local men, women and children who desired to travel to or from locations that were not conveniently served by the buses. These illicit passengers, often visiting relations or friends, were usually accommodated in the guard's van but sometimes on the engine, with the train stopping at cottages or farms between stations when required. Such was one of the pleasant social aspects of a country branch goods line, as its workforce had a relaxed attitude to authority in consideration of the local small population.

Goods and potato trains trundled over the whole line for 10 years after the war, until early 1955, but with lorries having increasingly taken over much of that traffic; and particularly during the last few years of that period, there was little justification for keeping the line open. The end of the goods service was internally announced on 12th February, 1955, when a short letter from the BTC at Marylebone Road in London to Frank Hole of British Transport Hotels at St Pancras station contained a statement in reference to the 'Ayr-Girvan (via Maidens) Branch' that 'the Scottish Region are arranging for the freight train service over the above branch to be withdrawn as from 28th February, 1955'.

An indication of the facts and figures in operating the railway for the limited freight service, and set in relation to the proposed closure, had been presented by Mr T.F. Cameron, the Chief Regional Officer at Glasgow, in an undated report, which referred to the '12 months ending April 1951' - indicating that closure had been considered at least as far back as that year. For the whole line, the single-track route length was 19 miles and 42 chains and the total track length, with double sections, was 23 miles and 78 chains. The existing stations, goods yards and sidings on the line were: Alloway yard; Greenan Castle sidings; Heads of Ayr passenger station; Heads of Ayr yard; Dunure yard; Knoweside yard; Balchriston siding; Glenside yard; Maidens yard; Turnberry station and siding; Dipple sidings; and Grangeston private sidings for ICI. The proposals for the closure were:

(a) that the freight train service be withdrawn from the section Greenan Castle goods to Grangeston private siding; (b) that the track and other redundant assets between a point 20 chains south of Heads of Ayr passenger station and a point 2 miles, 7 chains south of Dipple goods depot be recovered [i.e. removed] - 14 miles, 44 chains (route) - 16 miles, 76 chains (track); (c) that only traffic in full truck loads be dealt with at Alloway and Greenan Castle.

Traffic receipts and tonnage that was handled - classed under 'forwarded' or taken away, and under 'received' or brought in - were given as:

Receipts: parcels - £640; freight - £12,261; total - £12,901. Tonnage, excluding Turnberry Hotel traffic: forwarded - 2,659 tons, mainly early potatoes from all branch stations and 359 head of livestock; received - 14,950 tons, mainly coal and minerals (phosphate for storage at Turnberry) and 132 head of livestock.

The 'estimated annual saving' by the withdrawal of the freight service was stated to be £16,085, which was reached by the difference between the small 'annual loss of receipts' and the large 'annual reduction in expenditure':

Annual loss of receipts: freight - £1,660. Extra cartage or other cost - nil. *Annual reduction in expenditure:* station staff - £2,834; train working - £6,860; civil engineering - £8,051; total £17,745. *Estimated annual saving: -* £16,085.

From the annual reduction in expenditure, the loss in staff employment along the line was:

Alloway - goods agent; *Dunure* - porter (junior); *Knoweside* - goods porter (part time); *Maidens* - station master, goods porter (part time), train regulator (part time); *Turnberry* - station master, porter (junior); *Dipple* - goods porter. Civil engineer's department: ganger, sub-ganger, 3 lengthmen.

Alternative facilities were necessarily considered. BTC road vehicles already delivered freight directly to the customers' premises, and these vehicles would be able to cover the whole area that was served by the branch stations. However, most traders made their own arrangements for delivering and uplifting full loads at the branch stations, and it was felt that this practice would continue at the three designated railheads for the district after the branch closure. These railheads were: Greenan Castle sidings, which, in being connected by rail because of the Butlin's services, would remain open; Maybole depot; and Girvan Bridge Mill sidings. Additionally, Alloway goods yard was also to be kept open, as would Grangeston private siding, but the yards and sidings of all the other stations were to be closed.

These four photographs show the sad and dilipidated state of four M&DLR stations in September 1955, with the line having closed in February, though there was continued use from Girvan to Grangeston and Turnberry until 1957 or even 1958. Turnberry, 1955, with the clearer track indicating the continued use to Girvan.

Dunbartonshire Archives, Kirkintilloch: McEwan Collection

Knoweside, 1955, with a car faintly seen at the level crossing but with the gates no longer having to be opened for any train.   *Dunbartonshire Archives, Kirkintilloch: McEwan Collection*

Heads of Ayr, 1955. The presence of rails and sleepers on the western side of the island platform is puzzling, as the original track on that side was removed during the 1930s, but possibly a short section was re-laid by the workmen of Connell of Coatbridge, the contractor, for their convenience in dismantling the line from 1955.
Dunbartonshire Archives, Kirkintilloch: McEwan Collection

Maidens, 1955, looking north-east, showing the subway stairs, railings and white-glazed brick wall.   *Dunbartonshire Archives, Kirkintilloch: McEwan Collection*

For the year ending 12th April, 1951, laundry hampers had formed regular freight between Turnberry Hotel and Ayr, numbering 1,249 hampers forwarded and 1,834 received. They necessitated 136 special trips by train engine between Girvan and Turnberry during the summer months, but in winter they were taken to Girvan by a hotel car, with the returning laundry delivered by the daily freight train from Ayr by the coastal line throughout the year. Additional forwarded traffic that had been conveyed by train, such as empties and refuse, from the hotel totalled 242 tons, and there were 223 parcels; while received traffic amounted 1,888 tons, consisting of 1,801 tons of coal, 14 tons of ashes and 73 tons of merchandise, and 381 parcels. On the closure of the railway, the whole of the hotel traffic would require to be conveyed by road, with the additional cost to the hotel and catering services estimated at £568 in respect of full load traffic, and at £785 for parcels, laundry hampers and sundries.

One other item of freight that was conveyed partly by the railway was phosphate, a salt or compound of phosphoric acid. According to Mr Cameron, 24,500 tons were stored in the remaining and otherwise-disused hangars of Turnberry airfield, and of this, 20,000 tons had been brought by road and the remaining 4,500 tons by rail to Maidens and then by road. Mr Cameron had added that nothing was known about the ultimate destination of the phosphate.

Although the branch served an agricultural area, no new developments to increase the rail traffic were anticipated, but the line was required to be retained between Ayr and Heads of Ayr because it catered for the Butlin's passengers and because of the volume of coal traffic at Alloway and Greenan, which were also within the Butlin's section, could not be conveniently accommodated elsewhere; while it was also necessary to retain the line between Girvan and Grangeston private siding to serve ICI.

Mr Cameron's report ended abruptly with the conclusion of what should happen: 'It is *recommended* that the freight train service be withdrawn and the line closed between a point 20 chains south of Heads of Ayr passenger station and a point 2 miles 7 chains south of Dipple goods depot.'

In mid-February 1955, BR(ScR) announced to the public that the line from Heads of Ayr to Dipple would be closed as early as Monday 28th February. The *Ayrshire Post*, and the *Ayr Advertiser*, with headlines respectively of 'Maidens Branch Line to be Closed' and 'Branch Line Stations Close This Month', provided notification that the following goods stations, yards and sidings would cease to be used: Heads of Ayr, Dunure, Knoweside, Balchriston siding, Glenside, Maidens, Turnberry and Dipple siding; while Alloway and Greenan Castle would remain open and 'deal only with freight train traffic (including livestock) in full truck loads'. Alternative facilities for passenger-rated parcels, merchandise traffic and freight-train traffic in less than truck loads to and from the districts of the affected stations would be available at Ayr or Maybole stations. For freight and livestock traffic in full truck loads, the alternative facilities would operate from Greenan, for accommodating the Heads of Ayr and Dunure districts; from Maybole, for the Knoweside, Balchriston, Glenside, Maidens and Turnberry districts; and from Girvan goods station or Bridge Mill depot, for the Dipple district. A collection and delivery service would also be available between the railheads of Ayr, Maybole and Girvan and the districts of the coastal line.

The *Ayrshire Post*, in its issue of 4th March and under the heading of 'Once Busy Line is Derelict', produced an admirable tribute that was sympathetic and evocative in bidding farewell to the line and its last special goods service in fine weather:

> The sun shone out of a cloudless sky on Wednesday [2nd March] as a short goods train threaded its way slowly along the picturesque Ayr-Girvan coast railway. The train's

return journey marked the end of an era in Ayrshire railway history, for it was the last time that the 14-miles stretch of line between Heads of Ayr and Turnberry would ever carry rolling stock, passenger or goods.

As the train stopped at each station on the doomed line, furniture and station fittings were loaded on to trucks. Then the forlorn little expedition set off for the next stop and the process was repeated. Passenger traffic will continue on the section of line from Ayr to the new Heads of Ayr station, serving Butlin's Holiday Camp, and the portion from Girvan to the Alginate Industries factory at Dipple will remain in use for freight traffic. The stations left derelict after the last train ran on Wednesday were Knoweside, Glenside, Maidens and Turnberry.

Yesterday a miscellany of old clocks, signal-lamps, old-fashioned clerking desks and station seats was being catalogued at Ayr, but among the fittings removed from the station buildings there was nothing of any antiquarian interest. The probable reason for this is that every scrap was removed during the war.

Many of the platform seats recovered are in good condition and they are to be used as replacements for stations in the Ayr district. The closing of the line involves only four railway employees, two station masters and two porters who are to be employed elsewhere in the district.

Laid down in 1906, the line was designed to further residential development of the south Ayrshire coast. Expresses once ran non-stop from Glasgow to Turnberry Hotel, but passenger traffic was suspended in 1930 as road transport gained in popularity. For a number of years potato traffic continued, but the boom of lorry transport outmoded the railway's usefulness in this respect also. Now rusting rails are all that is left of a once bustling branch line.

However, that last goods train was not strictly the very last train that proceeded over the 14 miles of line between Heads of Ayr and Turnberry, because a number of runs were still required to uplift the track, and the first of these necessarily traversed those full 14 miles. The very leisurely dismantling of the line from Heads of Ayr to Turnberry was carried out from north to south between 1955 and 1957, or even 1958, starting immediately south of Butlin's Heads of Ayr station, where a short section of track remained south of the Butlin's railway bridge for the stabling of passenger coaches when required. The track south of Butlin's was removed by the iron and steel merchant James N. Connell of Coatbridge, who possessed a foundry and large scrapyard, and the rails were cut in half while in position and were lifted onto flat-bed railway wagons that had been brought - necessarily pushed - from the Girvan direction by an engine to a point a few hundred yards south of the broken stretch of track, with the engine able to depart back to Girvan. The wagons were left to be filled by Connell's men, as the wagons moved progressively southwards, being pushed by a large tractor and crane that was aligned over the track, with a chain coupled between the tractor and the wagons to prevent them running away. The engine returned to collect the wagons, perhaps the next day, or several days later, before further uplifting could be continued, and the yards or sidings were able to be used for the storage of the loaded wagons, or of the next set of empty wagons. After the gradual lifting of the rails, the other parts of the track - sleepers, chairs, bolts, fishplates and wedges - were conveyed by a lorry that headed more and more southwards along the by-now lifted railway, entering and leaving from the yards or from any other suitable points of access on the route of the line. The ballast was left behind, in being of no interest to a metal merchant.

After the 1955 goods closure of the M&DLR south of Heads of Ayr Butlin's station, a section of track was left intact for a distance of 460 yards, or slightly more than a quarter of a mile, beyond the station, to produce what was effectively a long headshunt that ended on an embankment 65 yards west of the bridge at Laigh

The remains of Balchriston siding and loading bank in September 1955, looking south, as the line curves through the cutting towards the Culzean tunnel.
Dunbartonshire Archives, Kirkintilloch: McEwan Collection

The remains of Balchriston level crossing's southern gate in the late 1950s, having survived for a few years after the 1955 closure of the line.   *G&SWR Association*

The remains of Maidens goods yard in September 1955, looking north with the closed M&DLR out of sight to the left, the left-hand siding led to a goods loading platform on the far-left, with the right-hand siding terminating at the goods shed. A third siding, discernible among the weeds, diverged further to the right and was not in existence at the opening of the M&DLR, as it is not shown on the 6-inch and 25-inch Ordnance Survey maps of 1908 and 1909.   *Dunbartonshire Archives, Kirkintilloch: McEwan Collection*

Kyleston farm. The headshunt was used to accommodate two successive services when they were timed to leave Heads of Ayr station within a relatively short interval, while it was also conveniently used in connection with excursion trains to Butlin's, especially when two arrived on the same day.

Also from the 1955 closure, which was initially between Heads of Ayr and Turnberry only, the line remained in use from Girvan to Turnberry until 1957 or 1958 because the dismantling had not reached Turnberry before then, such that the services for the hotel and for Grangeston were able to be maintained. During this period, on the withdrawal of the station master's post at Turnberry and the removal of the electric-token signalling, the staff was used for the Girvan-Turnberry goods and Girvan-Grangeston goods trains. Finally, as the dismantling proceeded south of Turnberry, both services ceased on unspecified dates - Grangeston first, in spite of being further south - and, thus, the last section of the Maidens & Dunure Light Railway south of Butlin's Heads of Ayr station closed for goods traffic. On the disuse of Turnberry station, the glass canopy was bought by Dumbarton Football Club, transported to the club's Boghead Park and erected by the club's supporters to form part of a covered enclosure.

All that was now left in use of the M&DLR was the electric-tablet section from Alloway Junction to Butlin's, primarily for the passenger traffic but also for goods traffic at Alloway and Greenan Castle. However, the truncated and little-used goods service lasted another four years and nine months after the principal 1955 severance, and the *Ayr Advertiser* announced the imminent closure of Alloway and Greenan on the front page of in its issue of 26th November, 1959, under the heading of 'The Axe Falls on Two "Ghost Depots"'. The paper reported that there was insufficient traffic to justify the depots being kept open and that they were to close officially on Monday 7th December, adding that Alloway 'was once a busy goods depot handling coal, livestock and produce' but that road traffic had gradually taken over, with only coal brought into the yard. The closure report was accompanied by a photograph of the sad and desolate scene after the removal of the two southernmost and longest sidings, while also showing the solitary employee, 64-year-old porter Elijah Bishop. With the implication that the yard was no longer in use at the time of the photograph, the caption stated: 'Elijah Bishop, the last railwayman at Alloway, shifts the points for the last time on the tracks which have carried their last trains.' Elijah, who had been the head shunter at Ayr harbour, was to be transferred to Kilmarnock station for the remaining few months before his retirement; and, although not stated in the paper, he had arrived in Ayr during World War I as a soldier, having originated from Newfoundland, which was a separate country until its union with Canada in 1949.

Towards the end of the service, Alloway and Greenan had been served by a coal train that was called 'The Squeeb' ('Squib'), running from Ayr harbour to the local coal lyes (yards) at the sidings in and to the south of the town, after the coal had been brought by trains from the Ayrshire pits to the harbour. The name derived from the train 'jumping about, back and forth' over short distances, and its route from the harbour was 'in and out of' the lyes at Townhead, Newtonhead, Glengall, Dalrymple, Alloway and perhaps Greenan, and then back to Belmont, before returning to Falkland yard or the harbour. 'The Squeeb' was essentially worked by the former CR standard goods tank engines of McIntosh design, which were '782' class 0-6-0Ts that were termed '3F' by the LMS and then by BR. Containing 4 ft 6 in. driving wheels, they were built between 1898 and 1922, to become the next most numerous CR class after the 'Jumbos'. Ayr had a small allocation of these '3Fs' of the ex-CR '782' class during the 1930s, with a maximum of six in 1950 and a reduction to four in 1959.

The *Ayr Advertiser* completed its account of the closure by indicating 'busier days at Alloway when the tracks glinted in the sun', but that now 'the lines are rusty and weed-choked', with the only future traffic being the Butlin's trains - 'and the ghost trains'. The Butlin's section was the last survivor of any part of the M&DLR; and while the passenger trains no doubt carried occasional light goods to and from Butlin's in the guard's van, the branch was not officially a goods line. Although Heads of Ayr Butlin's station was situated inside the camp, anyone could use the trains to and from there without visiting the camp. The station and the branch belonged to British Railways, which was why non-Butlin's passengers were permitted, but only Butlin's passengers could proceed from the station into the camp.

A poor image from the *Ayr Advertiser* of the last railwayman at Alloway, Elijah Bishop, as he views the sad and desolate scene at Alloway goods yard in November 1959 before the official closure of the yard on 7th December. The camera looks south-west.

J. Russell, and Ayrshire Weekly Press

Chapter Seventeen

The Butlin's Passenger Services
and their Locomotives, 1947-1968

During the first few years after the opening of the Butlin's passenger service in 1947, there was a general increase in the number of trains over the branch. Following a total of 13 trains in 1947, with six to and seven from Heads of Ayr, and 18 trains in 1948, with nine in each direction, came a total of 20 in 1950, 22 in 1951, and 21 in 1952 and 1953, but with an imbalance of more trains to Heads of Ayr than in the opposite direction during those first three years of the 1950s. The differences in each direction for the three years were as follows, to and from Heads of Ayr respectively: 11 and nine for 1950; 13 and nine for 1951; 13 and nine for 1952; and 12 and nine for 1953. These totals were high for what was, in reality, a small rural terminus station that consisted of one platform, in spite of its considerable length and in accommodating long-distance trains to and from cities.

The Butlin's services were to last for 21 years after the opening in 1947. How they developed and declined over the period of the line, for a selection of years from 1948 to its closure in 1968, is summarized by a composite timetable that portrays the trains and their variations to and from Heads of Ayr, Ayr, Kilmarnock, Glasgow, Edinburgh, Newcastle and Leeds. The representative services were extracted mainly from the summer issues of the official BR timetables - usually June to September - though the local services and the through services for Glasgow and Edinburgh started in May each year and, therefore, they were sometimes extracted from the timetable that ended in the preceding May. The Newcastle and Leeds trains encompassed a slightly lesser extent of the summer timetable period - for example, from mid- or late June to early or mid-September - than the trains to and from Glasgow St Enoch and Edinburgh Princes Street. British Railways also became known as British Rail and began using 24-hour times in 1965, but 12-hour times are shown in the composite timetable for uniformity.

Where no through trains to and from places in England were indicated in the BR timetables, connections for all the principal English cities were available at Kilmarnock and Glasgow. Some Kilmarnock-Ayr trains were extended to, and some were started from, Heads of Ayr to provide connections with the South, while more distant direct services to Edinburgh, Newcastle and Leeds developed in accordance with the growing popularity of the camp in the successive years. Other Glasgow-Ayr and Kilmarnock-Ayr Monday-Friday trains in the earlier years may have worked to and from Heads of Ayr on summer Saturdays, but it is not always certain which ones did so. The doubt is caused by the Heads of Ayr services being shown in the same timetable column as the Glasgow-Ayr and Kilmarnock-Ayr services, without distinction or notification about whether such trains were also sometimes through services to and from Heads of Ayr. Thus, more of those trains may have been through services to and from Glasgow and Kilmarnock than are indicated in the composite timetable. Corridor-trains served Edinburgh, Newcastle and Leeds, and non-corridor trains served Glasgow, which were Saturday extensions of the Glasgow-Ayr local services that ran Mondays to Saturdays.

Except for the local services between Ayr and Heads of Ayr, which were known by the train crews as the 'shuttle', all the Butlin's trains, including the locals that were extended to and from Kilmarnock, used the Ayr main line through platforms,

Composite Timetable Summary of Butlin's Services, 1948 to 1968

	1948	1950	1951	1952	1953	1957	1962	1964	1965	1966	1967	1968
Dep. times from Ayr (am) for Heads of Ayr	6.15K	7.15	7.15	7.15	7.15	7.15	7.15	7.15	7.15	7.15	7.15	7.15
		9.00	9.00	9.00	9.00	9.00	9.00	9.00	9.00	9.00	8.40G	8.30G
	10.08	10.10	10.10	10.10	10.10	10.07	10.12	10.12	10.12	10.12		
	11.31G	11.30G	11.30	11.30	11.30	11.17G	10.57G	10.48G	10.48G	10.48G	11.05G	11.05G
			11.45	11.47G								
Dep. times from Ayr (pm) for Heads of Ayr	1.04	12.08N	12.08N	12.08N	12.08N	12.08N	12.08N	12.08N		12.39N	12.39N	12.39N
		12.39E	12.39E	12.39E	12.58E	12.58E		12.51E				
		1.35	1.35G	1.35G	1.48G	1.48	1.53	1.50	1.50	1.50		
			2.43K	2.43	2.43	2.43	2.46	2.40	2.42			
									2.53E			
	3.32K	3.40	3.40	3.40K	3.40				3.20	3.22		
	4.40	4.50	4.40K	4.50K	4.50	4.50	4.50	4.40	4.40	4.40	4.05	4.05G
	5.47											
		6.15	6.15	6.15	6.15	6.15	6.30	6.30	6.30	6.30	6.10	6.11G
	7.55									7.22		
		8.05	8.05	8.10K	8.10	8.10		8.00	8.00			
	10.00											
Dep. times from Heads of Ayr (am)	8.39K	8.20N	8.20N	8.20N	8.10N	8.10N	8.05N	8.05N	8.00N	8.00N	8.00N	8.00N
		8.35L	8.35L	8.35L	8.35L	8.35L	8.20L					
	9.45G	9.45G	9.45G	9.45G	9.25G	9.25E	9.20E	9.20E	9.20E	9.57G	9.52G	9.52G
						9.45G	9.45G	9.57G	9.57G			
	10.40	10.55	10.55	10.55	10.55	10.55	10.40	10.40	10.40	10.40		
									11.55G		11.55G	11.55G
Dep. times from Heads of Ayr (pm)	12.30	12.00G	12.00G	12.00G	12.00G	12.00G	12.00G	12.00G		12.00G		
	1.50	1.25	1.10	1.10	1.35	1.35	1.35	1.35	1.20	1.20	1.20	1.20
		2.00	2.00	2.00	2.10	2.10	2.15	2.15	2.15	2.15		
		3.05	3.05	3.05	3.05	3.05	3.05	3.05	3.15	3.15	3.15	3.15
	4.25	4.20G	4.20	4.20	4.20	4.20	4.20	3.55	3.55	3.55		
	5.40											
	6.33K											
	8.30											

Notes: E - Edinburgh. G - Glasgow. K - Kilmarnock. L - Leeds. N - Newcastle. No letter beside a service indicates the local Ayr-Heads of Ayr service, but some of these trains may also have been through-services to and from Glasgow or Kilmarnock.

3 northbound and 5 southbound. The shuttle generally used dock platform 4, which was the original fifth platform of 1902 at the south-eastern end of the station, as a starting and terminating point, but the opposite loop platform 6, built in 1913 at the south-western end, was used occasionally. The journey time between Ayr and Heads of Ayr was generally 12 minutes for the five-mile distance, with any variations from the 12 minutes being nominal, and there was often an ample connection time of 12 to 18 minutes at Ayr between distant and local trains.

The Butlin's Edinburgh trains travelled over the former Caledonian line through Shotts, Holytown and Bellshill, all in Lanarkshire, with a stop at Holytown station, which was situated in the neighbouring town of New Stevenston, allowing local connections with the nearby large Lanarkshire towns, such as Hamilton, Motherwell and Coatbridge. Then the route was across the southern side of central Glasgow to Shields Junction and Paisley Gilmour Street, and via Kilwinning to Ayr. The through trains between Edinburgh and Heads of Ayr in one or both directions were a regular feature from 1950 to 1965. Furthermore, in 1957 - within the peak period for rail-borne holiday traffic between the years of post-war austerity and the encroachment by motor transport, there was another Saturdays-only train which ran during the summer from Edinburgh to Ayr and back but not Heads of Ayr. This service departed from Edinburgh Princes Street at 3.05 pm to reach Ayr at 5.41, and it left Ayr at 6.05 pm to arrive in Edinburgh at 8.55. Whether or not it was used much in either direction by Butlin's passengers, it allowed them an alternative time of day, from and to Edinburgh, to begin and end their holiday.

		A	B				A	B
		am	*pm*				*am*	*pm*
Edinburgh	*dep.*	10.30	3.05	Heads of Ayr	*dep.*		9.25	
Ayr	*arr.*	12.52	5.41	Ayr	*arr.*		9.37	
Ayr	*dep.*	12.58		6.15	Ayr	*dep.*	9.42	6.05
Heads of Ayr	*arr.*	1.10		6.27	Edinburgh	*arr.*	12.00	8.55

Notes: A - Via Bellshill and Uddingston, intermediate stops Shotts, Holytown, Paisley Gilmour St, Troon and Prestwick. B - Via Motherwell and Hamilton, intermediate stops Shotts, Holytown, Motherwell, Hamilton Central, Hamilton West, Blantyre, Paisley Gilmour St, Troon, Prestwick and Newton-on-Ayr.

A composite timetable of the arrival and departure times of the Heads of Ayr through trains and local trains in both directions during the period from 17th June to 15th September, 1957 illustrates the frequency of the service to and from the Butlin's terminus.

		am	*am*	*am*	*am*	*am*	*am*	*pm*	*pm*	*pm*	*pm*	*pm*
Edinburgh	*d.*						10.30					
Glasgow	*d.*				9.55							
Paisley	*d.*				10.10		11.57					
Newcastle	*d.*					8.15						
Carlisle	*d.*					9.54						
Dumfries	*d.*					10.39						
Ayr	*a.*				11.11	12.00	12.52					
Ayr	*d.*	7.15	9.00	10.07	11.17	12.08	12.58	1.48	2.43	3.40	4.50	6.15
Heads of Ayr	*a.*	7.27	9.12	10.19	11.29	12.20	1.10	2.01	2.55	3.52	5.02	6.27

Ex-CR '294' class as ex-LMS class '2F' 0-6-0 'Jumbo', and as BR No. 57284, with a three-coach Butlin's shuttle service near Ayr station's platform 5 on 2nd July, 1949.   *H. Stevenson*

Ex-CR '294' class and ex-LMS class '2F', 0-6-0 'Jumbo', as BR No. 57234, with a three-coach Butlin's shuttle at Ayr station's platform 5 in 1950. The driver, on the left, is Nick Armstrong, and the fireman is Bob Smillie, and in the background is part of the Station Hotel.   *R.H. Smillie*

		am	am	am	am	am	noon	pm	pm	pm	pm
Heads of Ayr	d.	8.10	8.35	9.25	9.45	10.55	12.00	1.35	2.10	3.5	4.20
Ayr	a.	8.22	8.47	9.37	9.57	11.07	12.12	1.47	2.22	3.17	4.32
Ayr	d.	8.25	8.52	9.42	10.01						
Kilmarnock	d.		9.30								
Dumfries	d.		10.02								
Carlisle	d.		10.54	11.27							
Newcastle	a.		12.29								
Leeds	a.		2.02								
Paisley	a.			10.32	10.42						
Glasgow	a.				10.57						
Edinburgh	a.			12.00							

Note: No northbound through service Leeds-Kilmarnock-Heads of Ayr

The Leeds through service ran only in the one direction, from Heads of Ayr; but for most of the summers from 1951, the Newcastle through service ran in both directions. On at least one occasion in 1954, a double-headed Heads of Ayr-Leeds train was extended to London St Pancras, hauling 11 coaches on 31st July, as was observed on that day by railway enthusiast David L. Smith, who wrote in his notebook: 'Very sparse from Butlin's. Lot[s] joined at Ayr, but quite comfortably seated'. The extension to London - which would have been known in advance and justified by advanced bookings from Ayr, as opposed to being decided on the day - presented the opportunity for the Heads of Ayr station master to have proclaimed, proudly, that the train at his station was destined for London. In 1957, Leeds was able to be served northbound by the 10.20 am from Leeds to Glasgow St Enoch, which called at Carlisle at 1.19 pm and arrived in Kilmarnock at 3.13 pm, connecting with the 4.00 pm from Kilmarnock that ran through to Heads of Ayr, departing from Ayr at 4.50 and reaching Heads of Ayr 5.2. The 9.08 am from Sheffield to Glasgow St Enoch, which ran about 15 minutes behind the Leeds train, made the same connection at Kilmarnock for Heads of Ayr.

The 'bias' towards southbound-only trains is also shown for an 8.43 am service from Ayr to Liverpool and Manchester in a separate composite timetable for three services to English destinations during the summer Saturdays of 1957. These were the Saturdays-only morning southbound trains from Heads of Ayr to Newcastle, from Ayr to Liverpool and Manchester, and from Heads of Ayr to Leeds; and they travelled over the former G&SWR main line in close succession, with varying station stops that also enabled the trains partly to serve the local south-western Scotland area and be semi-fast-running for the English connections. However, they ran sufficiently close together - albeit conveniently for the Butlin's passengers - that the Heads of Ayr single-line branch and its loop and headshunt could not have accommodated all of them in the short interval that was required; and therefore, in relieving the 'congestion', the middle train, to Liverpool and Manchester, was started from Ayr instead of Heads of Ayr. Like the southbound service from Heads of Ayr to Leeds, the southbound service from Ayr to Liverpool and Manchester did not have an equivalent in the northbound direction. Nevertheless, the latter service offered a connection at Ayr for passengers from Butlin's who, in heading south of Carlisle and at least as far as Liverpool and Manchester, could change at Ayr from the 8.10 am Heads of Ayr-Newcastle.

LMS class '2P' 4-4-0, as BR No. 40647, with an Ayr-Heads of Ayr shuttle in August 1958 passes Greenan sidings, which officially closed the following year. The engine and its two coaches also represented the typical appearance of a Girvan-Turnberry shuttle between 1931 and 1942.

D. Cross

LMS class '2P' 4-4-0, as BR No. 40664, reversing as it rounds its 1.48 pm ex-Ayr shuttle of two coaches at Heads of Ayr Butlin's station on 30th May, 1959 for a tender-first service back to Ayr.

H. Stevenson

		A	B	A
		am	*am*	*am*
Heads of Ayr	*dep.*	8.10		8.35
Ayr	*arr.*	8.22		8.47
Ayr	*dep.*	8.25	8.43	8.52
Newton-on-Ayr	*dep.*			8.56
Prestwick	*dep.*		8.50	9.01
Troon	*dep.*		8.57	9.09
Barassie	*dep.*			9.13
Kilmarnock	*arr.*		9.13	9.25
Kilmarnock	*dep.*		9.18	9.30
Dumfries	*arr.*	9.57	10.28	
Dumfries	*dep.*	10.02	10.32	
Annan	*dep.*	10.23		10.59
Carlisle	*arr.*	10.46	11.11	11.18
Carlisle	*dep.*	10.54	11.18	11.27
Newcastle	*arr.*	12.29		
Manchester Victoria	*arr.*		2.31	
Liverpool Exchange	*arr.*		2.48	
Leeds City	*arr.*			2.02

Notes:
A - 22nd June to 31st August. B - 29th June to 24th August.

Although BR(ScR) appeared to have a preference for providing through trains to bring some passengers home from Butlin's instead of taking them there, it is not clear why this one-way operation was adopted, which, if not balanced in return, would have resulted in certain empty coaching stock, or ECS, workings and, consequently, non-revenue-earning runs. However, the process may have been balanced by the working of non-Butlin's service or relief trains from England to Ayr, which, if regular, would have been listed in the working timetable that was not issued to the public, or, if occasional, would have appeared in the Special Traffic Notices. The timetables indicated that there were ECS workings between Ayr's various carriage sidings and Heads of Ayr station from the early years to allow for unbalanced local workings and for storage, maintenance and cleaning of the corridor trains between revenue-earning turns.

The 7.15 am from Ayr, as a local shuttle service, was a long train because of its specific returning role from Heads of Ayr, but it carried either a handful of passengers at the most, who may have been Butlin's staff not living on the camp, or no passengers at all, and, accordingly, the train may have been ostensibly judged by the public as a pointless run and treated by the railway authorities as an ECS.

Nevertheless, the reason for the 7.15 am service was that it formed one of the two English services from Heads of Ayr. No trains were stabled at Heads of Ayr on the Friday overnight into Saturday because there were no facilities for the locomotives and coaches, and it was therefore necessary to run the two trains to Heads of Ayr early in the morning, having had proper maintenance, while the crews also needed to be conveyed from Ayr to Heads of Ayr. Furthermore, the responsibility of Butlin's security did not extend to trains at the station. The 7.15 am train, although the first to arrive at Heads of Ayr, was the second to depart, and this was for Leeds at 8.35 am during the 1950s, to become 8.20 am by 1962. The second of the two trains to arrive at Heads of Ayr, formed the Newcastle service at 8.20 am and 8.10 am during

LMS class '2P' 4-4-0, as BR No. 40647, at Heads of Ayr Butlin's station with a two-coach shuttle service on 8th August, 1959.   *S. Sellar*

A view of Heads of Ayr Butlin's station on 18th June, 1960, looking south, with the roof of the covered walkway discernible, leading down to the camp to terminate opposite the building on the right. Unfortunately, the tender-first position obscures the engine that was stated to be an LMS class '4F' 0-6-0, as BR No. 44331, which was one of four of the class built at Glasgow St Rollox works in 1928 and allocated to Ayr in 1959. The '4Fs' were goods engines with no steam heating, but they were able to work the summer-only passenger services of the Butlin's shuttle, likely from 1959 to 1962. On the other side of the white gates, a path led down to the camp, facilitating the use of luggage barrows, but this path was not in existence during the early years of the station (*see the aerial photograph on page 202*)   *G&SWR Association*

the 1950s, but at 8.05 am by 1962 and thereafter at 8.00 am. It consisted of ECS and arrived soon after - and probably only a few minutes behind - the first train, for both were needed at Heads of Ayr so that the marshalling could be achieved quickly in readiness for the two English services; the additional part of the marshalling equation being that the engines changed trains.

The procedure was as follows (with 'N' and 'L' representing both the engine and coaches that formed the Newcastle and Leeds services, for ease of explanation). The 7.15 am service train proceeded from Ayr tender-first with its coaches ('L') to Heads of Ayr and the engine ('N'), before reaching the western end of the loop, positioned the coaches by the platform. The engine ('N') next uncoupled and backed beyond the loop and then ran forward again, through the loop to the eastern end of the coaches ('L'), to back onto the other end of the coaches and push them well beyond the junction with the western end of the loop, onto the section or extension of the track to the west of the station. The engine ('N') proceeded into the loop again and remained there, to await the arrival of the second train of ECS. These coaches ('N') were also hauled tender-first, to be positioned beside the platform, and the engine ('L') of this train was uncoupled, to reverse beyond the western end of the loop and couple with the coaches ('L') in the extension track, acting as a headshunt. The engine ('L') was coupled to these coaches ('L'), to form the Leeds train; and the first engine ('N') next proceeded forward through the loop and then reversed back, coupling with the coaches ('N') at the platform, to form the Newcastle train. Both engines were therefore facing forwards and ready to take their trains to the two English cities.

The headshunt, which could be used for other combinations of departing trains in close succession - for example, for Edinburgh and Glasgow - was protected by signals, such that, after the departure of the train in the platform, the train in the headshunt moved into the platform only when signalled to do so. Before the closure of the goods service in 1955, the Butlin's extension track was effectively a headshunt solely because of its facility of short-term passenger train storage west of the station, along the start of the route to Turnberry that used its own signalling system beyond the Butlin's signalling limit. Then, after the end of the goods service, the branch was severed ¼ mile west of Heads of Ayr Butlin's station and the track was lifted, with the remaining extension becoming a headshunt in the standard sense - albeit longer than average - having buffers installed at what became the end of the Heads of Ayr Butlin's branch. The buffers were situated on the part of the embankment immediately west of the underbridge at Laigh Kyleston farm (now Heads of Ayr Farm Park), and the reason for the headshunt being retained for the long ¼-mile distance was that it allowed the storing of two trains when required, especially in connection with the increasing excursion specials to Butlin's.

The constant 7.15 am Ayr-Heads of Ayr train served another useful purpose, in that it conveyed suitcases under the facility of 'Passengers' Luggage in Advance', whereby travellers could have their luggage sent ahead to save themselves carrying it. For holidaymakers to Butlin's at Ayr, their luggage, which was collected from their home by a British Railways' lorry and left the nearest station on the Thursday, was ultimately placed on board the Saturday 7.15 am train to Heads of Ayr.

From the start of the Butlin's English through services - in 1950 to Newcastle and Leeds, but to Leeds only in the southbound direction - two routes were used from Ayr through central Ayrshire towards Mauchline, where they converged. The Leeds trains proceeded circuitously northwards by Troon and Kilmarnock, offering a local service, which produced a distance between Ayr and Mauchline of 25¼ miles; while the Newcastle trains cut more directly eastwards from Newton-on-Ayr and by

LMS class '5' 4-6-0, as BR No. 45356, passes the closed Greenan sidings with a Heads of Ayr-Glasgow St Enoch eight-coach train on 3rd June, 1961. The bridge over the railway carries the Ayr-Dunure road.   *D. Cross*

LMS class '5P4F' 2-6-0, as BR class '6P5F' and BR No. 42802, and known as a 'Mogul' or a 'Horwich Crab', runs tender-first with a shuttle to Ayr, in passing milepost 45 from Glasgow, west of the former Greenan aidings, on 3rd June, 1961. The two coaches are of LNER Edward Thompson types, with many of them built after 1948 but before BR standard designs appeared in 1951-52, being a brake second next to the engine and a semi-corridor composite containing a lavatory that is indicated by the white oval window. The Heads of Ayr cliffs are vividly outlined in the background.   *D. Cross*

Annbank towards Mauchline, allowing no local service and a much shorter distance between Ayr and Mauchline of 11½ miles. The use of the route from Ayr to Mauchline via Kilmarnock also allowed the Heads of Ayr-Leeds train to serve selected additional stations in central Ayrshire - in particular, the county's largest town, Kilmarnock - and, thus, to provide an extra local service and a connection with England at a negligible extra running cost. However, this was not the case with the Newcastle trains in either direction; and why the Leeds trains ran via Kilmarnock and the Newcastle trains ran via Annbank is not known for certain; but one possibility for the Leeds service having been routed by Kilmarnock was that there had always been a direct railway connection between them traditionally, by virtue of the G&SWR-Midland Railway partnership from the pre-Grouping period. More speculative is why BR, from the start of the Leeds service did not provide a corresponding northbound train, since the locomotives and coaches would have to return somehow, though whether as one-way traffic is again not known. A representation of the direct Heads of Ayr-Newcastle trains, in both directions, and the direct Heads of Ayr-Leeds trains, in the southbound-only direction, for the years 1950, 1957 and 1962, is given in the following table:

		1950 A		1957 C		1962 E	
		am	am	am	am	am	am
Heads of Ayr	dep.	8.20	8.35	8.10	8.35	8.05	8.20
Ayr	arr.	8.32	8.47	8.22	8.47	8.17	8.32
Ayr	dep.	8.37	8.52	8.25	8.52	8.20	8.37
Kilmarnock	arr.		9.27		9.25		9.08
Kilmarnock	dep.		9.30		9.30		9.11
Dumfries	arr.	10.05		9.57		9.55	10.28
Dumfries	dep.	10.10		10.02		10.02	10.31
Carlisle	dep.	11.00	11.26	10.54	11.27	10.53*	11.18
Newcastle	arr.	12.35		12.29		12.29	
Leeds	arr.		2.05		2.02		2.02

		1950 B	1957 D	1962 F
		am	am	am
Newcastle	dep.	8.10	8.15	8.15
Carlisle	dep.	9.50	9.54	9.54
Dumfries	arr.		10.34	10.33
Dumfries	dep.		10.39	10.39
Ayr	arr.	12.01	12.00	12.02
Ayr	dep.	12.08	12.08	12.08
Heads of Ayr	arr.	12.20	12.20	12.20

Notes: 1950 timetable period 24th June to 2nd September:
A - Until 2nd September. B - Until 26th August.
1957 timetable period 17th June to 15th September:
C - Until 31st August. D - Until 24th August.
1962 timetable period 18th June to 9th September:
E - Until 1st September. F - Until 25th August.
* Interpolated dep. time.
Heads of Ayr-Newcastle services and Newcastle-Heads of Ayr operated via Annbank.
Heads of Ayr-Leeds operated via Kilmarnock.

LMS class '5' 0-6-0, as BR No. 45160, has passed under the Longhill Avenue road bridge at Alloway and is soon to cross the Doon viaduct with a Heads of Ayr-Edinburgh Princes Street train in July 1962.   *D. Cross*

LMS class '5' 4-6-0, No. 44723, running tender first, crosses Alloway Junction from the main Ayr-Girvan line to traverse the Butlin's branch with eight coaches of empty LNER and BR stock that will form a Heads of Ayr-Edinburgh Princes Street service in the summer of 1962.   *D. Cross*

For the Butlin's trains in operating over the four miles between Heads of Ayr, Ayr station and any of the Ayr sidings, the direction of the locomotive followed procedure that was only occasionally varied. It was usual for the locomotive on an inbound or outbound through train to haul the ECS tender-first on the empty run meaning that the engine ran backwards with the ECS and forwards with the passenger service. The local shuttle was hauled in whichever direction the engine happened to be facing, which often didn't matter, but in wild westerly weather, the train would usually not proceed tender-first into the blustery and rainy conditions, with the driver deciding the direction to suit the circumstances. Engines were turned and serviced at Ayr depot, at Newton-on-Ayr, within the large triangle of Hawkhill Junction, Newton Junction and Blackhouse Junction, uniting the lines from Ayr, Glasgow and Mauchline. Although Ayr possessed a 60 ft-diameter manual turntable, the practice was to use the triangle for turning the engines, as it was more convenient. The engines ran forward from Ayr station to Newton Junction, reversing into Blackhouse Junction, and forward again towards Ayr station, but then with another reversal when proceeding into the depot before later heading for the station.

The engine crews and the guards of the Butlin's Edinburgh services were changed at West Street Junction in Glasgow, as Ayr men operated the trains between Heads of Ayr and West Street, while Edinburgh men worked between Princes Street and West Street. The engines were also watered at West Street, which lay on the short line between Shields Junction and Gushetfaulds Junction, in connecting the Ayr line with the Glasgow-Edinburgh route via Rutherglen, Uddingston and Shotts. The Ayr and Edinburgh crews did not proceed beyond West Street from their home depots.

The engine crews and guards of the Butlin's Newcastle and Leeds services, who were from Ayr or Carlisle Kingmoor, were changed at Carlisle, which meant that the Ayr men worked between Heads of Ayr and Carlisle and the Carlisle men worked between Newcastle and Carlisle and between Leeds and Carlisle. However, in the instances where Carlisle men brought the train to Ayr, they did not proceed onto the Heads of Ayr branch because they were not familiar with that road, and a 'driver-conductor' from Ayr went aboard. If the return working of a Butlin's Newcastle or Leeds train - indeed, as with any train - was going to take the Ayr or Carlisle crews over their eight hours' duty, they had to be relieved and travelled back on a passenger train, referred to by the colloquial term of 'on the cushions', though the crews returned on any goods or parcels train that was conveniently available for them.

With the Butlin's Newcastle services operating for only one day a week for 10 to 12 weeks of the 15 or 16 weeks of the Butlin's season, there was not usually a train for the engine to haul in the opposite direction after it had taken the Butlin's train to Carlisle or Heads of Ayr. Therefore, a light-engine working occurred in such cases when returning to the Ayr or Carlisle depot, even if this was also inevitably inefficient because it hauled no train. There were no other direct passenger services between Ayr and Carlisle, but the returning engine could have been placed on a goods or parcels train, if this happened to be opportune on rare occasions.

Although the Butlin's services operated only on Saturdays, the railway staff worked on Mondays to Saturdays, and they were located in the railway booking office in the camp. On Mondays to Fridays, there were the station master, a clerk and, covering each of the two shifts of the day, a porter-signalman, who were augmented by two relief porters on Saturdays, when the station building was in use, with the station master and the porter-signalman for the shift in attendance at the station. The reason for three staff on a shift when there were no trains running for

Ayr depot's favoured ex-LNER class 'B1' 4-6-0, as BR No. 61261, leaves Ayr station with the Heads of Ayr-Edinburgh Princes Street service on 1st June, 1963, as the Station Hotel, of red freestone, dominates the background. *D. Cross*

The Ayr-Dunure road bridge beside Greenan sidings was one of Derek Cross' favourite locations, with the viewpoint allowing the Heads of Ayr cliffs to be seen prominently. Ex-LNER 'B1' class 4-6-0, as BR No. 61245 *Murray of Elibank*, hauls the 9.20 am Heads of Ayr-Edinburgh Princes Street services of 10 LMS corridor coaches in June 1964, with the engine passing milepost 45. *D. Cross*

five of the six days was because the railway booking office was effectively a busy travel-and-tourist-information centre for the campers, where inquiries were answered by the railway staff, who also organized the Butlin's bus tours for the campers. There were tours every day, except Saturdays, and sometimes several tours in the one day to diverse locations, including these as the most popular: Culzean Castle; the Burns Country in Ayrshire and in Dumfriesshire; Glen Trool in Wigtownshire; Glasgow; Edinburgh; and Loch Lomond and the Trossachs, extending from Dunbartonshire through Stirlingshire into Perthshire. Additionally, the railway staff provided essential information to the campers in connection with their journeys home and with luggage-in-advance arrangements.

The ceremonial first train to Butlin's on 17th May, 1947, which was welcomed by the female Redcoats, was hauled by LMS Stanier class '5' 4-6-0, No. 5157, *The Glasgow Highlander*. It was built by the large engineering firm of Armstrong Whitworth of Newcastle in 1935 and named in 1936, and appeared to have been a special selection for the opening occasion to portray a Scottish flavour. The class '5s', known as 'Black Fives', were designed by William Stanier - later, Sir William - the chief mechanical engineer of the LMS, and they were one of the first of his new modern designs that were introduced on the LMS in 1934, after his transfer and promotion in 1932 from the position of assistant to the chief mechanical engineer of the GWR to become the chief mechanical engineer of the LMS until 1944. The 'Black Fives' were among the most numerous and successful steam locomotives ever to run on Britain's railways, and after the total of 842 by 1951, another 172 of the similar but updated British Railways Standard version followed during the 1950s. They could be seen anywhere over the length of Britain, from Bournemouth to Thurso, and their duties included regular appearances on the Butlin's Heads of Ayr trains from the opening of the branch through most of its lifetime. Strangely, from a total of 842 'Black Fives' that were built from 1934 to 1951, only five were given names, and all these honoured Scottish regiments. They were No. 5154, *Lanarkshire Yeomanry*, named in 1937; No. 5155, *Queens Edinburgh*, named in 1942, with the name removed in 1944; No. 5156, *Ayrshire Yeomanry*, named in 1936; No. 5157, *The Glasgow Highlander*, named in 1936; and No. 5158, *Glasgow Yeomanry*, named in 1936; and all were built by Armstrong Whitworth. An allocation list of January 1946 showed all five of the named 'Black Fives' to have been at Glasgow St Rollox shed, which would not normally have supplied locomotives for Ayrshire services. No. 5158, *Glasgow Yeomanry* later went to Dumfries shed and could have taken an occasional turn to Heads of Ayr.

The LNER equivalent of the 'Black Five' was also used on some Butlin's trains, and this was the class 'B1' 4-6-0, which was of much the same size and power. The driving wheels were 6 ft 2 in. in diameter, whereas the 'Black Five' had 6 ft 0 in. wheels. The 'B1' was a 1942 design by Edward Thompson, who had become chief mechanical engineer of the LNER the previous year on the death of Sir Nigel Gresley. Mr Thompson, formerly of the North Eastern Railway, favoured the simplicity of two cylinders, but, in addition, the 'B1' was produced with wartime standardization and ease of maintenance as being paramount, with the aim of eliminating older outdated classes. Construction continued into the early British Railways period, with the final delivery being in June 1952. There were 410 members of the class built, but only a maximum of 409 existed together at any one time, as No. 61057 was so severely damaged in an accident in 1950 that it was scrapped.

Six of the 410 members of the 'B1' class - Nos. 61134, 61197, 61243, 61261, 61355 and 61396 - were unusual allocations to the former G&SWR system from 1963 to 1965. They were transferred as a result of partial dieselization from Eastfield in

In a view looking west on 22nd June, 1963, a Heads of Ayr-Glasgow St Enoch train, hauled by BR Standard class '4' 2-6-4T, No. 80025, passes between the former station and the higher-level goods yard at Alloway, in ascending the 1 in 80 gradient towards Alloway Junction. The station is hidden by the train's coaches, and the yard extends beyond the left of the view   *D. Cross*

From the background of the Heads of Ayr cliffs, the particularly impressive sight is formed by the steam power of a double-headed, 10-coach train on the short Heads of Ayr branch on 24th August, 1963. BR Standard class '4' 2-6-0 No. 76097, and LMS class '5' 4-6-0 No. 45164, with a Heads of Ayr-Newcastle train, comprising a combination of LMS and LNER coaches, pass milepost 45, from Glasgow, west of the former Greenan sidings.   *D. Cross*

Glasgow, which was the principal shed of the former North British Railway, to the G&SWR's Corkerhill shed, and they were recorded there in January 1963. They were 'foreign' to Corkerhill, which probably had no work for them, and nine months later, all six were at Ayr shed. The reason for the transfer to Ayr was thought to be that they were intended as replacements for the LMS 2-6-0s, which were 20 years older; but the 'B1s' were not popular with the crews on coal trains, as they were alleged to have 'nae brakes' - a standard cry of condemnation by the Ayr crews for unfamiliar or less effective engines. There was an accident on the southern approach to Ayr, owing to one of the 'B1s' running away with a coal train from Waterside, after which they were banned from the Waterside coal trains. Nevertheless, the shed staff liked at least one member of the 'B1' sextet: No. 61261, of which Derek Cross, a renowned railway photographer who was living near Maybole, wrote several times as being Ayr's pet 'B1'; and the pet was kept clean and used on the Butlin's trains throughout the summer of 1963. For the Butlin's services in 1963 and perhaps in 1964, the 'B1s' worked not only the shuttle between Ayr and Heads of Ayr and other local Heads of Ayr runs, such as to and from Kilmarnock, but also the 9.20 am from Heads of Ayr to Edinburgh Princes Street. This turn was arranged by the engine hauling the train tender-first as the 9.00 am local from Ayr to Heads of Ayr. The 9.20 crossed the 10.30 Edinburgh-Heads of Ayr between Holytown and Shotts if both were on time.

Three of the Ayr 'B1s' were withdrawn in 1964 - No. 61243 in May and Nos. 61197 and 61155 in June - but the older 2-6-0s were increased from 10 to 12 in allocation around that period. Two of the 2-6-0 withdrawals were replaced by transfers, while another two joined them, and others lasted until the end of steam in Ayrshire in 1966. However, the 'B1s' on the Butlin's line was only a transitory phase for them, and by May 1965, the three survivors - Nos. 61134, 61396 and 61261 - had been transferred to finish their days at the sheds at Edinburgh Dalry Road, ex-CR; Edinburgh St Margarets, ex-NBR; and Thornton, Fife, ex-NBR. Coincidentally, or perhaps ironically, it is possible that a named member of the 'B1' class from Edinburgh Dalry Road between October 1963 and May 1965 - No. 61245, *Murray of Elibank*, after an LNER Director - was at Ayr shed between its Edinburgh duties at the same time as the Ayr 'B1s' were at Edinburgh. It was photographed near Greenan by Derek Cross in June 1964, hauling 10 coaches on a Butlin's Heads of Ayr-Edinburgh service, and it would certainly have met some of its fellow members of the class at Ayr shed between turns.

Indeed, it was principally because of the enthusiasm and dedication of Derek Cross that an abundant and valuable visual representation of the activity on the Butlin's Heads of Ayr branch during the 1960s became available for posterity through his photographs; and while other railway enthusiasts fortunately were able to capture the line and its workings, no one was able to apply such an intensity of photography to the small branch. It was convenient for Derek that he lived nearby, in working two neighbouring farms - firstly Breek and then Knockdon - midway between Heads of Ayr and Maybole, on the slopes south-east of Brown Carrick Hill, with his farms additionally midway between the Heads of Ayr branch and the main Ayr-Girvan line through Maybole. In Ayrshire and south-western Scotland generally, and where appropriate for the Butlin's line, Derek recorded all types of steam and diesel locomotives with their different trains that carried service and excursion passengers, goods, parcels and minerals and the permanent way maintenance trains. One of Derek's earliest Turnberry-road photographs was of a southbound potato train, hauled tender-first by a Caley '3F', on the high ground near the deep curved cutting to the south of Dunure, in July 1950.

Other LMS standard engines which had operated on the G&SWR system, and which had a share in the working of the Butlin's trains, were the class '4' Midland 'Compound' 4-4-0s and the class '4' Hughes-Fowler 'Mogul' 2-6-0s.

The 'Compounds' formed a 1924 LMS development that was the equivalent of the Midland Railway '1000' class, and they were originally painted in the full-lined, crimson lake, passenger livery, but, in outline, they looked similar to the inside-cylindered, black-painted LMS '2P' 4-4-0s, and, like the '2Ps', they had 6 ft 9 in. driving wheels. In the first LMS phase from 1923 to 1928, nearly all the passenger engines were painted in lined crimson lake, but from 1928 an economy measure meant that the number of 'red' classes was reduced drastically. Mixed-traffic and secondary-passenger types became black with simpler lining, and goods types became unlined black, but the total of 195 'Compounds' formed one of the express classes that kept their crimson livery. The hidden power difference of the 'Compounds' was the third cylinder between the frames receiving high-pressure steam from the boiler, which was then exhausted to the low-pressure outside cylinders, and the compound expansion of the steam, in two stages, was the reason for the class nickname. By the late 1940s, the 'Compounds' had been superseded on principal passenger expresses by LMS 4-6-0s, but on 10th July, 1954, No. 41138, which was one of the last survivors, brought the Newcastle-Heads of Ayr train from Carlisle. It was withdrawn later in 1954; and the last 'Compound' at a Scottish shed, No. 41149, finished in 1955, although dwindling numbers remained in England until 1961.

The 'Moguls' were an excellent all-traffic type of engine that was built between 1926 and 1932, at the former Lancashire & Yorkshire's Railway's (L&YR) works in Horwich, Lancashire, and at Crewe. Containing 5 ft 6 in. driving wheels and a modern front-end cylinder and valve layout, they had been designed by George Hughes, chief mechanical engineer of the L&YR from 1904 to 1922 and of the LMS from 1923 to 1925. However, they appeared after Mr Hughes had retired and incorporated certain MR specifications by Sir Henry Fowler - who, formerly chief mechanical engineer of the MR, had succeeded Mr Hughes in that position within the LMS in 1925 until 1931 - and, accordingly, they were known as 'Hughes-Fowler Moguls'. The crews, particularly on the former G&SWR system, called them 'Moguls'; but they were also known as 'Horwich Crabs', particularly among railway enthusiasts, on account of the high running-plate that was upswept over the large outside cylinders and valve gear, which spuriously suggested a sideways waddling gait, like a crab. The cylinders had to be set higher than usual and inclined, because of their size and to maintain clearance at station platforms. The official LMS arbitrary power classification for them was '5P4F', which implied that they were slightly more effective on passenger trains than on freight trains.

Ayr shed extensively used its allocation of the 2-6-0s on goods and mineral work, especially for the trains that brought coal from the pits at Waterside. It is also possible that the 'Moguls' occasionally operated on the Turnberry road's goods service during the post-war period, but if so, the instances were rare because they were more valuable on heavier trains. On passenger trains, they could attain 60 mph freely, with their efficient front-end design, and they were used on the Butlin's services, mainly hauling the heavier and longer-distance trains - to Glasgow, Edinburgh, Newcastle and Leeds - as opposed to the lighter local shuttle, though they occasionally worked the latter. They were popular with the crews at Ayr.

LMS class '5X' 4-6-0s were slightly more powerful than the class '5s' and were used from time to time on through trains - for example, 'Patriot' class No. 45542 on the train from Edinburgh on 10th June, 1950 and 'Jubilee' class No. 45679 on the train from Newcastle on 11th August, 1956 - but it appears that these were more occasional visitors than the other classes. All the '5X' 4-6-0 types had 6 ft 9 in. driving wheels for express passenger work. The '5X' classification of the LMS was changed to '6' in early BR days, with a general reclassification one stage up of existing power classes '6' and '7' to classes '7' and '8'. This was an administrative exercise which included giving LMS type power classifications to locomotives of the other three railways of the Grouping - LNER, GWR and SR. There was no change to the previous '5X' type, except that they changed to '6' on repainting.

The Butlin's local shuttle service, running several times per day in each direction, was generally hauled by an LMS '2P' 4-4-0, until the Ayr allocation became extinct about 1960-61, but sometimes by a vacuum-braked goods engine, such as a former CR class '2F' 0-6-0 'Jumbo'. The CR '3Fs' may also have been used, but, if so, they were probably not common, only because they were more useful on other work. For the services, two or three non-corridor coaches of LMS or sometimes LNER origin were used - a favourite combined branch-set in Scotland being an LNER brake-third and a semi-corridor lavatory composite even on ex-LMS routes. During the 1950s, third-class coaches were re-designated second class, because the 19th century, second-class, intermediate standard of comfort, between 'first' luxury class and 'second' basic class had long been abolished in line with improvements to third-class coaches. Another CR locomotive was known to have worked the shuttle. Since 1895, the CR had standardized the 0-4-4T wheel arrangement for local passenger work and a batch of 10 John McIntosh '439' class engines to the final design were built in 1925. Two of them were based at Ayr - LMS No. 15261 for part of its life and No. 15262 for its whole life - and David L. Smith recorded the latter, carrying its BR number, 55262, at Ayr in working the shuttle on 26th May, 1955.

The corridor trains on the Butlin's services - usually of eight coaches but sometimes of 10 or 11 - were generally given class '5' locomotive power of BR or LMS, or LNER 'B1' class, sometimes double-headed with a class '4' pilot. The class '5' could be a variety of types from different depots - even a BR class '6' 4-6-2 'Clan' from Carlisle, since the Butlin's trains worked only on Saturdays and any spare engines could be used. BR 'Standard' class '4' 2-6-0s and 2-6-4Ts, with 5 ft 3 in. and 5 ft 8 in. driving wheels respectively, were used as pilots or on shorter workings. Before the introduction of the BR 2-6-4Ts, the similar LMS Fairburn 2-6-4Ts, from which the BR engines were derived, were numerous on the former G&SWR system, including a small allocation at Ayr. There were 277 Fairburn 2-6-4Ts that were built to a 1945 design by Charles Fairburn, who, from Sir William Stanier's retirement, became the chief mechanical engineer of the LMS from 1944 to 1945, and they did much good work on the former LMS system until premature replacement by diesel multiple units (dmus) reduced the work available for them. Withdrawal was steady from 1962, and one last survivor, No. 42274, was present at the end of steam traction in Scotland in 1967. It was similar for the BR Standard tanks, as the work for them was reduced in stages until the last survivors were carriage pilots at Glasgow Central in April 1967. It is likely that the Fairburn tanks, comprising 5 ft 9 in. driving wheels, worked to Heads of Ayr on the morning 9.55 through train from Glasgow, with the shuttle service usually operated by an LMS '2P' 4-4-0 or a CR 'Jumbo' 0-6-0.

BR class '6' 4-6-2 'Clans' from Carlisle were also stated to have worked to Heads of Ayr, from Newcastle or Leeds, with these services always having changed engines at Carlisle. 'Clans' operated on the Stranraer-Ayr-Newcastle route, but one working on which Heads of Ayr passengers northbound to Glasgow could have travelled, by

Alloway Junction signal box, photographed by one of the authors from the 10.30 am Edinburgh Princes Street-Heads of Ayr train on 22nd August, 1964, being the only remaining M&DLR box in existence at that time and only 58 years old. The Ayr-Maybole-Girvan line lies beyond the box.

S. Rankin

BR Standard class '4' 2-6-0, No. 76096, at Heads of Ayr station after arriving with the 12.35 pm from Edinburgh Princes Street on 7th August, 1965. This was four Saturdays before the last Princes Street-Heads of Ayr service on 4th September, because of the transfer of the Edinburgh-Heads of Ayr services to Waverley from 11th September.

W.S. Sellar

joining at Ayr, was the 2.50 pm boat train from Stranraer Harbour to Glasgow on a summer Saturday in 1956, which changed engines at Ayr, and the Ayr-Glasgow engine appears to have been a Carlisle turn, No. 72007, *Clan Mackintosh*. Another example of this class occurred with No. 72006 *Clan Mackenzie* on the 8.15 am from Newcastle to Heads of Ayr on 25th June, 1960. The 'Clans', containing 6 ft 2 in. driving wheels, were often viewed by critics as a redundant part of the BR Standard steam locomotive plan, and although of class '6' in power, they were regarded as little better than a class '5' 4-6-0, frequently working on class '5' equivalent traffic. Only 10 were built - all named after Scottish clans - with an order for a further 10 being cancelled.

There were excursions to Heads of Ayr from various towns and cities, including Blackpool, Perth, Dundee and Aberdeen, and occasionally on days other than Saturdays. For example, a Dundee train, hauled by an LNER 'A2' class 4-6-2 locomotive and piloted by a 'Black Five' from Ayr, was photographed by Derek Cross on Tuesday 27th July, 1965, as it entered the branch at Alloway Junction. Such non-Saturday excursions posed no problem for operating the branch because Alloway junction signal box was already manned as a block post for the main line southwards and a porter-signalman was employed Mondays to Fridays at Heads of Ayr in the railway booking office inside Butlin's camp.

The 'A2' locomotive was No. 60528, *Tudor Minstrel*, which was one of the small total of 15 for the class. The first of them entered service in December 1947 and the other 14 from January to August 1948, with *Tudor Minstrel* in February, and the photograph verified that locomotives even of that size were permitted on the branch. For the section from Ayr to Heads of Ayr, class '5' No. 45465, running tender first, was necessary as a pilot because extra power was required for the heavy train of the 'A2' on the continuous ascents for nearly a mile each of 1 in 170 from Ayr to Belmont and of 1 in 88 to Alloway Junction, with a short rise of 1 in 70 before the start of the branch. The 'A2' locomotives at Dundee were often 'spare' without fixed 'diagrams', or scheduled services, and were frequently used on excursions or fast goods or parcels trains. The 'A2's', which consisted of 6 ft 2 in. driving wheels and which had been allocated LNER numbers from 525 to 539, with *Tudor Minstrel* as No. 528, were designed by Arthur Peppercorn, who had succeeded Edward Thompson as chief mechanical engineer of the LNER in 1946.

From the summer of 1959, the majority of the Glasgow-Ayr-Girvan-Stranraer and Glasgow-Ardrossan-Largs services were operated by dmus, although some relief steam workings continued for most of the remainder of that year. The dmus were of the Swindon class '126', known as Inter-City sets, built by BR at Swindon in Wiltshire; and, after an introductory trial operation in July 1959, they entered partial service, in August, based at Ayr depot, running mainly as three-car units which also ran in multiples of three to become six-car and nine-car units. Thereafter, the remaining irregular steam services between Glasgow and Ayr were gradually withdrawn and replaced by dmus, allowing shorter turnaround times because of their convenient reversibility; and it was at the beginning of November 1959 that the dmus took over completely from the steam trains on the Glasgow-Ayr service, but the Saturdays-only Butlin's shuttle continued in the meantime as separate steam-locomotive-hauled services. In the summer of 1962, there was a Glasgow-Heads of Ayr dmu working through in both directions, with the dmu leaving Ayr at 10.57 am and Heads of Ayr at 12.00 noon, succeeding the steam service that had run at similar times during the previous few years; and more dmus and diesel locomotives were used increasingly on the Glasgow-Heads of Ayr and Kilmarnock-Heads of Ayr services during the mid-1960s. From 1966, with the reduction of steam traction to its cessation on 30th April, 1967, the trains between Heads of Ayr and Carlisle were more often diesel-hauled by medium-powered locomotives of type '1' with 1,000 hp (later known as class '20'), and of type '2' with 1,160 and 1,250 hp (later classes '26' and '27'). As was the case with the steam locomotives, the diesels and their crews on the Newcastle services were changed at Carlisle.

Stuart Rankin, one of the authors, travelled to Heads of Ayr station from Shotts on Saturday 22nd August, 1964 by the 10.30 am steam-hauled service from Edinburgh Princes Street. The journey was made using a 'Freedom of Scotland' rover ticket, and the station of Shotts was chosen as the farthest east that the train could be joined by morning travel from home in Greenock without going to Edinburgh, while it also offered the opportunity to travel over part of the former CR route between Edinburgh and Glasgow, westwards from Shotts. The engine was a grubby but mechanically-sound LMS 'Black Five' 4-6-0, No. 44786 from Motherwell shed. The train consisted of a total of eight LMS side-corridor coaches, arranged as follows behind the tender: brake second; second; second; composite; first; second; second; and brake second. It ran from Shotts three minutes late, past the junction with the line from Wishaw to pause at Holytown station for six minutes, where No. 44786 took water. From there, southern Glasgow, it was half an hour's journey to Paisley Gilmour Street on the Ayr line, and, after passing through Uddingston and Rutherglen, the train used the CR connecting line from Gushetfaulds Junction that led to Shields Junction and the main Glasgow-Paisley line. On this short link line, a three-minute halt was made at West Street Junction to change the footplate crew and guard, before proceeding through Shields Junction; and after a call at Paisley, the train had a non-stop run on the former G&SWR until Troon, with about 15 miles having been run at over 60 mph and reaching a top speed of 68 mph. From the smart running between Paisley and Troon, the train recovered the three minutes of lateness at Shotts; and then it catered for local passengers at Troon, with calls at Prestwick, Newton-on-Ayr and Ayr, before the departure from Ayr at 12.51, and the arrival at Heads of Ayr on time at 1.05 pm.

Having arrived at Heads of Ayr from Edinburgh on that Saturday in August 1964, class '5' No. 44786 ran-round its train and, tender first, formed the 1.35 pm local shuttle back to Ayr; and, before his return trip on the branch, Stuart photographed the engine and tender, while, on passing Alloway Junction, he managed to photograph the signal box. From Ayr, the empty carriages of the Edinburgh train could have proceeded to Falkland sidings or Belmont siding for stabling and cleaning, perhaps to wait until the following Saturday to return by the 9.20 am service to Edinburgh. As a teenager, he had no prior knowledge of the history of the Heads of Ayr branch nor of holiday camps - the timetable map showing the line only as a short stub - and he simply wished to travel on as many threatened lines as possible before the impending closures under the dreaded Dr Beeching regime. On transferring at Ayr from the 1.35 - and delighted to have been able to travel on the branch - Stuart boarded the 2.07 pm local service from Ayr to Kilmarnock, which was operated by a four-wheel single-coach diesel railbus, built by Park Royal Vehicles Ltd of London.

Chapter Eighteen

Towards the Branch Closure, 1966-1968

The 1950s and 1960s were contrasting decades for Britain's railway network, as optimism was followed by pessimism. After a narrow Labour victory in the 1950 general election, there was another general election in 1951, when the Conservatives returned to power, based on a policy of 'setting the country free of state control'. The Conservative victory was achieved only narrowly over a drained Labour with little more to offer the country after the exertions of nationalization during the previous six years, and Winston Churchill became Prime Minister for the second time. However, British Railways remained nationalized, to be managed for each of the Regions that had been established from 1948 by Area Boards, under the overall supervision of the BTC.

During the late 1950s and the early 1960s, BR had been accumulating large financial operating losses, from declining traffic, and such a state of affairs could not be allowed to continue, as the road-favouring Conservative government, led by Prime Minister Harold Macmillan, produced a 'remedy', ultimately with drastic consequences for the railways. By the Transport Act of 1962 the British Railways Board (BRB) superseded the BTC and attained control of the country's railways, formally from 1st January, 1963. Dr Richard Beeching, a physicist and engineer and formerly the Technical Director of ICI, was the Chairman of the BRB, having occupied the same post within the BTC from 1961; and under the Conservative government's directive of making the railways pay by 1970, his aim was to close many loss-making branch railways and some secondary main lines to allow profitability to be achieved from the retained trunk routes. The Beeching report, entitled *The Reshaping of British Railways*, was published on 27th March, 1963 and consisted of a booklet of 148 pages, accompanied by 12 maps, showing the proposed closures and modifications of rail services throughout Britain. The report brought shock to the whole country, for, altogether, the plan proposed the closure of about 5,000 route miles from a total of nearly 18,000, which also meant more than two-thirds of Scotland's stations were intended to be closed.

Among the many lines in Scotland that were proposed for complete closure were those between Ayr and Stranraer and between Dumfries and Stranraer, leaving Stranraer with no services; while the Glasgow-Barrhead-Kilmarnock and the Kilmarnock-Dumfries-Carlisle routes were to lose their local passenger services. Additionally within Ayrshire, the other passenger services to be withdrawn were those from Ayr to Kilmarnock, from Ayr to Dalmellington, from Kilmarnock to Irvine, and from Kilmarnock to Darvel. However, the Heads of Ayr branch was not included in the Beeching closure proposals - perhaps surprisingly, in view of its short length and limited traffic, but, in reality, counterbalanced by its special purpose in accommodating the Butlin's passengers. Its retention meant that the only passenger trains that would run south of Ayr - though only as far as Alloway Junction and Heads of Ayr - would be those conveying the Butlin's holidaymakers.

From the Beeching cuts, the passenger services from Ayr to Dalmellington, from Kilmarnock to Irvine, and from Kilmarnock to Darvel were withdrawn on 6th April, 1964, but the Ayr-Kilmarnock passenger services continued because of their significance in connecting Ayr, Prestwick and Troon with Kilmarnock, Dumfries and the cities in England, while also providing Kilmarnock with a connection to Northern Ireland. With the threat of closure to the Dumfries-Stranraer and Ayr-Stranraer lines having been present through the second half of 1963 and the first half of 1964, a welcome surprise, in part, was announced by the Conservative government in mid-July 1964: that the Ayr-Stranraer route was to be retained, to continue to serve the Stranraer-Larne steamer services. Unfortunately, the Dumfries-Stranraer route was not to be reprieved, and this meant that all traffic between the two towns would be diverted circuitously via Mauchline, Annbank, Ayr and Girvan, in conjunction with the use of the remaining stretch west of Glenluce between Challoch Junction and Stranraer - thereby running by two sides of the Dumfries-Ayr-Stranraer 'Sou'-west triangle', instead of one side. This diverted traffic included the continuation of the London Euston-Stranraer Harbour overnight passenger service, which was affectionately known as 'The Paddy', operating in connection with the Stranraer-Larne ferries; and the train would make a stop at Ayr in each direction, presenting the town with a direct London service.

The retention of the Ayr-Stranraer line naturally brought a reaction of delight in Ayr, Maybole and Girvan, and particularly in Girvan, where some of the strongest opposition to the closure had existed because the town depended to a large extent on holiday trade from Glasgow and from Northern Ireland by way of Stranraer. The Dumfries-Challoch Junction line closed to passengers and goods on 14th June, 1965, unjustly depriving the people of Galloway of their rail connection with Stranraer, Glasgow and England, but the people of Stranraer, while also having to suffer the loss of their direct railway to England, were nevertheless relieved to keep their line to Ayr, Glasgow and the rest of Scotland.

The general election of October 1964 - within the crucial period of the Beeching proposals - had been won, but only narrowly, by Labour, when Harold Wilson became Prime Minister in succeeding the Conservative's leader Sir Alec Douglas-Home, and this victory was Labour's first since 1950, after losing the 1951, 1955 and 1959 general elections. Hopes were high that many of the Beeching cuts would be reversed throughout Britain, but Labour, after pre-election condemnation of the proposed closures and promises of a good future for the railways, allowed closures to proceed, from the 1964 victory and from another in the general election of 1966, by a larger margin under Harold Wilson's leadership.

The Heads of Ayr branch, in spite of having experienced a decline in traffic during the early-to-mid-1960s, remained unscathed from the Beeching cuts, but the future looked ominous as methods of travel for holidays had changed. When Butlin's camp at Heads of Ayr had opened back in 1947, which was only two years after the end of World War II, the train was still the most popular form of travel for holidays in Britain, whether or not holiday camps were the destination, and this popularity continued through the 1950s. However, the threat from road transport was increasing.

During most of the 1950s, the motor car, though having steadily gained in popularity during the first half of the century, was still not within the reach of most families, and the motor coach, while now being faster and covering greater distances than during the previous two or three decades, was not yet able to compete with the train for speed and for the increasingly-longer distances across Britain that were traversed by holidaymakers. In 1950, about half of the holidaymakers within Britain travelled by train, with the remainder divided almost equally between the two forms of road transport, the car and the coach; but, during the 1950s, with the decline in the use of the train and the rise of both the car and the coach, the situation had changed significantly and quickly, and the three forms of transport accounted for a third each by the late 1950s. It was from this period that the car began to stretch ahead - and dramatically so compared with 1950 - to reach nearly half at the start of the 1960s and nearly 60 per cent by 1964. Meanwhile - if perhaps unexpectedly - from the late 1950s to the early 1960s, the coach had lessened in popularity - but this was also explained in consequence of the large rise of the car; while the train, during that period, had also declined but remained higher than the bus until 1964, when the train and the bus were both at 20 per cent. In 1966, the figures were even more dismal for the railway interests, falling to 18 per cent, while the car - now within the affordability of many more families in a more prosperous period fully two decades after the end of the war - had risen to 63 per cent, with the coach remaining at 20 per cent.

The decline in holiday traffic by rail that was reflected in the national figures had a considerable impact on the holiday service on the Heads of Ayr branch, and it was in late 1966 that serious consideration was taken of the decreasing passengers on it. The following ominous letter, dated 7th December of that year, from British Railways Scottish Region in Glasgow was sent to Billy Butlin - who, in 1964, had become Sir William or, as he preferred, Sir Billy Butlin - at the Butlin's headquarters in Oxford Street in London:

Dear Sir:
Passenger Train Service: Ayr-Heads of Ayr Branch
A recent examination into the economics of the above service, which runs over about 1½ miles of the main Ayr-Stranraer line and then over the 4¼ mile [correctly, 3¼ mile] long single line branch from Alloway Junction to Heads of Ayr station, has indicated that it is incurring a loss of several thousand pounds per year.

You will appreciate that no commercial undertaking can allow such a situation to continue indefinitely and it is, therefore, our intention to invoke the statutory procedure for the withdrawal of the passenger service from the Heads of Ayr branch. Before initiating any action, however, I felt it proper to acquaint you of our intention so that you can let us have any comments you may have to make. The branch is virtually a private siding for the conveyance of people visiting the holiday camp and, therefore, you may wish to consider the question of making good the loss which we are incurring. Alternatively, you would no doubt wish to collaborate in formulating proposed alternative arrangements for conveying passengers and their luggage between Ayr station and the camp.

The Ayr-Heads of Ayr service will continue to operate during the 1967 season. In the event of a withdrawal proposal receiving the consent of the Minister of Transport any alternative arrangements would be operative as from the beginning of the 1968 season.

I shall be glad to hear from you at your convenience.
Yours faithfully,
    G.W. Stewart
    Assistant General Manager

No one could have faulted BR Scottish Region for conveying such negative news to Billy Butlin and his large company, for no one could argue against the fact that the Heads of Ayr branch, in effect, constituted a railway that existed solely for the use of Butlin's camp. While the arrangement had been satisfactory to BR(ScR) when the line was a paying concern, the position had to be viewed differently, in the changed economics, when the railway company was making a loss for the convenience and benefit of the holiday company. A set of statistics from a BR(ScR) document soon conveyed the dismal scenario for the Heads of Ayr branch during the 1967 season, confirming the declining passenger traffic by rail to Butlin's camp. While the number of holidaymakers to the camp had increased significantly since it opened, the per centage travelling by rail to Heads of Ayr had decreased during the 1960s, approximately in line with the national figure. In 1957, 55 per cent of the campers at Heads of Ayr had travelled by rail, compared with the national figure of 50 per cent by rail for holidays in general; but the Butlin's figure for 1967 was only 13 per cent, against the national figure of 15 per cent. In 1967, from a total of nearly 72,000 campers at Heads of Ayr, the number who travelled by rail was 9,236, whereas 18,478 used buses and 44,000 used cars. It was also acknowledged that the number of passengers using the rail service fluctuated considerably during the season, such that, also in 1967, there were 169 on Saturday 20th May and 2,412 on Saturday 15th July, though it was also significantly realised that the latter date was at the start of the Glasgow holiday fortnight, known as the 'Glasgow Fair'.

Meetings between BR(ScR) and Butlin's in late 1967 initially indicated that the latter were prepared to pay a subsidy for the continuation of the service and for railway staff costs, rather than have the branch closed; but, ultimately, a change of mind prevailed, and a further meeting on 23rd November, 1967 confirmed that Butlin's were now, unfortunately, 'not prepared to meet the deficiency in operating the service to enable it to continue after the 1968 season'. Thus, under the Transport Act, 1962, BR(ScR) formally announced in December 1967 that they would withdraw passenger services from the branch after the 1968 season; and, because it was not a goods line, this meant that it would be closed entirely. The decision to close the Heads of Ayr branch had been forced on BR(ScR) primarily by the large increase in cars and secondarily by Butlin's lack of support to keep the line running, but, understandably, Butlin's did not want to contribute to keeping the railway open when most of their holidaymakers did not travel by rail. Motor transport now reigned, but, with the closure in view, some consolation remained because rail passengers would still be able to travel to Ayr station, which would become the railhead for Butlin's, however unsatisfactory this would be in comparison to Heads of Ayr station inside the camp.

In December 1967, the closure notice from BR(ScR) was posted at Heads of Ayr and Ayr stations and at 24 other stations throughout Scotland, from Prestwick, Troon, Kilwinning and Kilmarnock to as far north as Aberdeen and Inverness, with a copy of the notice sent to local authorities, MPs and newspapers. Under the heading 'British Railways Board, Public Notice, Transport Act, 1962, Withdrawal of Railway Passenger Services', the announcement began:

> The Scottish Region of British Railways hereby give notice in accordance with Section 56171 of the Transport Act, 1962, that they propose to withdraw the railway passenger service between Ayr and Heads of Ayr and to close the following station:
> *Heads of Ayr.* This service is operated on Saturdays only during the summer holiday period from May to September.
> In consequence of this proposal ALL passenger services between Alloway Junction and Heads of Ayr will be discontinued.

The withdrawal notice stated that passenger services would continue to be available at Ayr station and that Western SMT operated bus services in the area between Ayr and Heads of Ayr and between Ayr and Maybole via Dunure, while special bus journeys in connection with certain train services would run between Ayr and Heads of Ayr. Objections to the closure were required to be lodged in writing not later than 9th February, 1968, addressed to the Transport Users' Consultative Committee (TUCC) for Scotland in Edinburgh, and if no objections were received, the service would be discontinued after the end of the 1968 holiday season.

Notably, there was little overall concern about the closure locally, from Butlin's, from the local population and from the local authorities. While the lack of financial help from Butlin's had already been made evident, it was also unfortunate that, from the nature of the service, the line was not able to benefit the local people, such that they could not be blamed for not supporting it; but it was particularly sad that the local authorities were not only apathetic to saving the line but were lying in wait for it to be closed, to seize its route for their own convenience. This was because there were plans for the trackbed to be converted into a possible projected fourth and final stage of the new bypass road from the northern side of Prestwick, curving south-eastwards by Whitletts, to the southern side of Ayr. The fourth stage had been discussed without further development only because of the presence of the railway.

However, anxiety about the closure was in evidence from some members of Ayr County Council at a meeting on 30th January when they expressed the view that 'the withdrawal of the service could lead to a very considerable congestion both at Ayr railway station and at the entrance to Butlin's camp on Saturdays at the height of the holiday season'. This, they said, would cause hardship not only to holidaymakers but to road users generally. The County Council agreed to ask Ayr Town Council, Maybole District Council and the Butlin's management at Heads of Ayr for their views before deciding whether they should make an objection, but no formal objection was ultimately raised by the County Council.

Three objections to the closure were received by the TUCC for Scotland - two from railway associations whose aims were in promoting rail transport, and the other from an individual member of the public. These were from the Scottish Railway Development Association (SRDA), initially with an interim objection pending more information on the closure; from the North-Eastern Branch of the Railway Invigoration Society (RIS) in England; and from a gentleman in Edinburgh, Michael Thurlow.

Following the receipt of more information, the SRDA withdrew their interim objection, with Thomas Hart, the Honorary Secretary, declaring their reason to the TUCC that the proposed withdrawal would cause only inconvenience rather than hardship to the existing users. Nevertheless, Mr Hart added cautionary words to all those who were intent on closing the line but who, unfortunately, would likely pay no heed to them, no doubt in their satisfaction that the SRDA would not be protesting after all:

> I should make it clear, however, that, in withdrawing our objection, we do not intend to suggest that this service should be withdrawn. Our view is that the future of this line must be judged against the growing problems of reconciling amenity and recreational value with the pressures arising from car use in coastal areas. These problems will be most severe in coastal areas adjacent to major population concentrations and the Heads of Ayr area is adjacent to the combined 2.5 million population of Clydeside and Ayrshire. Compared to the potential *future use* of the line for coastal visitors (as part of a comprehensive policy for the the Ayrshire coast), the fact that withdrawal of the current service would or would not cause hardship to *existing users* is of little significance.

For the North-Eastern Branch of the Railway Invigoration Society, Mr A.H. Whitehall of Whitley Bay in Northumberland, the Secretary and Chairman, stated the case for retaining the line on the basis of the special service to and from Newcastle that also served Hexham, Haltwhistle and Carlisle, and implied in his letter was the matter of the luggage that the Butlin's holidaymakers needed to carry with them for their period of stay:

> The branch wishes to protest most strongly about the proposed closure of Heads of Ayr station on behalf of those who travel on the summer Saturday only 08.15 train from Newcastle to Heads of Ayr.
> Even if the above train were to terminate at Ayr and the return train were to start from Ayr (last year it left Heads of Ayr at 08.05), there would be considerable difficulty in

travelling the four miles between the two places by road. Most of those who use the above train do so in connection with at least one week's holiday at the holiday camp.

Should it be the intention to completely withdraw the above trains, considerable hardship would be caused to the above users as they would have to change at Carlisle, Kilmarnock and Ayr, and most important the journey times as well as the fares would be increased substantially.

Michael Thurlow, as the sole individual objector, wrote a brief letter to the TUCC to outline his own experiences and how he believed the proposed closure would affect others:

> During the past four years I have made seven journeys to Heads of Ayr by train, both to visit Butlin's Holiday Camp and to visit the locality. Whenever I have had to make the journey by road, from Ayr, this has taken a longer time due to road congestion, has been less comfortable, and has also required a walk from the railway station to the bus stance in Ayr. This walk in Ayr, with heavy luggage sometimes, is most inconvenient compared with the through train services at present provided.
>
> If the service is withdrawn, road congestion must increase and thus journey times become longer. Combined with the change of transport at Ayr this will certainly cause railway users hardship.

The Transport Act, 1947 had established a Central Transport Consultative Committee (CTCC) and a network of regional committees - one each for Scotland, Wales and London, and eight others for England - with the aim of considering public suggestions for, and disagreements about, the services that were under the operation of the British Transport Commission. The CTCC and the TUCCs were independent bodies initially during a period when there were few large-scale disputes and protests, and also few complaints that were significant to justify contacting transport committees. Moreover, this was before the sudden shock of the Beeching Report; and, possibly in anticipation of the outcry of the numerous intended closures, the Transport Act, 1962 lessened the powers of the TUCCs, which, in any case, had not previously been brought into substantial effect, leaving the emphasis from 1962 to be firmly placed on TUCCs expressing only the resulting hardship aspects of the closures, without having authority to stop them altogether. The limited voice of TUCCs, in combination with the vital and usually-ignored matter of who actually pays to keep railways open, often left the public and railway-promoting organizations bewildered in thinking that no proper fight against a closure had occurred. Thus, unfortunately, the TUCC for Scotland had no power whatsoever to force Butlin's or BR(ScR) to retain the Heads of Ayr branch, with no finance forthcoming from other individual or combined authorities; and under such circumstances, how could the line be expected to remain open?

A document, dated 22nd February, 1968, from BR(ScR) to the TUCC for Scotland declared that there was little to comment on the two remaining objections. To the hardship that was contended by the North-Eastern Branch of the RIS, the response from BR(ScR) was that their observations did not suggest that quantities of luggage were excessive and that the proposed alternative arrangements would adequately cater for this aspect; and that while thousands of holidaymakers each year journeyed by bus, the withdrawal of the through trains between Newcastle and Ayr was not included in the proposal. To Michael Thurlow's objection in suggesting that the Heads of Ayr service was used by visitors to the locality as well as to the holiday camp, BR(ScR) replied that this was 'a most infrequent occurrence' because Heads of Ayr station was located within the camp and the Butlin's staff maintained a check on alighting passengers to confirm that they held reservations or paid the entrance fee of 10 shillings for the day. Furthermore, the reference to the walk from Ayr station to the bus stance exaggerated the position, for the stances concerned in the new proposal were adjacent to the station forecourt, with Mr Thurlow having referred to the more distant bus station of the town.

The TUCC for Scotland, therefore, could only look at the objections without bias to the situation generally and with respect to hardship specifically, in spite of what would be thought about their decision in relation to the unfortunate possibility of the closure of the line. After a TUCC meeting on 1st March, 1968, their report, dated 15th March of that year, to the Minister of Transport, Barbara Castle, explained the circumstances of the closure. Passenger services would continue to be available at Ayr station, four miles by road from Heads of Ayr; and regular services on a half-hour frequency, with additional trains at peak periods, operated between Ayr and Glasgow; while trains were also available between Ayr and Kilmarnock, with 13 trains in each direction on Saturdays, but that this service was also the subject of a separate withdrawal proposal on which a decision was awaited. By road, Western SMT Ltd operated a bus service between Ayr and Heads of Ayr holiday camp via Doonfoot during the summer season, calling at the entrance to Ayr station forecourt, while the Ayr-Dunure-Maybole service was also routed via Ayr station and Heads of Ayr holiday camp, such that the increase in the journey time for passengers would be marginal. It was proposed that special bus journeys in connection with certain train services would be run between Ayr and Heads of Ayr on Saturdays during the holiday season and that through rail tickets to and from Heads of Ayr would be valid only on these special buses. Passengers' Luggage in Advance arrangements would continue to be available and special arrangements would be made to convey passengers' accompanied luggage at the times when the special buses were in operation. It was also significant to the committee that neither the local authorities nor Butlin's had objected to the closure, and it was unanimously agreed that, in view of the adequate alternative transport arrangements, no hardship would be incurred to users by the discontinuation of the passenger services to Heads of Ayr.

On 12th June, 1968 at Butlin's camp, a meeting took place with one representative each of Butlin's Ltd, British Rail Scottish Region, the Scottish Bus Group and their constituent Western SMT Ltd. They were Mr J. Gower, Manager of Butlin's Camp, Ayr; Mr R. Robb, the railway area manager at Ayr; Mr J. Tweedie; and Mr G. Ramsay for the bus interests. It was stated that Butlin's had accepted the closure as inevitable. Figures were produced showing a decline in the number of holidaymakers to the camp, with 81,000 people in 1966 and 71,000 in 1967, and with a forecast of 60,000 for 1968. However, Butlin's hoped to stem the decline in 1969 when, still in accordance with their general policy, they would introduce 'self-service flatlets'; while it was agreed by the meeting's members that 'only a fairly small proportion of campers travelled by rail', such that the problem of the railway closure 'was not an immense one'. Therefore, the buses would easily cater for the passengers between Ayr station and the camp.

One admirable organization of railway enthusiasts had been kept well informed about the recent sad news of the Heads of Ayr branch. They were the members of the Branch Line Society (BLS), established in 1955, whose aim was to communicate mainly topical and often additional historical information about Britain's railways - not just branch lines but also main routes. Special attention was given to news of services, unusual occurrences, and closures, re-openings and new openings of stations and lines for passengers and freight, while tours along lines and visits to railway sites were also

arranged. The news-sheet of the BLS was *Branch Line News* (*BLN*), and in its issues back
on 28th September, 1967 and on 10th January, 1968, there had been references to the
Heads of Ayr-Alloway Junction closure as an addition to the Beeching 'reshaping'
plan. Then, on 27th March, 1968, *BLN* had recorded - unfortunately incorrectly, but
also believed to be correct elsewhere independently - that no objections had been
received to the proposal to close the Heads of Ayr line and - correctly - that it was
expected to close in September. On 1st May, 1968, *BLN* communicated, in its typical
format, that the last train would run on 7th September, 1968:

Heads of Ayr-Alloway Jn, ScR(GSW), 7.9.68, P‡
[P‡ = Seasonal passenger train service - date shown is last day of operation.]

Sadly, the two objections were of no consequence in attempting to justify
overturning the railway-closure proposal, with both under-publicized objections
readily countered by the intended provision of buses between Ayr station and
Butlin's. The worthy attempt from the RIS was also answered by the fact that direct
trains would continue to run between Newcastle and Ayr. No public hearing was
therefore necessary in regard to the closure, which is probably why it was generally
believed that there had been no objections; and on 10th July, 1968, BR(ScR) officially
announced that the Minister of Transport, Richard Marsh - having succeeded
Barbara Castle in early April in Harold Wilson's government - had given his consent
to the closure. The *Ayr Advertiser* of 18th July summarized the decision under the
heading of 'End Near for Butlin Line':

The Transport Minister, Mr Richard Marsh, has given his consent to the withdrawal of the
Ayr to Heads of Ayr passenger train service. This means that the 'Butlin's' line will close.
  In recent years there has been a marked decline in the numbers of passengers using the
railway service - and an increase in road passengers using bus services and private cars.
  In their report to the Minister, the Transport Users' Consultative Committee and the
Scottish Economic Planning Council stated that in view of the adequate alternative
arrangements no hardship would result from the closure.
  The closure will not take place until the additional bus services have been authorized
by road service licences under the Road Traffic Acts 1960-62, and until all necessary
arrangements have been made to ensure that these services will be available to the
public from May to September each year.
  The present bus services operated by the Western SMT Company Limited are Ayr-
Heads of Ayr (Butlin's Camp) and Ayr-Dunure-Maybole, and special Saturday services
used by patrons of the holiday camp.

Similar information was conveyed by the *Ayrshire Post* of 19th July under the
heading 'Rail Closure Decision', but this paper, in its previous week's issue, had
carried a short article that was entitled - seemingly with hope - 'What Future for Ayr-
Turnberry Light Railway?' However, the subject was not about saving the line, and,
instead, was - tediously and depressingly for railway supporters - again concerned
with the possibility of the line being converted to a road.
  The letter from the Ministry of Transport in London to the British Railways Board
in London, confirming the closure, was dated 3rd July and ultimately formed the
official public notification at stations and in the newspapers, appearing under
'Public Notices' in the *Ayr Advertiser* of 1st August and the *Ayrshire Post* of 2nd
August, for these single issues only. Headed 'British Railways Board, Public Notice,
Transport Act, 1962, Withdrawal of Railway Passenger Services', the contents began:

Reproduced below is a letter from the Ministry of Transport intimating the Minister's consent to the discontinuance of the railway passenger service between Ayr and Heads of Ayr and to the closure of the following passenger station:

Heads of Ayr. In consequence of this decision ALL passenger services will be discontinued between Alloway Junction and Heads of Ayr.

Then came the standard withdrawal-notice letter in officialese to amplify the closure decision; and the long account was concluded by a short and direct statement that left no doubt about what would occur and when:

British Railways, Scottish Region, announce that the passenger service will be withdrawn and Heads of Ayr station will be closed on and from Monday, 9th September, 1968.

From the issue of the notification, there was the sad fact that only a few weeks remained before the closure would take place. The official closure date would be counted as Monday 9th September, but the last trains were intended to be run on the preceding Saturday, the 7th. However, it was ironical that, possibly unknown to BR(ScR) in Glasgow, Butlin's had extended their holiday season that year by a week, from 7th to 14th September, and the apparent anomaly of the closure date of the railway in relation to the closure date of the camp was recognized by the area manager at Ayr station, Ronnie Robb, who, on his transfer to there from the Glasgow headquarters in 1965, had become the first of British Rail's area managers. Ronnie soon informed the divisional manager in Glasgow of the difference in closure dates, to the effect that 'while the last trains bringing campers to the camp will be run on Saturday, 7th September, it is necessary that trains to Glasgow and the South should be available on Saturday, 14th September for the dispersal of the campers', and he therefore requested BR(ScR) in Glasgow to arrange 'the necessary alteration to the effective date of the withdrawal of passenger train services'. The response and solution from Glasgow was:

The date of closure will require to stand at 9.9.68 because the publicity is already prepared and partly distributed. However, trains requested by the Area Manager, Ayr, to run from Heads of Ayr on Saturday, 14th September can be run as a special arrangement and the Area Manager, Ayr, has been requested to submit his proposals.

Ronnie Robb was requested to inform Glasgow of the number of passengers who would be travelling on the last day to their various destinations.

In its issue of 7th August, 1968, *Branch Line News* had noted the intended closure of the Heads of Ayr branch on 9th September, with the simple statement of 'Closure Approved by the Minister of Transport: Heads of Ayr-Alloway Jn (Ayr), ScR(GSW) 9.9.68'. However, the enlightening *BLN*, whose output resulted from observant and knowledgeable contributors, was able to state in its issue of 4th September - with the information having, therefore, been known to *BLN* before then - that the closure date would be amended. This read:

*Heads of Ayr-Ayr (Alloway Jn), ScR(GSW), 16.9.1968, P(All),
[P = Closed to passengers. (All) = Closed to all traffic. * = Amended entry - cancels previous entry.]

Heads of Ayr. As Butlin's camp is not closing until Saturday, 14th September, limited services will operate on this date. The services will be a 0910 and 0952 from Heads of Ayr, forming the 0930 Ayr-Kilmarnock and the 1010 Ayr-Glasgow respectively. This follows the practice of the last couple of years.

Chapter Nineteen

The End of the Line, 1968

With its imminent permanent closure in the autumn of 1968, the Heads of Ayr branch, having operated from 1947, had provided a distinctive railway service over the short stretch between Ayrshire's county town and the extreme northern Carrick coast, as local and long-distance trains conveyed holidaymakers to and from Butlin's camp. Now, the service was to be discontinued and consigned to history; but the line had indeed developed its own history in attaining regular direct services between Heads of Ayr and four cities - Glasgow, Edinburgh, Newcastle and Leeds - during most of that period, while also receiving excursions from other cities and towns in Scotland and England.

The Newcastle-Heads of Ayr service had operated from 1950 until the end of the scheduled timetable in 1968, with a gap in 1965 when the service was changed to a Newcastle-Stranraer service for that one year, on the same train path to and from Ayr, which meant that a change of train, to and from the Ayr-Heads of Ayr shuttle, was required at Ayr for Butlin's Newcastle passengers, in both directions. This was the same summer as the closure of the Dumfries-Stranraer line for passengers and goods, and the possible reason for the Newcastle-Stranraer service, instead of Newcastle-Heads of Ayr, was in association with the closure of the line through Galloway, in the sense that the two services were simply combined to Ayr, as a possible short-term 'solution' to the Galloway closure. However, the idea appeared not to have been a success, perhaps after complaints from Butlin's about their passengers having to change trains at Ayr with their holiday luggage, such that the direct Newcastle-Heads of Ayr service was restored in 1966. In 1968, on the Saturdays from 6th July to 17th August, the Newcastle-Heads of Ayr train conveyed through carriages to Stranraer Harbour, but there were no through carriages from Stranraer joining the Heads of Ayr-Newcastle service at Ayr.

Also under the Beeching cuts, the once-busy Edinburgh Princes Street station had officially closed on Monday 6th September, 1965, with the remaining services from the station transferred to Waverley station. The Butlin's timetabled trains to and from Edinburgh were thereafter discontinued, perhaps with the view to the run-down and eventual closure of the Heads of Ayr branch; and apart from possible non-timetabled excursion trains from Edinburgh to Heads of Ayr after 1965 - and there may not have been any - Waverley was not used for the Butlin's services. A further drastic effect of the Beeching report occurred in the following year with the unexpected closure of Glasgow St Enoch station on Monday 27th June, 1966, with the Ayr, Ardrossan, Largs, Girvan and Stranraer services transferred to Central station. This meant that the last St Enoch-Heads of Ayr trains ran on Saturday 25th June, and that from Saturday 2nd July, Central station was used for the Butlin's services.

The trains for Leeds, running in the southbound direction only, had commenced in 1950, like the Newcastle service, but during the early to mid-1960s, the Leeds service had become supplementary or non-timetabled and had been reduced in frequency during the season. Thus, in each of the last two years of the line, there was only an isolated service from Heads of Ayr to Leeds, on 29th July, 1967 and 27th July, 1968, containing as few as 77 and 25 passengers respectively.

A BR 'Swindon' class '126' three-car diesel-multiple-unit at Heads of Ayr station with a Glasgow Central train on 7th September, 1968, a week before the last services on the branch. *W.S. Sellar*

The Butlin's trains for Newcastle and Leeds, and special excursions from elsewhere to Heads of Ayr, had been more often diesel-hauled in 1966, owing to the rapid reduction of steam power; and, with the official date of cessation of steam traction in Scotland having been 1st May, 1967, the last time that steam trains had operated on the branch was the late summer of 1966, while the end of steam at Ayr shed had been on Saturday 1st October, 1966. An example of a special service to Butlin's during the diesel era was a Perth-Heads of Ayr excursion, hauled by a type '2', No. 5310, that was photographed by Derek Cross at Alloway on Thursday 1st June, 1967.

The last year of service on the branch produced the following timetable of through services that, as part of the period from 6th May, 1968 to 4th May, 1969 of the BR(ScR) timetable, covered the Butlin's season from 18th May to 7th September, 1968, which was extended to 14th September but with a specially-arranged reduced timetable for that day:

		A	A	A	B	C	A	A	A
		am	*am*	*am*	*pm*	*am*	*pm*	*pm*	*pm*
Newcastle	dep.					8.15			
Glasgow Central	dep.		7.30	10.00			1.30	3.00	5.12
Ayr	arr.		8.35	11.00		12.23	2.35	4.00	6.06
Ayr	dep.	7.15	8.40	11.05	12.39	12.39	2.40	4.05	6.11
Heads of Ayr	arr.	7.27	8.52	11.17	12.51	12.51	2.52	4.17	6.24

		D	E	A	A	F	A
		am	*am*	*am*	*am*	*pm*	*pm*
Heads of Ayr	dep.	8.00	8.00	9.52	11.55	1.20	3.15
Ayr	arr.	8.12	8.12	10.04	12.07	1.32	3.27
Ayr	dep.		8.21	10.10	12.10		
Glasgow Central	arr.			11.10	1.10		
Newcastle	arr.		12.43				

Notes: A - 18th May to 7th September. B - 18th May to 31st August, and extended to 7th September. C - 15th June to 31st August, and extended to 7th September, conveys through coaches from Newcastle, calling at Kilmarnock, Troon, Prestwick and Newton-on-Ayr; and 6th July to 17th August, conveys through coaches to Stranraer Harbour. D - 18th May to 15th June. E - 22nd June to 7th September, conveys through coaches to Newcastle, calling at Newton-on-Ayr, Prestwick, Troon and Kilmarnock. F - 18th May to 24th August.

BR English Electric type '1' diesel (later class '20'), No. D8124, at Heads of Ayr station on 14th September, 1968, with the second-last passenger train on the last day of the Butlin's branch, forming the 9.10 am service to Kilmarnock and having connections to Leeds and London by the 'Thames-Clyde Express'. With the train having arrived from Ayr, departing passengers wait for the locomotive to round the coaches using the loop, before they can board for the return journey to Ayr and Kilmarnock. The view is east along the railway.   *D. Cross*

In the view west along the railway, the train has rounded the coaches, to run cab-first. On the right is a pylon for the Butlin's chairlift ropeway that, running above the railway, connects the camp with both the main entrance and the Heads of Ayr Hotel on the higher ground to the left.
                                                                                                   D. Cross

While Saturday 7th September, 1968 was the last day of the regular timetabled service on the Heads of Ayr branch, there remained two specially-requested services that would run on the following Saturday as the last-ever day of service. Thus, the end of the Butlin's railway service, the Heads of Ayr branch and Heads of Ayr passenger station came on the morning of Saturday 14th September, 1968, after 21½ years; and it was also the end of the remaining section of the former Maidens & Dunure Light Railway after 62½ years. On that last day, the final two trains were scheduled as planned. The first consisted of three BR standard non-corridor coaches that were hauled by a BR English Electric type '1' locomotive, No. D8124, on the 9.10 am service to Kilmarnock that would provide a connection with the southbound 9.35 am Glasgow-London 'Thames-Clyde Express', departing from Kilmarnock at 10.11, for Leeds and London St Pancras, and from which Newcastle passengers would change at Carlisle. The second and final passenger train from Heads of Ayr station was a nine-car class '126' dmu that formed the 9.52 am to Glasgow Central.

Derek Cross was present at Heads of Ayr station to photograph the 9.10, but he did not wait to photograph the 9.52, perhaps because he was aware that it would be a dmu. Though Derek had also photographed the last-ever through train from Heads of Ayr to Newcastle - the 8.00 am - on the previous Saturday at Greenan, which was hauled by a BR type '2' diesel, No. D5356 - he was not an enthusiast of diesel locomotives, and even less so of dmus; but it is nevertheless fortunate for railway history that he had been able to record the penultimate train.

Both trains from Heads of Ayr, as specials for the last departing rail-borne campers, would have been intended to work as empty coaching stock from Ayr to Heads of Ayr, but a few railway enthusiasts had been kindly allowed to travel on the first of them to the camp to be able to say farewell to the line in both directions. The *Ayr Advertiser* aptly summarized the morning's events:

> *The Last Day of the Heads of Ayr Branch Railway Line.* Only a handful of railway enthusiasts were at Heads of Ayr station on Saturday to watch the last passenger train travel over the picturesque branch line.
>
> With the co-operation of British Rail, they were able to travel up on the first train in the morning. This train left Heads of Ayr at 9.10 am for Kilmarnock with several items of furniture from the station master's office stacked in the guard's van.
>
> Soon afterwards, the last train from Ayr arrived, a nine-coach diesel multiple unit. Unlike so many 'last train' journeys, there were over 250 passengers travelling to Ayr or further up the line to Glasgow.
>
> Exactly on time, the last train left at 9.52 am. The only difference between this and a normal journey was the sharp report of three warning detonators going off, one after another - a sad but traditional feature of every last departure.
>
> Shortly after 10 am, the train drew into Ayr station, bringing to an end a service which had survived a number of vicissitudes, from its humble beginning as the Maidens & Dunure Light Railway in May 1906.

The line was officially closed on Monday 16th September, with a Monday formal closure for stations having been frequent practice after last trains had run on a Saturday. Sadly, no more would long and short passenger trains convey happy holidaymakers over the iron road to Butlin's at Heads of Ayr, and no more would any part of the old Maidens & Dunure Light Railway remain in use, having spanned far back in the haziness and romanticism of time, when passenger trains and goods and potato trains had leisurely wound their way along the scenic, atmospheric and invigorating Carrick coast, past Heads of Ayr, Dunure, Culzean, Maidens and

Turnberry. In the wake of the line's assorted closures and re-openings from 1930 to 1959, every stretch of it would now be erased from the railway timetables, as that summer season of 1968 came to an end.

On Sunday 29th September, two weeks after the last Butlin's trains had run, Alloway Junction signal box was closed, as there was no longer any purpose for it; but the usefulness of the railway office inside Butlin's camp meant that it would be retained for at least the 1969 season. *Branch Line News* recorded on 23rd October, 1968:

> *Heads of Ayr*. Although the train service has been withdrawn between Ayr and Heads of Ayr, and Heads of Ayr station closed, the British Railways booking office within the camp will remain in operation next summer. Buses, hired by British Railways, will operate between Ayr station and Butlin's camp at Heads of Ayr and through bookings will exist between numerous BR stations and Butlin's camp, rail tickets only being acceptable on the replacement buses.

On 2nd April, 1969, *BLN* reported:

> *Ayr*. Alloway Jn signal box was closed on 29th September and the branch to Heads of Ayr, the last remaining portion of the Maidens & Dunure Light Railway, finally 'put out of use'. Lifting is expected to commence shortly. On the main line the [signalling] section is now Belmont-Dalrymple Jn, and even this line may be singled in the future, right through to Girvan.

Then, in a final recognition of the old line, the Branch Line Society recorded in their *Annual Report 1968-9*, in connection with a BLS brake van tour from Ayr to Waterside and the lifting of the track of the Heads of Ayr branch:

> *Reports of Brake Van trips: Ayr-Waterside*. The morning of Monday, 1st September [1969] saw 5 members of the BLS making a brisk walk from Ayr station to Ayr Harbour where they boarded the brake van of the 0920 hours to Waterside. Departure, behind D5358 and D5412 and 55 empty wagons, was only 2 minutes late. The first part of the route, though Ayr, via Ayr Harbour Junction, Newton Junction and Hawkhill Junction, was somewhat slow due to signal checks to allow passage of the 0830 passenger train from Glasgow to Stranraer. After Ayr, the site of Alloway Junction was noted, where the coastal route to Girvan once diverged. This line was cut back to serve only Heads of Ayr Holiday Camp, but was closed at the end of the summer season [1968]. The track has been lifted and no trace remains now of the junction signal box.

In December 1968, Ronnie Robb had written to Glasgow to inquire whether Newcastle-Ayr Saturdays-only trains would be run in the summer of 1969 for Butlin's camp, and if so, whether they would run 'via Kilmarnock, as in the past' - meaning the recent past to and from Heads of Ayr, and in 1968 for certain. The two-part answer had been: 'Yes, via Mauchline'; which, in spite of Mauchline being on the route to Ayr both via Kilmarnock and Annbank, meant the Annbank route, though nevertheless ambiguously. If the Kilmarnock route was to be used, the reply would likely have been simply 'Yes', or 'Yes, via Kilmarnock'; whereas the wording 'Yes, via Mauchline' stipulated 'branching at Mauchline and running via Annbank' - for, otherwise, why had there been the need to mention Mauchline?

Soon afterwards, another Ayrshire rail service - over a route that had been associated with the Butlin's services - sadly ended, as a delayed laceration from the Beeching surgery, after the years of survival and uncertainty from the Doctor's initial plan to sever it; for passenger traffic was withdrawn between Ayr and Kilmarnock on 3rd March, 1969. It was an absurd decision in the gloomy post-Beeching era that robbed the county of valuable services: firstly, the county's two largest towns - Kilmarnock with 52,000 and Ayr with 48,000 people - of trains connecting each other; and, secondly, western and central Ayrshire of their direct rail connection to, respectively, England and Northern Ireland. Ayr and Kilmarnock were 16 railway miles apart, though it was only the section of eight miles between Barassie and Kilmarnock that lost the passenger service but with the retention of freight trains and the line to passenger standards to allow for the possibility of Glasgow-Ayr passenger trains being diverted via Kilmarnock.

Unlike in 1968 for the Newcastle-Heads of Ayr service running via Kilmarnock, the 1969 Newcastle-Ayr service, primarily to accommodate the Butlin's passengers, was routed via Annbank. The 1969 timetable did not show a call at Kilmarnock in either direction, but confirmation of the Annbank route was provided, for example, from the running time of the southbound train, in that it departed from Ayr at 9.00 am and arrived in Dumfries at 10.8, which was much too short a duration for the Kilmarnock route, with a requirement of nearer 1hr 40 min. It is possible that, in part, the Annbank route was used to discourage the non-essential use of the Kilmarnock-Barassie route for passenger trains, on the basis of preventing a return of the local Ayr-Kilmarnock service.

A set of figures, after the closure of the line, referred to the percentage of the Butlin's campers who had travelled by rail and road during the 1967 and 1968 seasons. While the figures that had been given at the meeting on 12th June, 1968 of the representatives of Butlin's and the rail and bus companies were 71,000 for 1967 and an estimated 60,000 for 1968, the total number of residential bookings that were compiled after the 1968 season became 66,458 for 1967 and 63,099 for 1968. The official figures were 16.7 per cent by rail and 83.3 per cent by road in 1967, and 14.9 per cent and 85.1 per cent respectively in 1968, albeit with the percentages not in absolute agreement with the totals. Nevertheless, the figures portrayed the decline of passengers to Butlin's at Heads of Ayr.

Such a decline was significant on its own but it was compounded by the separate problems facing the Butlin's organization throughout the country. The peak era for that style of holiday occurred between the mid-1950s and the mid-1960s, but towards the end of the 1960s, a new trend in holidays for British people was in evidence, for the British holiday camps and the British holiday resorts had experienced competition from the new overseas holiday destinations for the British people, who now had more money at their disposal for spending on exotic holidays abroad, which were no longer only for wealthy people. The holiday trend had changed after three decades, and Butlin's had to adapt to survive.

Bookings had fallen dramatically in 1967, and the ideal opportunity for change coincided with the retirement in 1968 of Billy Butlin and the succession of the business by his son, Bobby, as Chairman and Managing Director, who carried out changes and modernizations, which, in reducing staff costs, included the self-catering accommodation and self-service restaurants. In 1972, more people than ever before were spending their holidays at Butlin's, and it was a good time to sell the Butlin's empire. This happened in September 1972 with the purchase by the Rank Organisation, which was a British film and cinema company before expanding into a massive multi-national holiday and leisure enterprise. The Butlin's name was retained, with Bobby Butlin still in charge; but, unfortunately, during the remainder of the 1970s, the accelerating popularity of affordable package holidays abroad by air travel caused a reduction once more in the numbers of holidaymakers to the Butlin's camps.

In 1980, Sir Billy Butlin died of a heart attack. He was buried in his resident Jersey, and a large and impressive monument in the cemetery there outlined his life and achievements, with the final words of the epitaph declaring: 'He was never too tall to stoop to help the underprivileged.' The headstone of the memorial was also engraved with a composite illustration that represented the principal creations of his life: an amusement park with funfair rides and a holiday-camp with chalets and a swimming pool. Billy Butlin was not just an exceptionally wealthy showman but one who always delivered his promises, and more. Aside from his principal fame in providing affordable seaside holidays to the many working-class people, he was also a philanthropist, and much of his admirable work in that capacity was directed towards benefiting underprivileged, sick and handicapped children. His individual benefactions to many charities were never known exactly, but they totalled in excess of £5 million.

It was from 1980 that the Rank Organisation started to counteract the decline of their Butlin's now-termed holiday centres by a substantial series of investments, including at Ayr, through the early- to mid-1980s. Then, after the Scottish Tourist Board had promised financial support, it was announced in 1987 that a larger Butlin's renovation programme at Heads of Ayr would proceed; and the Butlin's leisure and holiday complex, called Wonderwest World, opened in 1988.

A year before the decision had been made to create the new Wonderwest World at Heads of Ayr, the town of Ayr, and part of the county, had started to benefit from another modernization, in the form of a transformed and faster rail service. This originated from the Ayrshire railway electrification scheme that had been proposed back in 1979; and with the late-1950s rolling stock of Swindon class '126' and Metro-Cammell class '101' dmus nearing the end of their working life, it had been vital for the BR and the Glasgow-based Strathclyde Regional Council (SRC), in admirable co-operation, to consider the electrification of the Ayrshire lines. However, the large obstacle, not surprisingly, was the cost, and BR and SRC were not in a position to be able to undertake the full cost together, such that other financial support was essential. The government promised support through the Scottish Development Department of the Scottish Office if an application for a grant from the European Regional Development Fund was also sought; and in October 1982, it was announced that a grant from Europe would be forthcoming. Back in 1967, the Glasgow-Paisley section had been modernized as part of the Glasgow electrification project to Paisley, Port Glasgow, Greenock, Gourock and Wemyss Bay, and, therefore, the Ayrshire electrification scheme would commence from Paisley. The £84 million investment to complete the scheme led to the first of the Ayrshire electric trains - of class '318' electric multiple units (emus), which were built by British Rail Engineering Limited at York - serving Ayr on 29th September, 1986, having been completed in under four years and six months ahead of schedule; while the electrification to Ardrossan and Largs opened on 19th January, 1987.

It was in association with the electrification of the line to Ayr that suggestions of its extension to Alloway, Greenan and Heads of Ayr were put forward in late 1987. Unfortunately, no material progress resulted, but four years later, the project was revived, and, by early February 1992, the *Ayrshire Post* was able to record the renewed interest from Glasgow 'in a plan to reopen a rail link to Alloway and Greenan', with the proposal, as part of the Strathclyde Rail Plan, originating from Strathclyde Passenger Transport Executive in a report to Strathclyde Regional

Council. The scheme was considered feasible, involving the provision of stations at Belmont, Alloway and Greenan, on the basis of the extensive building of new houses from Alloway to Doonfoot spreading towards Burton and Greenan; while only a short distance further west, Butlin's had shown interest in seeing the line once more serving their new holiday complex. There was also the possibility of a station to serve the new Ayr Hospital that had opened in 1991 to the south-east of High Glengall farm and immediately south of the psychiatric Ailsa Hospital, which formerly had its own very short goods branch that curved north-eastwards from the Ayr-Maybole line at what was Glengall Junction, facing Ayr. The issue of *Branch Line News* of 1st August, 1992 implied that 'the proposal to extend electrification southwards from Ayr to Alloway, with intermediate stations at Belmont and Ailsa Hospital', was still in contemplation by then, and that:

> This would involve the reopening of 1 mile 374 yards of the old Maidens & Dunure Light Railway from Alloway Jn to Alloway, the former station site being adjacent to the Robert Burns Heritage Centre, the 'tourist' centre of Alloway. (The Heritage Centre grounds include the former Alloway goods yards, which was at a higher level than the passenger platform 'Doon' in the cutting.)

The railway extension was seen as being significant for Butlin's Wonderwest World during the summer months because of their controversial plan in early 1992 for a vast multi-million-pound enlargement at Heads of Ayr; but the holiday scheme was defeated by strong public protests locally, because the belief was that it was too big and that it would destroy the local environment. The prevention of the scheme was unfortunately ironical from the railway viewpoint in two ways - one connected with the past and the other with the present. The first was from the fears of the objectors that the Wonderwest enlargement, if allowed, 'would open the floodgates for developers all down this stretch of the Ayrshire coast', whereas the very lack of developments along the Carrick coast, apart from those at Turnberry, had been a principal reason why the M&DLR had been forced to close many years previously. The second resulted in the situation having transpired that Butlin's, in having done nothing to stop the closure of the Heads of Ayr branch back in 1968, were denied - deservedly, dare it be said? - the ideal opportunity of acquiring a revived railway, in direct connection with Ayr and Glasgow, to their Wonderwest World.

Unfortunately, there were doubts about the viability of the electrified extension to Alloway, Greenan and Butlin's, in relation to the expense of building it and to the possibility of an insufficient number of passengers who would use it: essentially about whether an increased permanent residential and a temporary holiday population in the area was significant enough to justify its construction. As such, the project did not proceed beyond the discussion stage.

In 1999, after yet another large investment plan by the Rank Organisation, Wonderwest World at Ayr, in ceasing to use the Butlin's name, was transferred to Haven Holidays, another company within the Rank Organisation, and it became a Haven All-Action Holiday Park, opening in April of that year. For this refurbishment, the remaining chalets, other well-established buildings, and long-famous features of entertainments and amusements, including the chairlift and the miniature railway had been demolished, to make way for new two-storied, more modern chalets, other self-catering apartment accommodation, luxury static caravans, and contemporary forms and facilities for holidays, with the emphasis on attracting more of the younger families. In 2000, the complex at Heads of Ayr was

Ayr Townhead sidings, immediately south of Ayr station, on Monday, 19th October, 1964. The little 'Brighton Terrier' *Martello*, having reached Ayr from Eastleigh works, near Southampton, is being lifted by two cranes from the low-loader railway wagon, to be placed on a Pickfords low-loader transporter for conveyance by road to Butlin's camp. The tender of *Duchess of Sutherland* was conveyed to Butlin's on the next day from the sidings in the same manner.　　　*D. Cross*

Alloway Junction on Wednesday 21st October, 1964. Running backwards, the *Duchess* is hauled and propelled by two diesel shunters from Ayr depot to Greenan sidings, to be loaded onto the Pickfords low-loader road transporter for conveyance along the final short distance to Butlin's camp. This view is south-westwards from the signal box, looking onto the start of the Heads of Ayr branch and the former M&DLR.　　　*D. Cross*

then acquired by the large holiday company Bourne Leisure Ltd as part of their purchase of the whole holiday division of the Rank Organisation; and, under the subsidiary Haven Holidays, it was given a new name that was chosen after a small outcrop of rocks, called Craig Tara, that lay on the shore immediately north of the site.

Craig Tara Holiday Park remains active today on the sloping ground of the former Butlin's camp as a popular family holiday location; but, sadly, it has no railway connection, though service buses run directly into the centre of the complex. Unfortunately, very little remains of the Heads of Ayr Butlin's station, but the abutments of the bridge and the railway embankment to the west remain as a vestige of the railway that once served the Carrick coast between Ayr and Girvan from 1906 and between Ayr and Heads of Ayr from 1947, until complete closure in 1968. A quarter of a mile west of the entrance to Craig Tara is the entrance to Heads of Ayr Farm Park which presents visitors with the opportunity to see farm, pet and exotic animals and which also contains indoor and outdoor-adventure and playground attractions for children. In the vicinity, beside what was then Laigh Kyleston farm, was the underbridge - with only the abutments now remaining - where the ¼-mile-long headshunt of the Butlin's branch ended on the embankment, 65 yards west of the bridge.

The Butlin's Heads of Ayr Exhibition Locomotives

In January 1963, towards the end of the steam era, the significance of steam locomotive preservation was realised - only in an indirect sense, but nevertheless, fortunately - by Billy Butlin and Butlin's Ltd, and, appropriate to obtaining something else of 'the unusual' for the camps, the idea resulted in Butlin's purchasing several steam locomotives for use as static displays in some of the camps, to provide another attraction for the holidaymakers. Ultimately, four large former LMS passenger locomotives and four small former southern-England tank locomotives were quickly allocated to four camps at Ayr, Minehead, Pwllhelli and Skegness, with each of these camps receiving one large and one small locomotive. The restored exhibition locomotives that were displayed within Butlin's camp at Ayr from 1964 to 1971 were: LMS 'Princess Coronation' class 4-6-2 No. 6233 Duchess of Sutherland which had arrived in Ayr from BR's Crewe works; and a small tank engine, known as a 'Brighton Terrier', of 'A1' and later 'A1X' class of the London, Brighton & South Coast Railway (LB&SC), which was 0-6-0T, No. 62 Martello, which had reached Ayr from BR's Eastleigh works.

The news in the autumn of 1964 of the transfer of the majestic Duchess of Sutherland to Heads of Ayr was of intense interest to one man in particular at Ayr depot, both in his ongoing capacity as a locomotive engineer and from his boyhood memories of having excitedly observed, at Carstairs in Lanarkshire, this class in working the Glasgow-London express passenger services. Bill Bennett, initially as the shed master and then as depot engineer at Ayr, obtained the honour of overseeing all the local movements to and from Heads of Ayr in 1964 and 1971. Additionally, Bill's foresight and his voluntary dedication, independently of his everyday railway duties, ensured that he and his staff at Ayr depot made periodical visits to Butlin's camp during those years to apply grease and oil to all the moving parts of the Duchess and Martello. This was because of the open-air display site that exposed the locomotives to the moist and salty air of the Firth of Clyde; for, otherwise, the longer-

The dramatic sight of a large locomotive at the entrance to Butlin's camp, Heads of Ayr, on Sunday 25th October, 1964. Having been hauled directly on the rails from Ayr depot to the former Greenan sidings and then by the Ayr-Dunure road, from behind the camera's position, the *Duchess* faces Butlin's Camp as the tractor-lorry and low-loader transporter reverse into the entrance. *D. Cross*

The impressive display of the *Duchess* and *Martello* in 1968, as typically seen from the Ayr-Dunure road between 1964 and 1971, with many thousands of Butlin's residential campers and day visitors having obtained the opportunity of viewing and examining the two preserved exhibition locomotives and standing on the footplates. The liveries were LMS crimson lake for the *Duchess* and LB&SC yellow ochre for *Martello*. *W.S. Sellar*

term preservation of both locomotives, as foreseen by Bill beyond their possession by Butlin's, would have been much more difficult and expensive. Happily, both locomotives are in full steam service today, and in 2002, 2003 and 2007, the *Duchess* visited Glasgow on steam railtours, in allowing Bill and innumerable other enthusiasts the opportunities to witness the impressive sight in Scotland of the big locomotive that Bill helped to preserve by the simple use of grease and oil.

Butlin's Ayr Locomotive Data

Duchess of Sutherland: 4-6-2 LMS 'Princess Coronation'; LMS No. 6233; BR No. 46233; built Crewe, 1938; withdrawn from service February 1964; arrival and departure Butlin's Ayr, October 1964 and February 1971; sold by Butlin's to Bressingham Steam Museum, Diss, Norfolk, 1989; present location, Princess Royal Class Locomotive Trust, Butterley, Derbyshire. Origin of locomotive name: after Duchess Eileen, daughter of Charles Butler, seventh Earl of Lanesborough of Swithland Hall, Leicestershire, and wife of George Sutherland-Leveson-Gore (pronounced 'Looson-Gore'), fifth Duke of Sutherland of Dunrobin Castle, Sutherland, and of Trentham Hall, Staffordshire.

Martello: 0-6-0 'A1' and later 'A1X' class; LB&SC No. 62, No. 662; SR No. B662, 2662; BR No. 32662; built Brighton, 1875; withdrawn from service November 1963; arrival and departure Butlin's Ayr, October 1964 and February 1971; sold by Butlin's to Bressingham Steam Museum, Diss, Norfolk, 1989; present location, Bressingham Steam Museum, Diss, Norfolk. Origin of locomotive name: after the 74 Martello towers, or round stone forts, that were built along the coast from Seaford in Sussex to Folkestone in Kent as a defence against the threat of invasion from Emperor Napoleon of France in the early 19th century.

A part of the sad but inevitable departure of the *Duchess*, twisting through Ayr, after a journey of 3½ miles from Butlin's, on Wednesday 24th February, 1971, as the tractor lorry of Sunter Brothers of Northallerton, Yorkshire, turns towards Townhead sidings, hauling the *Duchess* on a low-loader transporter. The tender and *Martello* had been conveyed the previous day - all three by road because of the closure of the Heads of Ayr branch in 1968 - and both locomotives were transferred to Bressingham Steam Museum in Norfolk.

D. Cross

Chapter Twenty

Memories of the Line, 1930s-1950s

During and after their lifetimes, the original Maidens & Dunure Light Railway and its Butlin's branch continuation in time have unjustifiably received scant attention in railway literature, while also having been comparatively-little photographed overall - apart from the many admirable and historically-valuable photographs by Derek Cross for the Butlin's trains during the 1960s. This dearth of coverage is particularly puzzling in consideration of the diversity of the workings over both the M&DLR and the Butlin's section and of the wonderful scenery of the route. Indeed, the old railway to Turnberry has been closed for such a long time that there are now few people who remember it even in its later goods-only period, while the Butlin's railway workings have largely also been forgotten. With its highly-scenic route, what might have transpired if the M&DLR had managed to survive into the 1960s, in terms of a possible outcry to closing it? The early railway preservationists would then have been able to raise strong objections, though it would still have been very difficult to combat the closure, for even the short Butlin's branch could not be saved as late as 1968. Nevertheless, and happily, the authors of this first-ever book about the M&DLR were able to discover much of the story of the line from a number of 'preservationists' in another sense - railway and non-railway people - who, through their remarkable memories, relayed facts, experiences, stories and scenes from the line's history from the 1930s to the 1950s, including significant details recorded from outside officially-documented sources. The railwaymen additionally provided valuable information on the line's operational side, as already described in this book.

Someone who journeyed over the whole line on the 1938 special train for the Empire Exhibition in Glasgow was Bill Tait of Girvan, the golfing correspondent of the present *Carrick Gazette* and a long-established member of Turnberry Golf Club. In recalling his journey, Bill thought that he was aged about eight or nine at the time, but discussion with him suggested that he was only aged five when the 1938 special, as the only passenger train on which he could have travelled, had run along the line. His aunt had asked him at Girvan station whether he wanted to travel by the pretty route, via Dunure, or by the quick route, via Maybole, and Bill's answer had been unhesitatingly the pretty route. Even at such a young age, he remembered Turnberry station and 'the wonderful sweep down to Dunure which gave magnificent views across the Clyde'.

Thirteen years older than Bill Tait, Robert Logan was born at Drumbeg Cottages, by Turnberry, and he also travelled on the 1938 excursion train. Robert joined the train at his local Turnberry station, where 'a carriage-load' of people waited to travel, with most passengers, not surprisingly and except for Girvan, boarding at Turnberry, Maidens and Dunure. One of his other memories of the railway was in seeing what he and others called the 'caddies' train', being the daily goods train, with its guard's van carrying illicit passengers in the form of young caddies in connection with the golf at Turnberry. In 1935, Robert worked as a labourer at the nearby Shanter farm and he told of himself attending to four big Clydesdale horses being unloaded from a railway horse-box directly onto the platform at Turnberry station, and then riding on one of them while leading the other three along the Maidens road to the farm. Robert remembered one of the Turnberry station masters as David Grierson and one of the Maidens 'station masters' - or, rather, goods agent - as Robert Lees.

Fergus Gibson, as a boy of six from New Cumnock, also visited the Empire Exhibition of 1938, though he was not a traveller on the special train over the Turnberry railway. However, that same year, he went on a 'railway holiday' with his parents to Alloway station, for the novel reason that there were two railway camping coaches in what was formerly the northern line of the loop through the island platform and what was, by 1938, a siding that terminated at a buffer. The camping coaches were converted into railway carriages that were used as rented accommodation for holidaymakers in the Alloway area, and they were typical of others that were placed at certain 'camp sites' at quiet railway stations in coastal and rural districts of Britain. Fergus recalled that the coach at Alloway consisted of three or possibly four bedrooms, a sitting-room, and a kitchen, and the use of the station toilet, with the station then closed to passenger traffic. He was also given a run over a short distance of the railway on the guard's van of the goods train, through the tunnel and across the Doon bridge, though he cannot recall how far he went along the line. Fergus attained a career in railway management, and after serving in a variety of posts, he became the passenger manager for British Railways Scottish Region from 1982 until his retirement in 1987.

In 1940, Peter Urie, at the age of 12, moved with his parents and brothers and sisters from Low Coylton, east of Ayr, to Balchriston Cottages, midway between Balchriston farm and Balchriston siding, when his father began working for William Lyburn at the farm. Peter obtained exemption from Carrick Academy in Maybole to work full time at the farm because he was ahead in his schooling, and from 1940 to 1942, part of his farm work consisted of loading the early potatoes onto the train at the siding. He remembered long trains of 40 wagons, operating from Girvan to Ayr, calling by the small siding to transport the crop, and he asserted that the siding was long enough to accommodate as many as six wagons, with three or four wagons regularly there. He was able to picture the scene of the engine of the potato train drawing immediately north of the siding and forward of the level crossing and then reversing into the siding to pick up the wagons filled with the potatoes. The train returned in the afternoon to Ayr, loaded with the crop, and ran back to Girvan in the evening, either empty or with manure that was to be used as fertiliser for the fields of the coastal farms. This included pulling into Balchriston siding with wagons of manure, which Peter had to shovel onto a trailer and drive by tractor to the farm, but he said that he enjoyed the work for its therapeutic value!

While living at Balchriston Cottages, Peter often headed into Ayr by bus on a Saturday afternoon to go to 'the pictures', but, firstly, he had to walk northwards along a mile of the railway and across the Rancleugh viaduct to Knoweside, and from there, he travelled on the local double-decker Western SMT bus that ran between Knoweside and Ayr via Dunure. He was never scared in walking across the Rancleugh viaduct, even in darkness, because of its solid structure; and when he went for walks further north along the coast, he also crossed the Croy viaduct, or Knoweside viaduct, as he knew it, readily witnessing the optical illusion of the Electric Brae from it.

During the last few years of the Turnberry railway's goods service, Mrs Elma Cowan of Ayr, as the young Elma McWhirter, lived locally to the line at Heads of Ayr in one of the three railway cottages, and nearby at Lagg. During her childhood years, Elma became familiar with the area of the line at Heads of Ayr and Lagg, and when she was aged six to 11, she recalled seeing the trains go by, which would have been the daily goods and the seasonal potato workings. She and her younger sister, Linda, and a few pals would look and listen for the trains before running down from their cottages by the Ayr-Dunure road at Lagg and crossing the fields towards the railway to wave excitedly to the passing trains, in the style of the TV series and subsequent film versions of *The Railway Children*, from the Edith Nesbit novel. Elma added that the whistle of the train was always blown on the approach to the Bracken Bay cutting; and also in regard to the cutting, she was told about her father being engulfed there, while trying to walk through it in a big snow drift in the severe winter of 1947.

The railway evoked a few other memories for Elma. When the goods train reached the curve on the ascent towards the cutting, lumps of coal, which were piled high on the tender or on the wagons, would sometimes fall off to land by the line; and the young Elma sensibly decided that she and Linda could carry the coal home for the fire. Elma went to school at Fisherton crossroads, which served the surrounding area, including Dunure village, with the school situated close to Dunure station, and she remembered seeing wagons in the goods yard, and she was aware of the two railway cottages immediately opposite the school on the Ayr-Dunure road. Because of the rise of the road at Lagg, Elma and Linda obtained a good view of the railway from the cottage and then from the bungalow, with Bracken Bay and the Heads of Ayr cliffs behind. They were sad when the goods service ceased, with the silence and overall strangeness of the trains no longer passing, after which they and their pals played at the deserted Heads of Ayr station.

Nigel Macmillan of Glasgow was aged 14 to 16 from 1944 to 1946 when he spent three weeks on holiday in the summers of those years living beside Dunure station, in lodging with the Simpson family at Fisherton. Mrs Simpson was a friend of his mother, and one of her sons became famous in the role of Dr Finlay, of the 1960s' popular television series *Dr Finlay's Casebook*. Nigel was soon drawn to the station, rushing out after breakfast to see, on the first day, an LMS class '2P' 4-4-0 on the daily goods service, and, to his excitement, he was given a run on the engine a short distance beyond the deep and curved cutting south of Dunure. On the next day, a Caley 'Jumbo' class '2F' 0-6-0 took him as far as Maidens, though he had to walk much further back along the line than on the previous day, and when he was halfway through the deep cutting again, he heard a locomotive approaching from the north that made him flee back along the cutting until he found an niche in which he crouched, terrified, at what turned out to be a potato special passing slowly. After that, he smartly took his bicycle and had it placed on the top of the tender, as the morning footplate ride became a daily routine for him, as he was allowed to drive the engine. He also witnessed the Electric Brae's optical illusion.

Nigel was as an illicit passenger, and he remembered the goods train carrying other people. On one occasion in shunting at Glenside, there was a woman with a baby in her arms on the footplate, and from Nigel's carelessness in allowing too much water into the boiler, the engine started 'priming', or producing a dirty-water exhaust, resulting in the baby's face being covered in black spots and the mother exclaiming: 'Look at my wean!' (pronounced 'wane', meaning baby). On another occasion, there was nearly an accident with a potato train, as Nigel described from being on board. Six empty wagons were shunted at Knoweside and then pushed by the engine southwards, to be placed into Balchriston siding for the loading of potatoes there, with the rest of the wagons pulled behind the tender. However, only the fireman and Nigel were on the footplate, with the driver in the guard's van, playing cards with several illicit passengers, but, unfortunately, the gates at

Balchriston had remained closed because no one had heard the whistle of the approaching engine. Suddenly, the fireman shut the steam off and slammed the reverse lever, and Nigel quickly wound the tender brake, as the six wagons in front jerked taut and the rest buffered up behind. The train managed to stop in time, but Nigel remembered eight shaken people, after having finished in a heap at the front of the van, climbing down to see what had happened.

Nigel recalled that Turnberry was the only station not to be derelict and that it was clean and still displaying its pre-war posters. He added that it was like a preserved station and that it felt ghostly.

Ultimately, Nigel not only wanted to observe steam engines but to build them, and in 1949, he began an apprenticeship at the North British Locomotive Company in Glasgow, building steam and then diesel locomotives until 1957, when he left the railway works and became a machine-tool designer for various companies, including Hoover, and latterly a government inspector of oil rigs, before retiring in 1990. He also wrote two railway books: *The Campbeltown & Machrihanish Light Railway* and the autobiographical *Locomotive Apprentice at the North British Locomotive Company*.

Much of the story of the working of the line from the brake van of the 'K156' post-war goods and potato trains on the Turnberry road was provided to the authors by Joe Porteous of Ayr, who, from 1946, was a guard on goods trains on the lines of south-western Scotland; and without Joe's knowledge, such valuable information would not have been recorded for posterity. Joe's roster included the Turnberry road as a regular guard once every four weeks, Mondays to Saturdays, on the southbound goods service and on the seasonal potato trains in both directions. Then, while retaining his goods duties, he also became a guard on passenger trains in south-western Scotland, which included the Butlin's trains to and from Glasgow and Carlisle. As a guard on the freight services that traversed the Carrick coast, Joe was responsible for how the train was worked in relation to the arrangement of the wagons that were detached and collected at each of the yards; and from his duties on the potato trains, he reckoned that the number of wagons was often from 20 to 30 but that this sometimes reached 40, in thereby confirming Peter Urie's observations of such a high number.

Joe remembered a few of the employees on the Turnberry line and at the stations and yards. There was the senior guard John Hood, who, in gentlemanly fashion, allowed unofficial passengers to travel in the guard's van when no other transport was conveniently available to them. Such action was against the rules but was, nevertheless, very obliging in accommodating the local people, and Mr Hood impressed upon Joe and the other guards his wish to help such potential travellers. The station master at Alloway was John Rennie, who had been injured in the collapse of the footbridge in 1948 (*see Appendix Five*). At Dunure was Jocky Robertson, who resided across the road by the bridge by the station at Fisherton, and he was the 'goods controller', who, because of his artificial leg, saved himself unnecessary walking by standing on the bridge. He held out the appropriate red or green flag, depending on whether the goods train was required to stop at the disused platform to uplift bags of whelks from a local gatherer that were to be sent to Billingsgate fish market in London, with this stop independent of the train's business in Dunure goods yard. There was also Mary Shannon, the crossing-keeper at Knoweside, though Joe did not know her name, and Andrew Galloway, the porter at Glenside, having been an amateur boxer and the green-keeper at Turnberry Golf Club before the war. Joe also remembered Jim McVicar as the last goods agent at Maidens and David Grierson as the last station master at Turnberry.

With Joe having noted that lorries had taken over much of the goods and potato services, he recalled his sadness when the line was finally closed in 1955 that the quiet, rural and scenic branch line was no more a working part of the Carrick coast. He revisited in his mind, with much affection, the line and its stations and yards, and other features, including his 'memorable experiences' of crossing the spectacular 'rattly but not scary' Rancleugh viaduct, for Joe did not worry because he knew that it was a solid and massive component of what was, ironically, a 'light railway'. Travelling along the light railway - and the envy of many a hemmed-in office worker - was the fortunate Joe, in the freedom of his everyday work as the guard of the Turnberry goods train, amid the fresh and clean country and sea air. He enjoyed the idyllic atmosphere of the wonderful vistas in sunny weather and clear visibility, including the sparkling winter sight of Arran entirely covered in snow, and all gloriously viewed from his 'observation-car' veranda of the guard's van.

It was thanks to Joe's sharp memory and explicit descriptions that, six decades afterwards, he was able to relate so much vividly about the general operations of the line in the eras of the goods and potato traffic, as related elsewhere in the book. During part of Joe's period on the Turnberry road, he lived in one of the railway cottages at Maidens from 1949 to 1958, having the line immediately on the embankment beside his back garden. Andrew Galloway lived in the adjacent railway cottage, with Jim McVicar resident in the station master's house. In 1958, Joe moved to one of the railway cottages at Turnberry, opposite the embankment on the by-now closed line, and he remained there until 1962. The nearby station master's house was occupied, as previously, by David Grierson, who was, by then, employed at Girvan station. Joe continued his guard duties, still based in Ayr, but these ended in 1978 with his promotion to a relief supervisor at Ayr and then, from 1981, he held the position of station supervisor at Ayr, before retiring in 1991.

Bob Smillie, originally of Kilmarnock, had the privilege of being employed on the Turnberry line as a fireman and on the Butlin's services as a fireman and driver, while he also worked on the Girvan-Turnberry and Girvan-Grangeston goods services latterly. He fired on the Turnberry road from 1948 until 1951, though this was only occasionally; and while he never drove on the line officially, he did so unofficially as a fireman, depending on the driver being willing to take a turn at firing. One of his memories was steaming up the gradient to the Bracken cutting - or the Lagg cutting as he and the other railwaymen knew it - that lay between the two stations: 'A sharp blast of steam, or "sharpening up the blast", was needed to ascend, by opening up the regulator and giving the engine its greatest power, or "the works", as it was known to the railwaymen.'

Bob remembered the Knoweside crossing-keeper, Mary Shannon by name, in giving her coal unofficially for her cottage, and he relayed a story about Mary and the gates of the level crossing at Knoweside. One day in the 1940s, the gates had not been opened for the approaching goods train, which, with the driver expecting a clear road, failed to stop in time and demolished the gates. With no signal at Knoweside to tell him to stop before reaching the closed gates, because there was no signal box, the furious driver discovered that the crossing-keeper was calmly walking towards him with her hands behind her back. He asked why she had not opened the gates, whereupon Mary showed him a bunch of wild flowers that she had been picking in the field for the driver's wife, when the train had come along sooner than she had expected. The driver's further reaction was not recorded by Bob, but Mary, in asserting that the driver 'was not looking', nevertheless arranged, unofficially, for a local joiner to build new gates, though not to the original specifications. On an unconnected visit from the engineer's inspection train, the non-standard appearance of the gates was questioned, and Mary's pert reply, with irony, was: 'Up here, we look after our gates!'

Bob acknowledged the feeling of vertigo on crossing the Rancleugh viaduct, which, he added, was possibly the case with some of the other railwaymen too, even if they didn't admit it; and his description of it being 'scary' was because of the height and not of doubt about its solidity. He further remarked that it was spectacular in its own right and in offering views not only across the sea to the west but in the opposite direction up the impressive 'Rancor' gorge to the Carrick hills beyond.

The opening of the Butlin's passenger service provided Bob with a further opportunity to work over part of the original line to the new Heads of Ayr station, as a fireman and then as a driver as part of his coverage of the lines of south-western Scotland in general, including from Ayr to Glasgow, Stranraer and Carlisle, on both passenger and goods services. Bob drove the Butlin's passenger trains between Heads of Ayr and Glasgow in connection with Edinburgh, and between Heads of Ayr and Carlisle in connection with Newcastle and Leeds. He also fired and drove the Butlin's shuttle service numerous times, and he even provided a photograph of the shuttle at Ayr station in 1950, illustrating himself as the fireman and Nick Armstrong as the driver. Bob's work on the Butlin's services lasted until the branch closed in 1968, having also driven the dmus on the shuttle after they had taken over from the steam-hauled local trains.

For many years, Bob had additionally been involved in the trade-union side of railways, and he became the Chairman of the Ayr branch of the National Union of Railwaymen (NUR) and then the secretary before temporarily leaving train driving to work in the head office of the NUR in London from 1975 to 1979. In trying to prevent the closure of the Butlin's branch, he and his Ayr branch of the NUR were active in their campaign which argued the line's retention on several counts: in remaining convenient for long-distance passengers for Butlin's; in reducing traffic or counteracting the greater traffic on the roads; in providing a social service, as the town of Ayr gradually expanded in the general Butlin's direction to Alloway and Doonfoot, where the line ran; and, further to the preceding reason, in allowing the building of a new, unstaffed station at Alloway, at no cost to operate, in association with the Burns tourist environs. Sadly, as Bob commented, Butlin's 'were not too supportive' of retaining the railway because of the big increase of buses and cars. In 1980, Bob returned to Ayr to resume his driving, while again becoming the NUR branch Chairman, and he retired from railway work as a driver in 1993.

Like Bob, Dick Scott of Ayr was a fireman along the Turnberry road on the goods train and a fireman and a driver on the Butlin's services; but, later than Bob, Dick fired on the Turnberry line - or 'the shore road', as called it - in 1953 and 1954, within the last two years of the line's official closure for goods traffic, when lorries had taken over much of the traffic, especially the potatoes. Also like Bob, Dick was able to drive unofficially along the route - again dependent on the driver - including on the Girvan-Turnberry and Girvan-Grangeston services. It was Dick who provided information on the process of uncoupling wagons that were to be placed into the sidings by 'fly shunting' - or, 'slipping', as he termed it - with his specific memory of it having occurred at Heads of Ayr. In connection with the delivery of coal to Knoweside, he remembered that a woman operated the gates of the level crossing but he did not know her name - it was Mary Shannon - and he explained that part of the use for the coal at Knoweside was that it had to be used in the braziers beside the water tank column to stop the water freezing but that some was given unofficially to her for her own use.

However, with great significance for the chronology of the railway, Dick asserted that it was used from Girvan to Turnberry and Grangeston after the formal closure to goods in 1955. He worked on the line to Turnberry again in 1957, and possibly even into 1958, though without being able to ascertain in which of the two years the last working occurred. Nevertheless, the line was used from the Girvan direction as late as either of the years; and Dick was therefore one of the very last railwaymen to work on part of the original line south of Butlin's Heads of Ayr station.

Dick described a curiously wasted journey along the short section to Grangeston at the end of the service. He was the fireman and his driver was Ambrose 'Amby' Blyth, and they were informed that they were to proceed to Grangeston to collect two remaining wagons which were to be brought out full of scrap from the closing site. However, it closed sooner than the railway authorities expected, for when Dick and Ambrose arrived at Grangeston, the gate of the entrance was shut across the line and locked, and demolition of the buildings was already in progress. There was no sign of the two wagons, and, on the puzzled enginemen enquiring through the gates to some of the demolition contractors, no one had any indication of where the wagons were. As far as Dick was aware in telling the story, the wagons were never seen again; though even if they had still been on the property, Dick and Ambrose would not have been able to bring them out because the track inside the gates had been severed and parts of the sidings had been lifted, leaving only sleepers. Dick's conjecture of the situation was simply that, perhaps from the sudden availability of the demolition contractors, the opportunity was seized to close and demolish the establishment earlier than had been intended.

It was during the late 1950s and early 1960s that Dick worked as a fireman on the Butlin's services. However, in 1964, he became the last fireman at Ayr depot to be passed as a driver on steam locomotives because subsequent drivers were passed only on diesels. He remembered, from his periods of firing and driving, being on scheduled or excursion Butlin's trains to and from Glasgow or Carlisle for onward runs by other crews to or from Edinburgh, Aberdeen, Newcastle, Leeds and Blackpool. During the early 1980s, Dick also became a 'minder-driver', in teaching trainee drivers the practical aspects of driving operational trains; and this work was carried out initially on class '47' diesel locomotives between Ayr and Carlisle and between Ayr and Stranraer, and latterly, from 1986, on class '318' emus in connection with the electrification of the Ayr-Glasgow line. Dick retired in 1998.

The oldest railwayman to have been interviewed by the authors of was John Hastings of Ayr, who was born at Alloway in 1917, and it was firstly in 1939 and then regularly during the 1940s that John worked as a fireman on the Turnberry road - or 'the new road', as he referred to it, in contrast to the Maybole route. From his days on the Turnberry road, he remembered Jocky Robertson - 'the Controller' - on the road bridge above Dunure station, with his green or red flag. He recalled Mary Shannon by name at Knoweside, in being given lumps of coal, and she sometimes asked if one of her sons could be taken on the train and dropped off at Morriston farm to see his grandparents, as his grandfather worked there. John also observed the Electric Brae optical-illusion in the vicinity of Croy and Knoweside occurring on the railway as well as the road.

It was John who was one of the two firemen on the Girvan-Ayr section for the special double-headed excursion train that was organized to run along the coastal line for the British Empire Exhibition in Glasgow in 1938. The train of 'seven or eight non-corridor LMS coaches' - according to John, as he related the story for posterity - was to be hauled by two class '2P' LMS 4-4-0s. However, these engines constituted a problem for the signalman at Girvan station who ventured into a conversation involving the station master, the train crew and LMS officials from Glasgow who were seemingly present in a supervisory capacity because of the unusual occurrence of a passenger train heading by the coastal route. A declaration was then made by the signalman. 'This train's no' gaun ower that road. The engines are too heavy. They're no' allowed tae work there. Only class '2s' can go ower it.' His argument was that a class '2' of that particular class was not allowed; but, with the station master, crew and officials wondering what the signalman was meaning, John pointed to the side of one of the engines, and said 'Whit aboot that there?', indicating '2P' for passenger trains, and, therefore, that such engines were indeed suitable. John was correct, while the signalman had perhaps been confused in thinking of class '2F' Caley 0-6-0 'Jumbos' being allowed over the line with the usual freight trains but not with a passenger train, which was also correct - though he was wrong in thinking that the same ruling applied to the '2Ps. The difference was that the '2F' was restricted to freight traffic because it had steam brakes only for itself and not over its train, but, in contrast, the '2P' had vacuum-fitted brakes, meaning braking power from the engine through all the carriages, which was essential for safety on a passenger train. Ultimately, the signalman grudgingly conceded defeat and muttered: 'Well, Ah suppose it's OK.'

The '2Ps' were not too heavy for the line by reason of the 1931 M&DLR Amendment Order, but the signalman's interference had placed doubt in the minds of the LMS officials, and the outcome was that they needlessly arranged for the return working to proceed via Maybole and for the passengers from the localities of the coastal line to be conveyed home by bus from Girvan. However, if the train had returned by the coastal line, John would not have been able to claim that he was one of the crew on the last passenger train to convey the public over the whole route, because a different crew worked the return service. Although the railway enthusiast George Robin recollected that the LMS had run services of an 'evening cruise train' on Tuesdays during the mid-1930s from Glasgow to Girvan via Turnberry and back by Maybole, this statement gave no indication that the trains were run as late as the summer of 1938, and, therefore, John's claim of having worked on the last-ever passenger train on the Turnberry road seems valid. John recalled people gathered at the stations - particularly Maidens and Dunure - and along parts of the line to see the train and wave to the crew and passengers.

John also related a railway 'ghost story' as a tale of his own contrivance in his own district of Alloway, and it was aptly influenced by Robert Burns. The period was at the beginning of the Butlin's era, possibly in 1948, when a Saturday evening train from the South arrived very late at Ayr station and when John was the driver of the connecting service for Heads of Ayr. Certainly, in 1948, there was a 10 pm train from Ayr to Heads of Ayr, and it may have been that year and that train. John's fireman was a youth, aged about 18 or 19 and new to the branch. The time was approaching the midnight hour, as the train left Ayr, a mischievous idea simmered in John's mind, and he said to the young fireman: 'Ah hope we can get through the tunnel afore midnight.' The inevitable response was 'Why's that?' 'Well' continued John, 'the witches don't like being disturbed efter midnight', and he explained that the tunnel was built under the Auld Alloway Kirk's cemetery. The train steamed into the tunnel after midnight, and, suddenly, unseen by the fireman in the darkness, John stuck his head out of the cab and produced a blood-curdling yell, The petrified young fireman didn't speak until the train arrived at Butlin's: 'Ah'm no' gaun' back!' However, he did bravely go back but was dreading the tunnel again, and as the train passed through it, John repeated his blood-curdling yell, for he had to retain the consistency of the ghostliness. Unfortunately, John didn't obtain the chance to explain his mischievousness to the lad because they never happened to work together again.

In having become the first fireman to be passed as a full-time driver under BR Scottish Region, John ended his period as a driver in 1956, in being promoted to shift foreman, or train crew supervisor, at Hurlford, and he completed his railway career in that position until his retirement in 1982.

Whereas John Hastings was the oldest railwayman to provide memories of the line, Mary Shannon, being three years older than John, was the oldest railway*woman* to have been met by the authors. However, information was mostly provided in Mary's presence by Ronnie Shannon of Dunure, Mary's ex-railwayman son, as he helped her to recall events and other members of the Shannon family who had held railway, hotel and golf employment at Turnberry under the LMS. Ronnie's father, Jimmy, was the green-keeper at Turnberry, and he moved to Knoweside station cottages as a surfaceman in 1939, with Mary becoming the crossing-keeper. Ronnie's grandfather, Robert Shannon, was the station master at Turnberry during much of the 1930s, and Ronnie's uncle, Dick Shannon, was the head chauffeur at Turnberry Hotel during and after World War II, while Ronnie's aunt, Mrs Emma Hogg, was the porter at Glenside during the war years, in providing another female family connection with the railway. Mary was Knoweside's crossing-keeper from 1942 to 1955, and she remembered opening the gates for the wartime troop trains from 1942 to 1944 running about once per week - thereby providing confirmation that the trains from the Ayr direction had proceeded along the coast from Alloway Junction and not via Maybole and Girvan. Of the story about the smashed gates at Knoweside, Mary simply insisted that the driver was not looking.

Ronnie started work as the porter at Dunure yard in 1950, to remain there until early 1954, when he was transferred to Ayr No. 2 signal box, immediately south-west of the station, to train as a signalman. However, in remembering the Turnberry railway from his earlier boyhood days, Ronnie explained that it was Edward, his elder brother by a year, who, soon after the war, had been given most of the lifts on the goods train from Knoweside to Morriston farm, as recalled by John Hastings. Edward and Ronnie were often both illicit passengers on the footplate or guard's van of the goods train, with Edward usually heading mainly to Morriston to see his grandparents there, because his grandfather was foreman at the farm, and with Ronnie usually travelling the shorter distance to Glenside station, to see his aunt.

At Knoweside, Ronnie saw the goods train innumerable times, and he reflected on the train crews delivering coal to the family unofficially, adding that their kindness was reciprocated by his mother and father, as the 'self-sufficient' Jimmy and Mary Shannon - gardener and home-baker, and also poultry-keepers - provided the train crews with vegetables, cakes, scones and eggs. Ronnie often walked along the railway, including to Castlehill farm after school to buy milk before the era of its delivery by road to Knoweside, and these walks made him familiar with the Electric Brae effect from the line. Other less frequent walks occurred in severe snowy weather, when the grocery van could not reach Knoweside, and Ronnie's father, accompanied by Ronnie and Edward, walked along the railway to buy their provisions from the shop at Dunure harbour, two miles away, with supplies having to be brought from Ayr by fishing boats. During the severe winter of 1947, the snow drifts on the line reached the height of the telegraph wires by the railway embankment near Drumshang farm.

Ronnie took over the operation of Dunure yard after Jocky Robertson and he provided an indication of the limited work at a representative yard on the line at such a very late stage in the line's history. During Ronnie's period at Dunure, the goods train arrived at about 9.30 am, bringing the occasional wagon of coal or animal feeding coming into the yard, and other sundries, such as spare parts for farming machinery and packages of unknown items, which he sometimes delivered locally by bicycle. His shift was from 8 am to 4 pm, but he was at the yard principally for the arrival of the train, and, apart from some paper work, he had little else to do at the yard. However, during the summer season, Ronnie said that hundredweight bags of the early potatoes from the neighbouring farms were loaded into wagons at the yard and taken away by the afternoon train nearly every day during the season. He helped with the loading of the potatoes and then placed sheeting over the wagons to protect the crop. In the early part of the year, manure for the farms was brought into the yard by the goods train. Ronnie also recalled that, from the yard, the train picked up the three or four bags of whelks - each of perhaps about ½ or ¾ hundredweight - which had been gathered by Ronnie Findlay and his father Ozzy of Dunure, and which were sent to Billingsgate market usually every second day.

It was thanks to Ronnie's knowledge and memory that a description of the track being lifted was presented for posterity; and his statement that it was carried out approximately between 1955 and 1957, starting at the northern end from Heads of Ayr Butlin's station and gradually working southwards, did not disagree with Dick Scott's account of the section from Girvan to Turnberry still being in operation until 1957 and possibly 1958. Ronnie admitted that he did not know exactly when the extreme southern section was finally lifted, but he did know for sure that the company who removed the track was Connell's of Coatbridge.

Ronnie became a relief porter and relief shunter in Ayrshire, until leaving British Railways in 1966 to work for Post Office Telecommunications (later British Telecom), and he retired in 1992.

Three more railway employees - Graham Kirkpatrick, Ronnie Kidd and John Gibson - were able to provide information mainly on aspects of the Butlin's branch.

Graham Kirkpatrick of Glasgow, whose father and grandfather were employees of the G&SWR, moved to Ayr with his parents in 1932, when his father started work under the LMS at the District Goods and Passenger Manager's Office, which opened that year. As a boy in the 1930s, Graham was familiar with the Turnberry line's Alloway-Greenan section on foot, and he knew the Alloway station master, Matt Kerr, who was also in charge of Heads of Ayr and Dunure. Graham and Mr Kerr's son were pals, and after the daily goods train had passed, they walked along that section when there was only the goods train that was augmented in the summer by the potato trains.

It was in 1948 and 1949 that Graham worked in the parcels office that involved business with Butlin's in the earliest era of the train service, and he explained that they had a reputation of being very demanding in their dealings with the railway staff, as if no other railway business mattered to the railway authorities. He recalled that one of the commercial services that Butlin's offered was the taking of photographs of the campers with the Redcoats, and for the processing of the prints, Butlin's sent a consignment of films every Friday to London by the last passenger train from Ayr to Kilmarnock that connected with an overnight service from Kilmarnock to London. However, Butlin's were consistently late in bringing the films to Ayr station by motor transport, and they sometimes missed the Ayr-Kilmarnock train in the evening, and, consequently, the London train. Unreasonably, Butlin's complained, to the railway headquarters in Glasgow but Butlin's did not seem to take heed that their lateness was a regular occurrence and their own fault; and the never-changing ironical situation was that complaints were made by Butlin's to Glasgow but that no reprimands were made from Glasgow to Ayr because Ayr could not be faulted! Nevertheless, the saga of Butlin's sending their films by train presented an example of the fine balance that had to be maintained between railway and customer.

Graham mentioned a sundry road lorry that operated from Ayr to Butlin's, perhaps two or three days per week during the season, and the running of it into the camp was why the goods train did not need to call at Heads of Ayr station. The lorry carried all sorts of products and foodstuffs for the use of the camp and the campers, while it additionally served the neighbouring scattered farms and cottages, in conveying light goods and animal feeding and in serving the communities in the return direction when items needed to be carried to Ayr.

In Graham's period at Ayr, the station master at Butlin's Heads of Ayr was Bob Dunlop, who had been there from the opening of the station in 1947, and who was Graham's next-door neighbour at Newton-on-Ayr. Bob concurred with Graham that Butlin's had a most demanding management, and, no doubt, he experienced it in other ways at the Butlin's end of the branch. In 1949, Graham was transferred to Ayr harbour for two years and then to Troon harbour, with both posts in the capacity of harbour clerk and under railway employment, before moving to railway administrative work in London in 1957. He was made redundant by BR in 1971, but he soon regained employment in the National Health Service and remained there until his retirement in 1986.

Ronnie Kidd of Ayr had working connections with the original line and the Butlin's branch, though only for a week on the former. He eagerly went to Heads of Ayr station as a porter-signalman for the Butlin's seasons of 1951, 1952 and 1953. There were then four railway staff at Heads of Ayr, Mondays to Fridays, to cover the two shifts of the day: Bob Dunlop as station master; Quentin Wylie as clerk; and Ronnie or John Graham as porter-signalmen; and they were augmented by two relief porters on Saturdays. Ronnie described the station building as consisting of four sections, from the stairway west to east along the platform: two sets of toilets, a store room and the signal room. He also mentioned a 'railway duty' by Butlin's staff, in that, as a welcome to the new campers on Saturdays, one male and one female 'Redcoat' met every arriving train at the platform, including the shuttle. Ronnie's memory of the early 1950s provided the authors with a description of the marshalling of the first two trains of the day to and from Heads of Ayr, which departed for Newcastle and Leeds.

In 1954, Ronnie was transferred to Turnberry station as a relief porter for a week. In reality, the relief post should have been at Maidens, but because Ronnie was not familiar with the goods side of working, he was sent to Turnberry and the Turnberry porter went to Maidens. There were two staff at Turnberry - the station master, David Grierson, and the porter, and the shift was officially to last eight hours, but Mr Grierson kindly allowed him not to be there for the full shift because he was travelling from Ayr and because his week's transfer was only for the arrival of the goods train. Ronnie therefore obtained the distinction of working at the grandest station on the line, but neither he nor Mr Grierson realised that no staff would be working there by early in the following year.

Ronnie was a passenger train shunter at Ayr station from 1957 to 1960, and then he became a passenger guard on the local services that were centred on Ayr, including the Butlin's shuttle. In 1983, he was promoted to guard-inspector, and he remained in this post until his early retirement in 1993.

From Ronnie's outline of his duties at the booking office in the camp, he appeared more like an employee of Butlin's than of British Railways and more of a travel- and tourist-information officer than a railwayman, if enjoyably so, though his signalling operations firmly established the railway-operational responsibility. The same overall view and enjoyment, but without the signalling involvement, was acknowledged by another employee at Heads of Ayr station a few years later. John Gibson of Ayr was a clerk at Troon station in 1956 and 1957, and he became a relief clerk from 1957 to 1959, based in Ayr, when he had periods of duty at Heads of Ayr under the charge of Bob Blair as station master. John explained that it had been Bob Dunlop, the previous Heads of Ayr station master, who had tested him on dictation and arithmetic, which he had readily passed to become a junior clerk initially, and that he had been encouraged to obtain employment on the railway because his father knew Bob Dunlop. In the late 1940s and early 1950s, John had also known John Rennie, the station master at Alloway, and he was aware of Mr Rennie's connection with the Alloway footbridge accident of 1948.

Living close to the Butlin's branch in a cottage on the estate of Newark Castle, south-west of Alloway, John had been able to make an unusual use of travelling on part of the line during his period of working on Saturdays at Troon station in 1956 and 1957. At the end of his morning shift, he travelled home on the Edinburgh-Heads of Ayr service, which was the 12.08 pm from Troon in 1957, and he boarded the guard's van with his bicycle, having used it from Newark to Ayr on his outward journey, but his purpose was not to alight at Ayr or Heads of Ayr. Instead, his departure point was intermediate, a few hundred yards after the bridge at Longhill Avenue, and the Ayr drivers or conductor-drivers always obliged him by slowing almost to a stop to allow him to throw his bicycle onto the trackside, as he then carefully jumped down from the van, to head across the fields to his cottage. He recalled that the trains from Edinburgh also carried passengers from the Lanarkshire towns and that they were 'full to capacity'. He also accounted for there having been no need for a shelter or waiting room at Heads of Ayr station because the trains always arrived well before the departure times, allowing the passengers to board; and he remembered some Saturday 'work' that was unconnected with his own, when boys and occasionally girls conveyed the Butlin's campers' luggage in small carts between the station and the camp, in both directions, for the arriving and departing trains.

During the 1960s and 1970s, John worked successively in railway administration at Ayr, Glasgow, Irvine and back to Ayr on promotion to chief clerk. In the early 1980s, he was transferred to the large department of the Area Civil Engineer's Office in Glasgow, remaining there until his retirement in 1993.

As a last memory for the book, railway enthusiast Charles Armstrong provided valuable information about seeing a surprising train on the Turnberry road in 1953, when he was only five years of age. He lived in Springburn, Glasgow, beside the North British Locomotive Company's works, and, with his family, he went on holiday to Maidens that year and walked around the village with them. One day, his father took him along the road from where they could see a train at the station in the distance. They had never seen the station in use previously, but this time, it was occupied by a train consisting of what he described as two light-grey coaches but with no engine. He and his father watched for a short period from that distance, but nothing moved, and Charles lost interest and went back to his sandcastles. That evening, his parents speculated - albeit unrealistically - that the train heralded the introduction of a train service to Girvan, resulting in Charles asking if they could go there by train the next day! Charles added that his memory of the train remained unexplained until, many years later, he saw a photograph of the train at Ayr, in John Thomas' regional railway history book, *Scotland: the Lowlands and the Borders*, with the caption reading: 'An experimental diesel multiple unit built by ACV Sales in 1952, on test at Ayr on an Ayr-Dalmellington service.' The photograph was by Jim Aird.

From Charles' recollections becoming available to the authors, more information about the train was discovered to explain the sighting at Maidens, and some information had already been known. The train was manufactured in 1952 by Associated Commercial Vehicles (ACV) Ltd, formerly known as Associated Equipment Company (AEC) Ltd, of Southall, Middlesex, and famous for building London's buses. It was a three-car early and lightweight dmu or diesel railcar set, though Charles and his father had been able to see only two coaches from the distance, as acknowledged by Charles, in that a third coach was possibly hidden by trees; and its reason for being on the line was because it was on trial runs in Ayrshire. During 1952 and 1953, it had been on trial runs in England and Wales, and by mid-June 1953, it had reached Ayr for a fortnight of trials. It operated some of the services between Ayr and Dalmellington and between Ayr and Kilmarnock, and its presence on the Turnberry road, with limited goods traffic, was probably because the chance was offered to the railway authorities and engineers to try it unhindered by other traffic. Restricted to a maximum speed of 45 mph, the three-coach train, with each unit consisting of four wheels instead of twin bogies of four wheels, could seat 120 passengers and readily accommodate others standing. It was painted in two-tone grey, with a red lining or stripe along the length of the body, immediately below the windows.

The ACV dmu would have been ideal on the 25 mph limit of the Turnberry road, but there was no intention to reopen the route for passenger traffic. That proposal had been quashed in 1950; and in 1951, the line had already been considered for complete closure.

The southern end of the skewed Culzean tunnel. Pennyglen Avenue, the former main Culzean entrance, runs 45 degrees above the longer-than-necessary covered way. The photograph can be compared with the drawing on page 102 that represents the tunnel in early use for the M&DLR.   *S. Rankin*

Chapter Twenty-One

The Remains of the Line

Sadly, rails to Turnberry and Heads are no more and long gone, with more than 40 years having passed between the running of the line's last-ever trains to Butlin's and the publication of the story of the M&DLR and the Heads of Ayr branch. It is regrettable that the Carrick coast railway had closed so early, before the preservation era had been initiated, for it would have been a wonderful line for the operation of steam trains to connect Ayr and Girvan by way of the Burns country, Craig Tara Holiday Park, Heads of Ayr Farm Park, Culzean Castle and Turnberry Hotel, and simply to convey tourists and railway enthusiasts wishing a leisurely run along the beautiful coast with its superb sea views.

The entire length of the route is covered by the two sides of the appropriate present-day Ordnance Survey 'Explorer' series map, No. 326, entitled 'Ayr & Troon' and 'Girvan & Maybole', at a scale of 2½ inches to a mile, and admirable detail is discernible of the route, with indications of what is left of some of its structures.

The trackbed of the old line is still largely intact, but, owing to its increasing overgrowth, it is naturally in gradual decay from what it once was before its years of traffic withdrawal. Nevertheless, some of the most scenic sea vistas from the Carrick coast in the vicinity of the railway can still be admired, allowing enthusiastic observers of railway history the opportunity to imagine what the passengers and crews had spectacularly observed all those decades ago from the trains. In various combinations were the nearer views of the Carrick hills, the Heads of Ayr cliffs, Dunure village and its harbour and castle, Culzean Bay, Maidens village and its harbour, and Turnberry Lighthouse and golf links with the distant views west to Arran and Kintyre, south-west to Ailsa Craig and Northern Ireland, and north and north-west along the Ayrshire coast to Bute and Argyll. In contrast to so much of the railway's route having survived, it is particularly sad that the stations have been erased, with, among the overgrowth, only the island platform of Dunure visible, especially in winter, and a short section of the platform edge at Turnberry less discernible.

In recent years, three sections of the old line have become official pathways, while other sections - irrespective of the spectacular sea views that they offer - have, unfortunately, remained undeveloped as such.

The first of the official walking routes runs mainly through cuttings south-west of the main entrance to Culzean Castle. This 'Old Railway Walk' begins at the high Thomaston Avenue arched sandstone bridge, where a wooden stairway leads down to the trackbed, and proceeds for about ¾ mile to the square-cut, skewed and sloping covered way, or extended bridge, of concrete at the Morriston Avenue entrance to Culzean. Inside the covered way, the structure of the roof is easily observed, of alternating cast-iron girders and concrete arches, as at Alloway tunnel. The walk continues for almost another ¼ mile further to a tall and elegant skewed sandstone bridge and its dark-grey, brick-lined arch that carried the line over the farm road between Morriston and Ardlochan and Maidens, and the sudden appearance of light and sea after the preceding relative darkness is breathtaking, as Arran, Kintyre and Ailsa Craig burst into view on the approach to the tall arched bridge.

In 2004, for the second official railway walk, a clearance was made along a short section of the line from the Bracken Bay rock cutting to the west of the caravan site that spreads along the line on either side of the site of the original Heads of Ayr

The M&DLR in the landscape and seascape: a series of photographs portraying the picturesque rural coastal countryside and the spectacular views of the Firth of Clyde that were obtained from the trains on the M&DLR. The trackbed is included in each frame so that the perspective of railway to scenery can be appreciated. From the embankment west of the former Heads of Ayr station, looking west across Bracken Bay and reflectively showing Arran, the trackbed curves from the foreground of the view to the upper left to ascend to the Bracken Bay cutting, discerned immediately below the furthest-left clouds. This section, as far as the cutting, is now part of the Ayrshire Coastal Path.   *D. McConnell*

The trackbed is on the steep 1 in 70 ascent to the Bracken Bay cutting, with the view north-west to Arran.   *D. McConnell*

Running south of Dunure in a south-westerly direction, the trackbed points towards Ailsa Craig before turning more southerly, to be hidden round the hillside, in heading through the curve of the deepest rock cutting. Over 60 miles away, the Antrim coast of Northern Ireland, beyond both sides of Ailsa Craig and faintly discernible on the original print, is indicated by the formation of shallow cumulus clouds immediately above the horizon, induced by the greater heating of the land.   *D. McConnell*

A view from near Aucheninch bridge, showing the railway embankment to the south of the large Dunure cutting, looks north-west to Arran and Holy Island.   *D. McConnell*

The concrete piers of the Rancleugh viaduct, looking north-west, with Arran in the distance. The buildings near the centre are of Castlehill farm.   *D. McConnell*

The Alloway-Greenan cycleway over the Doon viaduct at Alloway in March 2009, as workmen from South Ayrshire Council fit the final sections of the balustrades to the tops of the concrete coping. Looking north-east, showing the single-track width of the viaduct and the double-track width of the tunnel.   *S. Rankin*

station, as part of the recently-established Ayrshire Coastal Path encompassing a distance of 100 miles for the official full extent of the route. Completed in the summer of 2008, the £70,000 project - a 'path' in the sense of a 'route', rather than a literal path - was proposed and promoted by Ayr Rotary Club and financed primarily by South Ayrshire Council, North Ayrshire Council and Scottish Natural Heritage.

The third official project resulted in a section of the M&DLR, from Alloway to Greenan, being transformed into a cycleway and walkway by the British cycling charity Sustrans, in promoting 'sustainable transport' to include using the trackbed through the Alloway tunnel and over the Doon viaduct to the Ayr-Dunure road. The plan was revived in 2005 when South Ayrshire Council, the owners of the route, received a funding of £40,000 from Sustrans through the Scottish Executive, and this sum was for the preliminary but still substantial remedial work in clearing the trackbed and rectifying the poor drainage. The remedial work was begun in early 2006, and later in 2006, a further Sustrans funding of £230,000 from the Scottish Executive became available to continue the project. The formation of the cycleway was started in the spring of 2007 by South Ayrshire Council and completed and opened that summer from Alloway to the site of the former Greenan sidings, covering a distance of 1½ miles. Although the tunnel was able to be traversed in its state of darkness during the early period of the cycleway's opening, lights were later installed on the roof for safer passage, and they allow a clear study of the structure of the tunnel roof, comprising the alternating cast-iron girders and concrete arches. In late 2008, parts of the castellated parapets of the Doon viaduct were restored with coping blocks to match the originals; and in the spring of 2010, the ¾ mile eastwards extension from Alloway was completed to the junction of the A79 and A77 Maybole roads - the admirable outcome being a tarmac cycleway over 2¼ miles of the former M&DLR between Greenan and a location ¼ mile south of the site of Alloway Junction.

Other stretches of the old railway, with and without sea views, can be walked, but they are counted as unofficial, and consideration must be given to the owners of the lands, who may not be receptive to such a use of their property. Therefore, recommendation cannot be given through the publication of this book to any potential railway walkers in taking the risk to trek, without permission, over any unofficial parts of the route. However, as if in part-compensation, some of the trackbed is vividly seen from stretches of the A719 coastal road south of Dunure, in presenting spectacular sea panoramas, from Aucheninch bridge, past Drumshang farm, via 'mysterious phenomenon' of the Croy Brae or Electric Brae; and from the eastern end of the Electric Brae, and past Knoweside farm to Castlehill Wood. Also south of Dunure, the line's largest cutting - 40 feet deep, through rock - is seen beside the Dunure road, west of Dunure Mains farm.

Of the railway infrastructure, little of great significance can be seen today. No station buildings exist, but in most cases, the sites of the former stations and goods yards are easily located, with Heads of Ayr, Knoweside, Glenside, Maidens and Dipple long established as caravan sites. Unfortunately, the girders and lattice parapets of the two largest and highest viaducts have long been dismantled, leaving only the sturdy concrete piers and abutments at Rancleugh and only the abutments at Croy. Ironically, in contrast, the smaller Dunduff bridge, north-east of Dunure village, still crosses the ravine and burn loftily in generally good condition. From the top of the bridge and the embankment, at a deceptively-commanding height, what a breathtaking sensation was instantly imparted to southbound passengers on viewing the Firth westwards and south-westwards. On the Culzean estate, apart from the three bridges on the 'Old Railway Walk', the short concrete-arched skewed

The western end of the 35 ft-deep Bracken Bay rock cutting, with the line turning south towards Dunure, as seen from the now-ramshackle timber bridge that was built by the G&SWR for farm animal accommodation. This photograph was taken in 2002 before the far end of the cutting was significantly infilled, to become impassable.   *D. McConnell*

The Dunduff bridge, looking west, with the depth to the ravine and burn greater than implied by the photograph. The steepness of the burn below the bridge is such that the difference in depth on looking down from the eastern and western parapets is readily noticed, and from the greater 55 ft height of the latter, a wonderful view is obtained seawards.   *D. McConnell*

Dunure station overbridge, showing the gap in the parapet panelling that is sealed with wire mesh at the drop where the long-demolished stairway led down to the island platform. The view is north-east to the most recent houses of Fisherton that are built on the site of the goods yard. *S. Rankin*

The overbridge at the Morriston Avenue entrance to Culzean, looking south-west, along the 'Old Railway Walk'. An optical illusion is created by the bridge because of the combined skew along and the descent over the railway - the latter from left to right - whereby the faraway vertical edge of the abutment on the right looks further from the camera than that on the left, but is nearer in reality, with the parapets also running parallel. As at Pennyglen Avenue and at Alloway, the single track of the railway ran under the western side of the structure. *D. McConnell*

The entrance to Maidens station subway, looking north-east, showing the wingwalls, girder lintel, parapet iron railing, and relatively recent replacement metal doors, with two caravans visible on the former station site above. *Inset:* The underside of the roof, showing the girder structure and the white-glazed brick wall. *S. Rankin*

Looking east through the M&DLR underbridge near Little Turnberry - formerly Turnberry farm - which was widened on its western side to carry the southernmost headshunt or siding for Turnberry aerodrome in World War I (*see map on page 128*). *D. McConnell*

tunnel or extended covered way, near Whiteston, still stands solidly, though this structure is not an official route.

Sadly too, nothing remains of the grandest station building on the line, at Turnberry - nor of its covered walkway and of the hotel's conservatory. During its lifetime, the hotel has had several owners. After the eras under the initial ownership of the G&SWR to the end of 1922 and then of the LMS to the end of 1947, the restored Turnberry Hotel returned to service on its 1950 reopening as part of the British Transport Commission's Hotels Executive, resulting from nationalization in 1948. With the abolition of the Hotels Executive in 1953, the responsibility was transferred to British Transport Hotels and Catering Services, as the replacement division of the BTC; and the hotel remained in railway ownership beyond the abolition of the BTC in 1962 to the succession by the British Railways Board in 1963 and their subsidiary British Transport Hotels Ltd (BTH). The hotel continued under BTH Ltd until after the passing of the Transport Act, 1981 that resulted from the Conservative government's privatization of BR's non-core, or indirect, railway business divisions, and it was sold to private enterprise in 1983.

Naturally, Turnberry is still dominated by golf and is indeed a paradise for golfers. There are two 18-hole championship-quality courses: the long-established and renowned Ailsa Course, of 6,976 yards, and the recently-constructed secondary Kintyre Course, of 6,853 yards, and both courses offer wonderful sea views to Arran, Ailsa Craig, Kintyre and Northern Ireland.

The more coastal Ailsa Course, in taking the golfers alongside the distinctive Turnberry Lighthouse and the ruins of Robert the Bruce's Turnberry Castle, is one of the world's best for play, and when Turnberry was added to the rota of locations for the Open Championship, it became the venue for the prestige competition in 1977, 1986, 1994 and 2009.

Unfortunately for Turnberry's history, no photographs appear to exist of the opening day celebrations in 1906 of the railway and the hotel, including the historic ceremonial train at Turnberry station, leaving only reasoned speculation and imagination to provide an indication of the grand arrival. Whether any photographs were taken and lost through time or never taken at all is not known and may never be known. However, given the prestige of Turnberry Hotel and its golf courses at the time of the opening, it seems inconceivable that photographs were not taken and preserved, but the question must be asked: did the G&SWR Directors fail to arrange that a photographic record was made of the grand occasion for posterity? That this was the case cannot be discounted, from photographs not having been discovered after an exhaustive search.

Nevertheless, for a small village in a small district, Turnberry possesses history that is astonishing in its diversity and significance.

In conclusion of the story of the Turnberry railway, because the line passed through the heart of the Burns Country at Alloway, here is contemplation with respect to the great enlightened and enlightening poet. What would he have written about the line had his life coincided with its existence, and can it be doubted that, being a progressive thinker, traveller romanticist and observer, he would have written of it other than favourably and sentimentally, and even humorously? Thus, he might have written something like this about Alloway's 'great ugly black-stained, wooden, goods shed':

O muckle ugly shack, what use for ye,   [muckle - great]
Than shelter ae rail wagon, or whiles three.   [ae - one; whiles - sometimes]
Auld Nick, frae Alloway's haunted kirk,   [Auld Nick - the Devil; frae - from]
Maun laugh at man's contorted work.   [Maun - Must]

MAIDENS & DUNURE LIGHT RAILWAY

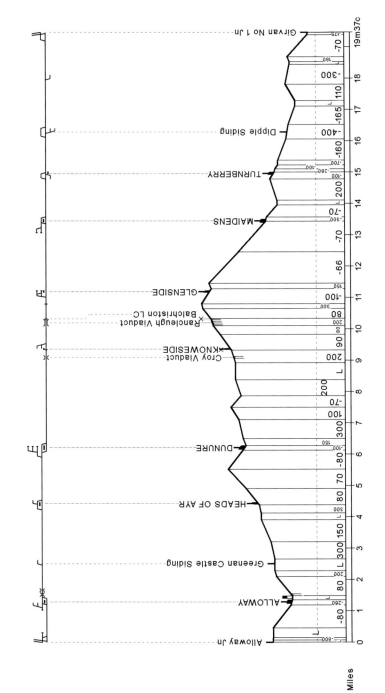

M&DLR gradient profile, clearly showing the summit between Balchriston and Glenside, plus other secondary summits and the steepest and longest incline from Glenside to beyond Maidens (*see also page 81*).

Drawn by A. Laing

Appendix One

M&DLR Gradients and Summits

Over 19½ miles of the M&DLR, there were seven gradients ultimately leading to and from the overall summit of the line and three secondary summits that could be termed 'principal secondary' after the true summit. From Alloway Junction, the first two steep gradients occurred on either side of Alloway tunnel, where there was a descent of 1 in 80 for a distance of ¾ mile before the tunnel, a level run through the tunnel and an ascent of 1 in 80 for ¾ mile after the tunnel. Over the three miles from the tunnel to Heads of Ayr station, there was an almost continuous ascent which became steeper, west of the station, for a mile at 1 in 80 and 1 in 70, in proceeding beyond the Bracken Bay cutting. The line reached the first principal secondary summit of 230 ft above sea level in a shallow cutting east of Fisherton Cottage and descended at 1 in 80 for ½ mile to Dunure station. A rise from the station at 1 in 100 and 1 in 80 for a mile carried the line to another principal secondary summit of 215 ft at the northern entrance of the deep and curved rock cutting, south of Dunure, and for the next ¼ mile, there was a descent at 1 in 70. However, a general rise from Drumshang farm followed for the next three miles, mainly at 1 in 200 to 1 in 80, which conveyed the line, by way of the Croy and Rancleugh viaducts, to the overall summit of 305 feet at the northern entrance of the Culzean tunnel. Then, it was downhill, initially at 1 in 100, and, being broken only by a short rise of 1 in 180 after Glenside station, the returning gradient from the Glenside rock cutting became the steepest and longest on the line, by far, lasting for a mile at 1 in 66 and then another mile and a half mostly at 1 in 70, to take the line to Shanter farm, half a mile beyond Maidens station. A rise at 1 in 200 for ¾ mile then carried the line to another principal secondary summit of 110 feet at Turnberry Big Wood, north of the station. The steepest gradient south of Turnberry was a descent of 1 in 70 for ¾ mile between Chapeldonan farm and the junction with the Ayr-Maybole-Girvan line.

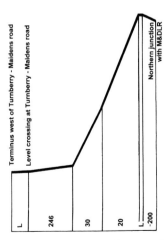

Turnberry aerodrome branch gradient profile, on a larger scale than the M&DLR profile. Slightly beyond midway along the 1 in 200 section from the northern junction with the M&DLR was the raised level crossing at the small road to Turnberry Cottage (*see also page 128*). *Drawn by S. Rankin*

M&DLR Distances

	Section Distances		Distances from Ayr No. 2		Distances from Girvan No. 3		Distances from Alloway Jn		Distances from Girvan No. 1	
	m.	ch.	m.	ch.	m.	ch.	m.	ch.	m.	ch.
Ayr No. 2	-	-	-	-	21	48	1	47	21	1
Alloway Junction	1	47	1	47	20	1	-	-	19	34
Alloway	1	17	2	64	18	64	1	17	18	17
Greenan Castle	0	69	3	53	17	75	1	86	17	28
Heads of Ayr LMS	1	18	4	71	16	57	3	24	16	10
Heads of Ayr G&SWR	1	13	6	4	15	44	4	37	14	77
Dunure	1	66	7	70	13	58	6	23	13	11
Knoweside	3	10	11	0	10	48	9	33	10	1
Balchriston	0	76	11	76	9	52	10	29	9	5
Glenside	0	72	12	68	8	60	11	21	8	13
Maidens	2	19	15	7	6	41	13	40	5	74
Turnberry	1	38	16	45	5	3	14	78	4	36
Dipple	1	41	18	6	3	42	16	39	2	75
Girvan No. 1	2	75	21	1	0	47	19	34	-	-
Girvan No. 2	0	30	21	31	0	17	19	64	0	30
Girvan No. 3	0	17	21	48	-	-	20	1	0	47

Notes:

Distances taken or calculated from the appendix tables of the G&SWR and LMS working timetables.

'Section Distances' refer to the block sections or non-block sections between one location and the preceding location in the table, as in 1 mile, 47 chains for the section between Ayr No. 2 and Alloway Junction signal boxes, and 1 mile, 17 chains between Alloway Junction and Alloway station signal boxes.

Location of Ayr and Girvan signal boxes: Ayr No. 2 was to the south of the station, on the western side of the Ayr-Maybole-Girvan line; Girvan No. 1 was in the vee of the junction of the M&DLR and the Ayr-Maybole-Girvan line; Girvan No. 2 was in the vee of the junction of the main line and the goods and harbour branch; and Girvan No. 3 was on the western platform at the southern end of the station.

Distances via Maybole for comparison: Ayr No. 1 to Maybole – 8 miles 61 chains; Maybole to Girvan No. 1 – 11 miles 64 chains; Ayr No. 1 to Girvan No. 1 via Maybole – 20 miles 45 chains.

Appendix Three

M&DLR Opening & Closing Dates

Line sections	Opened for		Closed for	
	passengers	goods	passengers	goods
Alloway Jn-Girvan No. 1 Jn	17.5.1906	17.5.1906		
Alloway Jn-Turnberry			1.12.1930	28.2.1955
	*4.7.1932		2.4.1933	
Girvan-Turnberry			2.3.1942	1957/58
Alloway Jn-Heads of Ayr LMS	17.5.1947		16.9.1968	

Stations, yards and sidings	Opened for		Closed for	
	passengers	goods	passengers	goods
Alloway	17.5.1906	17.5.1906	1.12.1930	7.12.1959
Greenan Castle sidings	–	17.5.1906	–	7.12.1959
Heads of Ayr G&SWR	17.5.1906	17.5.1906	1.12.1930	28.2.1955
Heads of Ayr LMS	17.5.1947	–	16.9.1968	–
Dunure	17.5.1906	17.5.1906	1.12.1930	28.2.1955
Knoweside	17.5.1906	17.5.1906	1.12.1930	28.2.1955
Balchriston Halt	†By 6.1910	–	1.12.1930	
Balchriston siding	–	5/6.1933	–	28.2.1955
Glenside	17.5.1906	17.5.1906	1.12.1930	28.2.1955
Maidens	17.5.1906	17.5.1906	1.12.1930	28.2.1955
Turnberry	17.5.1906	17.5.1906	2.3.1942	1957/58
Dipple sidings	–	17.5.1906	–	28.2.1955
Grangeston siding	–	By 10.1942	–	1957/58

Signal boxes	Opened	Closed	
Alloway Jn	17.5.1906	29.9.1968	
Alloway	17.5.1906	16.6.1936	Then ground frame to 7.12.1959
Greenan Castle	–	–	g/f 17.5.1906 to 28.2.1955
Heads of Ayr G&SWR (1)	17.5.1906	15.6.1914	Then replaced and repositioned
Heads of Ayr G&SWR (2)	15.6.1914	16.6.1936	Then g/f to 28.2.1955
Heads of Ayr LMS	28.5.1947	16.9.1968	
Dunure	17.5.1906	16.6.1936	g/f operation to yard 17.5.1906 to 28.2.1955
Knoweside	–	–	g/f 17.5.1906 to 28.2.1955
Balchriston	–	–	g/f c.1932-35 to 28.2.1955
Glenside	17.5.1906	16.6.1936	Then g/f to 28.2.1955
Maidens	17.5.1906	16.12.1936	Then g/f to 28.2.1955
Turnberry	17.5.1906	16.12.1936	Then g/f to 1957/58
Dipple	15.6.1914	21.9.1925	g/f before 15.6.1914
	Reopened 20.6.1932	16.12.1936	Then g/f to 28.2.1955
Grangeston	–	–	g/f 1942 to 1957/58
Girvan No. 1	17.5.1906	23.6.1935	

Key
* Re-opened for Turnberry station only, † for railway staff only, g/f = ground frame.

Notes: See overleaf.

Notes on opening and closing dates:

The stated opening and closing dates of the stations, yards, sidings and signal boxes do not necessarily coincide with the occurrence of the first and last passenger or goods trains over the respective sections of line, and these dates are either official or inferred with reasoned and justified assessment. It was also usually in the nature of railway closure dates that they were officially counted as occurring on the first Monday after the last train had run.

The official or public opening date of the stations and signal boxes in 1906 is given as Thursday 17th May, but the first 'passenger' train to run over the line was on Tuesday 15th May specially to carry some of the G&SWR Directors and officials to Turnberry Hotel for the ceremonial opening on Wednesday 16th May, when the ceremonial train that conveyed more G&SWR representatives and invited guests ran on the day before the public opening of the line and the hotel. However, while the line, the signal boxes and Turnberry station received a passenger train on 15th and 16th May, before the public opening on 17th May, it is the date of the service to the public, of 17th May, that constituted the recognised opening of the line and the hotel.

Balchriston Halt was never a public station and was used only for the convenience of railway staff at the cottage for the crossing and other passengers in the vicinity. The 'opening date' of the halt is not known, but one train called in each direction 'at Balchriston Level Crossing' from June 1910, as recorded in the Working Timetable, and the train possibly called before then, though there was no mention back in the June 1909 Working Timetable of trains calling there. Whether or not a halt was present at the level crossing in or before June 1910 cannot be determined, and the trains may have initially stopped without the need for a halt, which was observed to have existed in 1930, immediately before the closure to passengers of the Alloway Junction-Turnberry section. The short platform was likely constructed for the reason of safety, especially to assist the railway family of the crossing cottage and other residents of the locality, including schoolchildren; and, with it never having been mentioned in the public timetables, it was always referred to as 'Balchriston Level Crossing' in the working timetables. Its unofficial 'classification' as a halt, in having minor public-station status, probably originated later from railway enthusiasts and not from railway employees; and the enthusiast Jim Aird provided evidence for the existence of the halt in describing it as a tiny platform when he travelled on the last train of the whole M&DLR service on 29th November, 1930 and witnessed a stout elderly lady slipping on and sliding down the frosty ramp.

Heads of Ayr M&DLR station changed from a single platform to an island platform on 15th June, 1914, with the construction of a line on the southern side of the station to form a loop. The platform was not lengthened but it was widened by about six ft at each end and by about 11 ft in the middle section to accommodate passengers on the new southern side of the retained station building. However, a canopy, although planned, was not added to the building on its southern side, such that, unlike the original island-station buildings at Alloway, Dunure and Maidens, the building at Heads of Ayr was not symmetrical. The canopy may have been intended before the G&SWR realised that there were no access doors on the southern side of the building, with the company then deciding that the construction of doors and lintels in the wall, with other changes required internally, was not justified by the extra expense for the degree of use to be gained at a station that had few passengers. The public entrance to the station was by the path which branched from the station road and led to the ramp at the western end of the island platform. The path had existed from the opening in 1906 but was slightly realigned in June 1914 to cross the southern track of the loop at 45 degrees, instead of the more gentle angle towards the original 1906 single platform, which meant that passengers had to walk over the new track with care. However, the few passengers at Heads of Ayr would have been guided by the station staff, though particular care would have been required if passengers happened to be thinking of crossing when a southbound Turnberry express was due to 'career' through the station at 20-25 mph. Passengers were not affected by trains using the northern track of the loop.

The original signal box at Heads of Ayr M&DLR station, which was situated immediately beyond the ramp at the eastern end of the platform, was dismantled and replaced on 15th June, 1914 by one that was built on the platform close to the station building on its eastern side and on the centre line of the new island platform. The new signal box was larger to accommodate more levers and was more central for the modified station, as there were new loop points at the western end where none had existed previously.

Although the date of the last passenger train of regular service to run over the whole of the M&DLR was Saturday 29th November, 1930, to produce a passenger-closure date of Monday, 1st December from Alloway Junction to Turnberry, the last-ever passenger train to traverse the whole line occurred on Friday 20th May, 1938, forming the excursion from Girvan to Glasgow for the Empire Exhibition. The train called at Turnberry, Maidens, Glenside, Knoweside, Dunure and Alloway, with Turnberry the only station on the line that was still open, because of the Girvan shuttle service, but the other five stations, although not used since their 1930 closure, were able to be accommodated for that day. While the train was expected to return by the same route, it ultimately operated only in the northbound direction over the M&DLR, as has already been recounted.

The reopening period of 4th July, 1932 to 2nd April, 1933 from Alloway Junction to Girvan for passengers occurred solely for the operation of the experimental service of one morning train and one evening train from Girvan via Turnberry to Kilmarnock, with each having a connection at Kilmarnock for London via Leeds. Turnberry was the only M&DLR station that was used for the two northbound trains, which ran with no services in the return direction.

Balchriston siding and loading bank were authorized on 16th May, 1933, and it is likely that they were constructed very soon afterwards, in late May or early June, to accommodate the imminent early-potato crop.

On the closure of Girvan No. 1 signal box in 1935, which was situated at the junction of the M&DLR and the Ayr-Maybole-Girvan line, Girvan No. 2 and Girvan No. 3 signal boxes were renumbered No. 1 and No. 2. The original No. 2 and No. 3 had opened in 1893, in conjunction with the new passenger station at Girvan. The original No. 2 lay south of No. 1 at the junction for the goods and harbour branch that formerly contained the original Girvan passenger station and later goods station, while No. 3 was built further south at the replacement Girvan passenger station. It was the original No. 2, in being renamed No. 1, that controlled the M&DLR from 1935 after the simplification from a double-line junction to a single-line junction with a crossover; and on its closure in 1973 - which, by then, was of no relevance to the long-closed M&DLR - the box at the passenger station was renamed Girvan, without a number, and is still in use.

The closure date of 16th June, 1936 of most of the M&DLR signal boxes represented the beginning of 'one engine in steam' working until the goods closure of 28th February, 1955. After the 1936 closures, the Turnberry ground frame controlled the points and signals, which were necessary for the continued operation of the shuttle passenger service between Girvan and Turnberry until 1942 and also for military passenger trains over the section between Alloway Junction and Turnberry during World War II.

Although officially closed for goods services on 28th February, 1955, the line remained in use for goods services between Girvan and Turnberry and between Girvan and Grangeston until an indeterminate closure date in 1957 or 1958, because of the slow dismantling of the line from north to south.

The official closure date of the Heads of Ayr branch and Heads of Ayr Butlin's station was intended to have been Monday 9th September, 1968, with the last trains of the regular timetabled service having run on Saturday, 7th. However, with the extension of the Butlin's season by a week, the official closure date became Monday, 16th, with the last trains of a special non-timetabled service having run on Saturday, 14th. Therefore, strictly, the 9th was the last date of the regular timetable, while the last trains on the 14th were officially counted as 'specials' after the closing date. Nevertheless, 16th September, 1968 is generally accepted as the closure date of the Heads of Ayr branch and Heads of Ayr station.

Appendix Four

M&DLR Station Buildings

As on the Cairn Valley Light Railway (CVLR), the stations on the M&DLR were neat chalet buildings with opaque canopies, except at Turnberry, with its grander structure and glazed canopy, and at Knoweside, with no building. The original island platforms of Alloway, Dunure and Maidens possessed buildings that were similar to each other - or identical, in the case of Dunure and Maidens. The design of the buildings, except for Turnberry, was the same, irrespective of whether situated on island or single platforms or of the dimensions of the buildings. The lengths of the station buildings were: 36 ft for Heads of Ayr, Dunure and Maidens; 51 ft for Alloway; 45 ft for Glenside; and 86ft for Turnberry; while all the buildings were 12 ft 6 in. wide. Alloway's station building, with its separate station master's office, was longer than those at Dunure and Maidens, as was its platform, and the likely reason for both extra lengths was the expected excursion traffic for the Robert Burns' tourist attractions.

Heads of Ayr, Dunure and Maidens comprised two rooms, which were a booking office and a waiting room, while there were three rooms at Alloway and Glenside, with, respectively, a separate office for the station master and a waiting room for the Marquis of Ailsa. Alloway, Dunure and Maidens possessed doors and windows that were arranged as mirror images on the opposite platform-facing sides of the building - meaning that each door and window on one side of the building directly faced a corresponding door and window on the opposite side. These three stations also possessed a window to one side only of the chimney breast at one end of the building - Alloway on the southern side and Dunure and Maidens on the northern side, with the window to the side of the chimney that resulted in the window facing left to the approaching line.

At Heads of Ayr, where there was originally a single platform, and at Glenside, where there was always a single platform, the building contained no window at either end. When Heads of Ayr became an island platform in 1914, no changes were made to any part of the building that faced the new widened platform, such that the building remained 'single-sided' on the island platform, without a canopy on that side. It would have been laborious and expensive to construct doors and windows and their lintels into the existing building, especially for a station with a small amount of passenger traffic. Although Glenside was generally a request station, its importance to the G&SWR was increased because it was 'the Marquis' station', with a private room for his accommodation at the southern end of the building. As such, Glenside was longer than the other similar style of stations, though not as long as Alloway, and, with this extra length, it had a similar appearance to the extended version of Moniaive station on the CVLR, as drawn by Stuart Rankin in Ian Kirkpatrick's book *The Cairn Valley Light Railway* (Oakwood Press, 2000).

Until about 1900, the G&SWR timber station buildings and timber signal boxes were painted a dull red, but the M&DLR and the CVLR station buildings were painted cream on the horizontal wooden panels above the foundation level of red brick, which extended as high as the lower level of the windows. The ends of the buildings, supporting the chimney breasts of red brick, also contained horizontal wooden panels on both sides of the chimney or a window on one side, and the panels or windows were surmounted left, right and above by chocolate-coloured frames, or beams, between the chimney and the extremity of the building; while additional vertical beams, close together, formed the apex of the roof. The attractive colour scheme of the stations included the roof and canopy being composed of red tiles. Unfortunately, the colours of the station doors and window frames are not known for certain, but possibly they were brown and cream respectively. In addition to the tinted photograph of Dunure station on the back cover of the present book, a colour-tinted photograph of Moniaive station on the front cover of *The Cairn Valley Light Railway* illustrates the colour scheme of the stations on both railways.

The smallest original station was Knoweside, but later came the even smaller Balchriston halt. Knoweside was not provided with a station building but only with a small hut as a shelter, having dimensions assessed at 9 ft x 5 ft 6 in. By the late 1930s, there was a gap in the station fence, corresponding to a small structure on the 25 in. ordnance Survey map of 1909; and, from the same design of the chalet station buildings on the M&DLR and the CVLR, the shelter is surmised to have been built of a corrugated-iron, with a curved roof, similar to the shelters at Kirkland, Crossford and Stepford stations on the CVLR. Balchriston halt probably consisted of only a small timber platform, with no shelter, and the position of the platform, which was not shown on any map, was most likely situated adjacent to the crossing-keeper's cottage.

Not surprisingly, Turnberry was the largest and most attractive station, containing the most accommodating facilities for the hotel and golfing clientele, with the covered walkway leading from the hotel to the northern end of the station. The glass canopy of the platform, which was longer than the station building, commenced running southwards from the covered walkway for a total distance of 148 ft, being slightly more than a third of the platform's 400 ft length. The first 12 ft length of the canopy from its northern end extended from the passage between the covered walkway and the northern end of the station building; and then the canopy continued along the full length of the station building, which was 86 ft long, and then along another 50 ft beyond the southern end of the station building. This 50 ft extension was supported by a 'curtain wall' that stood on its own, south of the station building, and presented the impression from the trains that the station building was longer than it was. After the fire of 1926, the station building was rebuilt to the original plans, but with the principal difference that the new canopy consisted of gables of solid wood instead of frames of glass. The non-hotel public and all vehicles reached the station by the access road from the Kirkoswald-Turnberry road, with the station entrance at the back of the building and facing onto the station forecourt, adjacent to where the covered walkway met the station platform.

A closer study of the postcard view of Alloway station reproduced on page 97, focusing on the station building, signal box, water tank and station master's house.

G&SWR Association

Appendix Five

The Alloway Footbridge Accident, 1948

At the start of the era of British Railways, a special passenger train ran along the line from Alloway Junction to Alloway station, only to be associated with a distressing and tragic repercussion. The occasion was the first time since the era of World War II that Alloway station, which had officially closed in 1930 for regular passenger traffic, had been used for an excursion train, and during the war, it had been used as a depot of the Army's Royal Engineers. On Wednesday 16th June, 1948, Troon Old Parish Church began their annual Sunday School outing on a chartered train from Troon to Alloway. The train was well loaded, with 703 passengers, comprising 256 adults and 447 children, including babies, who were intent on enjoying a summer's day picnic at Burns' Cottage. Little did the travellers realise that, in spite of their train displaying celebratory balloons and streamers on its departure from Troon, the result of their trip would ultimately be one of injury, and, later, for one person, of fatality.

Although the length of the train was not recorded, the number of people on board represented 10 non-corridor LMSR nine-compartment coaches, and Alloway, with a 550-feet-long platform, was the only station on the Carrick coast line – the later Butlin's station excepted - that could accommodate such a length. The train arrived at Alloway station shortly after 11 am, and the travellers, happy in the anticipation of the picnic, immediately began streaming out of the carriages and along the former island platform to climb the stairs of the footbridge at the end of the platform. After about a third of the total number of people had crossed completely, the upper part of the footbridge that led to the road bridge and street level suddenly collapsed, when mostly women and children were passing over it, and 19 people of them immediately fell through the gap from a height varying between nine and 15 feet, to land on the solid platform ramp. They were taken in ambulances and in a police van to Ayr County Hospital to be treated for shock and serious injuries, though only four women were detained beyond the day. Sadly, the most serious case became fatal five days later when Mrs Jean Henry, a widow aged 72, died from severe multiple injuries. With the death of Mrs Henry, a Fatal Accident Inquiry was arranged for 24th August, 1948 at Ayr Sheriff Court, when evidence was heard from several witnesses before Sheriff Robert MacInnes and a jury of six men and one woman.

John Rennie, the Alloway goods agent – but loosely termed the 'station master' - told the inquiry that he had been assisting a man with prams to the top of the stairs of the bridge, when, suddenly, the stairs gave way below, resulting in Mr Rennie falling to the platform and suffering a broken wrist. John Findlay Smith, the Sunday School Superintendent, had been helping a lady to cross the bridge with her pram, when he heard a thud and screams and saw a gaping space in the bridge and a number of people lying on the slope of the platform. Among them, he saw Mrs Annie Miller still grasping her baby daughter in her arms, and she recalled her harrowing experience. She was carrying her daughter, aged 10 months, to the top of the stair, and she had her two little older boys with her, one in front and one behind. Near the top, she felt the stairway moving, and then the baby was thrown out of her arms as she fell. Naturally, her first thought was for the baby, who, fortunately and astonishingly, was lying beside Mrs Miller, and generally safe and sound, with only bruising in the baby's head, with the mother's sufferance of a broken ankle thereby of little consequence in relation to her painful initial thoughts about what had become of her daughter. Her two sons were not physically injured. Mrs Margaret Reid was detained for 10 days in Ayr County Hospital with concussion and bruises, and she vaguely recalled the collapse of the stairs and the screams of the people.

Other evidence was given by witnesses who had not been present at the accident but who, nevertheless, had been involved in testing the bridge, before or after its collapse. James Telfer of Irvine, the railway works inspector, explained that, because of the forthcoming excursion, he and James Howat, the railway area foreman of buildings and structures, had jointly carried out what he contended was a thorough inspection of the bridge on 22nd March, having tested the steps by jumping on them together and having tested the bridge with knives for rotten wood. Mr Telfer was satisfied that the bridge was in a good condition and that the stairway was safe, with the exception of three steps, which he ordered to be renewed in the top half of the bridge. The Procurator Fiscal (the public prosecutor in Scotland), Mr W.K. MacFadyean, asked Mr Telfer about the wooden 'stringers' of the bridge. They were long pieces of framework that ran from the top to the bottom of the bridge, parallel to and underneath the stairway, supporting the steps and being supported along their length by 'angle irons' – probably of L-shaped angle – underneath the stringers as a reinforcement. One of the upper stringers from the top of the bridge to the short landing, half-way down, had split along its whole length down to the landing, and the angle iron, which was bolted to it, had given way too, as the upper half of the stairway collapsed. Mr Telfer agreed that if the stringer had been strengthened, the bridge would not have collapsed.

Mr Telfer was not able to explain to the Fiscal why the test in March had failed to reveal the weak parts in the bridge, but corroborative evidence to Mr Telfer's testimony - that the bridge had not then been in a decomposed state - was provided by Francis Thompson of Ayr, railway joiner, who had replaced the steps on 4th May. He stated that he and a labourer had to use crowbars to remove the steps from the stringer and that a great deal of effort had been exerted because of them holding so well. They had examined the stringer thoroughly underneath and had not found it to be rotten.

However, two independent witnesses from the building trade were called by the Fiscal from their recent inspection of the footbridge, and they provided evidence of a different nature from that given by Mr Telfer and Mr Thompson. Quintin Clark, master builder and joiner, of Ayr, who had attained 50 years' experience of all types of constructional work, had examined the bridge on 22nd June, accompanied by his foreman joiner, Stephen McKergow of Ayr.

Mr Clark's examination of the stringers revealed that they were very much rotten; and having examined the debris of wood that was lying on the platform, he added that it could be broken with your fingers because it was so rotten. The Fiscal asked him if he thought that such had been the condition before the accident happened, and should the defects have been revealed. Mr Clark answered yes, and that, to find the defects, it would not have taken an experienced tradesman – only an apprentice - and he added that the wood on the stringers could not have deteriorated between the time of the accident and March. Indeed, Mr Clark discovered widespread decay on the stringers and he could not find a solid part on them, while he had also found other stringers on the bridge in a very decomposed state. Mr Clark would certainly have condemned the whole bridge as it stood and he believed that Mr Telfer and Mr Thompson had made only a superficial inspection because the timber was deficient. In summary, his opinion was that the bridge had collapsed because the wooden stringer that held the steps in position was rotten and had cracked along its length. Mr McKergow agreed entirely with Mr Clark, and, in essence, they asserted that the bridge had collapsed from stringer weakness from rot and lack of support by the relevant angle iron because of rusted corrosion.

The final witness was James Howat, who had carried out the inspection with James Telfer, and he explained that he had made routine visits to Alloway station in October 1947 and February 1948, and then, because of the excursion, in March 1948 with Mr Telfer. He insisted that they had found the bridge in good condition, with no portion obviously rotting, and only three steps needing to be replaced. Mr Howat disagreed with Mr Clark and Mr McKergow and maintained that the stringer was not rotten visibly or to the touch.

Sheriff MacInnes, in stating that there was no doubt about how Mrs Henry had met her death from an accident, instructed the jury to return a formal verdict, which, in Scots law, meant accidental death or misadventure, with no apportioning of blame. However, in doing so, he prompted the jury to consider it singular that the woodwork of the bridge had collapsed when previous examinations had not disclosed deterioration. To the formal verdict, the jury added a rider, with which Sheriff MacInnes agreed: that more thorough examinations should take place at regular intervals, with examinations carried out by tradesmen under the supervision of a qualified architect.

The test of Mr Telfer and Mr Howat jumping on the bridge was greatly inadequate, for their combined weight, as they did so, was much less than the collective weight of the people crossing the bridge. In the situation of the Alloway footbridge, where the speed of impact was not a significant factor at the moment of collapse, the 'live load' or 'dynamic load', that resulted from the people's movement, could be counted, for simplicity, as being twice the 'dead load' or 'static load', resulting from no movement. In the former case, greater momentum was generated on the steps because of the people's movement, and the two men's test therefore produced a live load that was the equivalent of four men's weight, if four were standing and not jumping. Mr Telfer had already agreed that the largest number of people who could theoretically be accommodated on the stairway was 40, and therefore, their test had represented only 10 per cent of the supposed maximum of 40 people, whose collective weight could be absorbed by the stairway, if it was in proper condition. However, the problem was that the stairway was in such an unsatisfactory condition that fewer than 40 people would have been sufficient to cause the collapse of the stairway. Mr Telfer's opinion on the soundness of the timber was clearly not sound as an opinion, and he was simply in a position where he had to defend himself in not admitting liability, as was the case with Mr Howat and Mr Thompson. In opposition, Mr Clark, who was scathing about the state of the bridge and the lack of thoroughness of the inspection, had no fear in being forthright at the inquiry.

Iain Goldie of Troon, as a boy of 11 years, was involved in the accident, as was his mother and one of his two brothers, and he was able to relate their part in the story. Iain fell from a height of nine to 12 feet while carrying his two-year-old brother, Gordon, though his five-year-old brother, Alastair, had managed to reach the top of the bridge before its collapse. Iain's mother also fell from the bridge in carrying her pram, injuring her back, while Iain was instinctively able to provide protection for his baby brother in arms by breaking his fall in the frightening seconds of the collapse. Iain recalled the sudden shock and impact in falling from half the height of the bridge onto the hard platform ramp, and he was taken to hospital, though he was found not to be seriously injured. Most of the people were still on the platform and it is most likely that they had to scramble or be helped up the much overgrown side of the cutting into the goods yard and from there to the road. Iain recalled that once the injured people were taken to hospital, the picnic at Burns' Cottage proceeded as planned by the vast majority of the excursionists who had not been involved in the fall, but Iain hadn't managed to go to the picnic because of his hospital visit, though he was pleased to have been able to sit at the front of the ambulance beside the driver. After the picnic, the passengers returned home by a fleet of coaches that were hired by British Railways.

The collapsed footbridge stairway at Alloway station, as published in the *Ayrshire Post* of 18th June, 1948.

G&SWR Association,
and Scottish & Universal Newspapers

Appendix Six

The Electric Brae: Road and Railway

In the summer of 1901, before the construction of the M&DLR had started, the *Ayrshire Post* contained various correspondence about a 'mysterious phenomenon' that lay in the vicinity of the new line, near the Croy viaduct, on a specific part of the road midway between Dunure and Pennyglen. This referred to the 'Croy Brae' - 'brae' being the Scots word for 'hill' or 'slope' - and the stretch of road eventually became known as the 'Electric Brae', though it was not known by the electric term back in 1901. The effect of the Croy Brae, as an optical illusion, involved the road appearing to run uphill when its aspect was seemingly downhill, and vice versa; and the same trickery was found on the railway.

In the issue of 7th June, 1901, under the heading of 'Ayrshire Notes' and the sub-heading of 'Ayrshire's Hill of Mystery', an anonymous contributor to the paper, in stating that 'astonishing qualities have been ascribed to it', highlighted its main effects: that hundreds have cycled up the hill without any effort and have had to pedal hard to reach the bottom; and that water by the side of the road flowed uphill. The contributor listed a few of the theories to account for the effects, such as a mighty loadstone, a powerful electric current, a new comet, the position of Mars, and whisky, and then related that a party from Prestwick had set out the previous week to try to explain the phenomenon with measuring equipment. The members agreed that the road was 'a veritable hill' downwards, west to east, from the sea to the Croy tollhouse, and one of them rolled a bicycle wheel from the 'foot' of the incline, when, to his amazement, it sped all the way to the 'top' of the hill. The account continued under the sub-heading of 'The Problem Solved', when it was explained that a civil engineer in the party arranged for levels to be taken at both ends of the brae; and the engineer announced his findings to the party at the tollhouse end: that the road before them, from east to west, did not rise but fell, and that the 'hill of mystery', 24 chains or 528 yards in length, fell 17 feet, such that the slope from east to west was 1 in 92. Or, as this was the opposite to what was thought to be seen, the contributor, having referred to the phenomenon as 'a marvellous optical illusion', simply concluded: 'It's hard no' to believe your ain een [own eyes].'

Four years later, in June 1905, when the Maidens & Dunure Light Railway was well in progress of construction, a photograph of the Croy Brae, which was sent to 'Oculeus', the regular contributor of the *Ayrshire Post*, who then brought the readers' attention to one 'effect' of the brae in a light-hearted way, with the tale of an unfortunate navvy from the Maidens & Dunure line. On returning from Maybole one Saturday night and stumbling on the brae, to fall with his feet facing the letter T in the photograph on page 68, he had his boots wrenched from his feet by the magnetic force, and when his boots were found in a field at the top or the bottom of the brae, the tackets, or hobnails, were gone! From the photograph, which shows a sideways or west-to-east view of the brae from a location south of the small road to Croy shore, and with the unfinished railway visible, it can be seen that the Pennyglen-Dunure road on the hillside in the background appears to ascend from right to left towards the T - i.e., from east to west - rather than in the opposite direction, whereas, in reality, the gradient towards the T is downhill.

That the illusion of the brae was also experienced from the railway was confirmed to the authors by four observers: two who had travelled on the line and two who had walked along it. Nigel Macmillan, who, as a young railway enthusiast, was an illicit passenger on the footplate of the daily goods and seasonal potato trains during the summers of 1944 to 1946, recorded that it was uncanny to drift 'uphill' with the steam off. This statement suggested that Nigel had travelled northwards and, therefore, on the returning potato train on the true downhill gradient, while the Electric Brae effect made him think, falsely, that he was running on an uphill gradient in that direction. The effect was also regularly felt from the footplate by John Hastings, who had become a fireman on the southbound daily goods train in 1938 and who had fired on the northbound excursion train the same year to the Empire Exhibition in Glasgow. Nigel and John - who may have met each other on the footplate all those years ago, unknowingly - asserted that this downhill section of the railway, from south-east to north-west, seemed to be going uphill. Peter Urie, who lived and worked at Balchriston as a boy, and Ronnie Shannon, who lived at Knoweside as a boy and then worked at Dunure station yard, confirmed the Electric Brae effect from their walks along the route of the railway when they were boys.

Along the Electric Brae stretch of the line northwards from Castlehill farm, through Knoweside station, to the Croy viaduct, the gradient was downhill at 1 in 90 from the farm to the station and then downhill at 1 in 200 from the station to a short distance north of the viaduct. Therefore, the gradient of the railway, downhill from south-east to north-west, was in the same general orientation as the gradient of the Pennyglen-Dunure road, from east to west, that ran on the hillside higher than the railway.

The false effects of the Electric Brae, which were seen in the 1905 photograph, are still vividly in evidence: from the same direction and similar position; from the road on the brae itself, as the viewer looks 'up' or 'down' the slope; and also from the sea at Culzean Bay. Today, the Electric Brae continues to intrigue many people who respond by experimenting on it, uphill and downhill, with their cars and bicycles, even though the answer of an optical illusion has been long established and commonly accepted; and today, at the lay-by of the brae, a sign in granite explains its curiosity, thus:

'The Electric Brae' known locally as 'Croy Brae'. This runs the quarter mile from the bend overlooking Croy railway viaduct in the west (286 feet above Ordnance datum) to the wooded Craigencroy Glen (303 feet A.O.D.) to the east. Whilst there is this slope of 1 in 86 upwards from the bend to the glen, the configuration of the land on either side of the road provides an optical illusion, making it look as if the slope is going the other way. Therefore, a stationary car on the road with the brakes off will appear to move slowly uphill. The term 'Electric' dates from a time when it was incorrectly thought to be a phenomenon caused by electric or magnetic attraction within the brae.

The Electric Brae, c. 1930, looking east, as a car faces west and truly downhill, though on the wrong side of the road. The optical-illusion creates the undeniable impression that the road slopes downwards in the distance, but the road level is definitely higher in the distance than in the foreground.   *M. Chadwick*

Appendix Seven

The Principal M&DLR Promoter: the Marquis of Ailsa, 1847-1938

More than 30 years after the promotion of the M&DLR, the life of the principal promoter of the ambitious project came to an end. Archibald Kennedy, the third Marquis of Ailsa and the initiator of the whole Turnberry project, died at Culzean Castle on 9th April, 1938, in his 90th year, having held his family title for the astonishingly-long span of 68 years. With his general health having fallen steadily for a considerable period, he had been confined to a wheelchair because of arthritis, such that his death was not unexpected. On 13th April, he was buried beside his father in the family cemetery at Culzean, which was filled to overflowing by the presence of a vast gathering of mourners from diverse sections of society and profession. They included landowners, Members of Parliament, police officials, provosts, magistrates, town-council and county-council members, and - equally important as a measure of the high respect for the Marquis as a landlord - the employees and tenantry of farmers and fishermen, who were augmented by many members of the public from the vicinity and further afield. Also in attendance was Thomas Smith, the Marquis' long-standing and loyal factor, as another gentleman who had been deeply involved in the establishment of the light railway back in the late 1890s and early 1900s, effectively as administrator and co-ordinator on behalf of the Marquis for the route through the beautiful Culzean estate. The Marquis' second wife, Isabella, as the Marchioness of Ailsa, died in 1945.

The leisure activities of the Marquis were varied, particularly his concern and work in country matters, encompassing natural history, afforestation, wildlife and gardening on the Culzean estate and elsewhere, all from the scientific as well as the aesthetic and practical viewpoints; but he was best known for his most passionate pastimes and expertise of yachting, yacht-designing and boat-building. Although a man of retiring ways, he never refused to honour his public duties to the county of Ayr, albeit doing so in his quiet manner, and he readily admitted that he would rather build a boat than make a speech, in ultimately accomplishing the former professionally through his Culzean Shipbuilding & Engineering Company at Maidens initially and at his Ailsa Shipbuilding Company at Troon latterly. Apart from his endeavours in connection with the M&DLR and his directorship of the G&SWR from 1892 until the demise of the company at the end of 1922, his early enthusiasm for transport extended to seeing the importance of the motor car, and he was the first baron in Ayrshire to register under the Road Act of 1903, from his ownership of four cars, having the registration numbers of 'SD 1', 'SD 2', 'SD 3' from December 1903 and 'SD 4' from March 1904.

The extent of interest that the Marquis possessed in the affairs of Ayrshire and Carrick was portrayed by his involvement in administering various associations and committees, including the following: the Ayrshire Agricultural Association, as President; the County Council, as the representative for Kirkoswald; the County Road Board, as Chairman; the Parish Council of Kirkoswald, as Chairman; the Church of Scotland, as an elder of Kirkoswald Parish Church; Kirkoswald School Board; Maybole School Board; Carrick District Council; Ayr Harbour Trustees; and Girvan Harbour Board; while he was also Lord Lieutenant of the county and a Justice of the Peace. He was the recipient of an Honorary Degree of Doctor of Laws, LL.D, from the University of Glasgow; and, in addition to his position on the G&SWR Board, he was a director of the National Bank of Scotland and a director of the Scottish Board of the Royal Insurance Company.

Archibald Kennedy, the third Marquis of Ailsa, had accomplished much for the development and renown of Turnberry and the Carrick coast between Ayr and Girvan from the establishment of the railway, even if the locality was not able to be developed fully during his lifetime, but his legacies of Turnberry Hotel and Turnberry Golf Club survive, in enterprising fashion.

Acknowledgements

For photographs and other vital material that greatly contributed to the histories of the Maidens & Dunure Light Railway and the Heads of Ayr Butlin's branch, the authors appreciated the kindness and help of the following people, organizations and authorities:

David Cross - for photographs by his father and renowned railway photographer, the late Derek Cross, with the young David frequently an eager onlooker when Derek photographed the trains on the Butlin's services during the 1960s.
Malcolm Chadwick - for photographs, including on the back cover in colour.
Hamish Stevenson - for photographs, including by his father, the late James Stevenson.
Stuart Sellar - for photographs.
Ian Middleditch - for photographs.
Gordon Clark - for photographs.
David Stirling - for photograph and information about M&DLR signalling.
Bob Smillie - for photograph and M&DLR opening-day leaflet.
John Russell - for photograph, and for information about the Alloway yard closure.
Kathryn Holderness - for photograph.
Andrew Laing - for drawing.
Joe Porteous, Bob Smillie, Dick Scott, John Hastings, Ronnie Shannon, Mary Shannon, Graham Kirkpatrick, Ronnie Kidd, John Gibson, Fergus Gibson and Bill Bennett, as former railway employees, and Nigel Macmillan, as a railway enthusiast - for their memories of the line, including operational information.
Elma Cowan, Peter Urie, Bill Tait and Robert Logan, as interested onlookers - for their memories of the line.
Iain Goldie - for information about his involvement in the Alloway footbridge accident.
Charles Armstrong - for observational information of the ACV dmu.
Arnold Tortorella - for research information.
Michael Scott - for research information.
Tony Jervis - for information from *Branch Line News*.
Tom Paterson - for access to Turnberry Golf Club minute books.
Glasgow & South-Western Railway Association - for photographs, timetables and signalling diagrams. (www.gswrr.co.uk)
Great North of Scotland Railway Association - for photographs, including on the front cover.
Carnegie Library/South Ayrshire Council, Ayr - for photographs, OS and Bartholomew maps, access to newspapers, and access to G&SWR plans of the Alloway tunnel and the Doon viaduct.
Mitchell Library/Glasgow City Council - for photographs.
Royal Commission on the Ancient and Historical Monuments of Scotland (RCAHMS), Edinburgh - for photographs.
National Archives of Scotland (NAS), Edinburgh - for photograph, ticket on back cover in colour, and access to timetables and documents.
Dunbartonshire Archives/William Patrick Library, Kirkintilloch - for photographs.
Scottish & Universal Newspapers - for *Ayrshire Post* photographs.
Ayrshire Weekly Press - for *Ayr Advertiser* photographs.
Butlin's Memories - for photograph.
Ladies Golf Union, St Andrews - for photograph.
Cassillis & Culzean Estates, Maybole, and Ayrshire Archives, Ayr - for Glenside station plans and access to Kennedy documents.
National Library of Scotland (NLS) Map Library, Edinburgh, for OS maps.
Turnberry Hotel - for timetable.

Index